W9-CPH-244

MEN WHO LOST THE PRESIDENCY

Profiles Of The
29
Men Who Lost
Elections To Be
President Of
The United States

ALVA C. GOLDBERG

J M Press
A Division of
J M PRODUCTIONS, INC.
BRENTWOOD, TN 37024-1911
1-800-969-READ

Published by JM Press, a division of JM Productions, Inc.
P.O. Box 1911
Brentwood, Tennessee 37024-1911
(615) 373-4814

First edition 1992.

ISBN 0-939298-40-6

PRINTED IN THE UNITED STATES OF AMERICA

ACKNOWLEDGMENTS

I am first of all deeply indebted to the authors of the many books listed in the Bibliography. Indeed, I have borrowed liberally from each, and I could not have completed the brief biographies of the *MEN WHO LOST THE PRESIDENCY* without their prior research, which together with historic tradition has provided the foundation of this work.

Both the Chattanooga Public Library and the University of Tennessee at Chattanooga Library allowed me to borrow books for extensive periods of time. One begins to fully realize how valuable the services of a library are when researching a book such as this. Even these excellent institutions did not have all the books I needed. I called upon the Chattanooga Public Library for help through its Inner-Library Loan Program, and three sorely needed books were acquired quickly. I wish to thank three libraries for their assistance: the Memphis Public Library System for a book on Horatio Seymour, the Memphis State Library for a book on Alfred Landon and the Library of William and Mary College for a book on John W. Davis.

It is also necessary for me to acknowledge those who have in a significant way spurned my interest in American history. My love for its study began with my fifth grade elementary school teacher, Mr. Holmes, and continued in the sixth with Mrs. Weaver, in the eighth with Mrs. Burgess, in high school with Mrs. Walton, and in college at the University of Chattanooga (now the University of Tennessee at Chattanooga) with Dr. Smartt and Dr. Livingood. In addition, the trivial pursuit of the knowledge of American history has been with me since childhood, and I am indebted to both my childhood and adult families and to a host of friends who have helped keep an interest in American history alive.

A.C.G.

Chattanooga, Tennessee
December 31, 1991

INTRODUCTION

The idea for this book first came to me immediately after the Presidential Election of 1960. John F. Kennedy, during his news conference the day following his election, paid an obligatory tribute to Richard M. Nixon. "I congratulate Vice President Nixon on a race well run, and wish him well in the future." With these sparse remarks, the President-Elect summarily dismissed his political adversary — *who had just served as Vice President of the United States for eight years!* Unfortunately, the news media, historians and the nation-at-large were also ready to do the same: such is the fate of the loser.

I soon found, upon but cursory research, that the same was true of other candidates in other elections. American history textbooks might in footnotes mention the names of defeated candidates, but little is known of the men themselves or of their political philosophies. Over the years I read a good deal about these men, but due to a business career I did not take the time to pursue the writing of a book that I had long yearned to author — until 1986, when I decided that if I were ever going to complete my idea, I had better get on with it. At that time I began to read extensively about the *MEN WHO LOST THE PRESIDENCY*, and then I began writing the brief biographies contained herein. It is my tribute to men who, while losing, have helped preserve the greatest form of government yet created by man.

This book includes biographies only of the major unsuccessful candidates who never became President, and therefore there are no biographies of candidates from the elections of 1800 (John Adams and Jefferson), 1828 (John Quincy Adams and Jackson), 1836 and 1840 (Van Buren and Harrison), 1888 and 1892 (Cleveland and Harrison), 1912 (Teddy Roosevelt, Taft and Wilson), 1960 (Kennedy and Nixon), 1976 (Ford and Carter), and 1980 (Carter and Reagan). The biographies of the losers in these campaigns can be found in a number of works about Presidents of the United States.

Also, "third party" candidates are not included. For the election of 1860 I chose Stephen Douglas as the major candidate, even though he was not second in the Electoral College, since I deemed from an historical perspective that he was the most important foe of Abraham Lincoln. The biographies are written chronologically, and for that reason Henry Clay is sequenced first during the election of 1824, when he ran fourth in the Electoral College, though perhaps he should first be placed under the election of 1832. Of course, no biographies are included for the elections of 1788 and 1792, when George Washington was unopposed, or of 1820, when James Monroe had no opponent.

The purpose of this work is to simply provide knowledge of the *MEN WHO LOST THE PRESIDENCY*, and I have within the biographies themselves attempted only to narrate the lives of these men and relate their works and beliefs. I believe, by and large, that the better candidate won in most elections, but naturally the question arises as to whether some of the losers of the Chief Executive's position would have made good or great Presidents. One can merely conjecture about what would have happened if different men had been elected. In retrospect, I have the feeling that DeWitt Clinton, whom Thomas Jefferson thought at one point to be the most qualified man in the country to be President, had all the makings of a great leader. If Henry Clay had chosen not to side with John Quincy Adams in the election of 1824, when the integrity of Jackson's beloved Rachel was questioned by the forces of Quincy Adams, he might have been elected and made a great President. James G. Blaine - like Clay a Speaker of the House, Senator and Secretary of State – was also an effective leader, though there is some justification to suspect his character. Charles Evans Hughes was outstanding in every respect except being a politician. So were John W. Davis and Thomas E. Dewey (Dewey was great in New York politics but not so at the national level). Al Smith was a courageous man with unusual vision and an outstanding leader who may have changed the course of the ship of state.

For the most part, though, I feel the ship of state would not have changed all that much with different Presidents. There are, however, several who probably would have at least attempted to make profound changes. George McClellan, a weak leader who poked fun at Lincoln and called him a "gorilla," would probably have made peace with the

South in 1865 and perhaps even allowed the Confederate States of America to continue alongside the United States of America. William Jennings Bryan would with his populist outlook probably not have taken the United States into world affairs and the twentieth century as quickly as McKinley and Teddy Roosevelt, placing more emphasis on domestic economic matters. Barry Goldwater wanted to change the outcome of the Viet Nam War, and had he been elected, developments would certainly have been different than if LBJ remained President. Conversely, the cynical George McGovern, a World War II hero who gave up the ministry to go into politics and who seemed ready to give up the United States and all it stood for in order to be elected and end the same terrible conflict, would have led the United States in a direction far different than Richard Nixon, who defeated him over-whelmingly.

I thought at one time of naming this work *WHAT IF*, but, as already noted, while it is useful to wonder about what could have been, what has happened has happened. Under our system of government all of the men who were supposed to be President - except for Samuel Tilden - did win and served legally (albeit there are appropriate questions about the elections of 1876 and 1960 as well as about elections where the popular vote winner has been different than the Electoral College winner). The most amazing thing to wonder about, though, is how the United States has held a peaceful transfer of power every four years since the establishment of the Presidency. The *MEN WHO LOST THE PRESIDENCY* are very much responsible for this peaceful transfer and for preserving the greatest government in the annals of mankind.

Because our system of government continues to exist, the *MEN WHO LOST THE PRESIDENCY* should not be forgotten.

CONTENTS

To

Judy, Richard and Steven

Charles Cotesworth Pinckney
The Elections of 1804 and 1808

Hanging in the Frick Art Reference Library in New York City is a remarkable Gilbert Stuart portrait of a dashing, Revolutionary War general officer in resplendent uniform, standing next to a white horse and bearing an uncanny likeness to George Washington. This notable figure is Charles Cotesworth Pinckney, a successor to Washington both as President-General of the Society of Cincinnati and as a Federalist leader. Pinckney tried to succeed Washington as President, but this fate was not to befall him. "If I had a vein that did not beat for the love of my Country, I myself would open it," once said this Colonial patriot whose sacrifices helped establish the successful American experiment in democracy.

EARLY LIFE

C.C. Pinckney was born February 14, 1745 in the family's "Mansion House" in Charleston, South Carolina. His father, whose ancestors had been in South Carolina since 1692, was a second-generation lawyer and planter who had made many enterprising investments and established the Pinckney name throughout South Carolina. C.C. Pinckney's mother, the daughter of an English army officer, was Charles Pinckney's second wife and had come to South Carolina from Antigua. She had made quite a name for herself in her own right by performing the first successful experiments for the growth of indigo on the American continent.

The first eight years of C.C.'s life were spent under the strict tutelage of his parents, who were eager to see him become a public servant. He is supposed to have been able to read letters before being able to speak and to have been able to spell and read by the age of two. His devout Anglican Christian parents expected him to know his sermon text each Sunday and to come home from Church and promptly memorize the Sunday "collect." Their influence must have been profound, for Pinckney remained a devout Anglican throughout his life.

In 1753 the Pinckneys sailed for England, where C.C. was to spend the next sixteen years attending preparatory schools and college. He was a pupil first at the prestigious Westminister Preparatory School and then attended Christ Church College at Oxford. C.C.'s education was primarily in the classics and the law, and he had the unique opportunity to study the English legal system under the renowned William Blackstone, who was to author the famous *Commentaries* on English jurisprudence. He studied rigorously and with a constant reminder by his widowed mother (his father had passed away in 1758) that work and responsibility took precedence over pleasure and play. Experiencing some ill health, Pinckney took some time off from his studies to travel extensively on the European mainland. At Caen, France, he enrolled in the Royal Military Academy to studied military science. He perhaps anticipated a need to control slave uprisings and defend Crown interests in the New World; surely he did not dream that this training would in but a few years be used to make war against the land where he was receiving his basic education.

Pinckney returned to England from the Continent, completed his education in early 1769, and was admitted to the bar. He "rode the circuit" in England one time so that he would be able to return to America with a prestigious reputation. Having at this point spent twice as much of his life in England as in his native colony, the twenty-four year old Charles Cotesworth Pinckney returned to Charleston in the middle of 1769 to pursue his career.

He quickly settled into the aristocratic station that he had inherited. He found upon return to South Carolina a different treatment than he had had in all the years in England. The "hazing" for being a colonial American was gone, and the opportunity to be the leader for which he had trained was not only present but expected. Being of a prominent background meant that his family and friends were already plotting his future. Thus in December, 1769, Charles Cotesworth Pinckney was elected a representative to the Commons House (state legislature) from St. John's Parish. His political career had begun; less than seven years later he would be at the forefront of American resistance to the British.

REVOLUTIONARY ACTIVITIES

Why Pinckney, after spending so many years in England, joined in rebellion can be traced to several factors. One was the condescending display of conduct by the English natives to the Colonial boy who had "intruded" upon England for his education. Additionally, the Pinckney family had been angered for years by the actions of the royal system. A British royal governor had appointed C.C.'s father, a member of the Royal Council of South Carolina and a Chancery Court judge, to the position of interim Chief Justice, but the royal writ of mandamus confirming this was never executed. The coveted position went instead to a native British subject, whose qualifications were suspect and whose background in England had included electoral corruption.

Only recently returned from England and only newly elected to the Commons House, Pinckney became a model citizen, being devoted to the Church and various civic and charitable endeavors. He became a renowned botanist and also began his colonial military career as an Ensign in the Charles Town militia. His progress in the legislature was at first slow, but his name together with his abilities soon started his upward rise. He had returned at a time when the Governor and his Royal Council were at odds with the colonially elected legislature, just as was the case in so many other colonies. In South Carolina, the Royal Government held the responsibility of approving all legislative appropriation bills. As rancor over the royal policy increased, the Royal Governor in 1772 called for the legislators to meet — but at Beaufort rather than Charleston, an extra distance of some seventy-five miles for legislators to travel. The legislators dutifully made the trip only to find that the Governor had switched the session back to Charleston. The legislators quickly backtracked to Charleston, this to the consternation of the Royal Governor, who was already upset to have received a list of grievances from a legislative committee that included the brash, young Pinckney.

Though brash, Pinckney was not considered an out-and-out rabble rouser. In 1773 he was appointed a royal barrister (Assistant Attorney General), and he was on intimate terms with many royal officials. In 1774 he became a vestryman in his Episcopal congregation.

Also in 1774, Pinckney married Salley Middleton, whose background was significant enough for the *South Carolina Gazette* to state that "...an Alliance had been completed, between two as respectable Families as any in the province..." This was certainly true, for C.C.'s father-in-law owned twenty plantations and eight hundred slaves. Connections were enhanced when Edward Rutledge, a future Chief Justice, married the sister of Pinckney's wife.

Pinckney considered himself a loyal British subject working within the royal system to see that colonial subjects were treated equally with native subjects. Like so many other prominent Americans, he languished when the British government decreed a series of laws indifferent to the colonies. One after another these acts were enacted without any compassion: the "Tea Act" of 1773 to aid the East India Company at the expense of the colonies; in 1774 the "Intolerable Acts," and then the "Quartering Act," to retaliate against the Boston Tea Party; and the "Stamp Act." Such actions aroused the righteous indignation of an amazingly intelligent and able group of men throughout the colonies, men who were for the most part already active in colonial legislatures and who were particularly adept at the workings of committees and the writing and publication of their thoughts. When calls for Committees of Correspondence were issued, C.C. Pinckney's name naturally emerged from the list of able South Carolinians available to represent the cause. Pinckney met with the Continental Congress of 1774 and then returned to take the lead in the secret committees expressing colonial displeasures — and to consider possible new forms of colonial government. A new South Carolina constitution was declared on March 26, 1776, just five days after the news arrived at Charleston that Parliament had declared the colonies in rebellion. On April 22, Pinckney joined others in an act of outright but simple defiance. Hearing that the royal Governor was about to arm the local Tories, he and a group of patriots, without disguise, went during the evening hours to three magazines (powder houses) and seized the munitions, leaving the Governor temporarily powerless against the rebels.

During this period of time, South Carolinians learned of a British strategy to incite the insurrection of slaves and to employ the use of Indians in the conflict with the rebels. The South Carolina Provincial Congress in June, 1775, authorized the recruitment and training of three regiments to counter this measure. Officers were at that time elected by the ranks, and Pinckney, now a Lieutenant in the Charles Town militia, led the ballot and was elected ranking Captain of the South Carolina regiments. He promptly set about recruiting and drilling his men, hoping to earn a military reputation for himself. As relations between the British and the colonists worsened, orders were received from the Continental Congress to seize Fort Johnson, a strategic harbor barrier. Pinckney's troops were to be the lead assault force of this mission. The royal Governor, having learned of the plan, however, removed the fort's cannons and abandoned Charleston. South Carolina was now in the hands of colonial leaders.

WAR

Pinckney thirsted for military glory but was to be consistently denied his desire for it despite his diligent efforts to succeed. Wanting action, Pinckney applied to and was granted admittance to General Washington's staff and participated in the battles of Brandywine and Germantown. His performance was apparently lackluster, for Washington mentioned nothing in his official or private correspondence to cite any gallantry on C.C.'s part. After this service the Captain returned to South Carolina to help defend against impending British attack.

Pinckney had dual responsibilities as soldier and legislator but spent most of his time as a soldier. He participated in early campaigns designed to root the British out of southern bases in St. Augustine and Savannah. He also worked to bolster the enforcements of the Charleston harbor area against coming British attacks. When, after leading maneuvers and finding along with other officers that members of the South Carolina militia often deserted and considered themselves not subject to ordinary military discipline, Pinckney appeared in his legislative role before the Carolina House and argued successfully for the legal institution of military discipline. This greatly enhanced the ability of officers to control troops.

The forces of the colonial South were no match for the British forces. In late 1778 the British took Savannah and secured Georgia. By mid-1779, Pinckney's beloved Charleston was falling, and with this came many personal setbacks for him and his family. His brother's plantation was lost to the plundering of the British, who not only destroyed all of the personal papers and effects of his late father but confiscated the plantation slaves as well. The slaves at his mother's home were also taken. Magnanimously, C.C. instantly offered to divide his personal effects three ways among mother, brother and himself. For a while, things seemed brighter when a French armada appeared off the coast of Georgia to offer relief, but the French commander, unwilling to share any glory with the Americans, delayed action, allowing the British to reinforce and defeat him. Now, as a siege was staged by the British, the outlook for Charleston and South Carolina became extremely grim. A council of war was called by the American commander, General Benjamin Lincoln, to consider surrender. Pinckney's courage and character shone bright when he objected, later stating that death to any man was to eventually come, but death "useful to one's Country was the greatest felicity a patriotic soldier can hope for."

Nonetheless Lincoln surrendered, and Pinckney then had to suffer the humiliation of being a prisoner of war. To be sure, the conditions of the day offered amenities not available to modern prisoners. He often could visit his relatives, he kept his Negro servant, and he was able to correspond without interruption. His correspondence was used to seek an exchange of prisoners so that he could be honorably freed and again join the effort against the British. For two years, from 1780 to 1782, Pinckney languished. Adding to his misery during this period was the death by small pox of his only son, also named Charles Cotesworth. In March of 1782, an exchange was finally arranged, and Pinckney rushed back to South Carolina to engage the enemy. But the war there was all but over, and the military glory that he longed for could not be had. He must have felt great pride, though, when he learned as the war was coming to a close that he was being promoted to the rank of Brigadier General.

LEADER IN COLONIAL SOUTH CAROLINA

Upon the conclusion of the war in 1783, Pinckney resumed his legislative and cultural leadership in South Carolina. He was a conciliator of sorts upon return from action, arguing that confiscation and heavy taxation of the property of Tories should be minimized. Perhaps this was because C.C. had relatives in the Tory category, but more probably it was because the man's farsighted wisdom saw the necessity of rebuilding South Carolina's war torn economy.

Pinckney himself had suffered heavy losses in the Revolution, but he had his plantations as well as his legal profession to sustain himself. He began to speculate heavily in land ventures and invested also in some private canal projects. These transactions put him deeply in debt, and of necessity he began practicing law more actively. This proved to be a much more successful financial undertaking than planting. Pinckney, though not a flowery courtroom orator, was methodical and meticulous, and he quickly became the leading lawyer in Charleston.

Pinckney suffered another personal tragedy in 1784 when his beloved first wife suddenly died. He was to wait two years before remarrying, choosing as his helpmate Mary Stead, the daughter of a prominent Charleston merchant. She brought with her a handsome dowry of some £14,000, requiring C.C. to devote a considerable amount of his future time managing this fortune and barring him from accepting various federal appointments. He did stay active in the South Carolina legislature and saw to it that legislation was passed creating institutions of higher learning. Still active in cultural affairs, he served as the President of the Charleston Library Society. Although a planter, he opposed paper money schemes to alleviate the plight of indebted farmers because he considered the plans inflationary and the credit of the State and the planters themselves too valuable to be risked in such undertakings. Pinckney also wanted a sound currency system so that he could regain from South Carolina war loans he had made in the amount of £21,500, as well as some £1,950 for services rendered during the war.

Not in the tradition of later South Carolina secessionists such as Calhoun, but as a true Federalist at heart who felt that the interest of South Carolina was best protected by a strong national government, Pinckney was quick to join the national movement to reform the Articles of Confederation.

Accordingly, he was among a committee of five South Carolinians who journeyed to Philadelphia in 1787 to attend a Constitutional Convention. There he joined with other Founding Fathers to draft, debate, refine and publish the document which was to be the basis of the most lasting democracy in world history — the Constitution of the United States.

FOUNDING FATHER

Pinckney made many distinct contributions to the Constitution. First, he frankly informed the delegates that union could not be achieved without an accommodation for slavery in the South. This, explained Pinckney, was not a moral but an economic issue. The issue was finally compromised, with the convention accepting Pinckney's suggestion of the year 1808 as the future date to ban further importation of slaves. He pushed for a one-to-one ratio for slaves but accepted the three-fifths rule in the spirit of compromise.

Pinckney was also the force for not taxing exports. He promoted the cause of states rights not for the cause of states rights but so that the Constitution would receive the national strength needed for ratification. In another matter, Pinckney strongly favored the election of both Representatives and Senators by state legislatures, fearing too strong of a central government. He fought for four-year rather than six-year Senatorial terms and felt that Senators should serve without pay. Unsuccessful in this approach, he then argued that the states, whose wealth he felt the Senators were supposed to protect, should pay the Senators' stipends rather than the federal government.

Perhaps Pinckney's greatest contribution to the Constitution came when the great crisis between the big and small states arose over the division of power between the House and Senate. A vote taken on the issue resulted in a tie. Pinckney, sensing that all was lost unless a compromise was made, jumped to his feet and moved that a committee of one from each state be formed to meet and propose a solution. Opposition from James Madison ensued, but Pinckney's motion carried, and the committee was formulated that drafted the "Great Compromise" and offered all of the states the means of accepting the document. Pinckney himself became enthused about the Convention's work. When Elbridge Gerry (a future Vice President known best today for "gerrymandering") stated that he could not sign the new document, Pinckney replied that he "would support it with all his influence." He and other delegates affixed their signatures on September 17, 1787, and then he headed back to South Carolina to lead the difficult battle for ratification.

South Carolina was known to be divided into two political divisions: the low country surrounding Charleston, which was Federalist; and the up-country, composed mostly of planters, who feared the encroachments of a strong national government and who claimed that four-fifths of the state opposed a change in government. The vote for ratification was to be close. The first test came over the location of state convention. Pinckney, using all his parliamentary skills, led the fight in the legislature to hold the convention in pro-Federalist Charleston. This carried by only one vote — seventy-six to seventy-five. Surely this was a portend of a divisive battle at the convention itself. But here Pinckney and his fellow Federalists showed a high degree of political wisdom. Up-country delegates, who feared a "fixed convention," were treated with the utmost courtesy when they came to Charleston, with merchants holding "open house" while the Federalist delegates pushed their measures forward. On the sixth day of the convention came the electrifying news that Maryland had ratified the Constitution, and anti-Federalists began joining the cause. Promptly a vote was taken, and ratification passed by a majority of seventy-six.

CONSTITUTIONAL GOVERNMENT

President George Washington realized the necessity of a unified new government. Accordingly, he offered positions to Pinckney and to Edward Rutledge, members of the two most powerful South Carolina families and men who could bring the various factions in the South into a harmonious national experience. Because of financial investments, C.C. refused any appointment. He did not, however, abandon the affairs of South Carolina, remaining in the state legislature and becoming a delegate to a new state Constitutional Convention that fixed Columbia as the new state Capital.

Neither did Pinckney abandon his ties with Washington. He and Rutledge were chief advisors to the new President from the region and dispensed patronage liberally. When Washington made a grand tour of the South in 1791, Charles Cotesworth Pinckney was his Charleston host. This must have been a warm occasion for each. Pinckney had the opportunity to reciprocate Washington's previous welcomes to him at Mount Vernon, and he hosted the tumultuous outpouring of affection by the citizens of Charleston for the "Father of his Country." A special tribute was given Washington, the President-General of the Society of Cincinnati, when C.C. and other officers of the Revolution held a banquet in the former Commanding General's honor.

Before Washington left South Carolina, he tried to get either Pinckney or Rutledge to accept a Supreme Court appointment, but each declined. C.C.

later also rejected the position of Secretary of War, but his half-brother, Thomas, did accept an appointment as Minister to Great Britain. Pinckney maintained cordial relations with the President and for the most part was also on very friendly terms with Washington's chief protege, Alexander Hamilton. These two conducted a lively correspondence, in which Hamilton often spoke disparagingly of Thomas Jefferson.

The bloody French Revolution found Pinckney in a position not considered Federalist. He favored the new republic and did not openly criticize the bloodbath that ensued. When Citizen Genet made his tour through America, Pinckney was his South Carolina host. Not until Washington declared "Neutrality," with Genet in defiance attacking Washington and appealing direct to the American people for aid in the French cause against Britain, did Pinckney turn on Genet.

This same French action with Britain brought Pinckney back into uniform once again. South Carolina feared British intrusion and felt the necessity of equipping a larger army of two divisions. When the legislature deadlocked between Thomas Sumter and Francis Marion as the commanding general of one of the divisions, Pinckney was selected as a compromise commander and received the rank of Major General. He proceeded with obvious pleasure and vigor to drill and instruct his new command.

A particularly embarrassing moment for Pinckney surrounded the naming of John Jay as a special envoy to negotiate British differences while Charles Pinckney was still ambassador to the Court of St. James. C.C. did not publicize his feelings about Jay, but he was displeased. Later, when Jay negotiated a treaty with England that was so one-sided in favor of the British that many consider it the most infamous treaty in U.S. history (especially so in South Carolina because reparations for slaves taken during the Revolution was not even considered), Pinckney still maintained public silence, choosing not even to read the document so that he would not have to make any comment and leave the impression he was bitter over his brother's awkward position. Washington was concerned that Pinckney would be so offended by the affair that he might change political parties and move the internal balance of political power to the Republicans; the President thus offered Pinckney the position of Secretary of State, but the offer was refused, not because C.C. had changed parties, but because he did not wish to defend the Jay Treaty. Pinckney remained a Federalist even after he and other fellow party members in South Carolina received the additional shock of John Rutledge not being confirmed as Chief Justice by the Senate.

THE FRENCH

Pinckney now began to be involved in one of the most distasteful episodes in the entire history of American foreign relations. James Monroe, a confirmed Republican, was President Washington's envoy to France. Monroe, disregarding the President's strict instructions to stay neutral, warmly embraced the French and assured them on the word of the administration that the Jay Treaty contained no ill effects for French-American relations. When the treaty was published, the French were outraged and felt that Monroe was either a liar or had lost the confidence of his government. For his part Monroe was equally outraged at Washington, who, fearing the breakdown of his entire Neutrality policy, then decided to recall the future President. James Monroe's replacement was Charles Cotesworth Pinckney.

Pinckney's trip by sea to France was a stormy one, perhaps a predilection of things to come. The new French Directory, in a series of high-handed and imperious acts, desisted in recognizing Pinckney's appointment. The Directory then conducted a barrage of verbal assaults on C.C., reminding him that it *was* France that had saved America from Britain. Pinckney was denied free access around Paris and threatened with arrest. Finally, the French ordered him home, and he returned in March, 1797, just after President Adams had assumed office. In Adams' campaign there had been some attempted sabotage by Alexander Hamilton, who had tried to have C.C.'s half-brother, Thomas — the Federalist nominee for Vice President — elected in Adams' place. Thus Adams, though he despised France, was in no mood to be friendly to C.C. Pinckney. However, as things developed, the President named a three man commission, composed of John Marshall, Elbridge Gerry and C.C. Pinckney, to go to Paris and mend relations with the French.

What happened when the three envoys arrived in Paris was astounding. To begin with, the French demanded an apology for some offending remarks by President Adams. Next France wanted reimbursement for any debts due its citizens. A demand was also given for the United States to forgive any French damage to American shipping. Then France told the delegates that it would require a loan from the United States. Finally, the French Directory would expect a payment — or rather a bribe — of some $250,000 for the privilege of negotiating with and assisting the Americans. To his great credit, an indignant C.C. Pinckney replied, "No, no, not a sixpence!" This was the infamous XYZ affair that was to darken French-American relations for some time.

Unfortunately, Republican Elbridge Gerry, to his great discredit, held separate sessions with the French, believing that he could mollify their demands and lessen the amount of the bribery demand. Pinckney and Marshall grew more and more weary of the demands and of the snobbish insinuations that American liberty was due to the merciful intervention of France. The French, showing a deviousness rare in foreign diplomacy, threatened America with war if trade with the British were not discontinued or if the American loan were not made. Gerry continued to so patronize the French that Secretary of State Pickering finally commented that he wished that the French Directory would keep Gerry — for the guillotine! Pinckney and Marshall held steadfastly independent and were ordered by the French to leave the country.

Pinckney's actions made him a hero throughout the United States. War with France seemed imminent, and Adams called George Washington from retirement to act as Commander in Chief of a new force. Now aging, Washington knew that the appointment of other generals was critical. He therefore officially recommended to President Adams a chain of command having Alexander Hamilton as Major General, with C.C. Pinckney and Henry Knox, subordinate in that order, as Brigadier Generals. Washington described Pinckney as "...brave, intelligent, and enterprising,...[with] numerous and powerful connections..." Some felt that this statement was a signal for Hamilton to bow out of his position in favor of Pinckney, but this did not happen.

Just as Pinckney had in earlier South Carolina days agreed to be junior to General Pickens, he now readily "rejoiced" to do the same for Hamilton and "...would serve with pleasure under him."

Everywhere Pinckney went when he returned from France he was given a hero's welcome. Town after town toasted the man who had stood up to the French. Highest esteem was shown in his native Charleston, where cannon salutes, songs and plays, and many banquets and fetes were given in his honor. Pinckney received these with obvious pleasure and then went about his task of building up the Southern defenses. After a while, relations between France and the United States normalized, and the threat of war subsided. By this time, however, the election of 1800 was approaching, and the Federalists were in bad need of a ticket to carry the nation against the emerging Republicans of Thomas Jefferson.

Alexander Hamilton, no friend of John Adams, engaged in a cunning political intrigue for the nomination of Pinckney. He arranged for the nomination of both Adams and Pinckney on equal terms, so that respective sec-

nation of both Adams and Pinckney on equal terms, so that respective sections of the country would be tempted to vote for the ticket. It was the understanding of almost all, including Pinckney at first, that Adams was to have the chief spot. The unfortunate effect of Hamilton's scheme, which was to have Pinckney elected if the Federalists prevailed, created a divisive bitterness among the Federalists, upon which the Republicans capitalized, and which marked the beginning of the end of the Federalist Party.

Hamilton was not the only cunning political schemer in the election of 1800. His arch rival, Aaron Burr, decided to challenge Jefferson when no Republican elector failed to follow the practice of not listing Burr's name on the Electoral College ballot. The election was to be decided by the House of Representatives. Pinckney, angered over Jefferson's refusal to support armaments after the French affair, and further irritated by charges in the Republican press that he was an adulterer and a sycophant of Hamilton, persuaded the South Carolina delegation to support Burr. It was Hamilton, of course, who finally decided that Jefferson was the lesser of two evils and saw to it that Jefferson became President.

The South Carolina of the early nineteenth century was changing politically. No longer did the Federalists have political control of the state. Now it was the Republicans who were continually winning the statehouse and the legislature. The Federalists wanted to run C.C. for U.S. Senator, but he declined, knowing that a Federalist could not win. He retained, however, a Charleston Senate seat in the legislature. Pinckney was reviled by the Republican press, which charged that while in France he had fathered an illegitimate child.

THE ELECTION OF 1804

Pinckney consoled himself by spending almost a year at the Pinckney plantation some 100 miles from Charleston. Then in 1803, he took a five month New England tour, obviously to test political waters. While in Boston to receive an honorary Doctor of Laws degree from Harvard, he learned of plans by some radical New Englanders, who were upset by the certain re-election of Jefferson, to secede from the Union. However, more cautious Federalists were eager not to leave the impression of secession and thought a national hero from the South could lead a unified Federalist ticket. This belief led to the nomination of Pinckney as the Federalist Presidential candidate in 1804. Rufus King of Massachusetts, himself later to be another Federalist candidate, was chosen as the Vice Presidential nominee.

Pinckney did not even bother to campaign, and Jefferson won the election overwhelmingly, receiving 162 electoral votes to Pinckney's 14. Only Delaware and Connecticut voted Federalist. Not only South Carolina but even Charleston voted Republican. This outcome was no surprise to Pinckney, who for the most part had disappeared from the public eye. One issue in which he did engage during this period was to wage an unsuccessful attempt to have dueling outlawed after his political mentor, Alexander Hamilton, was mortally wounded by Aaron Burr. C.C. had himself in earlier years engaged in dueling and in fact been wounded in an encounter, but he now vehemently opposed the practice as "un-Christian." The death of Hamilton also found Pinckney assuming the role of President-General of the Society of Cincinnati.

THE ELECTION OF 1808

It was the French and the British who brought Pinckney into prominent consideration again for the Presidency. Again at war with each other in 1807, both countries began to impress American sailors and damage merchant shipping. When the British attacked the *Chesapeake,* Americans were indignant. What better man to stand up to the British or the French than — Charles Cotesworth Pinckney?

The nomination of 1808 was much harder to secure than in 1804. Federalists truly believed that with Jefferson's refusal to pursue war and the divisions within the Republican party, there was a real chance for victory. James Monroe, Rufus King, DeWitt Clinton of New York and John Marshall were considered the leading candidates besides Pinckney for the nomination. The Federalists, clinging to the hope that a national candidate and a soldier in the tradition of Washington could carry the election, nominated Pinckney again. Rufus King was also again nominated for Vice President.

Unlike the election of 1804, Pinckney this time campaigned with enthusiasm. He especially hoped to carry his native South Carolina, where his military reputation together with his past stands against both England and France were widely publicized. So serious was his challenge that his cousin Charles — a Republican governor — secretly had papers published claiming C.C. to be, among other things, not an authentic Revolutionary war hero, inexperienced in foreign affairs, not up-to-date on domestic affairs, illprepared to be a statesman, not to be trusted as a President because he was a military man, and too old to accept the duties of Chief Executive. Again Pinckney and the Federalists were rejected not only in Charleston and South Carolina, but throughout the land, this time by 122 electoral votes to 47. It was the end of the political career of Charles Cotesworth Pinckney.

RETIREMENT

Pinckney no longer engaged in direct political contests, offering advice only when solicited. He retired to his Pinckney Island plantation to be with his family. His beloved second wife, Mary, passed away after a lingering illness of several years in 1812.

Thereafter, C.C.'s activities seemed to be purely civic or cultural in nature. He continued to be active as President-General of the Society of Cincinnati, supported the Charleston Library Society, helped form the Charleston Museum, sponsored the Agricultural Society, became a student of medicine and other sciences, and remained to the end of his days a faithful communicant of the Episcopal Church. He also sponsored the establishment of the Charleston Bible Society.

In 1825 came the exciting news that the Marquis de LaFayette was to make a farewell grand tour of the United States. When he visited Charleston, the French hero gave the familiar French embrace and kiss to a true American hero as the citizens of Charleston paid one last rousing tribute to an aging, seventy-nine year old C.C. Pinckney. Two months later, on August 16, 1825, Charles Cotesworth Pinckney was dead.

His passing was mourned throughout the land but mostly in South Carolina, especially at Charleston. His remains were laid to rest in the church yard of his beloved St. Michael's parish. Inside the church hangs a plaque inscribed as follows:

TO THE MEMORY OF
GENERAL CHARLES COTESWORTH PINCKNEY
ONE OF THE FOUNDERS OF
THE AMERICAN REPUBLIC.

IN WAR
HE WAS THE COMPANION IN ARMS
AND THE FRIEND OF WASHINGTON.

IN PEACE
HE ENJOYED HIS UNCHANGING CONFIDENCE
AND MAINTAINED WITH ENLIGHTENED ZEAL
THE PRINCIPLES OF HIS ADMINISTRATION
AND OF THE CONSTITUTION.

AS A STATESMAN
HE BEQUEATHED TO HIS COUNTRY THE STATEMENT
MILLIONS FOR DEFENCE
NOT A CENT FOR TRIBUTE.

AS A LAWYER,
HIS LEARNING WAS VARIOUS AND PROFOUND
HIS PRINCIPLES PURE HIS PRACTICE LIBERAL.

WITH ALL THE ACCOMPLISHMENTS
OF THE GENTLEMAN
HE COMBINED THE VIRTUES OF THE PATRIOT
AND THE PIETY OF THE CHRISTIAN.

HIS NAME
IS RECORDED IN THE HISTORY OF HIS COUNTRY
INSCRIBED ON THE CHARTER OF HER LIBERTIES,
AND CHERISHED IN THE AFFECTIONS OF HER CITIZENS.

DeWitt Clinton
The Election of 1812

Perhaps if he had bided his time and not been quite so politically ambitious, DeWitt Clinton would have been President of the United States. He had inherited a New York political dynasty which also was known for having provided vital aid to the winning of Independence. Well educated and molded in the classical Greek concept of the whole man, like Jefferson, his hero, he was at one point thought of by the sage of Monticello as the best man in the country to become President. Unfortunately, he ran for President as a Federalist and came away empty handed. Today, except for New York state, DeWitt Clinton is largely forgotten by the nation at large, although he made invaluable contributions to its future growth.

YOUTH IN REVOLUTIONARY NEW YORK

DeWitt Clinton was born on March 2, 1769, just as the quest for American Independence was beginning. His ancestry can be traced to Charles I of England. A split of the Clinton family during Charles I's reign created royalist and rebel Clintons. DeWitt was descended from the rebel line; his forbearers, suppressed religiously, politically and economically, escaped to New York where they quickly became entrenched in the leadership of the political and economic institutions of the state, as well as the Presbyterian Church. DeWitt's father served as a General during the Revolutionary War, while his uncle, George, was a delegate to the Continental Congress that declared Independence. George Clinton then served as Revolutionary War Governor, becoming the "Father of New York." Ironically, a major adversary of these two fighters for American Independence was a distant relative, Sir Henry Clinton, the Commanding General of British forces in New York and a son of a former Royal Governor of New York.

Young DeWitt was too young to serve in the War, but family tradition holds that he wore an American uniform at the age of six. It is said he worried constantly about the safety and health of his father, who had suffered a bayonet wound at Quebec. When Independence came, the Clinton family held great political power in New York. His uncle was particularly powerful, being named Governor again and again. His father, not so outgoing, preferred not to indulge in day-to-day politics, choosing instead to be a family man and see to the proper upbringing of his sons.

The education of DeWitt brought about a significant educational change in New York. DeWitt's father announced that DeWitt was going to attend Princeton, in New Jersey, since no suitable university was available in New York. This so shocked New Yorkers, who felt that such an action amounted somewhat to sacrilege, that the former King's College was reinstituted, with a new name — Columbia. DeWitt Clinton was its first student and first recipient of a Bachelor's degree. His course of study included rhetoric, philosophy, astronomy, chemistry, geography and mathematics. Later he had the distinction of also being the first recipient of a Master's degree. This degree was awarded in the presence of George Washington, who chose the Colombia commencement as his first public appearance after his first inauguration, an event at which DeWitt Clinton had been present.

DeWitt Clinton engaged in the practice of law after graduation from Colombia. He served under a leading New York attorney, and his practice was a successful one from the beginning. His uncle, the Governor, recognized DeWitt's potential and began to groom him for future leadership. During this period of time, animosities arose in New York which were the beginnings of political parties in the United States. The Federalists, led by Hamilton and Jay, were pushing hard for ratification of the Constitution to replace the Articles of Confederation. The Clinton family were the prime anti-Federalists in New York and did not support ratification until Virginia became the tenth state to ratify and until proper assurances were given that the Bill of Rights would be adopted. Eighteen year old DeWitt Clinton was busy at this time writing answers to "Publius", the pseudonym used by Hamilton, Jay and Madison in *The Federalist Papers*.

After Washington began his duties as the nation's first Chief Executive, New York City became the center of the nation's political activities, and Gov. George Clinton, who had a son named George Washington Clinton, was naturally a prominent figure in the city. Young DeWitt continued to establish himself in the practice of law, and he began to also become involved in certain civic activities, including the Masons, a social club call the Black Friars, and the Tammany Society ("Columbian Order"). This organization was formed in opposition to the Society of Cincinnati, which was established by Washington, who was its first President-General. Ironically, Washington himself now became a member and Grand Sachem (chief) of Tammany. DeWitt Clinton became its Scribe. He also began to hold a number of other posts, including Secretary to the Governor. He was emerging as a political figure.

As Alexander Hamilton became more involved in the opposition to George Clinton and began to openly support other candidates, DeWitt became more anti-Federalist, and he began to speak more for Republican causes. Close ties with Washington faded as the Capital moved to Philadelphia. When Citizen Genet, who had appealed to the American people to support France over President Washington, married Gov. George Clinton's daughter, Federalist opposition to Gov. Clinton increased, and New York gubernatorial elections became closer and closer. The year 1796 was an eventful year for DeWitt Clinton. George Clinton decided not to run for re-election, and DeWitt, no longer able to serve as his uncle's Secretary, left public service and returned to his law practice. That year he also took as his wife Mary Franklin, daughter of a successful merchant whose house had been used as the Presidential Palace by Washington during his New York tenure.

INTO POLITICS

When Jefferson opposed Adams in 1796, Governor George Clinton was his running mate. DeWitt Clinton was now a confirmed Jeffersonian Republican. He himself ran for the state legislature in 1796 but was defeated. But his star began to rise when former Chief Justice John Jay, who had succeeded George Clinton as Governor, was vilified after the terms of the Jay Treaty with England were made public. DeWitt's next contest for the legislature was in 1797, and he was elected to the state body along with Aaron Burr. The Republicans were beginning, with President Adams misguiding the Federalists politically, to gain complete control of New York (and the nation). A number of events confirmed this: Robert Livingston swept Jay from the Governor's office in 1798; the Alien and Sedition laws created only alienation for the Federalists; and then Aaron Burr was both elected Governor of New York and selected as Jefferson's running mate in 1800. After Burr was named Vice President subsequent to his failed but macabre scheme to steal the Presidency, George Clinton again became Governor. At the same time, DeWitt Clinton became a state Senator and a member of the powerful Council of Appointment, which controlled municipal offices and patronage throughout the state. Gathering power quickly, DeWitt Clinton was, at the age of thirty-two, the leader of the Democratic-Republican Party in New York state. In less than a year, he would be United States Senator from New York and a national Republican leader.

UNITED STATES SENATOR

Clinton served as Senator in the new federal city of Washington during 1802-03. His actions in this office were not of an extraordinary impact, but he did author the twelfth amendment to the Constitution, which provided for new methods of electing Presidents and Vice Presidents. Clinton also began to do all he could to rid the nation and New York of Vice President Burr for his unparalleled chicanery in attempting to rob Jefferson of his seat as Chief Magistrate. This was to create a division among New York Republicans that lasts to this day. The schemer Burr arranged to have the Tammany Society, originally intended as a patriotic order, transformed into his partisan political machine. The Clinton faction of the Republican Party supported Jefferson, and Burr's influence declined. When Burr was removed as Jefferson's running mate in 1804, George Clinton was his replacement. In the same year Burr tried to regain the New York Gubernatorial seat, but the former Vice President was defeated, largely due to the Clintons. These events led Burr to use the Tammany Society (now better known as Tammany Hall) through the years as a scourge against DeWitt Clinton.

The division between Burr and the Clintons created a notable dueling incident for DeWitt during his term as Senator. A Burr supporter, John Swartwout, took offense at being removed as a Director of the Manhattan Bank. Apologies were demanded, but Clinton refused, though earnestly hoping to avoid a battle. His adversary finally provoked the duel, in which pistols were loaded and fired five times, with Clinton shooting Swartwout twice through the leg. After the first hit, Clinton tried to call off the affair, but his opponent insisted on continuing. Even after the second wound, the duel was almost continued, but finally it was stopped with Clinton not at all proud of himself or the results.

MAYOR OF NEW YORK

Before Burr's infamous act against Jefferson, the Clintons had joined him in the New York Republican landslide of 1800, with George Clinton being returned to the Governor's seat. When Burr's scurrilous plot was discovered and he was pushed aside by Jefferson, the Clintons rather than Burr were consulted on New York patronage matters. With his influence rising, DeWitt Clinton was selected to fill a vacancy in the office of Mayor in 1803. His salary was $15,000 plus fees; the position offered him great security for his growing family.

The results of Clinton's service as Mayor are truly astounding. One duty of the appointed position required him to act as Judge on civil and criminal matters, and he quickly became accepted for his fairness and intelligence. As an administrative officer, he was a model for any mayor, rendering both political and cultural leadership, and being especially adept at wielding influence with the state legislature, in which he simultaneously served as

State Senator. He led movements for free public education, for the establishment of the New York Historical Society, for better turnpikes throughout the state, for religious toleration of Catholics, for the manumission of slaves, for a public New York City hospital, for an "Almshouse" to treat the mentally ill (the beginning of Belvue), for the education of the Deaf and Dumb, for a supply of clean public water to fight disease (especially yellow fever), for the fortification of New York harbor and the better defense of New York (as the War of 1812 became imminent), for a Library, and other admirable causes. He also worked to create a home for the Academy of Arts, served as Grand Master of the Masons and was the leading patron of the arts and sciences, leading an attempt to house these institutions under one roof ("The New York Institute"). While Mayor he was also a personal friend and early supporter of steamboat builder Robert Fulton, and he became as well a close acquaintance of Commodore Perry, the Naval hero of the War of 1812. Though not continuously re-elected as Mayor, DeWitt Clinton was in office for such an extended period that he was regarded as the essential driving force behind the expansion of New York City into a major economic and cultural center. His dynamic leadership also propelled him into the limelight of national politics.

In 1810, Clinton was approached by the Federalists in New York for support of a canal system. Clinton immediately seized the initiative for the "Erie Canal," personally seeing that passage of a bill in state legislature was successful. He then served on its board. Its success became a passion with him, so much so that it eventually became know as "Clinton's Ditch." The successful building of the Erie Canal created a direct passageway for western trade, and New York prospered immensely. The Erie Canal assured DeWitt Clinton of a prominent place in American history.

THE ELECTION OF 1812

DeWitt Clinton had a falling-out with Jefferson Republicans when, first of all, his uncle was passed over for President in 1808 in favor of James Madison, and secondly, when President Madison offended him by refusing him a fighting command in the War of 1812 (he was commissioned a Major General without any command). A feud between the Clintons and Governor Daniel Tompkins, later Vice President under Monroe, ensued for many years because of this. When war was declared in 1812 and then prosecuted without much energy or success, the Federalist Party saw a chance to restore itself to power. Clinton had already been mentioned as a possible Republican candidate, but Madison was in control of this party. The Federalists, knowing that Clinton was, like most Northerners and New Englanders, only lukewarm for war against the British and also anxious to see a break-up of the "Virginia Dynasty," offered him their nomination. DeWitt Clinton accepted the nod and ran a spirited campaign, gaining more electoral votes than any of the Federalist candidates for President except John Adams. Madison prevailed, however, by 128 to 89 electoral votes, dashing the forty-three year old New Yorker's hopes to be Chief Executive of the land.

CONTINUED SERVICE AS MAYOR AND STATE SENATOR

Clinton had been supported by many who felt that the war was not being prosecuted properly and by others who felt that the war should not be being fought at all. He accepted defeat gracefully, hardly pausing before he began arming troops around New York and raising twice the number of troops in New York City as requested by the Federal government. He also used police force to resist attempts by some Republicans to dispose of former "Tories," not letting New York City become a city of blood.

The complicated in-fighting of New York politics continued. Rufus King, the Federalist candidate for Vice President in 1804 and 1808 and the future (1816) candidate for President, was re-elected to the Senate in 1813. A newcomer on the New York political named Martin Van Buren charged a political intrigue: DeWitt Clinton, he said, had supported King as a repayment for the Federalist nomination in 1812. Van Buren thus killed Clinton's re-election as Lieutenant Governor, a post he had attained in 1811. When Governor Tompkins became Vice President in 1817, Van Buren, now a Republican leader in New York, opposed Clinton's bid to be nominated for Governor. But Clinton had both the party and the people on his side, and he took the oath of office in 1817.

GOVERNOR (1817-23)

From the beginning of his governorship, Clinton pushed hard for the completion of the canal system. Tammany Hall, however, began to bring charges against the Governor and his canal, and petty party bickering ensued. When Clinton refused to discharge public servants in wholesale fashion, he received the wrath of both Republicans and Federalists. These divisions prevented Clinton from accomplishing many goals, and his achievements were less than when he was Mayor, although he did establish a state Library and initiated the annual New York observance of Thanksgiving. He opposed a movement for a new state constitution, supported Federalist Rufus King in his successful re-election, and had Van Buren removed as state Attorney General, a move that almost encouraged Vice President Tompkins, immensely popular in New York, to again run for Governor against Clinton. Tompkins, however, declined to run, and

Clinton was re-elected in 1820. During this term, a state constitutional convention was held, and a new document was adopted providing for new veto measures but reducing the term of governor from three years to two. The judiciary system was also revised. Clinton's second term saw the realignment of the Republicans; Van Buren was now firmly in command, and Clinton, being pragmatic, decided it best not to seek re-election to the Governor's office.

Van Buren would not let the retiring Governor live in peace or dignity. He manipulated the legislature into passing without debate a measure removing Clinton from his beloved Canal Board. This was especially harsh to Clinton, who had never received compensation from this service. The dismissal also came during a period of extreme difficulty for Clinton, who had recently lost his first wife, Mary, the mother of his ten children. A devoted and loving father, he had already suffered considerably when several of his children had died. To add to his woes, both his father and uncle-mentor had also both passed away in 1812, and he was without their counsel. Though he later remarried, many thought that much of the vigor for his well-rounded life was gone. This may have seemed so also because of an accident that saw his leg broken, which caused him to walk with a limp the rest of his life, and which eventually lead to the general failure of his health.

Martin Van Buren may have thought he had plotted Clinton's demise, but he soon found that that shoddy treatment did not end DeWitt Clinton's career. As the canal came closer to completion and was dedicated in October, 1825, Clinton received an outpouring of respect and affection that, together with his return to the Governor's chair, found him being considered seriously again for the Presidency. Thomas Jefferson was supposed to have remarked that "...the President of the United States ought to be the greatest man in America... D.W.C." Clinton was certainly qualified to be President, but 1824 was to be John Quincy Adams' year, even if by a "corrupt bargain." Many thought that DeWitt Clinton, probably the most able government servant in the country, would become Secretary of State and "heir apparent" to Adams, but that post went to Henry Clay, who had arranged Adams' election. Clinton was offered the position of Ambassador to Great Britain, but he declined the appointment.

His national stature increased, and he was now speaking in other states about internal improvements. He had sided as early as 1824 with Andrew Jackson, who had toasted him, to the chagrin of Van Buren and others, on a visit to Tammany Hall in 1819. In 1828 he was supporting the General for election, and Van Buren, a campaign manager for Jackson, was frantically patching up relations with the ever popular Clinton. Talk was rampant that DeWitt Clinton would be named as Secretary of State — and "heir apparent" — to Andrew Jackson when he was elected President in 1828.

UNTIMELY DEATH

Unfortunately, DeWitt Clinton's health failed just as the steps to appoint him were about to be put in motion. He suffered a case of severe influenza, made all the worse by a large gain in weight from his broken leg in 1818. His condition worsened until he died, probably from a heart attack, on February 8, 1828. A great outcry of shock and deep remorse swept the country, especially in New York state and New York City.

Yet when all the official mourning was over, it was discovered that DeWitt Clinton had died in debt. His estate was attached and his furniture sold to cover what he owed. His family was not provided for and no one came forward to offer help, although over the years he had devoted his life to many noble causes, giving countless sums to worthy aims. Finally, the state of New York passed a bill granting his family the unpaid portion of his salary as Governor and $10,000 cash. His old political enemies would not go for $20,000 — such was the case of partisan politics in New York.

Buried in a plot of a family friend, the man who had built New York's greatest wonder, the Erie Canal, was not publicly enshrined or recognized. Finally, in 1844, members of his family and other close friends removed his remains from the borrowed plot and placed them in a more suitable site in Brooklyn, complete with a full-sized bronze statue. It seems totally unfitting that it took sixteen years — almost as long as it took to construct the Erie Canal — for DeWitt Clinton, one of the great early leaders of New York and the United States, to receive a proper burial.

Rufus King
The Election of 1816

"You never heard such a speaker. In strength, and dignity, and fire; in ease, in natural effect, and gesture as well as manner, he is unequalled." So said none other than the renowned orator Daniel Webster of one of America's outstanding early leaders. From the time of the Revolution until the time of Jackson, Rufus King, now obscured by the passage of time, was a dominant and effective political leader. His unsuccessful candidacy for the Presidency in 1816 does not diminish the valuable contributions he made to his country.

COLONIAL MASSACHUSETTS LAD

King was born March 24, 1755, in Scarboro, Maine, which was at that time a subdivision of Massachusetts. His parents were of English stock and well established as merchants. His father held various political positions in his community, including Selectman. His connections were apparently very high, for none other than John Adams represented Rufus King's father in his legal affairs.

Young Rufus attended grammar school in Scarboro and then went off to Dummer Boarding School near Newburyport, Massachusetts. He received classical tutoring from professors who had graduated from Harvard, in which he himself enrolled in 1773. There King engaged in various student activities, particularly the Speaking Club, and graduated "with the first honors of the class of 1777, which was considered an excellent one. He was not only first in mathematics, the languages and oratory, but took the lead in every athletic sport, running, jumping, and swimming." While at Harvard, King also began a lifelong support of the Anglican Church, which was a departure from his Congregationalist upbringing.

King also departed from his loyalist upbringing. His father was a devoted Tory who at one point was forced by patriots to kneel at gunpoint and refute statements of loyalty to the Crown. King's early correspondence shows a clear sympathy for the Colonists, but some citizens in his home town of Scarboro decided that he was a Tory. When drummed-up charges of horse stealing were brought against King, he decided to keep his residence at Newburyport, where he was studying law and where his father's background may not have been as well known. He had received an excellent farm as an inheritance from his father, and he converted this through various transactions into cash which tided him over until the Revolution was over and he could establish himself as a lawyer.

Because King was a student during most of the Revolutionary War, he did not become a soldier until 1778, when he was twenty-three. He was an aide-de-camp with the rank of Major to General John Glover and saw service in the Newport, Rhode Island arena. Among those with whom he served were John Hancock and the (General) Marquis de LaFayette. He luckily escaped injury when he was sent from the officer's dining hall on an errand; the fellow officer who took his place at the kitchen mess table lost his leg when a cannonade struck the hall. With a commendable but inglorious military service (which he had not desired) behind him, King was discharged in 1779.

INTO POLITICS

After the Revolution, King continued his law studies and obtained his Massachusetts license to practice law. He practiced in the County Common Pleas Court for three years and then was admitted to practice before the Supreme Judicial Court. He soon obtained a reputation as a first-rate attorney, especially being noted for his ability to persuade through his speech. His cases were mostly civil, and more often than not he won. His financial success was established at an early age.

As he began to prosper, King entered into the civic affairs of Newburyport. He was a "visitor" of the town's schools, became a warden of St. Paul's Episcopal Church, became a Mason, and attended the various social events of the area. He became romantically involved with a local girl whom he desired to marry, but she ran off with another man, some said, because of an illicit affair. King entertained hopes of a reconciliation after her husband's death from small pox, but she also died shortly thereafter.

Predictably, the young attorney from Massachusetts who had graduated from Adams' Harvard would be a Federalist. In 1783, at age twenty-eight, he was selected to fill the unexpired term of a vacant Massachusetts state legislative seat and served there until 1786. Like C.C. Pinckney in South Carolina, he did not sympathize with the movement to confiscate Tory property. During this period, King and Elbridge Gerry opposed the Society of Cincinnati in Massachusetts. He also opposed certain legislation for imposing a tariff for federal revenues. His parliamentary skills coupled with his oratorical ability found him soon being elected to the Congress of the Confederation, that assemblage which first governed the new United States under the loosely constructed Articles of Confederation. King made two primary contributions while serving from 1784-87 in the Congress: first, he took the lead in supporting a financial bill that would give regular financial support from the states to the Congress; secondly, he joined none other than Thomas Jefferson in inserting an anti-slavery provision into the Northwest Ordinance, thereby prohibiting new states in the Northwest Territory from allowing slavery.

The Congress met first in Trenton, but that city could not accommodate the delegates properly since the New Jersey state legislature was also in session there. A move was made to move the site of the Congress, and New York won out over Boston. This proved to be a significant choice in the life of King. While in New York he grew close to Alexander Hamilton, John Jay and Robert Livingston, and he naturally became involved deeply in Federalist matters. He also met and fell in love with Mary Alsop, the eighteen year old daughter of a wealthy merchant who had been President of the New York Chamber of Commerce and a delegate to First and Second Continental Congresses (he withdrew after the Declaration of Independence, preferring a reconciliation with England). The inheritance and family ties of Mary Alsop King would secure King's future and eventually lead him to a permanent residence in New York City.

Of course, the Articles of Confederation were not a satisfactory basis for governing the new nation. King was a faithful member of the body, attaining perfect attendance in his first term, and missing meetings in his two other terms only when he had pressing business. He quickly recognized that the government under the Articles was too weak, especially when it came to the funding of the government. When a Convention was called to meet in Philadelphia to discuss ways to strengthen the Articles, King was a delegate from Massachusetts. Absent from Massachusetts at this meeting were John Adams (then Minister to England), Samuel Adams and John Hancock, all of whom had signed the Declaration of Independence. Present, however, was one signer of the Declaration, Elbridge Gerry, who is most remembered today for his "gerrymandering" schemes while Governor of The Bay Colony. He refused to sign the Constitution, fearing "too much democracy," but he did not later refuse to serve as Vice President (1813-14) under Madison. Gerry became the first sitting Vice President to die while in office.

King participated in all of the great debates of the Philadelphia meeting. He joined an early move to go further than just altering the Articles. His previous experience as an Articles Congressman showed him that a strong federal government was essential, and he went on record early as being in favor of a new document. His Federalist leanings were easily detectable: he favored seven year terms for the president (later he tried for a twenty year term, like a "prince"); he also favored an absolute executive veto; and he favored the Virginia Plan, which allowed greater power to the larger states than to the smaller states. When a tie vote occurred on the acceptability of this plan, King was chosen to represent Massachusetts on a select committee to work out a compromise. He bitterly opposed slavery but recognized that a plan had to be presented which would allow the South to retain its commercial position and the Northern smaller states to retain their voting rights. It was from this setting that the bicameral legislative system, the "three-fifths" formula with the 1808 expiration date for importing slaves, and the constitutional ban on taxing exports by states were approved. King also introduced the provision that ratification would occur with the approval of nine of the thirteen states rather than by approval of the Congress of the Articles of Confederation. By signing the document, King became immortalized as a "Founding Father" of the United States.

King returned to Newburyport, from which he had been absent for three years, and barely earned election to the state Constitutional Convention. In Boston he fervently defended the new document, explaining step-by-step the reasons the delegates at Philadelphia had adopted the various provisions. Several points arose that had to be addressed. First, the question of certain civil liberties was brought up by Gerry; this ultimately resulted in the consent of Massachusetts subject to the "Bill of Rights" being approved. Secondly, to achieve approval, John Hancock contrived a political scheme. In return for his pivotal support for the Constitution and the Bill of Rights, he would at the least be supported for Governor, for Vice President possibly, or for President *if* Virginia did not ratify the Constitution. This scheme was accepted, and Massachusetts ratified the document. This conclave provided an excellent example of King's ability to compromise positions that were in part repugnant to him so that the nation's overall best interests could be served.

MOVING TO NEW YORK

King returned to his wife in New York after Massachusetts ratified the new Constitution and pondered his future. After a short period of time, he returned to his home state to seek elective office. He found that, just as in Newburyport some years earlier, his popularity had faded. King decided to move to New York, and this proved to be a fortuitous move. Within ten days of moving to his adopted state, King was elected to the new state assembly. This body at that time was responsible for electing Senators, and King was chosen by compromise as one of New York's first two Senators when Alexander Hamilton decided that one nominee would not be as responsive to the cause of Federalism (and Hamilton) as would King. By drawing straws, King won a six year term rather than one for two years.

IN THE SENATE (1789-96)

Being a Senator, since it met at first in New York, was a truly enjoyable position for King. It not only provided him with a stimulating challenge but afforded him and his wife gratifying social callings. It was not unusual for President Washington, who particularly enjoyed entertaining guests, to have Senator and Mrs. King for evening dinner. It was also fashionable for the Vice President or Cabinet Members to entertain in the evenings, and Sen. and Mrs. King were always pleased to attend such events.

King's first term as Senator revealed him as a steady and reliable Federalist. Being not only a friend but a disciple of Hamilton, he supported especially those bills that called for a stronger national government. He was behind the movement to have the federal government assume the debts of the states. He later reluctantly supported, since he loved New York City so much, the compromise to move the nation's Capital to Philadelphia for ten years while the new federal Capital was being built in the District of Columbia. He also supported the first National Bank and was appointed to its Board of Directors, serving at the same time on the Board of the Bank of New York. King opposed the extension of slavery and was for the removal of the secret debates under which the Senate operated. He also believed in a strong national defense, voting for bills to strengthen frontier defenses against unfriendly Indians and to create West Point. Time and again, he voted for protective tariffs and interior improvements. So Federalist was King that he opposed the appointment of the eminently qualified Albert Gallatin as Ambassador to France, using the length of Gallatin's citizenship as his reason for opposition, though Gallatin's Republican leanings were the real reason.

The Republicans were making gains politically in New York, but King was an effective advocate for Federalism. In 1793 he supported John Jay, then Supreme Court Justice and considered a possible future Federalist candidate for President, against the incumbent, George Clinton, for Governor. Clinton's long tenure made him a vulnerable opponent, and Jay was the apparent victor over Clinton. Clinton, unwilling to cede his seat, however, challenged the votes in several counties and managed through questionable means to retain his position. When Clinton tried to obtain the Vice Presidency after Washington was elected to a second term, King led the opposition to Clinton and was greatly relieved when John Adams was re-elected.

King chose to support the Federalist cause on the most controversial treaty in American history — the Jay Treaty with Great Britain. This treaty gave the United States practically nothing in return for the United States waiving claims for damages to American shipping by the British. Aggravating the matter even further was Britain's refusal to refrain from the practice of impressing American seamen. The issue which created Jay's mission, that of trade with the West Indies, was not even addressed in the treaty. The Republican press was indignant, and the country was bitter. Attempts to explain the Treaty by Federalist spokesmen such as Hamilton were greeted with hisses and boos, and, on one occasion, a stoning. Washington astutely kept the treaty private until the New York gubernatorial election of 1796 was complete and Jay declared the winner. A series of newspaper debates ensued with Republican Robert Livingston using "Cato" and "Curtiurs" as pseudonyms, while Federalists Hamilton, King and Jay used "Camillus". Through King's management, the Senate, by a bare two-thirds minimum margin (20 to 10), passed the Jay Treaty. Many now believe that the passage of the Jay Treaty created irreparable damage to the Federalist cause and began that Party's downfall.

Another rousing issue of the day surrounded Citizen Edmond Genet, who landed in the United States at Charleston, South Carolina and began a tour northward explaining the rights of Frenchman. King was typical of many Federalists: he was horrified when the "Bloody" revolution occurred and the heads of monarchs and lesser members of the nobility rolled. Genet made many partisan Republican statements in his attempt to enlist American support for the French Revolution before committing a fatal mistake — he threatened to appeal to the American people over the head of George Washington, who had declared "Neutrality" between England and France in their latest war. It was King and John Jay who published articles revealing Genet's threats, and this caused Jefferson and the Republicans to back down from their previous support of the French troublemaker. Genet sued King and Jay for libel but later withdrew his complaint, quieting down considerably when he lost the support of the radical French government and was warned that he himself might be a candidate for the guillotine. He sought and received asylum in America, married the daughter of Governor George Clinton, and became considerably less vocal.

As the Presidential election of 1796 approached, King was persuaded by Hamilton to consider contenders other than John Adams for the Presidency. Hamilton did not, first of all, fully trust or admire Adams and, secondly, sincerely felt a Southerner was needed to win. After Patrick Henry was approached and found unwilling to serve, a scheme was concocted by Hamilton which was by any standard devious. He persuaded Thomas

Pinckney to run with Adams. Though everyone assumed Pinckney would be the Vice President on a successful Federalist ticket, Hamilton and King had other ideas. Their plan, if successful, would have had the Federalist electors place Pinckney's name first. As with so many macabre schemes, Hamilton and King were exposed, and the plot failed.

AMBASSADOR TO GREAT BRITAIN

King was getting tired of all the political debate and intrigue found in the Senate and desired a change of scene. He openly sought to be Ambassador to Great Britain. Washington was approached through Hamilton and others, and the appointment was readily made. After resigning from the Senate, one New York Congressman remarked that "he [King] is justly deemed the main pillar of that important branch [the Senate] of government." King left for England in June, 1796, and was to remain there until 1802.

The new Ambassador was able to settle into the life of London with relative ease. He began his service when Pitt was Prime Minister and Lord Grenville was Foreign Secretary. King became acquainted intimately with business leaders and members of the British government and was soon pleading the commercial causes of the states. He initiated a demand that Maryland be reimbursed for bank stock owned before the Revolution, and ultimately Maryland collected £200,000. He was also able to keep American merchants apprised of the English financial scene. In another matter dear to Americans, King worked successfully for the release of LaFayette from an Austrian prison.

But the primary duty of King while in England dealt with the intrusions of England first and France secondly into the naval affairs of American merchant and government vessels. Britain had begun to impress American seamen when her own naval population declined. King was extremely patient in pursuing matters with the imperious British, and he exhibited a high degree of skill and tact in his continuing negotiations. At one point he had an agreement with Lord Grenville for the cessation of the British actions, but then the Pitt government fell. Being a Federalist under the pro-British Adams, King's dealings with the British were always tolerant, and war with England was averted. When Adams was succeeded by the Republican Jefferson, King was retained in his post. France then began actions almost identical to England, but these acts of impressment and damage to American shipping were viewed with a more vehement attitude by King. The record of the French Directory, with its record of brutal executions, was no doubt his reason for a less tolerant attitude toward the French. A far more bitter resentment by Americans, however, resulted when bribes were demanded during the notorious XYZ Affair. King did all he could to encourage the United States to stand firm against the French. When the Irish tried to revolt in a manner similar to the French, however, King supported the British government, encouraging it not to allow members of that element to immigrate into the United States. He was also upset with a revolution in Santo Domingo, fearing a spread to the slaves in Jamaica and perhaps America. Yet King was in favor of South American independence, which was not in the interests of either the Spanish or the French, and which would also not benefit the English. King was also busy during the escapades of the Barbary Pirates and was instructed to purchase certain gifts of bribes. He utterly detested his role, warning "...our security against the Barbary powers must depend upon force and not upon Treaties, upon ships of war instead of Presents and subsidies."

An embarrassing moment for King arose after he had negotiated certain Mississippi River navigation rights with the British before the Louisiana Purchase. When the successful purchase from the French was made, the Senate rejected provisions in King's treaty with the British. Not fully aware of all the Franco-American negotiations over Louisiana, King felt snubbed by the Jefferson Administration's refusal to support his treaty negotiations and resigned as Ambassador. Ironically, it was King who personally brought back to the United States news of the Louisiana acquisition.

FEDERALIST LEADER AND VICE PRESIDENTIAL CANDIDATE

Returning home in 1803, King found that he was being considered for high office by the Federalist Party. The Republicans, who knew King to be both able and honest, feared he might be selected as the Presidential candidate. Federalists had already decided for the most part, though, to run King for Vice President under Charles Cotesworth Pinckney of South Carolina. An attempt to persuade King to run for Governor of New York was opposed by King himself because of the many personal affairs he had to attend to after being away for over five years.

On February 22, 1804 — Washington's birthday — a Federalist dinner meeting in Washington nominated Pinckney and King as their ticket. Their opposition was to be the incumbent Jefferson and a new Vice Presidential nominee, George Clinton, the long-time Republican foe from New York, to replace the infamous Aaron Burr. The election of 1804 was probably decided long before the Federalist candidates were nominated. The Republican Jefferson had greatly enhanced American prestige and pride with the Louisiana Purchase. Furthermore, Republicans were allowing more people to vote, irregardless of class. The Federalists were putting up a ticket more or less as a hope of better things to come.

An unfortunate by-product of this period of time was the demise of Alexander Hamilton. When Jefferson became disenchanted with Burr after his attempts to steal the Presidency in 1800, he had no choice but to drop him from the ticket in 1804. Burr then decided to run for Governor of New York that year. Hamilton approached King and begged him to run against the heinous Burr, who was garnering considerable Federalist support, but King realized he could not win and declined to run. Hamilton set about on one of his schemes to defeat Burr, in the process making remarks which Burr regarded as so derogatory that a challenge was issued. King advised Hamilton to disregard both Burr's demand for an explanation and his challenge to a duel. Hamilton's refusal to heed this advice cost him his life and plunged King into deep sorrow. The Federalist Party and the nation would sorely miss this effective but temperamental leader.

During this campaign period, former Secretary of State Timothy Pickering proposed that five New England states break away from the United States and form its own government. To his great credit, King privately opposed this movement, but he chose not to make a public statement. The entire country continued to turn Republican. King was secretly nominated in the state legislature for Senator but overwhelmingly lost to the Republican candidate. He held no illusions about the outcome of the 1804 Presidential election and was not in the least surprised at Jefferson's landslide, 162 to 14, in the Electoral College.

King settled back into his home life and civic work, wondering if he would get another call to public service. He became a warden of Trinity Episcopal Church and a charter member of the Academy of Fine Arts. He was a firm supporter of education, being a Trustee of Columbia College, where he led a successful movement to overturn Episcopalian domination, and was also a Trustee of Union Hall Academy as well as a commissioner of common schools.

Private citizen King became involved in public life again as a result of an old British practice: attacking American ships and impressing sailors. Jefferson wanted King to be an envoy to England, where he was respected, but King declined when Jefferson would not meet his demand that he have full control of negotiations and then let the President and the Senate decide their usefulness. When the British attacked a small boat near New York and killed one man, King and other Federalists became upset. The Federalists then became irate when the *Leopard* attacked the *Chesapeake,* killing and wounding some American sailors as well as impressing others. The entire country was up in arms against the British, and when Jefferson's Administration did not retaliate against the British, it was met with considerable opposition. A scheme was then hatched to nominate Vice President Clinton for President rather than James Madison, who was closely associated with the Embargo of 1807 that had financially damaged Federalist New York merchants, to succeed Jefferson. Clinton, however, was too repugnant to the Federalists, who met secretly in New York City in August, 1808, and renominated Pinckney and King. Unlike the election of 1804, the Federalists truly thought they could defeat Madison (who, incidentally, had Clinton as his running mate). But although the Federalists in 1808 were to improve their performance over 1804, the Republicans still controlled the White House, winning in the Electoral College by 122 to 47.

INTERIM PERIOD (1809-1816)

Without a political platform from which to operate in 1809, King still held respect as a "Founding Father" and senior statesman and was able to sound his views on various issues. He was predictably in favor of improving relations with England and was pleased when Jefferson negotiated a relaxed agreement with the British. Unfortunately the British chose to dishonor the entire agreement, claiming that they had the right to trade in American ports while forcing the United States to cancel French trade. This violation of American sovereignty offended even the normally pro-British King, who saw that American honor and reputation would diminish rapidly by accepting this British provision. King saw clearly through the scheme of the astute Napoleon Bonaparte, who was attempting a power play similar to that of the British. But Napoleon's moves proved to be more effective than England's. The British refused to rescind Orders of Council allowing impressment, while Napoleon agreed to release American ships if action against the British were taken. This soon happened when the Republican Congress led by the "War Hawks" (Clay and Calhoun) voted a new embargo which was a prelude to a declaration of war. War was declared after the British refused to accede to the new embargo's demands.

Except for Viet Nam, the War of 1812 was probably the most unpopular clash of arms in which the United States has engaged, and Rufus King was at the forefront of opposition. Coming from merchant oriented New York, his area suffered considerably in trade. It also had historically leaned toward England rather than France. The declaration of war in Congress had passed without overwhelming support, and the public was clearly not behind the effort, with King saying it was "...a war of party, and not of Country." Madison, who did not have the charisma of Jefferson, was soon faced with serious opposition for re-election in 1812. People from New England had long been trying to break the Virginia "dynasty," and Republican DeWitt Clinton saw an opportunity to unite both Federalists and Republicans throughout the country and especially in the New England area to unseat Madison. King was quite opposed to Clinton, thinking his true goal might be that of trying to get the Republican Vice Presidential nomination to succeed his uncle, who had died in office. Many Federalists wanted King to run in 1812, but he knew his cause would not be effective. A Federalist convention was held in New York City in September, 1812, and while it did not nominate a candidate, it found it expedient to support a candidate who might try to change the course of state. King apparently opposed this move, but Clinton for all practical purposes was the Federalist candidate in 1812. His race was the most successful for a Federalist since Adams; yet he too was defeated decisively in the Electoral College.

Shortly thereafter, King was again elected to the United States Senate. Coming so closely after the Federalist candidacy of Clinton, some, among them a young Congressman named Martin Van Buren, felt that a deal had been perpetrated between Clinton and King. However, a more likely story is that King received the support of influential bankers who could rely on favorable actions in the Senate by King.

In May, 1813, at age fifty-eight, King took the seat of a Senator once again. His Federalist Party was fading in influence, but his stature personally was to rise again, primarily due to the circumstances surrounding the War of 1812. Very soon, opportunities arose for King to make himself a primary spokesman against Madison. Madison appointed an Ambassador to Sweden unsuitable to King and others, and King had the nomination squashed. Then he successfully opposed the nomination of Gallatin as a peace commissioner, under the pretense that the Treasury Secretary could not hold two federal offices simultaneously. King also made a strong call for fortification of the New York harbor and later supported Maryland in its claim that its defenses were not adequate. The war was creating havoc with the American financial system; despite this, King would not for the most part support Madison's measures to raise taxes. When chances for peace arose, King was delighted that relations with Britain might be restored. He was also pleased to hear that Napoleon had fallen, though he realized that Britain might now be able to concentrate more effort on the United States. The United States had in fact already taken a beating by the British and was weary of the issues which had led it into war. The question of impressment was no longer of importance — if peace could be achieved. King was in fact playing politics, realizing that the credibility of the Republicans was sinking and that perhaps his chances in 1816 were ripe. His possibilities had been increased most by the burning and sacking of Washington. He was also gaining support for opposing, on constitutional grounds, the very unpopular idea of conscription, or the drafting, of soldiers. Rumors were rampant that

Madison might call King into the Cabinet and have all senior Cabinet members resign so that the pro-British King could become President and negotiate peace. However, two events changed this. The first was the Treaty of Ghent. The other was Andrew Jackson's fabulous victory at New Orleans, which restored American (and Republican) prestige after the War of 1812 had been settled.

Like Henry Clay, King changed his position on a National Bank, opposing the creation of one in 1814 although he had been a chief proponent of the first bank. He was hopeful that the treaty with England would restore the commercial success of the United States. He voted for a tariff but was opposed to a stronger military department. King was now the only "Founding Father" in the Senate, and he continually reminded other Senators of the intentions of the Constitution. He argued unsuccessfully at one point, for example, that it was the original intention of the Constitution to have Electors chosen by District rather than state.

In 1816, a secret Federalist caucus nominated King for Governor of New York. King was incensed at being selected, but was persuaded to run on the basis that DeWitt Clinton would run and defeat Governor (later Vice President) Tompkins, whom King respected more. When King consented to run, the Republicans promptly made him a target of many assertions: he had received British protection in New York in the Revolutionary War; he had refused to denounce Irish revolutionaries; his son, as an investigator of the treatment of American prisoners in the War of 1812, found no fault with the British actions; and he had personally misused the inheritance of a widow. King was overwhelmingly defeated.

THE ELECTION OF 1816

Though King had twice been unsuccessful as a Vice Presidential candidate and also unsuccessful as a candidate for Governor, he was still the most renowned Federalist in the country. Therefore, he was made an "unofficial" candidate in 1816 against James Monroe, who had served with King as a "Founding Father" in 1787, and who years earlier had also attended King's wedding in New York City. Monroe's running mate was Governor Tompkins. King made no effort to campaign or delude himself into thinking he would win. King later remarked that "...he had the zealous support of nobody..." Monroe's victory in the Electoral College was a landslide, 183 to 34.

SENATE LEADER

King's activities in the Senate became less political and more states-manlike. He opposed a "Home" Cabinet department and fought for protective tariffs. He pushed for American sea power and merchant shipping dominance. He was the prime supporter for a new Navigation Act. He pointed out that speculators were taking advantage of the new National Bank.

In June, 1819, King's wife of almost thirty years died after a lengthy illness. She had borne him five sons, all of whom would be successful: one would be Governor of New York; another an editor; one a merchant and banker; another a lawyer and Ohio legislator; and another a physician. Each was in some way an embodiment of the remarkable King. It is interesting to also note that a half-brother had been Governor of Maine.

King's final years in the Senate were quiet but determined. He retained his Federalist trade ideas as partisans crossed party lines during the "Era of Good Feelings." He supported Andrew Jackson's mission into Florida. In 1820 certain Republicans opposed King's re-election, but he prevailed after a long and arduous campaign. He was strongly supported by Martin Van Buren, and the two became close friends when Van Buren later became the junior Senator from New York.

The final thrust of King's Senate tenure was for the end of slavery. He opposed the Missouri Compromise, hoping that a schism would erupt to resolve this stigma once and for all. Some, including the retired Jefferson, thought King had a scheme to restore the Federalists, but King was through with national election hopes for his party and did not in 1820 speak against James Monroe, the only President besides Washington to run unopposed.

Rumblings in New York created a convention for a new state Constitution. King was a delegate to this meeting with a number of distinguished New Yorkers: Vice President Tompkins (the chairman); future President Van Buren; former Chief Justice John Jay; and former Presidential candidate DeWitt Clinton. Without much success he pushed his views against slavery. He tried to have property ownership as a requirement for voting but was not successful. On the whole, the new state Constitution was a Republican document which King did not support with glee. It passed on popular vote by a wide margin.

King decided to retire from the Senate and public life after his term expired in 1824. He also began resigning civic posts, such as Trustee of Colombia. He participated in a dinner for LaFayette when the French Marquis made his final triumphant tour of the United States and then, at age seventy, planned to settle down. President John Quincy Adams then prevailed upon him to once again become Minister to England, and he reluctantly accepted. In England, the elderly King was pleased to receive greetings from many whom he had known a quarter of a century earlier. But his duties were tiring to him, and his efforts to resolve damages, including slave indemnities, from the War of 1812 were all in vain. The British rebuffed him, and King resigned the post, stating his belief that he could not be effective.

The elder statesman was seriously ill as he began his journey by ship back to the states. Gravely weak upon arrival, he went first to his country home, but was soon moved to New York City, where his physician son could more closely care for him. There he died on April 29, 1827, a man never either popularly accepted by the people of his time or truly recognized by future generations as a "Founding Father" and sturdy proponent of the institutions of freedom which so many Americans have enjoyed.

Henry Clay

The Elections of 1824, 1832 and 1844

Eminently qualified as a Congressman, Speaker of the House, Senator and Secretary of State, Henry Clay was by any measure one of the most outstanding men ever to seek the Presidency. He made the mistake of acquiring Andrew Jackson as an enemy, and this cost him his life's goal. He still made so many major contributions to the nation, though, that he is today regarded as on one of the all-time great Americans.

VIRGINIA BIRTH

The United States was not yet one year old when on April 12, 1777, a boy — the fifth of seven children — was born to a poor Baptist minister and his wife in frontier Hanover County, Virginia. The neighborhood to which he was born was called the "Slashes," a name which seems retrospectively to portend the life of political romance than Henry Clay would lead.

Life on the frontier was not easy, and the life of his father was cut short, when Henry was only four. After a period of time the widow Clay married a Captain Harry Watkins, a move which would prove providential to Henry's fortunes. Henry attended school for a short time in a typical frontier one room log cabin, and at age fourteen, through the influence of his step-father, he secured a position as a "boy behind the counter" in a Richmond retail store. There Clay soon exhibited a knack for quick learning and excellent ability plus a remarkable affinity for reading and speaking easily with others. Captain Watkins, aware of the youth's outstanding talents, arranged a position for Henry as a supernumary in the High Court of Chancery. Clay undoubtedly realized that this was an opportunity that could not be wasted, and he set about to do his work with diligence, again showing an uncommon easiness with words. He often reported to work in ill-fitting, heavily starched clothing, leaving an awkward appearance in many respects, but he worked hard at self-improvement; while his colleagues partied at night, he "read books," probably realizing at this early age that the limits to his ambitions rested with his own efforts and talents.

Clay soon got a break of uncommon proportions. It happened that Chancellor George Wythe of the High Court of Chancery — that same George Wythe of Revolutionary War fame who had tutored and mentored the likes of Thomas Jefferson and John Marshall — noticed the efficiency of Clay and offered him a position as an amanuensis, to write out and record decisions of the High Court. Clay suddenly found himself in a position which required skill and offered the potential to expand his abilities while at the same time having contact with many of the stimulating intellectual figures in the new Republic.

It did not take Clay long to decide to become a lawyer or to pursue a notable career, as had others who had clerked for Wythe. He subsequently entered the office of Robert Brooke, the Virginia Attorney General, and received, after about a year's study, a license to practice law. Clay entered into the legal and social life of the new Virginia capital of Richmond with ease but found that making a living was not so easy. His mother and step-father had moved to Kentucky, and Henry decided to join them there and "grow up in the wilds."

KENTUCKY BEGINNINGS

Tradition has it that Clay, who had been a member of debating societies in Richmond, joined one upon arrival in Lexington, and while listening to a debate one evening, was overheard muttering that the debate had not been exhausted. The presiding officer called upon Clay to speak, and when he did, the new Kentuckian impressed all present with his ability to stand on his feet, reason and issue an impassioned plea.

He began his practice of law and defended one lady on murder charges by reason of "temporary delirium." Others charged with capital crimes sought his services, and none that he defended was ever sentenced to death. Later as a prosecutor, however, he was successful in securing death by hanging of a slave accused of killing a harsh overseer, a verdict that haunted Clay throughout his life. Clay also began a successful civil practice and began to take part in various social activities, particularly debating societies. It is said that he constantly rehearsed speeches so that he could outshine his opponents and was ready in a wink to take up almost any subject with full mastery.

In just a little over a year after having left Virginia, Clay at age twenty-two secured the hand of Lucretia Hart, a Kentucky belle with notable roots. She was most devoted to Henry, and together they had eleven children. The couple prospered, and soon they purchased Ashland, a 600 acre estate near Lexington. About this same time Clay, who seemed to have a penchant for being in the right place at the right time, began writing articles and making speeches for the emancipation of slaves in Kentucky, just as a call was being made for a state constitutional amendment to ban slavery.

Clay's anti-slavery pronouncements did not endear him to Kentucky frontiersmen, but when the French promulgated the infamous 1799 XYZ affair, he was able to magnetize Kentucky voters with his fiery oratorical denunciations of the French. In 1803, he won his first elective office, state legislator. At the Kentucky capital of Frankfort, Clay's reputation as a debater was quickly established.

Like many a politician in frontier days who spoke sharply, Clay participated in duels, but he was never injured. Clay had more than a passing acquaintance with Aaron Burr, actually even successfully defending him on charges of engaging in an unlawful enterprise with a foreign power with which the United States was at peace. Only later did Clay realize that he had been grievously misled by Burr.

EARLY WASHINGTON DAYS

In 1806 Clay was appointed to fill the unexpired term of a resigned United States Senator, and he journeyed to that center of American political life that was to occupy his energies and talents throughout the rest of his days. It is interesting to note that Clay may hold title to the distinction of being the youngest U.S. Senator ever, for he took his seat on December 29, 1806, which was some three months and seventeen days before his thirtieth birthday. No one bothered to raise a constitutional question about it, though, and Clay began his illustrious career in the Congress.

From Virginia and with the background of Wythe, Clay was quite naturally a Jefferson Republican. His early speeches showed an interest in internal improvements, and the foundation for the "American System" that he was later to introduce was laid. He was inspired by the mission of Lewis and Clark and was surely captivated when Jefferson spoke of *OUR CONTINENT!*

Clay's term ended in March, 1807. When he returned home, he was again elected to the state legislature. Rumblings in Europe between England and Napoleanic France had begun, and when England began to impress American sailors, President Jefferson found that in rural Kentucky a patriotic ardor of defiance against the British had erupted. At the forefront of the anti-British sentiment was young Henry Clay, ready to assault the Red Coats on almost any count, even proposing that the people of Kentucky wear no British made clothing.

Clay was then selected to fill the unexpired term of another resigned U.S. Senator. He showed interest in the advancement of "Home Industry" and became a confidant of Albert Gallatin, the Secretary of the Treasury. He also took a keen interest in the debates over the Spanish Cession of Florida and the National Bank.

On the Florida question, Clay, showing some initial signs of being a "War Hawk," was President Madison's instrument of defense in the Senate after one Federalist Senator complained that the South and West showed no sympathy for the British cause. "I shall leave the honourable gentleman from Delaware to mourn over the fortunes of the fallen Charles. My sympathies are reserved for the great masses of mankind...," said Clay, leaving no one in doubt as to his feelings about England.

The issue of the rechartering of a National Bank in 1811 found Clay, a Republican strict constructionist, voting with other Senators to defeat by one vote (it had passed in the house) the Bank's charter. Twenty years later, he would be fighting his indomitable foe, Andrew Jackson, in favor of a new National Bank.

SPEAKER OF THE HOUSE

Upon completion of his second temporary term as Senator, Clay was elected to the House of Representatives, taking his seat in December, 1811. Both fiery and flowery, Clay said he "preferred the turbulence of the House to the solemn stillness of the Senate." Clay was joined in the House by a new group of young Congressmen who were to be the "War Hawks," those who were tired of British impressment and English blockades, and whose sympathies were with America's oldest ally, France, in the European conflict. Among these Hawks was John C. Calhoun from South Carolina, who, like Clay, was to be a formidable force on the American political scene until the 1850's.

Clay's previous pronouncements about British activities in Florida were instrumental in the House electing him its Speaker. As soon as he was installed, he began a series of fiery tirades against the British, forever reminding his colleagues of the embarrassments of impressment and the British attack on an American frigate (the *Leopard*). He was instrumental in seeing that the U.S. had an extraordinarily large military buildup of the Army and Navy. At that time both the British and French, once again at conflict in Europe, were blockading American shipments at home and foreign ports, and the economic results to Americans as well as belligerent

Europeans were devastating. President Madison contrived the seemingly ingenious proposal of having the United States trade with whichever European adversary first broke the "non-intercourse" of trade with the United States. France moved first and trade between the U.S. and France began. Britain had the opportunity to alter its policies, but a dispatch from London to the British minister at Washington revealed that the dreaded British "Orders of Council," which forbade trade, would not be rescinded. Clay immediately incited a call for a declaration of war, certain in his own imagination that with the British occupied in Europe, the Americans could sweep through Canada and dictate terms of peace.

Of course that did not happen. The War of 1812 was not prosecuted properly by President Madison, and only a few victories, mostly in the West or the South, were won. Along the Canadian border, the U.S. scored some initial successes but then suffered several defeats. Of course, ultimate humiliation came with the burning of Washington and the White House as British retribution for the American burning of York (later Toronto). Had it not been for American successes in the South, the American reputation no doubt would have suffered drastically, and it is not inconceivable to think that Henry Clay may well not have kept a secure lease on political life had there not been the victory at New Orleans by his future nemesis — Andrew Jackson.

Clay had helped the U.S. into war, and he was called upon by President Madison to help conclude the hostilities. When the Emperor of Russia, an ally of Britain who was being invaded by France and who saw the advantage of not having Britain involved on the North American continent, offered to mediate the dispute, President Madison promptly accepted, nominating at first a temporary commission and then five permanent commissioners, among whom were John Quincy Adams and Henry Clay. For nearly five months, the British and American delegations bargained at Ghent in the Netherlands. Clay was not anxious to yield on certain British demands, such as free access to the Mississippi and fisheries off the Atlantic coast, even though the British at this time definitely held the advantage in the war. Clay did not accept British solicitations as generous; indeed, Clay maintained that it was the British who had brought on the hostilities through maritime indigressions. Calmer heads on the American side finally prevailed upon Clay to join them in signing a peace accord on December 24, 1814.

HOLD ON THE HOUSE

Clay was returned to the House by his Lexington constituents in 1815 and continued his long tenure as Speaker. He had ample opportunity to try other fields of government, being offered the post of Minister to Russia and then Secretary of War. But his tendency was to stay not just as Speaker — but Master — of the House, that body whose operations he understood better than any other man and whose agenda he could and did control.

Many of the issues confronting the House in these days, such the reduction of war debt, tariffs, and national defense, were routine, but others were momentous and of great historical significance.

One of the first was the old question of what to do about a National Bank. In 1811, Clay, as a Senator, had led the fight and cast the decisive vote against rechartering the Bank. In 1816 John C. Calhoun, who, like Clay, was becoming established as a political power, submitted a new proposal to recharter. Its differences between the defeated proposal of 1811 were very minor. Clay decided to support the measure but needed reasons to explain his switch. These he provided with an adroitness that few politicians in the history of the U.S. could match. First, he said that as a Senator in 1811 he had been instructed by the Kentucky legislature to oppose the bank, and he felt obligated to uphold that joint body's wishes. Secondly, he claimed the bank proposal in 1811 as well as the originally chartered bank were too political, while the 1816 proposal was not. Clay's third reason for switching was a bit more novel if not downright political double talk. The Speaker now issued a dissertation on the interpretation of the powers of the Congress. Clay, formerly considered a "strict constructionist," now explained that some powers were not delegated by the Constitution, and that Congressmen had the right and duty to interpret the times and change previous positions, acting, of course, in the national interest. It would not be the only time in Clay's long career that he changed a position and found the appropriate reason for doing so.

Another issue — and one that would haunt him throughout his career — was Florida, at that time a Spanish possession that was being used as a base for the harassment of U.S. citizens. Runaway slaves and Indians were marauding Southern citizens, but Andrew Jackson, the hero of New Orleans, knew how to handle the situation. Old Hickory simply raised an army on his own and invaded the territory. In the Seminole War, the Tennessee General overran the Spanish fort of St. Marks, hung the Indian chiefs and then executed, after a court-martial on shaky evidence, two white men in league with the Seminoles. Jackson did not stop there. He next proceeded to the Spanish capital of Pensacola, deposed the Spanish governor and installed his own. Satisfied, he returned home more popular now than after New Orleans.

Official Washington, except John Quincy Adams, was mortified. Jackson had violated both American and international law, but no one dared chastise the popular Jackson — except for Henry Clay. Clay thought Jackson was wrong, and he plainly stated this before the House. Clay, however, overplayed a resolution he introduced to condemn Jackson, a neither inexperienced nor inveterate politician who knew he had the popular advantage over Clay. Old Hickory savored the first of many political triumphs over the "Gallant Harry of the West."

THE MISSOURI COMPROMISE

The most important issue in the country during this period of Clay's tenure as Speaker, though, was the Missouri Compromise. Slavery was beginning to find broad and strong opposition throughout the land. Many founding fathers had tolerated the "peculiar institution" only as the lesser of two evils — slavery or the dreaded rule of King George. Now, to the consternation of Southerners, moral considerations had begun to control the descendents of the Northern founding fathers, and the nation was becoming bitterly divided.

The issues were rather easy for all to understand. Missouri had applied in 1818 for admission as a state. An amendment was approved by the House of Representative that further slavery in the territory be prohibited and that the children of all slaves within the territory be freed upon reaching age twenty-five. Fierce debate raged throughout the land, and the initial decision by the House for slavery to be allowed in the territory was defeated in the Senate. Arkansas was then organized as a territory, and the same motion arose again in the House. This time a vote referring the measure for reconsideration was tied — and then decided upon by the tie-breaking vote of Speaker Clay to stay the cause against slavery in Arkansas.

Missouri had in the meantime been admitted as a slave state, while Maine had been admitted as a free state to maintain the status quo. A new measure to ban slavery in Missouri was defeated. Southerners, now becoming both angry and distraught, were questioning Northern violations of the "federal compact" and wondering if breaking away might be necessary to save its economic system and way of life. Northerners were also thinking that a separation might be necessary. A measure was then introduced during the sixteenth Congress to forever ban slavery north of the southern border of Missouri (36° 30") but maintain the practice to the south. This was a position Clay, himself an owner of slaves but who had been catapulted into politics by calling for the ban of slavery, could latch onto and promote, since the South could be assured of keeping its institutions and the North could maintain its morality. Clay was tireless in moving the bill through the House and in speaking for its adoption, often using such ethnic terms as "negrophobia" and speaking of labor unfit for free men being fit for Negroes. But slavery was not his concern. His concern was to have a Union, one that could stay united (and possibly some day have a united leader), and to that end he rolled over all opposition. For example, the venerable John Randolph of Virginia, seeking to have the action of the House overturned, was rebuffed indifferently on three occasions by Clay, who ruled twice that Randolph's motions were out of order because other business was under consideration and then calmly informed his colleague, who had patiently waited until the conclusion of the normal business of the day, that the bill in the meantime had been passed from the House chambers on to the Senate, where passage was already accomplished and could no longer be considered for further motion..

Clay emerged from the Compromise of 1820 both reviled and revered. He also emerged, though eminently qualified, as an unelectable Presidential candidate that year. That he desired election was known throughout the land. He was well aware of his title as the "Great Pacificator," and he enjoyed the displays of affection that greeted him time and time again in towns all along the routes to and from his home and Washington. But with the firm belief that he could not be elected President in 1820, and because of personal financial difficulties, Clay decided to retire, take a lucrative position as general counsel for the Bank of the United States in Ohio and Kentucky, and wait several years to make his run for the top office.

However, party bickering broke out in Kentucky no sooner than Clay resigned, and he consented to stand for election again from his old Lexington district. There had also been bickering in the House over a new Speaker, but as soon as Clay appeared, the matter was settled: Clay was instantly re-elected Speaker.

THE AMERICAN SYSTEM

It was becoming a tradition for the Secretary of State to succeed to the Presidency. This had been true of Jefferson, Madison and Monroe. Now John Quincy Adams held the position, and he had been of wise and useful counsel to James Monroe, currently presiding over an "Era of Good Feelings." Clay, though a member of Monroe's Republican Party, knew that he needed to be his own man with his own programs. He began pushing legislation that would become his "American System," the first order of business being the national Cumberland Road. Monroe, taking the usual Republican "strict constructionist" viewpoint, vetoed this measure and immediately incurred Clay's wrath. The former strict constructionist used the same reasoning as during the debate over the Missouri Compromise: the Nation had changed and the Constitution offered ample powers to accommodate those changes. Then Clay introduced a bill to survey the need for a system of internal canals and other national roads. In the ensuing debate over the bill, Clay showed remarkable foresight, alluding in his arguments "...to the proud and happy period, distant as it may be, when circulation and association between the Atlantic and Pacific and the Mexican Gulf shall be as free and as perfect as they are this moment in England..." This bill passed both houses and was not vetoed by Monroe.

Soon the House held one of the most remarkable debates in its history. It arose over the question of tariffs and allowed Clay to fully explain his "American System." A financial crisis had struck the U.S. in the early 1820's. Inflation from the War of 1812, troubled war-time economies in England and France that made precious metals rare, depreciated domestic currencies, generally tight money for the American consumer, and, especially, cheap British imports, were all combining to play havoc with the American economy. Clay introduced a bill to raise tariffs on goods that would not interfere with the American home manufacturing system. Battle lines were immediately drawn, pitting Clay's Middle American forces of home manufacturers and free farmers against plant manufactures of the Northeast and the slave farmers of the South. Master parliamentarian and showman that he was, Clay declared a Committee of the Whole in the House with himself as Chairman. His chief adversary was young Daniel Webster of Massachusetts, likewise fluid in delivery if yet more deliberate and precise in speech. The debate lasted a full two months, and Clay expanded the question into a host of other economic questions: what of the balance of trade? of the value of currency to production? of the rate of exchange? and, principally, what of the right of protection of American products? The vote was close, but Clay carried by five votes. His "American System" was now ready to be presented at the national polls for approval.

THE ELECTION OF 1824

In addition to Quincy Adams and Clay, Andrew Jackson, John C. Calhoun and William Crawford of Georgia were contenders for the Presidency in 1824. Calhoun soon concluded that his future would be best served by making an alliance with all possible candidates and withdrew in favor of being on the tickets of Adams, Jackson and Crawford as Vice President. Crawford, Monroe's Secretary of War, was the Republican Party favorite, but he was very ill from a paralytic attack and thus not backed by many Republican leaders.

The 1824 election was full of rumors and innuendo. Various deals were attempted: to run Adams with Jackson or Crawford with Clay or Jackson with Clay. Thomas Hart Benton, who had attacked and shot Jackson in a Nashville hotel ten years earlier, was canvassing for Clay. Martin Van Buren was the campaign manager for Crawford. But the race narrowed between the tradition of electing an incumbent Secretary of State — Adams — or a victorious General — Andrew Jackson.

Election day produced no majority winner. Jackson, the military hero, led in both popular and electoral votes, while Adams was second, Clay a disappointing third, and Crawford trailing the field. Under the Constitution, the House would have to select the next President from the top three electoral vote recipients by state caucus. Here Clay experienced a calamity. Though Speaker, he could neither muster the sufficient votes nor scheme in any parliamentary way to achieve victory. He knew that he could, however, swing the election. His own Kentucky legislature had passed a resolution asking him to support Jackson, and he held several friendly exchanges with the General — the first such since his denunciation of Jackson's mission in Florida — to consider supporting the Hero of Horseshoe Bend, but because of the perception of Jackson's reckless and lawless behavior in Florida, he decided to give his support to Adams. With Clay's support, John Quincy Adams was selected the President of the United States by the House of Representatives on February 9, 1825.

Magnanimous in defeat, Jackson was one of the first to congratulate Adams on Inauguration Day in March. But history well records what followed: Adams appointed Clay Secretary of State — and Jackson charged "bargain and corruption." By October of 1825 Jackson had been nominated by the Tennessee legislature to run for the Presidency in 1828. The General immediately resigned from the Senate and entered upon his crusade to gain the Presidency for the people.

SECRETARY OF STATE

For the first time in many years, Clay had a boss: John Quincy Adams, sixth President of the United States. His position as Secretary of State involved more than foreign policy. Tradition held that members of the Cabinet were advisers to the President in all areas. Debates at Cabinet meetings were common, and Clay must surely have felt at home during these sessions. Adams had the utmost respect for Clay's abilities and character. The two worked together harmoniously, but the circumstances of the time did not allow Clay the potential to establish a name for himself at the State Department as he had in the House.

The primary forces working against Clay as Secretary of State were the upcoming election of 1828 and Andrew Jackson. Jackson had been on the attack against Clay from the time of his nomination as Secretary of State, first urging the Senate not to "advise and consent," and then parading throughout the land spreading the details of "corruption and bargain." It is interesting to find two future Presidents coming to the aid of Clay. Senator John Tyler of Virginia wrote a letter finding no fault with Clay's actions in the recent election. For this he gained the eternal enmity of Jackson's backers, and he found his path to the Presidency not through Jackson's wing of the Republican Party (now becoming named the Democrats) but through Clay's wing (the Whigs) as the successor of William Henry Harrison. In a separate, frivolous incident, Jackson announced that a member of the House was party and witness to the "corrupt and bargain" scheme of Clay for Adams. Pressed for identification, Jackson named a young Pennsylvania Congressman, James Buchanan. Buchanan refuted the charge, however, and Clay was certain that a knock-out punch had been delivered to Jackson. But that was not to be. The people felt simply and surely that Jackson had been wronged, and popular support was to continue in favor of Old Hickory.

In foreign policy, a fascinating connection was made between Clay and Simon Bolivar, the "Liberator of South America." Clay, the despiser of European despotism, was anxious to implement the Monroe Doctrine by showing the European powers that all of the new American republics would stand together. Accordingly, he called for a conference of American nations to discuss trade reciprocity, the elimination of Spanish influence in South America, mutual defense measures, the securing of religious and other liberties, and the end of slave trade. Jackson's forces promptly used this latter issue to negate any effective progress, and other countries maintaining slavery concurred. Clay and Bolivar maintained a cordial correspondence over the years, though, and their respect for each other was lifelong.

The British allowed Clay several opportunities for foreign policy success, but major opportunities for the most part were thwarted by Jackson. The mission to Ghent on which Clay had served still had one unsettled item, that of the British payment of reparations for the British capture and carrying away of American slaves. Emperor Alexander of Russia mediated, and a sum was established and finally paid the U.S., a success for Clay. In another matter, the British issued Orders of Council disbanding U.S. trade with the British West Indies. For a time tempers flared, but eventually, after the death of the conniving Lord Canning, diplomacy reversed the British directive, presenting Clay with another success. But in a strange turn of events, Clay, in a most unwise move politically, negotiated with the British on the mutual exchange both of British and American deserters in the War of 1812 and of slaves who had fled to the other country's territories. Jackson must have secretly chuckled at this part of Clay's diplomacy. Would the hero of New Orleans have waited for thirteen years to have the British pay their just debt? Would Old Hickory negotiate with a vanquished foe if trade were unilaterally abandoned? Would a slave holder from the South even consider proposing the exchange of former British subjects now living in American liberty for slaves who could not vote?

Clay's other forays into foreign affairs are hardly noteworthy. He sought unsuccessfully to purchase Texas from Spain. In trade, he followed the conventional policy of reciprocity, granting favor for favor. He concluded a host of trade treaties with foreign nations. Interestingly enough, Clay hinted at the establishment of Caribbean havens for the eventual movement of American slaves to freedom and self-government.

Clay had a close call with death when, after being attacked by John Randolph of Virginia in a House speech, he demanded "satisfaction." The two men met and exchanged one volley, with Randolph missing and Clay grazing Randolph's coat. Another volley was readied. This time Clay fired first and put a bullet through Randolph's coat. Randolph was free to fire upon the helpless Clay, but unlike Aaron Burr when dueling Alexander Hamilton, he fired his pistol into the air. The two shook hands and forgot the matter.

The four years that Clay spent in Adam's administration were not happy ones. He had not mastered circumstances in the manner to which he was accustomed. His tenure in Washington, now some twenty-five years, was beginning to make his health deteriorate. Moreover, he had been frustrated by the humiliating defeats at the hand of Jackson. When Jackson won over-whelmingly in 1828, carrying to Clay's shame every state that Clay had carried in 1824, the "Gallant Harry of the West" decided to once again retire to the peace and tranquility of Ashland.

THE ELECTION OF 1832

Clay, now age fifty-two, was out of official public life and thoroughly enjoying the private life of a gentlemen farmer. His prominence and his abilities could not be forgotten by his constituents, however, and his daily correspondence showed a keen interest in the political affairs of the day. He was already being beckoned by the likes of Senator Daniel Webster and other notable Whigs, and he knew he would oppose Jackson in 1832. On a goodwill tour down the Mississippi and to other parts of the South, he was greeted by affectionate throngs, though he could not help but notice the equal outcries against him. It did not take Clay too long to get his rest from officialdom; now his physical resiliency had him bouncing back from recent infirmities and feeling the old stirrings of a political fight. Master orator that he was, capable of thrilling either the galleries of the House or a political meeting both with his flowing voice and his flowery gestures of body and hands, Clay was definitely the most effective leader to take on Jackson.

His major problem in his quest against Jackson was not the issues of the day but Jackson himself, that bitter enemy who considered any enemy of himself an enemy of the country, who, like the dreaded British, ought to be conquered. During Jackson's terms as President and afterwards until his death, the two leaders opposed each other again and again on those great issues of the day which were tremulous in the history of the United States. Even those profound issues, however, did not enter into their battles nearly so much as their personalities.

Clay's second run seemed to begin earlier than Jackson's of four years earlier. He made a Washington speech three days after Jackson's inauguration indicating that the election of a military man was not good. Jackson soon thereafter began his "spoils" system, and Clay promptly decried this. After a New York Freeman threatening to publish the secret orders of the Masons was brutally murdered, Clay, himself a Mason but inactive in any lodge, uttered outrages, knowing that Jackson as an active Mason would make no statement to mollify the new, rapidly expanding Anti-Mason Party, whose support Clay was seeking.

That Jackson detested Clay can be seen in the actions surrounding Clay's relations with Jackson's allies. Clay returned to the Senate with a narrow victory over Col. Richard Johnson, a Jackson protege who had personally killed Chief Tecumseh at the Battle at Thames. While Clay may have claimed a temporary victory, he was to later see Johnson elected Vice President under Martin Van Buren, who also experienced Clay's vindictiveness in the famous incident where Van Buren, formerly Crawford's campaign manager but now a firm Jackson supporter, had resigned as Secretary of State to show support for Senator Eaton's wife, the subject of snubs by Mrs. John C. Calhoun and other Cabinet wives because she was of questionable virtue. Jackson appointed Van Buren Minister to England, but Senator Clay arranged for the Senate to not only not "advise and consent," but to do so by having the infamous Vice President Calhoun personally cast the tie-breaker against Van Buren. Old Hickory got his revenge, though, by simply stuffing Van Buren down the throats of Clay and his allies as the Vice Presidential nominee in 1832 and the successor Presidential candidate in 1836.

Clay opposed and lost to Jackson on key domestic issues, guessing wrong again as to the public impact that Jackson had in elections. One issue involved tariffs, and more broadly, the national budget and treasury. Jackson opened up the sale of western lands, reducing the price per acre from $2.00 to $1.25. This was so successful that the government eventually required payment only in gold, and prosperity abounded. Jackson, seeing no need to have the government collect money just for the sake of hoarding it, decided it might be well to relax import duties. This, of course, was a direct threat to the protectionism of Clay's "American System," and he would not idly stand by to see the ruination of his dreams for American expansion. Clay decided that "free trade" was to be opposed, as was cheap land in the West, never grasping as did Jackson that raw-boned farmers striking out to the west to make new ways in life on cheaply bought dirt would support Old Hickory. Clay did himself little credit also by attacking the venerable Albert Gallatin, an able and honest public servant since the administration of President Jefferson, requesting that he return to his native Europe and practice his "unpatriotic" acts there.

Jackson brought forth and disposed of another domestic issue, the National Bank, with a classic display of political savvy. In 1830, a full six years before recharter, Jackson proposed that a new charter not be issued, simply because he knew the Bank was controlled by his personal and political enemies. Clay, who opposed rechartering in 1811 but then supported it in 1816, mustered the forces in the Congress to gain favorable Bank reports and see that the Congress voted for the Bank and against the President. A bill was passed by both houses in July, 1832, just some four months before the election, authorizing a new charter, and Clay was jubilant, thinking Jackson would be defeated. But again he completely misjudged "Old Hickory." Now Jackson mustered his forces, led by Senator Thomas Hart Benton, a former Clay ally and Jackson enemy. The President vetoed the bill and issued a vintage campaign document that claimed a bank monopoly was in force, making the rich richer and the poor poorer. He also claimed the bill was unconstitutional, quite conveniently using Clay's 1811 arguments as proof. The veto was sustained.

When the election ballots were tabulated in November, Jackson had won an overwhelming victory, claiming 219 of 288 electoral votes to Clay's mere 49. Clay had made the mistake of thinking the people would choose the bank over a military hero. And Clay erred grievously on the issue of tariffs and western lands. The people stuck with Jackson, who had the immense satisfaction of being rid of Calhoun and seeing Van Buren preside over the "great triumvirate" of Clay, Webster, and Calhoun, as well as seeing Nicholas Biddle of the National Bank die a broken man both politically and economically.

SENATOR FOR LIFE AND COMPROMISER AGAIN

Crushed by defeat, Clay returned to the Senate to perform some of his most valuable work at a time when issues of the day called for a great leader in the Senate, one who could master the diverse elements of the darkening American political picture.

President Jackson, though firmly in control, had bitter enemies on every issue. One of these enemies was John C. Calhoun, recently discarded as Vice President but elected Senator from South Carolina. The issue Calhoun raised — nullification — involved the survival of the Union itself. The story is familiar: South Carolina wanted protective tariffs but Jackson opposed this and prevailed; Calhoun issued "manifestos" saying that states rights were greater than the Union's; Jackson's ire arose and he threatened to hang Calhoun for treason; the situation was tense indeed, and a solution was desperately needed.

A compromise was needed or blood would be shed. And who should come forth with a plan but the "Great Compromiser" himself, Henry Clay. It was a peculiar position for Clay. He had no stomach for Jackson, and the plan he would propose was an anathema to his beloved "American System." It proposed a graduated reduction of tariffs to twenty percent, another flip-flop for Clay, who had just a few years earlier viciously attacked Albert Gallatin for a similar proposal. But Clay knew the art of compromise, and he knew that the protection of American manufacturing was secondary to the beloved Union. Coupled with the tariff reduction was the "Force Bill" or "Bloody Bill" against South Carolinians, a bill passed on Jackson's birthday which authorized the President to use troops against nullifiers. Calhoun gave in, and a crisis was averted.

The next great issue in Clay's tenure in the Senate surrounded the "removal of the deposits" by Jackson from Nicholas Biddle's National Bank. The act was a purely partisan one by Jackson, who saw the bank as his personal enemy and thus the enemy of his Country. His action would precipitate great questions as to the constitutional powers of the Presidency, but these questions were trivial to the Hero of New Orleans and Horseshoe Bend, of the conqueror of Spanish Florida, of the victor in the most recent Presidential election where the bank itself was _the_ issue. And so Jackson announced his plan to remove the federal deposits and place them into "pet" state banks owned by the friends of his party.

Such action promptly created a financial panic, especially among Clay's manufacturing friends. The clamor called for a great debate, and naturally

Clay was at the forefront. He was joined by Webster and Calhoun, whose thunderous objections are said to have been some of the loudest in the history of the august body. "Distress" petitions were circulated throughout the land and brought to the Senate as evidence that a financial calamity was being wrought by "King Andrew." Certain special elections for the House resulted in the election of anti-Jackson men. And a resolution to censure the President was being led through the Senate by Clay, leading many to wonder if impeachment were to be the next item of business. A curious sidelight to this incident occurred when Clay delivered an explosive charge to Vice President Van Buren, demanding that the Senate's presiding officer deliver the wishes of the people to the President. Said Senator Thomas Hart Benton, "During the delivery, the Vice President maintained the utmost decorum of countenance, looking respectfully and innocently at the speaker all the while, as if treasuring every word he said, to be faithfully delivered to the President. After it was over... he [Van Buren] went up to Mr. Clay and asked him for a pinch of his fine maccaboy snuff, and, having received it, walked away." The friends of Jackson may have had use for Clay's snuff — but not for Clay himself.

Clay managed a successful resolution of censure in the Senate but unresourcefully lost his sense of timing in the matter. As time played along, Jackson's "common" man came to realize that he was not suffering as was the upper, manufacturing class. And then an ironic event galvanized the Jackson support. Congress adjourned in mid-1834, and a convention of Clay's supporters took the name "Whig" in opposition to King Andy. Their mistake was to try to place the title of Tory to Jackson and his followers. The common man knew better. A young Jackson protege from Tennessee, James K. Polk, just starting to show his abilities in the House, led a successful fight against censure in the House. During this period of time, Jackson nominated Roger Taney as Secretary of Treasury, but Clay mustered the forces not to "advise and consent." A furious Jackson would have final say, though, just as he had had with Van Buren: Roger Taney would later be nominated by Jackson, and confirmed by the Senate, to serve as Chief Justice of the Supreme Court.

Many other issues arose between Clay and Jackson during this era, including French problems, a "tenure of office" question, and the removal of the Cherokees in the infamous "Trail of Tears." Clay's successes against Jackson were very few, and he must have indeed been a happy man to see the upcoming 1836 election. Had Clay been a better prophet, he would have not run against Jackson in 1832 but waited to take on Van Buren in 1836. But the Whigs that year nominated William Henry Harrison, who, though a military hero, could not upstage Jackson's protege, Martin Van Buren (the only Vice President in American history until George Bush to succeed a President of the same party by an election of the people. Such was the popularity and success of Jackson). Indeed, before Jackson left office, Sen. Thomas Hart Benton led a successful fight to expunge Clay's censure of Jackson, the resolution actually requiring that the official document sponsored by Clay be crossed through with bold strokes of an ink pen.

Van Buren, as we know, was no Jackson, and he faced devastating financial problems no sooner than elected. Though Clay was to be at the forefront of opposition to Van Buren, it was not — could not — be with the same degree of vindictiveness as with Jackson. The yearnings to be President seemed to revive again, and his hopes for success in 1840 were not waning. But events had already done him in. He was a two time loser and was burdened as well with the issues of the National Bank and slavery. Even during Van Buren's term, he would again be drawn into another Bank debate. And the South would always wonder how a slave holder could compromise as well as how a Southerner could have a Northern outlook. The Whigs therefore nominated William Henry Harrison again in 1840, and he took as his running mate a Democrat, John Tyler, riding to victory with the catchy phrase "Tippacanoe, and Tyler, Too!" Clay campaigned hard for the ticket, and when the Whigs won an overwhelming victory, 234 electoral votes to 60, a feeling of religious deliverance was felt.

Harrison offered Clay the position of Secretary of State, but Clay knew his effectiveness lay in the Senate. Friends of Clay were, however, named to each Cabinet position, with Daniel Webster receiving the most coveted position of Secretary of State. Unfortunately Harrison died after only a month in office, and the Whigs had to deal with Democrat John Tyler, a Republican of the old school and a "strict constructionist." Problems began at once over the proper address for Tyler. The Cabinet, announcing Harrison's death, addressed the "Vice President." Former President John Q. Adams suggested "Vice President, acting as President." Clay preferred "Regent." Tyler ordered President, however, and that title rightfully became accepted.

Upon assuming his duties, Democrat Tyler was advised by his close confidants to dump his Cabinet except for Webster; to oppose any national bank; to oppose protective tariffs; to oppose the distribution of revenues from the sale of public lands to states; to annex Texas; to reform relations with Great Britain — to, in effect be the Democrat he was rather than a Whig. Tyler's character was one of principle rather than conciliation. While he would keep his old Republican principles, he could not dismiss the Cabinet wholesale. This was in time to change, but only after issues rather than personalities were the cause.

Clay had felt that he could control the "Regent" and at first enjoyed a cordial relationship with the new President. Their correspondence indicated a desire to be amicable, but Tyler was never conclusive in any committment to the support of programs that violated his strict constructionist views. Clay engineered through the Congress the passage of a new National Bank. All through the proceedings he had felt in control of Tyler, once remarking, "Tyler dares not resist. I will drive him before me." But when the bill was presented to Tyler, he vetoed it. The outcry of Clay and the Whigs was vociferous, Clay stating that Tyler should have followed the same path as when a Senator and resigned rather than not obeying the will of his constituents. (This had been done by Tyler when he had been instructed by the Virginia legislature to vote to expunge the censure resolution of Andrew Jackson.) Another bill for a bank, this time the "Fiscal Corporation Act," was passed, but Tyler did not let the name change affect him, and he again vetoed the measure. Now Whig leader Clay invoked a most devious plan against Tyler. He met with Tyler's Whig cabinet members and instructed them to resign, and all, except Webster, did. His broader plan, at which he was successful, was to isolate the Whig party (except for Webster) from Tyler and make another run for the Presidency. But a critical mistake had been made when Webster had refused to resign; future Whig divisiveness would cost Clay dearly, especially in New England.

THE ELECTION OF 1844

In March of 1842 Clay announced that he was resigning once again from the Senate. Many thought the 62 year old Clay would be retiring permanently from public life. His "last" speech to the Senate was an event of keen excitement and a matter of national reverence. Clay's performance was superb: he apologized for his rash outbursts over the years, allowing that they were due to principle and not personality; if he had wounded his fellow Senators, he begged apology; the Senate was august and grand; the United States was the most noble form of government ever; he was deeply grateful for the fidelity of so many. At its conclusion, Clay was hailed, many an eye shedding tears. Even Calhoun, now also aging and perhaps reminenscing a bit, for the first time in years greeted Clay and shook his hand.

Clay returned to Ashland but not to retire. His speech was considered a hallmark of statesmanship, and the Whigs, like modern Republicans with Richard Nixon, were almost unanimous in believing that Clay had earned the right to be President. In April, 1842 state Whig conventions began nominating the "Old Prince" to run in 1844, and by September a convention of some 100,000 people present met in Dayton, Ohio to nominate Clay. The official nomination came at Baltimore in May of 1844 at the Whig National Convention.

But Clay's past and his inability to catch the issues of the day were to doom him once again. First, his old nemesis, Andrew Jackson, retired but still interested in both the affairs of state and Henry Clay, arranged for the Democratic nomination of "Young Hickory," James K. Polk, along with George Dallas of Pennsylvania for Vice President. Jackson next persuaded President Tyler of the futility of seeking election, thus unifying the Democratic Party. Then the "Liberty" party named James G. Birney as a candidate, costing "slave holder" Clay rather than "slave holder" Polk the crucial state of New York.

Undoubtedly, the decisive issue of the campaign was Texas. Clay had to tread carefully on this, for it was tied to slavery and he had all too often in the past lost the Southern vote by being a Northern man. He found it convenient in this campaign to tread lightly on all the issues of the past — slavery, tariffs, protectionism, and the national bank. Though Polk was Speaker of the House, he was relatively unknown, and the Whigs, thinking they would easily win, made the dreadful mistake of asking, "Who is Polk?" and then derisively laughing. Jackson, almost dead, then brought forth again the "corruption and bargain" charges of 1824. Simultaneously, the "Native American" movement, which was aimed primarily at Catholics, became active, and it was no secret that Theodore Frelinghysen, Clay's running mate from New Jersey, was virulently anti-Catholic. While this would cost critical votes, Clay then capped everything by writing the so called "Alabama" letter, in which he not only stated his favor of annexing Texas but noted that he owed abolitionists nothing since ..."No man in the United States has been half as much abused by them as I have been." This provided the revolt among Whig abolitionists that Polk needed. Clay for the third time, though running a closer election than before, was denied the Presidency. "I am afraid that it will be yet be a long time, if ever, that the people recover from the corrupting influence and effects of Jacksonism. I pray God to give them a happy deliverance."

LAST YEARS IN THE SENATE AND THE COMPROMISE OF 1850

Clay retired again to Ashland only to find the next few years bitter ones. The war with Texas would claim the life of his favorite son, Henry Clay, Jr. He had already lost all of his daughters. Becoming aware of his frailties and advanced age, he was baptized into the Episcopal Church.

Of course, a man of Clay's background could not be a recluse. He traveled and spoke extensively. His counsel was sought by men of prominence throughout the land. It was not too long before some again mentioned Clay as a Presidential candidate in 1848, but this was not to be. The Mexican War would produce new military heroes, and this time the Whigs rather than the Jacksonians would claim a winner.

Clay had not paid too much attention to his financial affairs over the years and was in danger of losing Ashland. He was astonished to find that a secret gift, so secret that he could never find the donor(s) had been made to save his homeplace. Only with reluctance was he persuaded that nothing was ill-conceived and that acceptance would not be a violation of his character.

As Clay spoke more and more, he received more and more backing for the nomination of 1848. Unfortunately, his friends in the Whig Party would do him in. Leading on the first ballot over Zachary Taylor, he mistakenly thought he had the key state of Ohio committed to him, but to his chagrin, it was not, and then, alas, even his beloved Kentucky cast a majority for Taylor. Feeling betrayed, Clay did not campaign for his party's ticket. The Whigs won that November, but it was to be their last Presidential victory.

The "Old Prince" was now very aged. In its seventy-first year, his body was beginning to show the ravages of time. He suffered constantly with a hacking cough from the tuberculosis that would eventually take him. His mind was still agile, however, and his will to be heard great. Though not in Washington, he kept abreast of the current events: of Texas and California and other territories bargaining for statehood at the expense of either slavery or abolition; of the Mexican treaty settlements such as the Wilmot Proviso or the Treaty of Guadaloupe Hidalgo; and of the makeup of President Taylor's Cabinet, which was disturbingly composed mostly of slave holders, as was Taylor himself.

In 1849 Kentucky had a constitutional convention to consider the abolition of slavery, as it had in 1799. This was the event that had sprung Clay into political office, and it would return him to the Senate once again, though he was just as ambivalent on the slavery issue as fifty years before. Still a slave holder, he spoke in favor of abolition; yet in a grandiose scheme, he proposed that freed slaves be sent to Liberia, there to work out their own social problems. Rumblings began to reach Washington that Clay might be returned to the Senate; some men of prominence hoped otherwise. These included President Taylor's son-in-law, Jefferson Davis, and Alexander Stephens of Georgia, the future Confederate Vice President. All too many

Whigs feared the domineering Clay would hold too much power over the inexperienced Taylor.

Nonetheless Clay took a seat in December, 1849. He knew that the greatest issue of the day was slavery but was astonished to find "...the feeling of disunion among some intemperate Southern politicians." In the Senate he was surrounded by a host of the brightest stars in its history: Webster, Calhoun, Benton, Sam Houston, Davis of Mississippi and Davis of Massachusetts, future Vice President Hannibal Hamlin, John P. Hale, Stephen Douglas of Illinois, former Presidential candidate Lewis Cass, and future Lincoln Cabinet members Salmon Chase and William Seward. Amidst this array, the "Great Compromiser" plotted a program to save that which he cherished most — the Union.

Clay succinctly described the problem. "Here are five bleeding wounds [counting them on the fingers of his left hand]: first, there is California; there are the territories, second; there is the question of the boundary of Texas, the third; there is the fugitive slave law, the fourth; and there is the question of the slave trade in the District of Columbia, fifth." Clay's resolutions were seven months in passing, encompassing probably the greatest debate in the history of the Senate. Clay himself led the debate with a masterly but exhausting two-day oration, begging for conciliation and continued Union. Then other Senators spoke frankly, some bitterly. Calhoun delivered his last manifesto, a stinging denunciation of abolition and a warning of disunion to come. Webster was the only Senator to inch towards a compromise, but his bending brought forth charges of being a fallen archangel. On and on the Senators labored, Jeff Davis offering no concession and Seward refusing any future compromise whatsoever. The death of President Taylor, coupled with a Nashville convention calling for a compromise, finally provided the impetus for movement. Webster became Fillmore's Secretary of State and provided momentum for passage of Clay's measures. In his closing speech on the matter, Clay stated, "I know no South, no North, no East, no West, to which I owe my allegiance." Confronted by a South Carolina Senator that a certain Mr. Rhett of that state might hoist the flag of secession, Clay jumped up in an instant, declaring "...he will be a traitor, and I hope he will meet the fate of a traitor." He outrightly declared that even his beloved Kentucky would not stand between him and his Union. It was Henry Clay's finest hour!

Tired and extremely ill and also bitterly disappointed, Clay decided to vacation, believing his bill to be dead. Then the improbable happened. One by one the various measures, which he had consolidated in one "Omnibus" bill, passed individually. The Compromise of 1850 was law.

Clay remained a Senator, but his activities were now restricted severely by mental and physical weaknesses. He saw the disruption of his 1850 Compromise and pleaded, with no success, that both sides try to conciliate. He traveled and spoke when he could, and there was a cry for him to run for President again in 1852. His response was frank: he was too weak and would not be around to serve. He traveled to Cuba to seek relief for his cough; that proved of no value, so he returned to Ashland. He then made one last trip to Washington for one last Senate appearance, but he was bedridden throughout the session. One last presidential campaign was to be started before he passed. He wanted Webster for the Whigs, but General Scott, an anti-slavery Whig, was nominated. The Democrats ran a "dark horse," Franklin Pierce, a Northern man with Southern principles. In this campaign, while he was on his deathbed, both parties adopted the compromise politics that Henry Clay had so long espoused.

Death came on June 29, 1852. He was taken to the Senate to lie in state. After funeral orations, he was transported by train back to Ashland, stops being made at all the towns along the way so that the entire populace could join in the national mourning. The "Mill Boy of the Marshes," "Gallant Harry of the West," "The Pacificator," the "Old Prince," "The Great Compromiser" and the lover of the Union was no longer available to conciliate and compromise for the domestic peace and tranquility of the Union he loved so much.

Lewis Cass
The Election of 1848

Lewis Cass was the last Presidential candidate to carry forth the legacy of Andrew Jackson. For years he was a Michigan and Northwestern leader; then the social disorder surrounding the wives of Jackson's Cabinet members created a shuffle which brought Cass to the national scene. From that period in the early 1830's until the beginning of the War Between the States, the venerable Cass served with distinction among many of the nation's giants. His bid for the Presidency in 1848 was for him extremely bad timing — had he been nominated in either 1844 or 1852, he probably would have been elected, and he may well have forestalled the terrible tragedy of civil war.

COLONIAL MASSACHUSETTS UPBRINGING

Both of the parents of Lewis Cass traced their roots to England, and his father's ancestry settled in Massachusetts. The Cass' station in life must not have been too substantial, for Jonathan Cass, the father of Lewis, was but a blacksmith at the outbreak of the Revolutionary War. He dropped his trade to fight for the Colonial cause, participating in the battles of Bunker Hill, Trenton and Princeton. In 1781 he married Mary Gilman, who bore him a son in the city of Boston on October 9, 1782. That son, Lewis, was the eldest of six children born to the couple.

At age ten, Lewis Cass entered the Exeter Academy in Massachusetts, spending the next seven years in a rather classical study of English, French, Latin, Greek, geography, arithmetic and practical geometry. During this period Cass' father re-entered the army, attaining the rank of Major. Eventually Major Cass moved his family to Marietta, Ohio, then western wilderness country organized under the rules of the Northwest Ordinance. In rural Ohio young Lewis began studying law while simultaneously being educated in the philosophies of the Federalist and Jeffersonian Democratic parties. His legal studies must have been quite impressive, for he was the first person licensed to practice law in Ohio after it became a state. His political identity became somewhat of a personal struggle, since his parents were from Federalist New England and his father had served under Washington. Young Cass was impressed by the philosophy of Thomas Jefferson, however, and he became a Democrat for life.

Cass' law practice was a successful one. His reputation was so good that he soon found himself being elected to the Ohio legislature, just before he turned the mandatory age of twenty-five. It was during this time that the infamous Aaron Burr engaged in his plan to establish a new government, and he paid a visit to Ohio to promote his treasonous cause. Though Cass' relationship with Burr is not quite clear, he is apparently the person who first reported Burr's illicit activities; Jefferson himself spoke of the "first blow" being delivered in Ohio. Cass himself later introduced a bill calling for ties to the Union with no sympathy for rebels.

President Jefferson in 1806 rewarded Cass by appointing him as U.S. Marshall for Ohio, a position he held until the outbreak of the War of 1812. During this period, Cass married Elizabeth Spencer, daughter of a Revolutionary War General. Theirs was a long marriage, with several children being born to the devoted couple.

THE WAR OF 1812

As war between the United States and Great Britain loomed once again, Ohio was called upon for volunteers, and 1,200 men responded. These men were divided into three regiments, and Lewis Cass commanded one of the three, holding the rank of Colonel. One of the objectives of "War Hawks" such as Henry Clay and John C. Calhoun was to conquer Canada. This goal, coupled with the British influence over certain Indian tribes occupying the Northwest, made the Michigan territory a significant military outpost in the War of 1812. Cass was placed under the command of Brigadier General Thomas Hull, a former Governor of the Michigan territory who unfortunately proved to be an ineffective military leader. The young Col. Cass distinguished himself on several occasions, becoming known as the "Hero of the Tarontee" after one battle. The bravery and eagerness for action by Cass and his fellow troops from Ohio were to no avail, though, for Hull refused to either take the initiative or pursue military objectives. Finally, Cass and his fellow officers plotted the "court-martial" of Hull, whose refusal to attack saw Canada not only vanish as an objective but found the British successfully invading Michigan and capturing Detroit. Cass himself was captured by the British during this invasion. Later paroled, he had no compulsion in testifying against Hull, who was prosecuted by a young Judge-Advocate named Martin Van Buren.

Cass was subsequently promoted to Major General in the Ohio militia and then Colonel and Brigadier General in the regular army. He saw service in a bloody campaign against the British and Indians as the Americans tried to recapture Detroit. He was an aide-de-camp to the "Hero of Tippacanoe,"

General (and future President) William Henry Harrison. He also served with a future Vice President, Col. Richard Johnson, who personally killed the fierce Indian chief, Tecumseh, at the Battle of the Thames. This theatre of action also was famous for the naval defeat of the British by Commodore Perry, who proclaimed, "We have met the enemy, and they are ours!"

GOVERNOR OF MICHIGAN

For his distinguished military service, Cass at age thirty-two was rewarded by President Madison with the appointment of Governor of the Michigan territory. This was a position he was to hold for some twenty-two years, carefully guiding the rugged Northwest area (which at that time consisted of lands far beyond present day Michigan) from a territory thought by many to be infested with savages and bad land into a state settled by solid citizens who were able to cultivate the rugged but fertile Michigan dirt.

While hostilities had formally ceased with the Treaty of Ghent, Cass was still faced with the activities of Indian tribes, who were incited by the British and could find safe haven, when necessary, a short distance away in Canada. Though Jefferson's Louisiana Purchase had been in effect for over a decade, there was still some hostile French influence there also. Cass approached the problem of the Indians with unusual tact. He often gave hungry tribes provisions, and he did not hesitate to negotiate with them. Once he went alone without arms into an Indian settlement to demand an end to hostile actions. The Indian chiefs were so impressed with Cass' bravery that one hostile Indian who tried to shoot Cass (his firearm misfired) was severely beaten by the Indians themselves. "The Great Father at Detroit" became revered by the tribes. Cass was critical of whites who gave savages whiskey and once, to prevent abuse by devious settlers, used an axe to break open casks of whiskey in front of thirsty warriors. He also brought to justice any white man who murdered or wrongfully abused any Indians.

The Indians felt threatened, of course, by the continuous immigration of white settlers. It was Cass who had encouraged this, getting the Congress to pass a bill offering Michigan farm land as bounty to former soldiers. Easterners, hesitant at first to come to a frozen land they thought incapable of farming, finally came in droves. The white population then became so strong that the influence of the Indians was diminished, although skirmishes continued to take place for many years.

Cass, an early disciple of Jefferson, worked hard to bring public education to the Michigan territory, and his system was copied in many other territories. His actions provided for land to start the "College of Detroit."

He also strove to implement a unified code of justice, which appropriately became known as the "Cass Code." Somewhat of a scholar, Cass also wrote the first history of the Michigan area.

Governor Cass also led the movement for the statehood of Michigan. As soon as the number of settlers required for statehood had moved into the territory, he called for an election, but the influence of French settlers prevented entrance. More and more settlers from Massachusetts, New York and other New England states moved into the territory, and the push for statehood could not be denied. Finally, in 1837, after Cass had gone to Washington as Secretary of War, his beloved Michigan gained entrance as the twenty-sixth state of the Union.

SECRETARY OF WAR

Improbable events led to the selection of Cass as a member of Andrew Jackson's Cabinet. Jackson learned that his Vice President, John C. Calhoun, had years before argued in secret Cabinet meetings that Jackson's actions in occupying Florida were illegal and that Jackson should have been dismissed. The enraged and unforgiving Jackson would never again tolerate Calhoun — or his friends. Several members of the Cabinet were Calhoun sympathizers. They chose to uphold Calhoun's display of chivalry when he supported the actions of the wives of other Cabinet members who socially snubbed the wife of Secretary of War Eaton, whose marriage to the young and beautiful Mrs. Eaton after the death of his first wife was not considered the social etiquette of the day. They forgot that similar questions had also been raised about Jackson's marriage to his beloved Rachel.

Of course Jackson finally saw to it that his entire Cabinet "resigned." Judge Hugh White of Tennessee was asked to become Secretary of War, but he declined the appointment, and Lewis Cass was selected in his place. Cass, who had little intimate knowledge of Jackson, was propelled to the center stage of American politics, a position he was to occupy for the next twenty-five years. He was also to convert from a Jeffersonian to a Jacksonian Democrat and to become a protege and part of the legacy of "Old Hickory."

Some of the more important events in the nation's history were to take place while Cass was Secretary of War. All of the events surrounding the efforts of Calhoun and the state of South Carolina to claim "States Rights" and the right of nullification occurred. The Force Bill was passed and ready to be enforced, with General Winfield Scott, the future Mexican War hero and (unsuccessful) Presidential candidate, being placed under Cass' command to execute the bill. Of course, the challenge of Calhoun was put down before Jackson hanged the South Carolinian. Cass himself played a conciliatory role in the matter, conveying to certain Virginia elements that Jackson was not as thirsty for blood as popularly believed and leading other elements to understand that Jackson would accept the compromise eventually proposed by Henry Clay which allowed for a Force Bill together with a gradual reduction of tariffs.

A tragic policy that was formulated during this period was the "Trail of Tears." This was the forced removal of Indians, particularly Cherokees, to the West, together with the takeover of their land and possessions. Those Indians who would be moved were for the most part highly cultivated, but the determined Jackson, whose now deceased wife had migrated to Nashville by the Tennessee River where savages had raided boats, had no sympathy for the Red Man. Ironically, Cass, who had been the great friend of the Northwest Indians, acquiesced to Jackson's policy and supported the forced removal.

Perhaps this was because of a certain fondness and respect that Cass had immediately developed for the hero of the War of 1812. Cass revered Jackson, though the reverse was not quite the case. Still Jackson must have greatly respected Cass, for years later a bust of Cass was displayed at the Hermitage. After Jackson prevailed in the South Carolina episode, Cass accompanied the Chief Executive on a Northeastern tour, and each was widely acclaimed.

Cass did disagree with the President on one important matter, the removal of deposits from Nicholas Biddle's National Bank. Meeting with the President privately, an understanding was reached where Jackson agreed to take responsibility for any action and relieve the Cabinet of any pressures. Cass remained as Secretary of War until near the close of Jackson's administration, when the President appointed him Minister to France.

FRENCH AMBASSADOR

This appointment was made not only out of respect but because the sedentary Washington life that Cass was leading was causing his health to deteriorate. Also, Jackson, long a hater of the British, knew that Cass too was a great critic of the British and could be counted upon to use his influence in Paris to maintain a proper balance of power. Jackson also had a very pressing problem. He had negotiated a treaty with the French for reparations to American commerce dating back to the days of Napolean, and, becoming irate when the French had refused to pay, he threatened war to collect the sums due. Although the money was paid, relations were still edgy, and Jackson now needed someone to soothe feelings. Cass was that man.

After Cass took a long European vacation, visiting many ancient historical sites, he began his tenure in Paris. His personality was so pleasing to the French that they soon regarded him as the most affable Ambassador since Benjamin Franklin. This was in no small part because Cass, who had amassed a large fortune in Michigan, was able to entertain the French Court in an elegant and tasteful style.

For the most part Cass' stay in Paris was uneventful. But problems with the British found Cass in the center of controversies that would bring him to the forefront of American politics. One incident came about because the British, still unable to fully accept the outcome of the Revolutionary War and the War of 1812, permitted citizens in Canada undue leeway in crossing the American border to create disturbances. One such occurrence resulted in the death of an American citizen by a British subject, who crossed the border back to Canada. Later, the same man reappeared in New York, was apprehended by New York state authorities and held for trial on murder charges. The British were outraged, and for a while war seemed imminent over this incident, but the Ashburton Treaty was negotiated to avoid future border disputes.

In yet a far more significant incident, the British together with France, Prussia, Russia and Austria, signed a five-party treaty stating that they would no longer honor slave trading. The British compounded the problems of the United States when it stated that it would use its Navy, then the world's most powerful, to prevent the extension of this practice, hinting that it might board American vessels to enforce the treaty's provisions.

Cass, who always thought the British arrogant and who had not changed his mind while visiting the Isles (he was on hand to witness the coronation of Victoria), quickly assumed a posture that enhanced his political future. While New England Secretary of State Daniel Webster thought the United States should tread slowly, the fervent Cass indignantly opposed the British, and wrote a paper which made the question of American freedom on the seas the paramount political issue of the day. Without directly taking a posture for or against slavery, Cass was able to secure for himself a loyal Northern following and a sympathetic Southern following at the same time. When soon afterwards he was called back from his diplomatic appointment following six years of service, he was in the position to seek the nation's highest executive office.

PRESIDENTIAL CANDIDATE

Cass returned from his post in France to be hailed as a genuine hero. From Boston to New York to Washington and thence at many stops enroute to his Michigan home, he was feted time and again for his defense of U.S. rights on the high seas against the infamous British. Soon calls were being heard that he should run for President, and clubs were being organized to bring this about in 1844.

The Whig Party, which had elected William Henry Harrison in 1840 only to have Democrat John Tyler succeed him upon his death, was set to nominate Henry Clay as its nominee. The Democrats were having a more difficult time deciding upon a favorite. The leading candidates were former President Van Buren, former Vice President Richard Johnson, and Cass. Ironically, it was his hero, Andrew Jackson, who sealed the fate of Cass in 1844. The Texas annexation question had become the chief campaign issue. Jackson, nearing death in his retirement at the Hermitage but still too angry at Clay because of the 1824 election to let him assume the Presidency, took steps to decide the election. He first of all persuaded President Tyler to resist any "third party" temptations. Then, since Van Buren had made the fatal mistake of opposing Texas statehood, Jackson decided that a protege from Tennessee was necessary. Thus, "Young Hickory," James K. Polk, was drafted as the first "dark horse" nominee. Cass was denied the nomination in the year of Democratic success by the man he had so faithfully served and ardently revered.

Polk's term was a taxing one. The nation's expansionist mood saw a war with Mexico and an increase in its territory. "Manifest destiny" was becoming a reality. The energetic Polk, who preferred to handle all government details himself rather than delegate them, died from sheer exhaustion shortly after leaving office in 1849. He had decided not to seek re-election.

Cass was the early favorite to gain the 1848 Democratic nomination, his only serious opposition being Secretary of State (and future President) James Buchanan. He was nominated at Baltimore on the fourth ballot, and Gen. William O. Butler of Tennessee was selected as his Vice Presidential running mate. Unfortunately, the Mexican War had produced several very popular military heroes, and one, Gen. Zachary Taylor, was persuaded to accept the Whig nomination. Even more unfortunate for Cass was a split in the Democratic Party, brought about by former President Van Buren over the question of slavery. When the Democratic Convention did not heed his demands, the former Chief Executive formed a third party, while still a fourth party was formed under John P. Hale of New Hampshire. Taylor, a slave holder who was not known to have supported a party or even to have voted in the past, let the Democrats debate the slavery issue and the people think of his war record. "Old Rough 'n' Ready" won the Presidency with ease.

SENATOR

Cass, who had been elected to the Senate from Michigan in 1845, took defeat well and resumed his legislative duties. He was to serve in the Senate among many of that body's all-time great members: Henry Clay, Daniel Webster, John C. Calhoun, Thomas Hart Benton, Sam Houston, Charles Sumner, Stephen Douglas, Jefferson Davis, William Seward and Salmon P. Chase. Cass was an active participant in all the proceedings surrounding the great issues of the slavery question.

When Henry Clay introduced measures in 1850 to avoid conflict over the slavery issue, one of his chief allies and supporters was Lewis Cass. Cass himself assumed a role of leadership in the thirty-first session of the Congress, a truly historic body now remembered because Clay, racked by tuberculosis, and Calhoun, the aged and dying South Carolinian, were each presenting their last acts before the Senate and the American people.

The Compromise of 1850 passed, but it was only a short time before conflict once again seemed imminent. This time the problem lay in western territories that were possibly future states; the South wanted slave states to be admitted in equal proportion to free states so that the institution of slavery could be saved; the North wanted the converse so that the dreaded practice could be forever ended. Soon the Kansas-Nebraska bill was in the Senate, not sponsored either by Clay or Calhoun, who were now both dead, but by Stephen Douglas of Illinois, the future Presidential opponent of Abraham Lincoln.

Because he was more interested in the Union than slavery, Cass had a base of political support similar to many other Northern Democratic leaders of the day. President Pierce, for example, found it convenient not to support slavery but also not to oppose the Constitution, which allowed the practice. This made an alliance such that the election of a Northern Democrat with Southern ties was attainable; had Cass been a little bit more in tune with the South in 1848, he might have been President. Cass did not favor slavery — in fact, he opposed it, and so did the people of Michigan. In 1849, oddly, the legislators of Michigan were divided about Cass, and he won re-election to the Senate only by the close vote of 44 to 38, indicating that that state thought Cass was too lenient on the slavery question.

In reality the Michigan Senator was more interested in "Manifest Destiny" than slavery. He did, therefore, support the annexation of Texas and the resulting war with Mexico. He also supported the many treaties which saw the United States acquire great tracts of land at the expense of the defeated Mexicans. Additionally, he was quick to support those treaties which expanded the great Northwest boundary. However, when a plan emerged, sponsored by James Buchanan among others, to purchase Cuba and make five slave states of it, Cass denounced it.

When Doulgas's Kansas-Nebraska bill came to the Senate floor for a vote, Cass supported it for peculiar reasons. He first of all saw no advantage to the South to have states admitted equally. Secondly, he thought the western territories were not climatically suited for slavery to be economically feasible and that the system could not become entrenched there. He nonetheless concluded that the bill should be passed in order that the Union could be saved.

Of course, matters were getting more serious by the day. Cass was in the Senate when the Missouri Compromise was repealed, and he was also in the Senate when Congressman Brooks of South Carolina came on the Senate floor to "cane" Senator Sumner of Massachusetts nearly to death. (Cass had thought one of Sumner's speeches the most un-American and unpatriotic he had ever heard in the Senate). Cass did not find it within his power to either publicly condemn the caning or to find a way, while serving as a member of a Select Committee investigating the incident, to censure the Congressman from South Carolina.

SECRETARY OF STATE

When the Kansas-Nebraska bill passed, a new political party, the Republicans, emerged as a powerful new force, and John Charles Fremont was fielded as its first candidate in 1856. The Democrats nominated James Buchanan, who had the necessary Southern political ties for a Northern Democrat to win, since he had sponsored the five-state Cuban proposal. He was joined on the ticket by John Breckinridge of Kentucky, a future Confederate States General who has the distinction of having been the youngest Vice President in the nation's history. The Democrats retained the White House in 1856.

Buchanan's Cabinet had a decidedly Southern flavor. There were members from Georgia, Mississippi, Tennessee and Virginia. Only Northern men from Connecticut and Pennsylvania were available to join Cass, who received the top Cabinet appointment as Secretary of State. Buchanan was a timid, placid President who gave in all too often to the demands of the Southern Cabinet members in order to avoid personal conflicts.

Great Britain soon created distractions when she once again threatened to board American vessels to prevent slave trading. This enraged Cass, who hated the British worse than slavery. For a while, war with Britain appeared to be a possibility. The United States at one point sent armed vessels to encounter the British Navy, but negotiations achieved a peaceful result to this dispute.

In 1860 Lincoln was fielded as the Republican candidate while the Democrats, in disarray, fielded tickets headed by Stephen Douglas, Vice President Breckinridge and John Bell of Tennessee. Southern states spoke openly of secession if Lincoln won — which he did when the North went solidly Republican and the South divided its vote.

While Buchanan sat idly by, his Southern Cabinet members openly plotted secession. The Secretary of War gave a copy of Buchanan's annual message to Congress to Southern elements, for example. Others allowed munitions to be transported to the South and warned the President that his actions could lead to war. Buchanan himself thought it was unconstitutional for him to act against secession. Cass joined the President in supporting the preservation of slavery if that would preserve the Union.

Finally, the disciple of Jackson warned the Cabinet that "...he was not ready to yield every point [to the South] for the sake of avoiding trouble." Shortly thereafter, he demanded that the President reinforce Fort Sumter. The President refused, and Cass resigned as Secretary of State in December of 1860.

PRIVATE CITIZEN

Returning to Michigan, he was deeply grieved when the War Between the States broke out several months later. The Republicans attempted to convert him, but he was to remain a loyal Democrat to his death. He was also to remain a loyal American, leading efforts in Michigan to raise volunteers. In one lengthy speech, he proclaimed, "...He who is not **for** his country is **against** it. There is no neutral position to be occupied..." On another occasion he lamented, "I have loved the Union ever since the light of that bonfire [one lit in New Hampshire when the Republic was formed when he was but a boy] greeted my eyes. I have given fifty-five years of my life and my best efforts to its preservation..." His last public speech in 1862 was a call for volunteers to defend the Union.

Cass spent his last few years pursuing old friendships and scholarly studies. In 1866, at age 84, he succumbed to the ravages of time. Both Democrats and Republicans mourned his passing. He was buried in Detroit, where he had come as a young man to carve out a future. He had been Soldier, General, Governor, Secretary of War, French Ambassador, Senator, Secretary of State and Presidential candidate. Unsuccessful as the candidate for the Chief Executive and perhaps somewhat obscure today, his life still was exemplary both for the contributions made to American government and as a symbol of the achievements possible under the American system of government and way of life.

Winfield Scott

The Election of 1852

From the War of 1812 until the War Between the States, Winfield Scott loyally served the United States as its most illustrious soldier. He was brave in battle, innovative in military organization and exceptional in military leadership, rising to the coveted post of General-in-Chief with the three star rank of Lieutenant General, the first man since Washington to achieve such standing. He hoped, like Washington, to also become Commander in Chief and Chief Executive, but his disposition was not suited for political warfare, and he was denied this dream by the American people. His life both as a soldier and Presidential candidate are worthy of remembrance, though, by the American people whom he served for over fifty years.

A VIRGINIA LAD

Winfield Scott's ancestry can be traced to England, where his predecessors engaged in a civil uprising against the King. When that adventure against the monarch failed, refuge was sought in America, and a Scott clan migrated to Virginia. From this lineage came William Scott, who served as an officer in the Revolutionary War. He married Ann Mason of the famous Mason family of Virginia, and the couple's marriage produced six children. One of them, born on June 13, 1786, in post-Revolutionary Virginia, was Winfield Scott.

Scott was a towering boy of outstanding physical strength, a feature that was to be of benefit throughout his life. His early education, rudimentary at best, was received at a boarding school run by a Quaker and at a high school in Richmond, where he studied Greek and Latin classics, rhetoric, metaphysics, logic, mathematics and political economy. Although not a very good student, Scott liked reading and especially enjoyed poetry, which was to be a life-long passion for the soldier-to-be. After a year at the Richmond high school, Scott enrolled in William and Mary College at Williamsburg, the same school that Thomas Jefferson and other prominent Virginians had attended.

Scott studied to be an attorney, perusing the works of Blackstone in addition to taking courses in chemistry and philosophy. His passion for reading was expanded, and he delved into the lives of Caesar and Scipio. He read the works of Milton, Samuel Johnson, Goldsmith, Adam Smith, John Locke and Gibbon. He ardently read the poetic works of Dryden and learned to speak French fluently. A full curriculum was more than Scott was willing to endure, and he left William and Mary after one year to enter the law office of David Robertson of Petersburg. It was his intention to read books until he could be admitted to the bar. Several incidents of national political importance were, however, to change these plans.

INTO THE ARMY

The first incident was the attack of the U.S. frigate *Chesapeake* by the British. This occurred just as the trial for treason of Aaron Burr, Vice President during Jefferson's first term, was concluding. Scott had been an observer at this trial, viewing the likes of Burr, Chief Justice John Marshall, a frontier General named Andrew Jackson (who was not at all friendly to Jefferson and testifying for Burr), a fledgling New York reporter named Washington Irving, and a host of other national figures. The outrageous British action caused a patriotic fervor to sweep the country, and the twenty-one year old Winfield Scott interrupted his law career to answer the call of Virginia's Governor for volunteers. Although war was not declared over this incident, Scott did see some action, helping to capture some English sailors who tried to come ashore along the Chesapeake Bay. He was then assigned to the calvary and received a promotion to Lance Corporal.

Following his initial tour of duty, Scott decided to move to Charleston, South Carolina to continue his practice of law. His mind was not completely set on this career, however. When Congress in 1808 passed a law authorizing an increase in the numbers of both officers and enlisted men, Scott decided to earnestly pursue a military career. Going to Washington, Scott enlisted the aid of friendly Senators and Congressmen, who used their influence to have Scott commissioned a Captain in charge of a company of men in Light Artillery.

The new Captain was assigned to duty at Fort Norfolk (now Monroe) at New Orleans. The commander there was Brigadier General James Wilkinson, who was returning to the command of the Department of the West after testifying against Aaron Burr, and for whom Scott had acquired suspicious feelings after hearing his testimony. The garrison at New Orleans had responsibility for protecting New Orleans and for seeing to the affairs of the newly acquired Louisiana Territory. Conditions for soldiers in the swampy terrain were miserable, and Scott, displaying a canny ability for recognizing and dealing with unsanitary field conditions, soon began criticizing Wilkinson not only for the conditions at New Orleans but also for his testimony in the

Burr trial, calling the General a "...liar and a scoundrel." The Captain was promptly arrested and court-martialed. He personally defended himself of charges ranging from "Conduct unbecoming an Officer" to taking the pay of his men. The military court found Captain Scott guilty and suspended him from holding his commission or receiving pay for a year. A recommendation to reduce the sentence by nine months was not accepted by the War Department.

Before leaving Louisiana, the future General-in-Chief challenged a Doctor who had supplied information which led to his conviction to a duel. Scott fire his weapon and missed the Doctor, who took aim and fired, grazing Scott's scalp. The brash young Captain then returned to Virginia, where he spent a year receiving plaudits for speaking against General Wilkinson and also earnestly studying the military profession. Scott not only tried to be restored to duty early but even attempted to secure a promotion to Major. This was not granted, but the Captain was allowed to return to duty in 1811.

THE WAR OF 1812

Soon, another incident arose which was to alter Scott's future. In 1811, the "War Hawks" — Clay, Calhoun, and others — came to Congress and pushed for war, and before long, the War of 1812 was declared. Scott was promptly advanced to the rank of Lt. Colonel. Anxious for combat, he led two companies to the front along the Niagara River in New York state. There Col. Scott participated in several battles as the Americans tried to penetrate and capture Canada. In bloody action at Queenston, he distinguished himself for his bravery and military leadership, but his force was defeated, and he himself became a prisoner of war for a period of time. He was paroled and not supposed to return to action, but the U.S. government bypassed the parole by claiming he had been exchanged for British prisoners. (Had the British recaptured him, they surely would have executed him at once and without question.) After the parole, he traveled to Washington and was greeted as the "Hero of Queenston" at a White House reception. Soon, the gallant Colonel was reporting to President Madison and Secretary of State Monroe on various aspects of the Canadian military situation. His demeanor must have been impressive, for shortly thereafter he was promoted to full Colonel in the regular army.

Colonel Scott's new assignment was as Adjutant General to Gen. Henry Dearborn, who held the responsibility of attacking the British above the Niagara and capturing Toronto, the capital of Upper Canada. Dearborn was old and slow in his actions and gave Scott a free hand in organizing a general staff (a new concept in the army), training recruits and devising orders of battle. Scott went about his duties diligently and soon had a plan for encountering the British at Fort George, near Queenston, where he had been captured only a year before. Scott's plan was well drawn, for the British were completely routed. Scott himself personally led much of the fighting; during the action he suffered a broken collar bone when a magazine (powder house) that had been deliberately set afire by retreating British exploded as he was rushing it to capture precious and sorely needed powder for the American cause.

When the American effort sputtered, President Madison assigned Scott's old adversary, Gen. James Wilkinson, to take command of American forces in Upper Canada and plan an expedition to capture Montreal. Scott and Wilkinson agreed to let bygones be bygones, and Scott participated in further bloody actions along the St. Lawrence River. Despite his personal efforts, the Americans suffered further defeats as this effort also sputtered. The President, wanting a first hand report of the situation, decided to call Col. Scott, who seemed to come out of all the battles with his reputation enhanced, to Washington for consultations. Scott understood the political ramifications of his position and knew he could advise the President equally well on both military and political considerations. The President must have been impressed with the advice given, for soon Winfield Scott was promoted to Brigadier General. He was not quite twenty-eight years of age.

Scott's next mission was to organize a brigade and relieve New York of British intrusions along the Niagara. His troops consisted primarily of New York militia, whom he trained assiduously in close order drills. He also instituted camp sanitation, a practice not commonly employed at that time, with the result that his command had far fewer sick calls than others. When desertions became a problem, Scott held a public execution of several court-martialed offenders, and the practiced immediately diminished.

Gen. Scott's leadership was soon proven when he was ordered to attack once again at Fort George and proceed northward along the Niagara. His army was so well trained that the British thought they were fighting American regulars rather than militia. At the Battle of Chippewa on July 5, 1814, Scott's troops performed so bravely that the War Department ordered that the gray of their uniforms be adopted as the color of the uniforms worn thereafter by West Point cadets.

Scott's force pushed on and at Lundy Lane engaged in one of the most gruesome battles of the war. Each side alternately charged the other, and casualties were high. Scott himself had two horses shot from under him before being shot in the left shoulder and receiving a life-long disabling injury. While the British justifiably claimed victory, Scott maintained to the end of his life that Lundy Lane was an American victory. At the very least, he proved that American volunteers could be trained to do battle with the British. American morale was restored, and Scott himself was regarded as a genuine hero. After recovering sufficiently to travel, Scott headed toward Philadelphia to get expert medical treatment. At towns all along the way, he was greeted wildly, and he was bestowed with an honorary Master of Arts degree at Princeton. Other honors were also given: the Congress had a commemorative gold medal struck; the Legislatures of New York and Virginia voted resolutions of thanks and honorary swords; and President Madison appointed him Brevet Major General.

Scott was placed in command of the military district at Baltimore while receiving further care. Close to Washington, he was often called upon to give advice to the President. The new Major General gladly gave the President military counsel, advising that his drill tactics, patterned after the French, be implemented throughout the Army, a recommendation that was instituted. He also reorganized and enlarged the Corps of Engineers and gave the President a critical review of the Army's senior officers. He was considered for duty under Jackson in New Orleans, but his Doctor forbade that. When the war was concluded, his name was mentioned for both Secretary of War and Ambassador to France, but the twenty-nine year old General politely refused these offices. Instead, he served on an army board faced with reorganizing a peace time army. When the board's work was concluded, he became, with the permanent rank of Brigadier General, one of only six generals remaining in the army after the war.

PEACETIME SERVICE

Following his service on the army reorganization board, Scott applied for and received permission to take a long leave of absence and travel to Europe. While enroute, the Battle of Waterloo concluded, and Scott spent a great deal of his time in Paris studying the victorious European armies assembled there. He then returned to the United States to view the inauguration of James Monroe as the fifth President and to travel to Richmond, where he took as his wife Maria Mayo, the daughter of an army officer and a close friend of Dolly Madison.

The Scott's marriage was not a particularly happy one. Military duty, of course, required long separations. In addition, Mary Scott often traveled to Europe for extended stays (even dying there in Rome in 1862, while Scott was at home in the United States). Yet Scott maintained toward the end of his life that he had always been entirely faithful to his wife. The marriage produced two sons and five daughters.

All of his life Scott was prone to delivering remarks that were ill-advised and which would delay his advancement. This was first demonstrated in the case of Gen. Wilkinson in 1808. Nine years of service apparently did not teach Scott to hold his tongue against superiors, for in 1817 he charged, in language that amounted to a dressing-down of a superior, that Major General Andrew Jackson, the hero of New Orleans, had been guilty of insubordination to the President. "Old Hickory" became so angry at reading Scott's letter that he sent a reply to his "insolent" inferior requesting a duel; Scott, realizing that if he agreed to the challenge from the deadly serious Jackson he would be either dead or ruined (if he killed Jackson), courteously declined. Yet he apparently did not have a fear of dueling, for he issued a challenge to New York Gov. DeWitt Clinton, who had run for the Presidency against Madison in 1812, after further remarks were made about the inflamed matter. Affairs between Scott and Jackson did not improve until Jackson occupied the White House in 1829.

Another quarrel that Scott maintained for years was a question of seniority with a fellow General. In 1821 Congress reorganized the Army, with Scott and Gen. Edmond Pendleton Gaines becoming Brigadier Generals under Major General Jacob Brown. Gaines and Scott had each become Colonels and Brigadier Generals on the same date, but Gaines' name had always appeared on Army rosters above Scott's. However, Scott had become a Brevet Brigadier General over a month before Gaines, and because of this, he maintained that he was senior to Gaines. The two Generals engaged in a bitter and vicious rivalry for many years, each maneuvering to be the successor to Gen. Brown if or when he vacated the Major Generalcy. In 1822, Scott, perhaps a little weary of the military intrigues to which he was also a part, considered resigning his commission and either becoming an Ambassador or running for Congress, but President Monroe would not consent to the request. As the Presidential election of 1824 approached, Scott became an ardent supporter — and contributor to the tune of $500 — of John C. Calhoun, who promised him that he would be the next Commander of the Army. When John Quincy Adams became President in 1825, both Scott and Gaines besieged the new Chief Executive to designate himself as the superior. Scott boldly spoke of the pledge of Calhoun, now Vice President under Adams, to make him the superior officer, and then received a shock when Adams presented a letter to Gaines from Calhoun making a similar pledge. Adams ordered Scott and Gaines to desist from their pestering and infighting, and the two did so for about two years, but the contest began anew when Gen. Brown passed away in 1828. President

Adams, who had considered court-martialing each General for insubordination, temporarily resolved the question of succession by appointing a former General but current Colonel, Alexander Macomb, to become the new Major General.

If the President thought he had heard the last from the arrogant and outspoken Scott, he was mistaken. Scott now maintained that he was not required to obey the orders of Macomb, whom, he stated, was not his senior and should, since he issued orders to Scott, be arrested for "contempt and insubordination." He also demanded that legislation favorable to him be passed by Congress. The President patiently heard all the trivial arguments from Scott before finally removing him from his western Army command. When Andrew Jackson, who had the reputation for not putting up with such disputes as Scott was creating, assumed office in 1829, Scott decided to make another journey to Europe and, upon returning, he consented to the superiority of Macomb. His ego deflated, Scott was appointed to command the Army in the eastern United States.

With his future now resolved, Scott received several surprising but challenging assignments from his new Commander in Chief, Andrew Jackson. The first was to take command of the Black Hawk War. Jackson wanted an energetic fighter to fight the Indians and bypassed local commanders to enlist Scott. Before Scott could arrive on the scene, however, the action was already finished. Appointed to serve as a Peace Commissioner, he helped effect an agreement whereby the Sacs ceded nearly all their lands to the United States. While in this theatre, Scott acquired endearing affection from his troops when he personally attended them during a violent outbreak of cholera that proved more deadly than the enemy. He instituted sanitary practices, by now a custom of his, and conditions gradually improved.

A more serious assignment awaited Scott after the Black Hawk uprising. When South Carolina threatened nullification and secession, President Jackson detailed Gen. Scott to Charleston to implement measures to preserve the Union. Scott, a Southerner and former resident of Charleston, calmly but firmly deployed troops and ships to assure the collection of tariffs without insulting the South Carolinians. When a Customhouse with valuable sugar inside it caught fire, Scott sent his regulars to put out the fire; this action also put out some of the emotional fires in the city. Soon, with President Jackson threatening from Washington to personally hang Calhoun and with Scott making a quiet but forceful show in South Carolina, Calhoun decided to relinquish his demands.

The President next assigned Scott to take charge of fighting the Seminoles in Florida. This proved to be a difficult assignment since Scott's old adversary, Gen. Gaines, was also in Florida. Scott's area of command grew to include the Creeks in Georgia and Alabama. The General did not suffer any losses of significance and defeated the Creeks in Alabama, but his actions were not good enough to satisfy the General now sitting in the White House who had scored an easy victory over the Seminoles in 1818 and who had also defeated the Creeks. The President ordered a court of inquiry into Scott's failures to gain decisive victories and relieved the General from his command. When the court met, it heard vicious testimony from Gaines but discounted it because of the long dispute between the two bitter rivals. Scott was completely exonerated four days after Andrew Jackson left office.

The new President, Martin Van Buren, had been a friend of Scott's for nearly thirty years. Realizing perhaps that Scott could perform delicate military missions with diplomacy, as was the case in Charleston, Van Buren dispatched Scott on two occasions to the Canadian border after blood had been shed along the international boundary. Scott realized that, while the British were guilty of border violations and murder, many Americans were overly zealous for retribution against the Red Coats. He was able to mollify both sides, and each time the situation eased without general war being required to solve the disputes.

Scott also was assigned by Van Buren to carry out Andrew Jackson's wishes to move the Cherokees from Tennessee, North Carolina and Georgia to Oklahoma in the terrible saga now known as the "Trail of Tears." Realizing how sensitive his mission was, Scott ordered restraint in the treatment of the highly civilized Cherokees, but awful scenes of human brutality still occurred. A plan allowing the Cherokee chiefs to supervise the removal in lieu of being escorted by troops was agreed to by the General, who also agreed to have funds from a treaty with the Indians used under this arrangement. This did much to ease the misery of the Cherokees.

When the Whig Party was formed as the election of 1840 approached, Winfield Scott joined the movement and was immediately mentioned as a possible Presidential candidate for the party. Although on active duty, Scott did not dissuade his followers from promoting his name, and he eagerly sought the nod of his new party. But the real battle for the 1840 nomination was between Henry Clay and William Henry Harrison. Scott's managers (among them Thurlow Weed and William Seward) threw their support to Harrison to keep Clay away from the White House.

The Whig victory in 1840 and the death of Gen. Macomb in June of 1841 found Scott now in the position to achieve his long time goal of becoming

Major General and General-in-Chief of the Army. President Tyler decided that his best action, in order to avoid another dispute between Scott and Gaines, was to act quickly, and he did, appointing the fifty-five year old Scott immediately. The Senate, which had a Whig majority, confirmed the nomination on July 5.

The forthcoming Whig convention of 1844 found Scott's name being mentioned once again as the nominee for Chief Executive. The General-in-Chief had no problem with being both an active duty officer and a political candidate. But the Whigs were firmly in the control of Henry Clay, who was nominated by acclamation on the first ballot. To the dismay of the Whigs, though, James K. Polk, with the help of Andrew Jackson, became the eleventh President of the United States.

WAR WITH MEXICO

War with Mexico was a foregone conclusion as Polk assumed office in March of 1845. In addition to the problem of winning the war, Polk also wanted to make sure that a popular Whig general, such as Winfield Scott, did not gain enough battleground notoriety to launch a decisive campaign in 1848. But since there were no Democratic generals capable of directing the war, the President gave the assignment to the General-in-Chief.

Gen. Scott, who was so particular about details that he gained the nickname "Old Fuss and Feathers," began a deliberately slow and detailed planning process from his post in Washington, not realizing that the President expected him to go directly to Mexico and lead the war effort. Gentle hints that he do so were not heeded. Further pressure, including the creation of more Major General vacancies so that a Democrat might be selected to lead the war effort, brought from Scott a long, petty letter in which he not only defended his conduct in organizing the war but derided those above him who did not understand the principles of military strategy. Then he sarcastically stated he could not leave Washington for fear of having to fight the Mexicans on his front and others to his rear — an obvious reference to President Polk and the Democratic party. The President, who felt that Scott was not in favor of a quick end to the war, decided to turn the tables on Scott, accepting Scott's argument and announcing that another General would be chosen to go to Mexico. This startling news elicited a hasty response from Scott, who now profusely apologized to the President for his statements and offered to go to Mexico immediately.

Scott arrived in Mexico in February of 1847 with an impressive group of volunteer and regular soldiers. His officers would include some of the brightest graduates of West Point, among them Robert E. Lee, Ulysses S. Grant, P.G.T. Beauregard, George Meade, and Joseph E. Johnston, as well as one notable volunteer officer, Major General Franklin Pierce, who would be his opponent for the Presidency in 1852. Although in overall command of the Mexican War, Scott was leading a southern expedition and leaving the northern action in the hands of another Whig general who would soon be a very popular hero, Zachary Taylor. Scott at once captured the Mexican port city of Vera Cruz, considered to be the gateway to Mexico City. The General then began an advance toward the Mexican capital, scoring another impressive victory at Cerro Gordo, where his losses were only 431 while capturing over 3,000 enemy troops. The commanding general, who had cut his own supply and communications lines and was foraging off the Mexican farmlands, then paused at Puebla while Nicholas Trist, a peace commissioner from Washington, tried to negotiate a treaty with the Mexican government. Scott's propensity to create trouble for himself arose once again when he objected to not having the authority himself to conclude the treaty; at one point President Polk was about to recall his General and court-martial him, but he delayed such action. When the Mexicans refused to reach an agreement, Scott mounted an August campaign against Mexico City. Preliminary victories were gained at Conteras, Churubusco, Molino del Rey and Chapultepec. By mid-September, after a series of scintillating tactics and feats of individual heroism by his young West Point officers, the capital city itself capitulated. After this victory, the Mexican government promptly sued for peace, offering Scott the opportunity to be President of Mexico. He declined the offer, and the United States concluded a treaty that was most beneficial to the western growth of the nation.

While Gen. Scott could justifiably be proud of his Mexican achievement, he soon was faced with another major personal problem. Certain newspapers that had received copies of dispatches from Democratic officers to Washington officials began publishing articles which claimed that Scott's selection of routes, tactics and goals had been the creation of other generals who had formulated the successful battle plans rather than the commander himself. The incensed Scott immediately ordered his officers to quit making such reports. When they continued, he investigated the articles, and after he thought he had found the officers guilty of supplying the information, set about to court-martial them. President Polk then intervened, refusing to have his Democratic generals put on trial, and relieved Gen. Scott of his command and ordered a court of inquiry into the entire matter. The inquiry found no fault with Scott, but it did take up a great deal of his time, not concluding its work until the middle of 1848. In the meantime, Zachary Taylor, the hero of Buena Vista, secured the Whig nomination and won the Presidency.

After the court of inquiry was concluded, Scott was restored to his position of General-in-Chief, and more plaudits seemed to be in store for him when Congress in 1848 authorized the three star rank of Lieutenant General. It was naturally assumed that Scott would receive the rank as a reward for his services in Mexico, but the irascible Scott had also had his problems with the former army officer and new President, Zachary Taylor, as well as a number of other Washington officials. Consequently, no nomination was immediately submitted, and Scott was left to wonder concerning his future. When Taylor died suddenly in 1850, President Fillmore was much more friendly to Scott, even having the General-in-Chief serve as acting Secretary of War for a period of time, but the nomination for Lieutenant General was not forthcoming.

THE ELECTION OF 1852

As the 1852 Presidential election approached, the sixty-six year old Scott decided once again to be a contender for his party's nomination. In doing so, he had to challenge his Commander in Chief and the sitting President, Millard Fillmore, as well as the eminent Secretary of State from Massachusetts, Daniel Webster, who was also challenging his President. Interestingly enough, Fillmore took no personal offense toward either man. The Democrats held a nominating convention in Baltimore and after forty-nine ballots named as their nominee Franklin Pierce, a former Congressman, Senator and Mexican War Major General, whose war record had been commended by Scott. Baltimore would also be the site of the Whig convention, which would prove to be the undoing of Scott.

The great issue of the day was the preservation of the Union. Scott himself was a strong Unionist, and for that reason he endorsed Clay's Compromise of 1850, though not in such a way as to antagonize his support in the North. At the convention, however, the floor leaders of Fillmore and Webster pushed through a platform requiring the nominee to endorse the Compromise and the Fugitive Slave Law. Unwittingly, the Whig Party relegated itself to obscurity, for it never again won a Presidential election.

The balloting for the Presidential nomination was nip and tuck between Fillmore and Scott with Webster, who would not yield his delegates, always a distant third. On the forty-seventh ballot Scott began to make a breakthrough, and he was nominated by acclamation on the fifty-third roll call. William A. Graham, Secretary of the Navy from North Carolina, was named as the General's running mate.

Scott soon proved that he was no politician. His speeches were not polished or well written. Further, he could not hold together a divided Whig party which was also suffering from the passing of the venerable Henry Clay. While President Fillmore cheerfully supported him, Scott's court-martial and courts of inquiry were now resurrected with complete political embellishment. A final problem for Scott arose when the Free-Soilers refused to accept him as their nominee. Sensing something had to be done to salvage his candidacy, Scott decided to tour the country on a campaign swing, the first Presidential candidate to do so.

The Democrats had boasted that "We Polked you in 1844, and we will Pierce you in 1852," and their prophecy was telling, for Franklin Pierce trounced Scott on election day. Unable to carry even his native Virginia and but four states in all, Scott lost the popular vote decisively and the Electoral College overwhelmingly, by a vote of 254 to 42. The Democrats now labeled the Whig candidate "Lostfield" Scott.

PROMOTION TO LIEUTENANT GENERAL

Franklin Pierce was magnanimous in victory over Scott, allowing him not only to retain his position as General-in-Chief but also permitting him to transfer his headquarters to New York, where the General-in-Chief had accepted as a gift a house presented to him by friends. Pierce's Secretary of War, Jefferson Davis, was quite a different story. Davis challenged Scott's authority on many points and even personally audited the General-in-Chief's expense account, refusing to honor mileage expenses. Open hostility emerged when Scott submitted a voucher to close out his Mexican War account that included a five percent commission for himself on items he had personally handled, a practice that he maintained was common military custom. The matter was finally settled by the President, who allowed the General $6,149.86 of $11,584.56 requested.

In 1855 the Congress again approved the rank of Lieutenant General. Although Davis vehemently opposed the promotion of Scott, Pierce submitted his name to the Senate for ratification. A quick confirmation was granted, and, at age sixty-nine, Winfield Scott became the first officer since George Washington to wear the three stars of a Lieutenant General. Scott relished his personal accomplishment but wasted no time in submitting to Davis a voucher for back pay to the date in 1848 that he was breveted Lieutenant General. Davis denied the voucher, but the President sided with the new Lieutenant General, and once again a back payment, this time for $10,465.17, was allowed.

THE WAR BETWEEN THE STATES

Scott was greatly relieved when James Buchanan, who became President in 1857, did not retain Jefferson Davis as Secretary of War. The new Chief Executive and the General-in-Chief maintained cordial relations. When war with England was threatened over an Oregon boundary dispute, Buchanan dispatched the aging General to the scene. Scott withstood the rigors of the trip down the Atlantic, across the Isthmus of Panama, and up the Pacific coast quite well, and used his diplomatic skills to mediate the dispute and avoid war.

As conditions between the North and South worsened, Scott tried in vain to get the President to reinforce forts in the South, but Buchanan refused to act, stating that while it was unconstitutional for the South to secede, it was also unconstitutional for him to prevent secession. Scott was a witness as several Southern Cabinet officers exited their posts, boasting as they did so of the harm they had done the Union while serving under the docile Buchanan. The General-in-Chief was glad to see Buchanan leave office, though he was wary of the new President, Abraham Lincoln.

Lincoln was likewise wary of Scott, the Virginian of whose loyalty he was not certain. The old General realized this but went about his duties without bothering to answer either Northern of Southern inquiries as to where his loyalty would be if conflict erupted. Scott finally answered questions of his loyalty by posting troops at the Capitol after rumors had circulated that secessionists would try to disrupt the 1860 Electoral College's proceedings. He also called out troops on the day of Lincoln's inauguration. The General-in-Chief then recommended a reinforcement of Southern garrisons such as Fort Sumter. Southern sympathizers such as former President Tyler had hoped that Scott would eventually join the secessionists, but these overtures were put to rest firmly with the declaration. "...I have served my country, under the flag of the Union, for more than fifty years, and so long as God permits me to live, I will defend that flag with my sword, even if my native state assails it!"

Unable physically to personally lead troops in the field, Scott did his best to build a strong army. His main concern was the loss of officers to the South. It was Scott who encouraged Lincoln to give the command of the Northern army to Robert E. Lee; a private meeting between the old General and his devoted protege would not, however, change Lee's mind about not fighting against his native state.

It was also Scott who conceived the Anaconda Plan, which had as its purpose a slow squeezing of the South's resources and manpower until it would be forced to surrender, but this plan was not one that moved fast enough for President Lincoln. Lincoln respected his General-in-Chief but eventually decided that he would have to replace him. When the North suffered losses as Manassas, a cry for new military leadership forced the President to consider the replacement of the aging General-in-Chief. The Congress passed a bill which allowed Scott to gracefully retire with full pay, and he took official retirement in November of 1861.

FINAL SALUTE

He moved his official quarters to New York and spent the next five years traveling in Europe and writing his autobiography. When his replacement, George McClellan, began to falter, Lincoln visited Scott privately concerning a replacement, and the President took his advice on an appointment. When Ulysses S. Grant became a national hero and only the third American general to wear a three star epaulet, Scott sent him a copy of his autobiography with the inscription, "From the oldest to the Greatest General." After the war, Grant made a ceremonial visit to the former General-in-Chief while inspecting the cadets of West Point.

By 1866 the eighty year old Scott now residing at West Point had become very feeble and frail. His body was suffering both from the rigors of military life and from ailments brought on by his excessive drinking and gourmet diet. In late May, as an Episcopal Chaplain was reading to him from the Order of Visitation, Winfield Scott passed away.

While a simple service was held at the West Point Chapel, the nation expressed its grief symbolically. Government buildings in Washington were closed; flags flew at half-mast; and salutes by minute guns were rendered at Army posts throughout the land. The West Point mourners included a host of Generals, most notably the new General-in-Chief and next President of the United States, Ulysses S. Grant.

And, of course, the cadets of West Point were also at the funeral. Following taps, they marched back to their barracks in perfect cadence, their bearing solemn but dignified, showing the highest respect for a fallen leader. Of particular note on this solemn occasion were the dress uniforms of the cadets. Their color was gray —the same gray as the uniforms of the American troops which had defeated the British at the Battle of Chippewa in the War of 1812 -- and the same gray worn since that time by the cadets of "The Long Gray Line" to epitomize the bravery demonstrated by Winfield Scott.

John Charles Fremont
The Election of 1856

John Charles Fremont -- "The Pathfinder" -- was the greatest trailblazer of his day, but when if came to blazing a path to the White House the frontier scout was completely lost. Though inept at politics, he nonetheless made invaluable contributions to the nation, and the story of his life is yet another of the fabulous stories of opportunity and success that the American system of government affords its citizens.

OF DUBIOUS HERITAGE

Of all candidates for President, John Charles Fremont began life with less chance of success than any other. His mother, who was descended from Revolutionary War stock, had had her marriage arranged by her financially destitute parents. Unfortunately, they had chosen for Anne Beverly Whiting an elderly gentleman who had fought as an officer under George Washington. The marriage between the young bride and her older mate simply did not work; soon Major Pryor had filed for divorce in the Virginia legislature. For her part, Mrs. Pryor entered into a secret romance with an immigrant of the French revolution named Jean Charles Fremon, who had supported the French King and fled to Santo Domingo when the royal government failed. Events finally placed Fremon in Williamsburg, where he taught French at William and Mary. The love affair between the two was passionate, for soon a child was conceived out of wedlock. Confronted by her husband, Anne Whiting Pryor decided to escape the pressures of Virginia. She and Fremon eloped to Savannah, Georgia, where two illegitimate children were born. The second, a boy, was delivered on January 21, 1813, and named John Charles Fremon. Forty-three years later, he would be called upon to be the first nominee of the political party that would become a symbol of privilege to many in the United States.

Fremon's parents were not in very good shape financially, his mother taking in boarders while his father took various teaching positions. The family moved from place to place throughout the South. Once, while staying in Nashville, the infant John Charles Fremon, lying in his crib, barely escaped death from a stray bullet fired during the duel between Andrew Jackson, who was almost killed, and Thomas Hart Benton and his brothers. Ironically, Thomas Hart Benton would become the father-in-law of John Charles Fremon.

Finally, word arrived that Major Pryor, the legal husband of Fremon's mother, had died, allowing his mother and father to wed and legitimize their three bastard children. Unfortunately, Fremon's father died soon after, leaving Mrs. Fremon the difficult task of rearing the children alone. Rather than return to her native Virginia, Mrs. Fremon moved to Charleston, South Carolina, where she again took in boarders to support the meager family.

EXPLORER

The move to South Carolina proved to be fortuitous for Fremon. First, John Charles was given the opportunity to obtain an education, and he proved himself an able student. At age fourteen, good fortune indeed struck when a Charleston attorney offered Fremon a clerkship in his office and agreed to pay for the bright young lad's education to be an Episcopal priest. Fremon (the "t" was not added until he was twenty-five) again proved himself a capable student, excelling in Greek and Latin, and displaying a good ability at essays. He entered Charleston College but was distracted by a beautiful Creole girl from Santo Domingo. The two apparently had a torrid affair, and Fremont was expelled from his school. The affair ended in time, and the restless young man, only seventeen years of age, decided to take a position as a schoolteacher. Fremont's schoolmaster allowed the new teacher the use of his library, and John Charles began a serious study of the lives of famous explorers and of astronomy and exploration. It was a study that was to be lifelong.

Fremont's residence in Charleston allowed him the good fortune also of meeting Joel Roberts Poinsett, who had just returned to his home after serving as Ambassador to Mexico, and who would in the future serve as President Van Buren's Secretary of War. Poinsett took a liking to Fremont and used his influence to secure him a position as a mathematics instructor aboard the *Natchez,* a sloop of war sailing for South America for two years. On the same boat with Fremont was Lieutenant (later Admiral) David Farragut. Also on board was a rowdy midshipmen with whom Fremont quarreled so much that a challenge for satisfaction was issued; fortunately, the seconds for each man prevailed on the two hotheaded young men not to go through the actual duel.

Upon his return from South America, Fremont applied for and received an appointment as an officer teaching mathematics in the Navy. In the meantime, however, another opportunity came to Fremont. The Army Topographical Corps needed an assistant engineer to help survey a railroad route between Charleston and Cincinnati. Fremont accepted this assignment and then took another surveying job in which he mapped, for the

Army's possible future use against the Indians, the Cherokee country of Tennessee and North Carolina. In addition to observing the habits of the Cherokees, which led him to agree with the "Trail of Tears" policy that forced the migration of the Cherokees to the west, Fremont also plotted such wild rivers as the Hiwassee and Nantahala. It was from this experience in the Cherokee wilderness that he was to begin his lifelong quest of the unknown outdoors that would ultimately mark him as "The Pathfinder."

In 1838 Fremont, through his old friend Joel Poinsett (now the Secretary of War), received a Lieutenant's commission to serve as the assistant to Joseph Nicolas Nicollet, a Frenchman by birth, whose services had been secured by the government to explore the great midwestern areas of the United States. Since the Louisiana Purchase under Jefferson, only the team of Lewis and Clark had made any significant progress in the area's exploration, and the government was anxious to provide more information to a growing population that was expansion minded. Nicollet, a former College Professor schooled in mathematics and astronomy and recognized as a leader in the field of exploration, was expected to widen the knowledge gained on earlier expeditions. John Charles Fremont, with experience from his Cherokee adventure and with excellent abilities in math and astronomy, would be the assistant to Nicollet on two journeys.

Each journey began from St. Louis and went northward up the Mississippi River to Minnesota and thence west over the Great Plains. Fremont soon acquainted himself with the natural wonders of the area as well as natural living habits and customs of Indian tribes, particularly the Sioux. He was awed when the earth trembled from passing herds in buffalo hunts, but the rumbling earth did not keep him from participating in buffalo hunts.

Fremont received quite a reputation as an explorer from these first two western experiences and was summoned to Washington, D.C., to meet President Martin Van Buren. While there, he also became acquainted with Missouri Senator Thomas Hart Benton, the same Senator who had almost ended his life while dueling Andrew Jackson. Senator Benton was one of the foremost exponents of American expansion to the Pacific, and he befriended the young explorer, often inviting him into his home for dinner and to engage in wide-reaching discussions of the arts, government, astronomy and exploration of the west. The Senator also introduced young Fremont to other influential Senators, Congressman and government leaders who were eager to hear of the west.

But by far the most important acquaintance made from this friendship was the Senator's daughter, Jessie. Only fifteen at their first meeting, it was "love at first site" for John Charles, who was attracted to whom was regarded as one of Washington's most beautiful belles. Sen. Benton and his wife were wary of the young army explorer, however, thinking him not an adequate match for their daughter, and finally forbade the two from courting.

Shortly after this, Fremont was commissioned to undertake his first personal exploration, a trip to map the Des Moines River in Iowa territory. This journey was of a short duration, only about three months, and not necessarily adventuresome, but it enhanced Fremont's reputation as an explorer. Since his mentor, Jean Nicollet, was now in declining health, it also gave Fremont a reputation as one of the foremost leaders of explorations in the United States.

When Fremont returned, he quickly made a courtesy call to Sen. Benton's home to give a report of his activities. This was but a pretense, of course, to visit Jessie Benton. The two young lovers soon resolved to be married, whether with the approval of her parents or not. Jessie arranged a trip to a friend's house, where Fremont waited with a Catholic priest who was to perform the wedding, with Kentucky Sen. J.J. Crittendon and his wife serving as attendants. The young couple kept the ceremony secret, with Jessie returning to her parent's home to live. Finally, the two confronted Sen. Benton with the news. The Senator, greatly upset, at first ordered Fremont out of his house, never to return, but when Jessie spoke up to her father and indicated she would also be leaving, her father relented on his words and asked Fremont to move into the family home. A lifelong bond of love and mutual respect then replaced the initial animosity.

THE PATHFINDER AND WAR HERO

Over the next eleven years, from 1843 to 1854, Fremont was to lead four extraordinary expeditions which were to be of the utmost importance to the expansion of the United States, and which would forever establish his fame and reputation. Taking up where Lewis and Clark left off after their 1806 westward trip, Fremont traveled from St. Louis to the Pacific Coast, mapping countless streams and ravines and plotting mountain after mountain. His guide on these journeys was the legendary Indian fighter Kit Carson, who often took scalps after encounters with Indians. Fremont was also accompanied by a host of surveyors, mappers, and other scientific adventurers, whose records were vital to the westward movement.

Fremont's expeditions were not just adventurous; they were full of all kinds of dangers and travails. On one journey, Fremont's troops were lost for an entire winter, traveling through the bitterly icy cold Sierra Nevada

Mountains and having to forage wild roots and berries for the most meager subsistence. Several men went raving wild from their hunger, while others froze to death. There is some evidence to indicate that cannibalism may also have been practiced by some members of Fremont's party.

Another journey, and the one which made Fremont a national hero, was his 1845-46 expedition to California. This sojourn began as war with Mexico seemed imminent. President Polk summoned Fremont to the White House for a confidential meeting, the contents of which have never been revealed. However, the historical evidence indicates that the President instructed Fremont to journey west to California under the pretense of mapping the area while actually being in a state of readiness for military action when hostilities in Mexico erupted. Fremont's detachment was in northern California when word reached him that war had been declared. With a group of rugged mountain men and experienced explorer-soldiers, he moved south and in grizzly fashion inflicted heavy losses on the Mexicans. After capturing Sonoma, where the Mexicans had enlisted Indians who were being paid by the number of scalps they took, his men soon unfurled a home-fashioned "Bear Flag," and California — the Bear Flag Republic — was declared. A short time later, the "Stars and Stripes" were also unfurled, and California was placed under the jurisdiction of the United States. Fremont moved his troops further south, and a link-up with General Stephen Kearney was effected, soon eliminating any further Mexican resistance in the Pacific state.

Unfortunately, major problems for Fremont were about to unfurl. Gen. Kearney had moved into California and considered himself the leader of all army forces there. Fremont, now a Lt. Colonel, felt that he was in command in California, with his authority being derived from a Navy Commodore who had appointed him Military Governor of California. Fremont soon had several confrontations over authority with Kearney. After the Commodore left California and word came from General-in-Chief Winfield Scott (who had himself been a candidate for the Presidency in 1852) that Kearney was indeed in command, Fremont finally yielded to the command of the General. Kearney wasted no time in gaining personal satisfaction. He ordered Fremont to accompany his forces to Fort Leavenworth, and there he had the Colonel placed under military arrest, to face court-martial charges of mutiny, insubordination and misconduct. Senator Benton called upon President Polk to intervene but found that there was resentment for both himself and his son-in-law. Since Sen. Benton could not practice before the court-martial tribunal, Fremont acted as his own attorney in defending himself. His defense was not successful, however. The military court found him guilty on all three charges, though it stated that Fremont had been placed in bad circumstances. The court dismissed Fremont from the Army but recommended that President Polk consider Fremont's valor and service and commute the sentence of dismissal. The President agreed to this, but Fremont, furious and feeling the whole affair was rigged, decided to resign his commission and undertake future missions through private financing. His father-in-law prevailed upon him to hold his tongue in order to obtain federal funds to finance certain projects, such as publishing his *Geographical Memoir upon Upper California.* Fremont's silence in the long run was a boost to his further exploration of the west.

All of the proceedings surrounding his court-martial had a profound effect upon the Army officer-explorer. Formerly outgoing and trusting, he now became introverted and suspicious. Where he had formerly depended entirely upon the government for his support and subsistence, he now looked to private sources. He began planning to become wealthy, established and more influential politically. When some businessman approached him about plotting a railroad route to California, he readily accepted this private venture. This mission was to be another harrowing experience. Fremont led his men through high mountain ranges enroute to California, and their supplies ran so low they had to resort to eating their mules in order to survive. Men soon became frostbitten in the icy winter snows, and some succumbed. After the last mule had been slaughtered, the mountaineers resorted to eating bugs, roots and even their moccasin soles. By the end of the expedition, one third of the men had died from the rigors of the winter trip.

Fremont decided that he should pursue wilderness travels no more. He brought his family, via the Isthmus of Panama, to San Francisco, where he and Jesse established a home. The former explorer began speculating in land and mines and acquired a bonanza when gold was found on his property. Overnight he and Jesse became rich and began to live a life of luxury.

UNITED STATE SENATOR

Because of his fame and stature, it was inevitable that Fremont would become active in politics. As California applied for statehood, he was approached by pro-slavery elements who assumed his Southern background and close connection to Sen. Benton would make him favorable to the "peculiar institution" and thus an ideal slavery candidate for US Senator. When Fremont emphasized his opposition to slavery, however, he was then chosen by anti-slavery elements to be one of California's first two Senators.

Sen. Fremont made the long trip to Washington to serve for only twenty-one days. Word came to him that he should return and canvass the state if he expected to retain his seat. Taking the long journey back by way of Panama, Fremont became ill with neuralgia and rheumatism. At the same time, he found that his property laden with gold had been overrun by squatters. Personal tragedy was compounded when a great fire struck San Francisco, burning down the family home. Fremont, beset by the loss of his Senate seat and personal assets, decided to take refuge with his wife on a trip to Europe.

For the most part, the Fremonts' 1852 trip was a blessed relief from the turmoils of the last two decades. He was honored in London by the Royal Geographical Society. He was a bit taken aback when he was arrested there because some drafts written on an 1847 expedition had bounced and the English creditors wanted him held personally liable. To his great relief, a future foe, Secretary of State James Buchanan, testified to Fremont's innocence, and he was released. Returning to the United States, Fremont was propositioned to lead an expedition in 1853-54 to plot a railroad route to the west. Fremont had hoped to obtain a government grant to do this, but Secretary of War Jefferson Davis, a pro-slavery man, ignored the request of "The Pathfinder." Like other escapades, this Fremont journey was also in the dead of winter. Soon mules and horses were slaughtered for food. Men walking mile after mile in bitter cold conditions found their boots deteriorating; walking barefoot in snow, they were soon frostbitten, and some died. Cactus leaves were foraged for food. After months of wandering about, the remnants of Fremont's fifth expedition finally reached safety in the Mormon town of Parowan. While some exploration success had again been achieved, Fremont now knew that his days as a pathfinder were over.

PRESIDENTIAL CANDIDATE

It was perhaps inevitable that the forty-three year old nationally famous adventurer famous would be drawn into the national political arena. He had lived in an age when men with a military background — Jackson, Taylor, Scott, Cass and Pierce — were prominent. Additionally, there was the family connection to Sen. Benton, whose influence in the Democratic Party was great, though he had not been returned to the Senate in 1851. Elements in the Democratic Party first approached him in 1852 about running for the Presidency, but Fremont, a staunch anti-slavery man, resisted all of their entreaties. He himself was against the Missouri Compromise, the Kansas-Nebraska bill and the Fugitive Slave Act. As these positions became nationally know, the newly formed Republican Party, seeking a candidate that could bring it national prominence at once, sought out Fremont as a candidate for the Presidency in 1856.

There were other candidates for the Republican nomination, some more suited to the maneuverings of politics and government. But in an age when the written press controlled images, Fremont's reputation found him more formidable than other personages such as Abraham Lincoln. Lincoln could not even garner the Vice Presidential nomination, which went to Sen. William L. Dayton of Ohio.

The Republicans had an anti-slavery platform and a famous name. To this they added campaign songs and a good slogan, "Fremont and Victory." But the Democrats, who bypassed Stephen A. Douglas to select James Buchanan, were far more experienced at campaigning and winning elections. Fremont was charged with being a Catholic because on one expedition he had painted a cross on a rock. His opponents charged that he had claimed to make discoveries on his expeditions that had been made by others. His financial dealings were called up for question, and he was charged with being a heavy drinker and a slave owner. Finally, his illegitimate birth was made an issue. Poor Fremont, never a politician to begin with, had little chance. As Southern Democrats put it, the Republicans stood for "Free soilers, Fremonters, free niggers, and freebooters."

Buchanan won, but not easily, with 1,832,955 popular votes to Fremont's 1,339,932. Former President Millard Fillmore, running as a Know-Nothing, gathered 871,731 votes, keeping the Democrats from claiming a popular majority. In the electoral college, Buchanan carried 174 electoral votes to Fremont's 114 and Fillmore's 8. Fremont carried the North but lost every slave state. Yet it was a strong showing for a new political party and showed the nation that the Republican Party with its platform for freedom would not be disappearing from the political scene.

Returning to California, Fremont found that his fortune earned from his gold mines was disappearing. Not only were expenses exceeding income, but claim jumpers had moved onto his property and refused to leave. Threats to his wife and family were made, and though Jesse Fremont refused to be intimidated, her husband decided to purchase land in San Francisco overlooking the Bay, where they moved in 1860. Fremont decided to take a trip to Europe to seek new capital for his venture and to get away from the stress of his operation. On the way he visited Abraham Lincoln in New York and offered his services for the impending civil war. He had hardly arrived in Europe before word reached him that hostilities had erupted at Fort Sumter in his native South Carolina.

WAR BETWEEN THE STATES

Lincoln issued Fremont a commission as a Major General and placed him in charge of the Department of the West, a significant position in a time of great national danger. But Fremont's services would be undistinguished. He created a political furor, first of all, when he issued an "Emancipation Proclamation" in 1861! Abolitionists were delighted that the 1856 Republican standard bearer was keeping the faith, but the politically savvy Lincoln, who wanted the issue of the war to be the union of the states rather than the freedom of the Negro, objected and soon relieved Fremont of his Departmental command.

Fremont was subsequently placed in command of the Mountain Department in Virginia where he led a detachment that attempted the rather impossible task of capturing a rail center at Knoxville, Tennessee and consolidating Union strength in East Tennessee. Lincoln then realized that Fremont was no brilliant military leader and rectified the situation by consolidating Fremont's command with several others to form the Army of Virginia. This command was to be pivotal in the rest of the war, but Fremont was neither to command this Army nor any other. He was no longer active in the War and finally resigned his commission in 1864.

FINANCIAL RUIN

After the war, Fremont, the "Pathfinder," lived the life of a successful businessman. Reputed to be a millionaire, he continued to invest in various ventures, particularly railroads. Never one to watch financial details all that close, and living an opulent life of luxury, he was dealt a stunning blow in 1873 when a "railroad panic" struck. Now Fremont, the former hero and former millionaire, was without any fortune. He was forced to sell not only his home in San Francisco but all of its furnishings and art. His wife, commenting on the life the couple had been leading, said that the new owners of their San Francisco home would "...find few shadows on the walls."

In 1878 President Rutherford B. Hayes appointed Fremont Governor of the Arizona Territory. His salary of $2,600 annually, it was hoped, would alleviate the misery of the Fremont family. However, Fremont and the people of Arizona, who felt that he attended to personal business too much and was away from the Territory too often, soon became disenchanted with each other. The sixty-eight year old former frontiersman resigned as Governor in 1881 to move to New York and rid himself of the bickering and rejoin his wife, whose poor health, which had been aggravated by the

Arizona weather, had already forced her to return east. In doing so, Fremont subjected himself and his wife to a state of poverty. In 1887 he moved to Washington in order to write his *Personal Memoirs,* hoping to make a fortune as Grant had, but this success was not forthcoming. Finally, his wife approached an old railroad friend and told him of their plight. Provisions were made to move Fremont, whose health now was very poor, to a better climate in California; money was also given to establish the Fremonts when they arrived. Still the Fremonts existed in a state of want. In 1890, a move was undertaken to restore Fremont's commission as a Major General, thereby allowing him to draw a pension. Fremont traveled to Washington to successfully lobby for this. He also petitioned Congress for payment on some land in California taken years before by the government without compensation, but this was unsuccessful.

While on this trip, Fremont made a detour to New York to place flowers on the grave of the son of a California friend. Riding a streetcar back to his hotel room, he suddenly became very ill. Doctors diagnosed his condition as peritonitis, caused either by appendicitis or a gastric ulcer. The next morning he was dead.

Burial was simple as he had requested. Dressed in a plain black suit and placed in a plain pine coffin, John Charles Fremont, the illegitimate child who became legendary as the "Pathfinder" and the first Republican candidate for President in 1856, was buried without fanfare in a donated plot at Pierpoint, New York.

Stephen A. Douglas

The Election of 1860

"Lincoln-Douglas" is synonymous with any American political debate, especially a presidential one. Lincoln is today well known, but many do not realize that for years he was obscured in Illinois by Stephen A. Douglas, a formidable party organizer, political thinker and outstanding orator and debater. In his quest for the Presidency, the extremely able Douglas was done in by a career replete with positions offensive to many voters, allowing Lincoln the opportunity to capture both the Presidency and one of the highest places in American history.

VERMONT NATIVE

The man who was to become known as a western man and who would push for expansion through "manifest destiny" began his life in the East, at Brandon, Vermont, where he was born April 23, 1813 of simple frontier parents. His Scotch ancestors had been in the country since the 1600's; some had participated in the French & Indian War, and others fought in the Revolution. Douglas's grandfather, who filled the role of father upon the death of Stephen's father when the child was only two months old, had served as a Vermont Assemblyman and was known as a speaker.

Growing upon a farm required that young Stephen fulfill all the necessary chores of early nineteenth century rural life, but he did find time to participate in such pastimes as fishing, swimming and exploring in nearby woods. Only three months per year were allowed for schooling, an experience the quick minded Douglas took to quickly, becoming particularly adept at mathematics and Latin grammar.

Stephen early in life showed an aptitude for woodworking and at age fifteen persuaded his mother to let him become apprenticed at a cabinet shop in Middlebury, Vermont, fourteen miles north of home. However, this arrangement was not totally satisfactory, perhaps because while in Middlebury in 1828, Douglas became involved in politics for the first time, during the Presidential campaign between Andrew Jackson and John Quincy Adams. Of course, Stephen was attracted by Jackson, who in time was to be revered by the young Democrat, and he participated in the campaign by tearing down campaign posters that shed a bad light on the Tennessee military hero. Unfortunately, Stephen's boss was an Adams supporter, and the young, headstrong Douglas was sent home after only eight months. He was to later state that his lifelong political creed was established during this period of his life.

Stephen secured another woodworking position in nearby Knowlton, where he worked for over a year, but he became seriously ill in late 1829 and was advised to give up cabinetmaking. His grandfather had passed away during this same period of time, and the young Stephen had to mature rapidly. Realizing that he must establish a future, he enrolled in Brandon Academy in preparation for college. At Brandon, Douglas was again an excellent student and especially enjoyed the study of history. Douglas also began to become involved in local politics.

Douglas' future was shaped further when in 1830 both his sister and mother married and moved to Canandiaigua in western New York. The seventeen year old Douglas followed the family and enrolled as a boarding student at Canandiaigua Academy, where he rigorously studied Latin, Greek, English, mathematics and French. Although he did not graduate from the Academy, his fundamentals were sound, and he did gain extracurricular skills from the debating club, where he practiced his defense of Jackson.

The young Jacksonian also made several acquaintances that surely impressed his politically active mind, including two Postmasters General, many Congressmen and state legislators, several judges, and a number of prominent lawyers. These surroundings probably induced young Douglas to desire to be a lawyer himself, and he secured a position "reading the law" in a local office. While this position provided him with experience and contacts, both legal and political, Douglas was impatient to be his own man and have his own practice. Realizing that it would be a considerable period of time before he could complete four years of study and three years of practice in order to take the New York bar exam, Douglas decided to seek better opportunities elsewhere. In 1833 at age twenty, with $300 in his pocket, Stephen A. Douglas boarded a stage for the west. Ten years later, he would be on the national political stage.

GETTING ESTABLISHED

Stopping first in Cleveland, Douglas used a letter of introduction from an attorney in Canandiaigua to secure a position with a local legal firm. Unfortunately, he was struck with an attack of fever and rheumatism which left him bedridden for several months. In the meantime the firm for which he was working secured other young lawyers, and Douglas decided he should move further west. He headed for St. Louis, now with only $30 in his pockets. There the young lawyer-to-be found legal employment non-existent. An attorney who interviewed him advised him that perhaps he could find employment in a smaller town. Almost broke, he heard that Illinois was growing, and he decided to head there for the small town of Jacksonville, named, appropriately enough, for his political hero.

Now with but $5 to his name and no law license, Douglas was desperate for employment but found positions in Jacksonville also very scarce. He sold his schoolbooks and clerked for $1 per day. He decided to head for an even smaller Illinois town, where he could practice law without a license, but the steamboat that was to transport him blew up. In late 1833, Douglas, now in dire straits for basic financial needs, walked to the small town of Winchester and formed a school through subscriptions to local families. This afforded him some much needed financial relief. He took quarters in an apartment behind the local general store and at night talked politics with local residents. Soon, he persuaded some of them to let him represent them before the local Justice of the Peace.

Douglas felt sufficiently established after a few months of legal practice to give up his school teaching and strike out full time as a lawyer. He went before a Judge of the Illinois Supreme Court in March of 1834 and was granted, at age twenty-one, a license to practice law. Douglas moved back to Jacksonville and began practicing law and politics. Jacksonville, a center of population in the 1830's Illinois, had neither a clearly defined Democratic Party organization nor a defender of Andrew Jackson. When the President made war on the second National Bank and a local meeting was called to discuss the issue, Stephen A. Douglas gave an hour long speech to rebut charges made against Old Hickory. So effective was this speech that the assembly unanimously passed several resolutions in defense of Jackson. It was Douglas' first political speech and showed that he was, in a time when political speeches and debates were cultural events, a gifted and natural orator of the highest order.

Douglas also had excellent organizational abilities as well as the ability to mix and mingle with the local population. As time went along, he proved himself capable of smoking cigars, drinking "hard cider," and conversing with the frontier men in coarse language. Short of stature and often slovenly dressed with seemingly uncultured manners, the young party loyalist determined to carve himself a political career in his new state. He worked hard for party causes and formed alliances within the party. In 1835 he entered his first political election and was elected District States Attorney, upsetting the incumbent.

The district which Douglas represented covered eight counties, and the new Attorney at first covered them all. He was now making $250 annually plus fees, and thought he would be making $500 to $600 per year. He was the object of ridicule to many of his adversaries, who considered him too young, uneducated and inexperienced to have his position. Although embarrassed many times, Douglas overcame these charges by working hard and by having the ability to organize with great detail.

He became so involved in party conventions and meetings that he soon neglected his office, but the Party recognized his loyalty and awarded him its nomination for State Representative in 1836. The young Democrat immediately hit the stump and campaigned vigorously, out-polling all other candidates in the race.

When Douglas took his seat in the Legislature, he found himself serving with five future Congressmen, two future Senators, and one future President of the United States — Abraham Lincoln. He also found himself a most active legislator and was appointed Chairman of the House Committee on Petitions. He soon took to the floor to defend attacks against Jackson, support a system of internal improvements which included a canal system, oppose, as any true Jacksonian would, an attempt to enlarge the state banking system, and participate in a move to relocate the state capital to Springfield. After three months of service, Douglas resigned from the Legislature and accepted an appointment from President Martin Van Buren as the federal Register of the Springfield Land Office.

Now Douglas commanded the handsome income of $3,000 annually, but perhaps more important to him was that he had a position that offered him the financial freedom to build his political career. At a time of rapid expansion in Illinois, the new Register was able to make many new acquaintances and extend many personal favors. Additionally, he had the time to attend all of the frontier town's social functions while simultaneously participating in his legal practice. The next session of the Legislature found Douglas at the state capital as a lobbyist pushing for the convention rather than a caucus system of nominating candidates. He also became more deeply involved in the party organization, and, together with several other party leaders, he purchased an interest in a newspaper that acted as a Democratic Party mouthpiece. A complaint to the Secretary of the Treasury from the local Congressman was soon filed stating that Douglas was using the Register's office to oust the incumbent. Denying that he did anything improper, Douglas kept active in Party affairs and was indeed nominated, in 1838 at the tender age of twenty-five, to run for the Congressman's seat after the incumbent had decided not to seek re-election.

Running against the underdog Douglas was a law partner of Abraham Lincoln, John Todd Stuart. The two foes, typical of frontier campaigning, traveled the District together, sharing the same meals (and often the same bed), and engaging in open debate before any group of voters they could assemble. With the ability to speak colloquially and straightforward, Douglas could control his audiences and proved to be a formidable candidate against his older and better know opponent. Though an economic panic had just struck the nation under Van Buren, Douglas, the party loyalist, continued to support the Party forcefully and effectively on all positions.

When Stuart became ill at Bloomington, tradition has it that his "fill in" was none other than Abe Lincoln, and this marked the first time the two giants of Illinois politics faced each other on the stump. Another story has it that Stuart, after being verbally bantered by the 5'-3" Douglas at one stop, picked up Douglas and put him under his arm and carried him around the town square; Douglas responded by biting Stuart and leaving a life-long scar on his thumb. The returns proved to be extremely close, with Douglas losing the contest by only 36 votes out of a total of over 36,000. Douglas at first claimed election irregularities and launched a protest, but when it became apparent that there were problems on his side, he quietly dropped his appeal.

He resumed his Register's position at Springfield and continued to engage in social affairs and the other party matters of the day. It was during this period of time that Mary Todd came to Springfield, and some historians believe that Douglas may have courted her; if so, he must have not done so seriously, for his heart seemed devoted to the Democratic Party before anything else. It would be some time before Douglas, who preferred the cavortings of politics foremost, would wed.

The Presidential Election of 1840 found Douglas again loyally supporting the national ticket. In Illinois, Abraham Lincoln challenged the Democrats to a debate. The Democratic Party accepted and announced that its speaker would be Stephen A. Douglas. For the next twenty years, the two men would dog each other from both local and national podiums. This rivalry would prove to be a truly American political classic.

The 1840 election itself proved interesting. On one occasion Douglas caned an opposition news editor. On another, Lincoln tried to make political mileage of a provision that would allow Negroes to vote but keep Revolutionary veterans from not doing so. Douglas campaigned hard throughout Illinois, and the State went Democratic. But the Whigs and General William Henry Harrison ousted Martin Van Buren and gained the White House.

Douglas' success was raising eyebrows among the Whigs, who decided to try to check the young Democrat's future by bringing suit against alien voters (especially Irish) who were overwhelmingly voting for Douglas and the Democrats. Douglas defended the aliens and had the case dismissed when he discovered a technical error (the Clerk had recorded 1839 rather than 1838 on a document). No sooner had he succeeded in this endeavor than was he called upon to represent the Democratic position in a matter affecting the eligibility of the Secretary of State to serve for life. The Democratic Governor was trying to get rid of a Whig who occupied the position. The Whig Supreme Court ruled against the Governor, but the incumbent Secretary was driven from office when he began drinking heavily and acting arrogantly. To replace the ousted Secretary, the Governor nominated the rising young star of the Democratic Party in Illinois — Stephen A. Douglas.

While being Secretary of State was politically important to the ambitious Douglas, its duties did not interest him very much. He had become quite successful as an attorney, winning notable cases and achieving a good success rate. The law and politics held his attention more than recording legal documents. When the Legislature reorganized the State Supreme Court in early 1841, Douglas sought and won election to this body. Not yet twenty-eight years old and with very little legal training, Stephen A. Douglas had risen to the top of the Illinois legal profession.

Douglas rode a Circuit in west central Illinois and quickly established a reputation as a hard working judge, clearing his docket while other judges had theirs pile up. Most of the cases he tried were simple in nature and received only brief legal opinions. Perhaps his most notable case involved a Doctor who had harbored a fugitive slave. While a federal case had maintained that apprehending a fugitive slave was not in a state's jurisdiction, Douglas found that this case involved the keeping of the peace in Illinois and fined the Doctor $400. An uproar arose, but Douglas' opinion was upheld by the State Supreme Court as a whole. Over a decade later the case was finally heard on appeal to the U.S. Supreme Court. Salmon P. Chase was representing the Appellants, but Douglas' decision was upheld by the highest tribunal in the land.

During this period of time Douglas was to establish some lasting relations with members of the Morman Church who had first moved into the area during the late 1830's. Douglas had viewed the group as prime Democratic voters and wooed them accordingly. When Joseph Smith was brought before his court to be returned to Missouri, where he was charged with treason and being a fugitive from justice, Douglas dismissed charges against him on procedural grounds. After Joseph Smith's murder, Douglas was appointed by the Illinois Governor to meet with Brigham Young and persuade the Mormans to move west. Considered a friend of the Mormans, he was contacted by them for many years afterward when help was needed.

ON TO WASHINGTON

Douglas' service on the bench may not have been the most distinguished, but it did provide him with the opportunity to broaden his political base. It also provided him with a lifelong title — Judge Douglas — a form of address that pleased him and which Lincoln, for example, would use during the famous debates of 1858. But forever pressing upward in his political march, Douglas would not remain on the bench much longer.

A vacancy in the Senate, to be filled by the Legislature, occurred in 1842, and although a friend had held the position for the last six years, Douglas at age twenty-nine determined that he should move on up the political ladder. Some of his close confidantes were already suggesting to him that he had a much larger role to play in American history, and little encouragement was needed for him to seek higher elective office. However, the Democratic caucus voted 56 to 51 in favor of an opponent, partly because Douglas would not have reached the constitutional age of thirty until well into the next session of Congress.

Another opportunity to go to Washington soon arose. The census of 1840 found Illinois eligible to elect four new Congressmen, and the district Democratic convention decided to nominate Judge Douglas (over both a former Governor and a former Senator) to fill the new Fifth Congressional District seat. Judge Douglas immediately resigned from the bench and waged a vigorous campaign against an older, but not necessarily more experienced, Whig, who charged that Douglas' record of service as a Legislator and Judge was undistinguished and that Douglas was a "political adventurer," hinting that Douglas would turn on former friends to seek a position, a charge that was not altogether untrue.

The two candidates agreed to engage in a series of joint meetings where Douglas would argue for the traditional Democratic values of hard money and low tariffs. His opponent would later admit that he was no match at these public meetings, where Douglas, with his folksy manners and dress, excelled. Douglas' hard campaigning paid off; he won the new seat by a margin of 461 votes out of 17,000 cast.

Douglas put his personal affairs in order and headed for Washington, retracing the same route that he had used just ten years before when he left his family with but $300 in his pocket. He took a seat in the House Chamber that included former President John Quincy Adams, future Vice President (under Lincoln) Hannibal Hamlin, future President Andrew Johnson, Alexander Stephens, the future Confederate Vice President, and John P. Hale, the New Hampshire abolitionist and future splinter party candidate for President.

The young Congressman from Illinois found Capitol living not too satisfactory. He joined a society of bachelors headed by Pennsylvania Senator James Buchanan. Many of this group were in special demand at the White House, where President Tyler held a dance every two weeks with the Marine Band present.

Much to his liking, though, was Capital politics. He wasted no time in addressing the body in favor of his hero, Andrew Jackson, who was having hard times in retirement. A bill to refund a $1,000 fine levied against Jackson during the Battle of New Orleans created considerable debate, an art at which Douglas quickly proved himself a master. This bill easily passed the House. Douglas was also at the front of debates over states rights, which he supported, and internal improvements for the west, which he also supported. Unfortunately, he became seriously ill shortly afterwards and could not participate completely in his first session in Congress.

Soon Douglas recovered his health and was in the midst of political forays again. He traveled to Nashville to speak and was thrilled to personally meet Andrew Jackson. As the Presidential Election of 1844 approached, he began to press for a candidate that would encompass his views on expansion. Douglas was to become a leading exponent of "manifest destiny," and he was all in favor of the annexation of Texas. Further, his statements over the years would show that he indeed favored a United States bigger than it actually became, for he wanted parts of Canada, Cuba, Mexico and portions of Central American added to the United States. Douglas supported James K. Polk — "Young Hickory" — as the Democratic nominee when Martin Van Buren refused to openly support Texas annexation. After Polk's nomination, Douglas campaigned for the Tennessean. Polk won big in Illinois in 1844 and carried the nation against Henry Clay. The 1844 campaign left Stephen A. Douglas, who had little trouble winning re-election to the House, as one of the leading Democrats not only in Illinois but also in the Northwest (where he was challenging Missouri Senator Thomas Hart Benton for leadership) and in the nation as a whole.

POPULAR SOVEREIGNTY

It was rumored after the 1844 Presidential Election that Douglas might be appointed Polk's Attorney General, but he announced his intention to stay in the House. He liked his Congressional bachelor life and sensed that his rise to power would be through the House and the Senate rather than the Cabinet.

When Texas applied for statehood, Douglas led the fight in the House for its admission. There were some legal arguments against the admission, including an 1819 Treaty with Spain, but Douglas conveniently found other arguments to blend with the tide of "manifest destiny," and a bill sponsored by him was enacted into law on the last day of the administration of President Tyler. Douglas in the meantime was pushing both for a territorial government in Oregon and for a Northern Oregon boundary of 54°40', even if this meant war with England. Douglas hated the English, whom he thought were encircling the United States militarily and plotting to take over Texas and Cuba. He himself wanted to annex portions of Canada for the United States. To connect the United States to the Oregon territory, he proposed a system of internal improvements, especially a Pacific railroad. To give protection to this railroad and settlers moving into Oregon, Douglas proposed a series of fortifications and the establishment of a new territory, Nebraska, to serve as a connector. When the U.S. had defeated the Mexicans, vast areas of land were surrendered to the U.S., and when President Polk requested approval of an agreement that would pay the Mexicans $2 million in exchange for the cession of certain other territories, Douglas was greatly heartened. The young Congressman had a vision of "an ocean bound republic," and now there seemed to be nothing except the wilderness to prevent this dream from becoming reality.

But then Democratic Pennsylvania Congressman David Wilmot introduced a bill, the "Wilmot Proviso," that would keep slavery from extending into any territory acquired from Mexico. With the introduction of this bill the nation began undergoing a constitutional crisis that would ultimately lead to civil war. The South quickly read into this act a loss of a delicate balance of power, for if free states only were to be admitted, the institution of slavery could be eventually banished. This, of course, was exactly what the North desired. With, Polk, a Southerner, in the White House, the North stood little chance at that time of prevailing in the dispute, but with the population balance of power favoring the North, any election could change the picture.

Douglas himself began formulating a doctrine he would entitle "Popular Sovereignty." Believing first that that a territory's economy would determine the need for or against slavery, and arguing secondly that the question of slavery should be left to the voters, Douglas was content to let each territory determine its own slavery policy. But since both the North and the South believed the other would flood a territory with voters for an oncoming statehood election, assurances were demanded by each side. The South insisted that the dividing line established in the Missouri Compromise of 1820 be carried to the Pacific and that a Constitutional Amendment be passed to assure this forever. Northern abolitionists wanted no further slavery, even if voters approved it at the polls.

It is interesting to note that Douglas himself had no particular concern for the slave. He spoke of the Constitution as having been written for descendents of European whites and felt that God had created blacks inferior, though they should not be mistreated. When he married the daughter of a North Carolina slave holder, he acquired as a dowry (though his wife held title for political reasons) a plantation in Mississippi. He hired a manager for the estate, but he kept close watch over its affairs and derived income from it. When his first wife died, the farm was passed to his children, but Douglas continued to keep check on its affairs and receive income from it until his death.

Douglas, who believed slaves to be property, never really considered that slaves should have any right to decide their future. Therefore, his arguments tended to favor the South until the late 1850's, when he realized that for the South slavery was more important than the Union, a principle which was anathema to Douglas, who, like Lincoln, felt that the Union was more important than sectionalism.

UNITED STATES SENATOR

Because of his theory that the Union should be preserved at all costs, in keeping with the tradition of his hero Jackson, but because he owned slaves and espoused territories that would enable the growth of slavery, Douglas became a powerful national figure and a figure that the people of Illinois were fond of. He easily won re-election to the House and campaigned for other Democrats throughout Illinois. When a Senator died in 1846, Douglas passed on the opportunity to be elected since the vacancy was only for the unexpired term of two years. He hatched his political alliances during the next two years and then received the unanimous endorsement of the Democratic caucus and was elected to the Senate in 1848. The "Little Giant," as he was now known not only in Illinois but throughout the United

States, was at thirty-five years of age a political figure of national proportions who certainly would have to be reckoned with in the future.

Devoted to politics, he had never had much time for women. He was, however, considered one of Washington's most eligible bachelors, and matches were constantly sought for him. In 1843, he met Martha Martin, an eighteen year old North Carolina maiden. After four years of courtship, Douglas and Miss Martin were wed in a North Carolina ceremony. Douglas' father-in-law offered a dowry of slaves, but Douglas, mindful of his political career, asked that they be maintained in his wife's name. The couple had three children. Shortly after the marriage, Douglas made the decision to change his Illinois residence to Chicago, which he recognized as the commercial crossroads of the West. Douglas purchased various tracts of land along the Chicago lakefront which would eventually yield him tidy profits.

Entering the Senate as Clay and Calhoun were ending their careers, the thirty-five year old Douglas became Chairman of the Committee on Territories (a position he had also held in the House) and thus became a central figure in the issues of slavery and western expansion. It was his Committee and often his own handwriting that proposed the creation of territorial governments for places such as Oregon, California, New Mexico, Nebraska, Iowa, Wisconsin and Deseret (a name which would be dropped for Utah). And it was Douglas' bills that proposed statehood for many of these same territories.

Douglas was very much present and active when Henry Clay presented his "Compromise of 1850." Along with Webster, Calhoun, Lewis Cass (the 1848 Democratic nominee), William Seward and Jefferson Davis, Stephen A. Douglas sought a means to reconcile the bitter differences which would not be resolved. To Southern demands for an extension of slavery to the Pacific, Douglas argued that the nature of the territories involved prohibited the extension of slavery. This position alienated Southern Senators, who felt that Douglas, who controlled slaves himself, was a bit overbearing in informing the South that it could not extend its slave influence to keep balance with Northern abolitionists bent upon the South's destruction.

Clay's "Compromise" would pass, but soon Clay and Webster and Calhoun would pass from the American political scene. Another figure who also left the Senate was Thomas Hart Benton of Missouri, considered the leader of the Northwest. With the passage of so many imminent Senators, leadership fell more and more to "The Little Giant." His oratory was so strong that when he was to address the Senate on an important matter, the galleries would fill, as it had done for Clay and Webster in the past, and a hush would come over the chamber as he spoke, in anticipation of the drama which he would unfold.

Douglas had supported Lewis Cass, a Northwesterner, for President in 1848. As the Election of 1852 approached, there was a considerable amount of talk for the "Young Giant" from Illinois to run. Douglas was only thirty-eight, but he was ambitious, and felt, due to the passage from the political scene of such figures as Clay, Webster, Calhoun and Benton, that he was the heir to political leadership in the United States. Because of this, he decided to explore the Presidential political arena.

As he sent feelers for support around the country, Douglas found that there was indeed a groundswell of support for him. Many seasoned politicians felt that the time was right for someone from the west, but who was born in the east, married to a Southern girl and who held a vision for a continental country, to be President. But the young Illinois Senator was a bit naive politically, soon finding that Lewis Cass, whom he had supported in 1848, was still interested in being Chief Executive. Also interested was James Buchanan, the bachelor from Pennsylvania who had been Polk's Secretary of State and who was quite experienced in political maneuverings. Douglas, Cass and Buchanan went to the Democratic convention in Baltimore without a clear consensus of the Party. Cass held an early delegate lead, but he soon faded with Buchanan taking the lead and Douglas in hot pursuit. Douglas eventually took the delegate lead and seemed destined to stampede the convention, but then Buchanan and Cass, fearing Douglas in the White House, threw their support to Franklin Pierce, the former Senator from New Hampshire, who had been quietly garnering Northern support to go with the support of Southern delegates who trusted him on the slavery question.

Douglas showed no public resentment toward Buchanan or Cass, and he campaigned vigorously for Pierce, who prevailed over Winfield Scott, the military hero of the Mexican War. In the meantime, he was himself elected to another six year Senate term. It was commonly felt that he was among the top leaders of the Democratic Party and that in 1856, if he maintained good relations with influential party members, he would be the Democratic candidate, since his philosophy was similar to President Pierce's. The Illinois Senator resumed his career in 1853, only to find that his influence with the new President or fellow Democratic Senators was not quite what it should be. Douglas was about to bring territorial matters to the floor of the Senate when his wife, who had just borne their third child, died from the complications of delivery. Deeply hurt, the grieving husband decided to tour Europe, where he met several monarchs, including the Czar of Russia.

The 1854 session of Congress proved to be one of the most important in the nation's history and one which would forever establish Stephen Douglas' place in American history. As Chairman of the Senate Committee on Territories, it was Douglas' duty to respond to the request of Nebraska residents for statehood. Douglas took steps in favor of Nebraska's admission, but a coalition of pro-slavery Senators blocked passage. Infuriated at the Southerners, but faced with the challenge of seeing the nation continue its westward expansion, Douglas fashioned a new bill, the "Kansas-Nebraska Act." This bill was the culmination of Douglas' "popular sovereignly" argument; he maintained that the bill would keep a balance of power by allowing people (other than slaves) to vote on the issue in Kansas, while slavery would be prohibited in Nebraska. Both pro-slavery and abolitionist interests initially voiced unwavering opposition to the bill, but Douglas, displaying both masterful oratorical and organizational skills, guided the bill through both houses of Congress.

Douglas would boast that "...I myself passed the Kansas-Nebraska bill...," and he did, but there were dire results for him because of it. In the 1854 elections, his party suffered significant losses, losing control of the House, and he personally received much of the blame. In his home state, the Democratic Party also suffered losses, and it would take his personal lobbying coupled with poor opposition from the Whigs for the Democrats to retain the other seat in the U.S. Senate. The nation became divided more and more over the slavery issue, and a new political party, the Republican, was formed from free-soiler Northern democrats and Whigs. This party would soon be making strident political gains by noting that "a house divided against itself cannot stand." Douglas himself found when Congress convened in 1856 that he had lost favor with party leaders, particularly in the Senate, where he lost his position as Chairman of the Committee on Territories, and where he was more or less ostracized by fellow Democratic Senators. Douglas had stated that questions of slavery had forever been removed from the Senate and House, but soon "bleeding Kansas" erupted into a cauldron of discontent, and the initial stages of civil war began.

1856 was to be another pivotal year in the political life of Stephen Douglas. He was encouraged by his allies, who admired his courage in the face of violent opposition, to take the initiative in running for President, but Douglas decided to withhold active campaigning, as he had done in 1852, until the nominating convention approached. His principal rivals were as in 1852: James Buchanan, Lewis Cass and the incumbent President, Franklin Pierce. Buchanan, who was Ambassador to Great Britain, quickly assumed the lead in the race, partly because Douglas would not announce and consolidate his position, and also because he had not been home either during the Kansas-Nebraska debate or the tumultuous tide of events that followed. Neither Cass nor the President could muster any enthusiasm. At the Cincinnati convention, Buchanan took the early delegate lead, but as more ballots were taken, Douglas edged closer to Buchanan, while Cass and President Pierce faded in strength. After sixteen ballots, Douglas, knowing he could not win, withdrew and gave the nomination to Buchanan. Southern delegates were greatly upset by the magnanimous gesture of Douglas, but they were mollified by the Vice Presidential nomination of Kentucky Senator John C. Breckinridge. Douglas campaigned long and hard for the ticket and was delighted at its election. He felt certain that he would play a major role in the government during the coming four years and that he would be supported by Buchanan as the logical candidate of the Democrats in 1860.

Douglas was absolutely wrong in this conclusion, and the next four years were to prove the most difficult of his life. President Buchanan, whom Douglas had called on "old fogy" in 1852, disliked and did not respect Douglas and refused to honor Douglas' requests on selections to the Cabinet or other positions of patronage. Douglas, realizing that this President was not going to help him in any way, soon broke most lines of communication with Buchanan.

Momentous issues occupied Douglas' agenda as Buchanan came to power, such issues as the Dred Scott decision and what to do with "bleeding Kansas." Douglas, the states rights man that he was, agreed with the Supreme Court interpretation on Dred Scott's freedom. He also fought efforts of Northern Senators to accept the pro-slavery constitution of Kansas, feeling that fraudulent documents had been submitted, and felt the North was obligated to support the Fugitive Slave Act, which was, after all, the law of the land. For these positions, Douglas was subjected to scathing criticisms; undaunted, he continued to fight for his position on "popular sovereignty."

When Douglas was to speak on an important issue, the Senate galleries would often be filled with eligible ladies who knew that the widower from Illinois was himself again eligible for matrimony. Douglas did not woo the ladies in attendance, but in 1856 he created a sensation when he suddenly took as his second wife Adele Cutts, daughter of a Washington clerk and a grand-niece of Dolley Madison. Adele was Catholic and this was to provide some political problems for the Illinois Senator, but she was to be an ideal political helpmate; although she disliked life in Illinois, she understood the demands that the Senator had and supported him completely in his complex political career.

In 1858 Douglas faced a formidable political challenge when he sought re-election to his Illinois Senate seat. The Republicans had made significant political inroads into Illinois, and they had nominated an old adversary, Abraham Lincoln, to oppose the incumbent. This is the campaign now remembered mostly for the famous "Lincoln-Douglas" debates, which epitomized the American values of democracy and free election. This was an election that also provided many challenges to Douglas as he tried to maintain both his Illinois and national influence.

Douglas found that opponents of slavery and the Kansas-Nebraska bill as well as Buchanan Democrats were out to get him. He rolled over the Buchanan supporters in the Democratic state convention. Lincoln, however, was providing voters with some eloquent and challenging campaign language. With the remark that the nation could not survive "half-slave and half-free," a distinct issue was drawn between the two. Campaigning hard, Douglas seemed to be winning when Lincoln, who had been traveling behind the "Little Giant's" entourage and making replies to the Senator's remarks, on July 24 issued a challenge that the two "...divide time, and address the same audiences during the present canvass?..." Douglas hesitated at first but did agree to seven joint appearances (the press wanted one hundred), the format not being a question and answer session presided over by moderators, but an arrangement where one candidate would speak for an extended period of time, fully explaining his positions and questioning the other's, and then the other replying in like kind.

In the debates Douglas scored points on his popular sovereignty ideas, but Lincoln also scored well, especially when arguing against Dred Scott or the Fugitive Slave Act and using Biblical references to substantiate his positions. The Republicans, though against slavery, were practical enough to be concerned politically when Douglas made statements to the effect that even if a Negro were not a slave, he was not the equal of the white man.

When the election results were tabulated, Douglas would have enough votes in the Legislature to retain his position. But a close analysis revealed that had the Senate seat been decided on the popular vote, Lincoln, whose legislative candidates gathered 125,430 popular votes to Douglas' 121,609, probably would have prevailed. The Illinois Legislature's vote, however, was 54 to 46 in favor of Douglas. It was another in a series of close electoral victories for the "Little Giant." Many wondered if there were any circumstances that could stop his goal of becoming President in 1860.

Douglas' personal life provided him a great deal of satisfaction during the turbulent times of the late 1850's. To the two sons from his first marriage,

Stephen and Adele would add a daughter, who, unfortunately, would die at eight months of age, just before the 1860 election. Douglas adored his family, and he was always concerned that his career kept him away from those closest to him. Always involved in different matters, Douglas became involved in many business deals in Illinois and other areas of the country to seek a fortune. The expenses of Senate life and Presidential politics were great, however, and often he would have to sell off some asset to meet some political obligation, such as publishing a pamphlet or meeting expenses of a newspaper in which he had invested for political reasons. Douglas was probably richer on paper than in reality, and his assets were used more to promote his philosophy than his life style.

THE ELECTION OF 1860

The Election of 1860 was to be Stephen Douglas's last campaign. After Senate re-election, many assumed that *this* Democrat, who had successfully prevailed over the Republican battle cries in 1858 and who not only had such considerable experience in government but had the ability to defend Democratic positions on states rights, was the logical candidate for the Party in 1860. Douglas himself felt that he was the best leader of all the Democrats to take the nation through the festering period which had already seen "bleeding Kansas," John Brown at Harper's Ferry, and the emotions surrounding the publication of *Uncle Tom's Cabin.*

His nomination would not come about without opposition or tribulation. Southern Democrats, who had seen him as the best compromise candidate in earlier years, now felt that a platform must be adopted that would offer no more compromise. Douglas attempted to adopt the 1856 platform, but this was thwarted. A definite and final break with the South came when Douglas maintained that his popular sovereignty theory did not mean that the South could require laws that prohibited free voting on the slavery question in new territories. Above all, Douglas was opposed to disunion and stated there was absolutely no compromise on that question, which was now at a fever pitch in the South. At the Democratic convention in Charleston, Southern delegates withdrew to try to force a compromise. Before ballots were taken, Douglas supporters tried to pass a resolution allowing a majority of the participating delegates determine the nominee, but the New York delegation, which felt that Douglas over the years had had too much of a states rights position, objected. When ballots were taken, Douglas commanded a large majority of delegates for the nomination, but he could not get the necessary two-thirds for nomination. After almost sixty ballots, the convention, in total disarray, adjourned to another meeting in Baltimore six weeks later.

The Southern delegates decided to hold a separate convention. Their nominee would be Vice President Breckinridge. Another Southern candidate, Senator John Bell of Tennessee, the former Whig, would lead a Constitution Union Party ticket. Of course, the Republicans would nominate Abraham Lincoln.

Meeting in Baltimore, the Democrats were still in disarray. Procedural questions arose over competing delegates, and a fight erupted over the convention platform. Southern delegates who had replaced those at Charleston were also wanting some accord on the slavery position, but Douglas refused to accommodate them. When the time for nominations came, the Southern delegates, about one-third of the convention, withdrew. Douglas then received all but eighteen votes on the first ballot and was declared the nominee. For Vice President Douglas preferred Alexander Stephens, the Georgia Congressman who would become Jefferson Davis' Vice President, but the convention chose Sen. Benjamin Fitzpatrick of Alabama. Things could not be worse for Douglas: two conventions had ended in turmoil, and Sen. Fitzpatrick, to add further to the disunity, refused to accept his nomination. The Democratic National Committee chose Herschel V. Johnson, a former Senator and Governor from Georgia, as the replacement.

Douglas, the organizational genius and untiring public speaker that he was, endeavored to spend all of his energies in his race for the White House. He traveled first through New York and the New England, preaching that secession was disunion and pledging to wipe out the disloyal elements of the Democratic Party. Both Lincoln and Breckinridge, said Douglas, were interventionists, and neither deserved election. Next, the nominee went South where he hoped to get enough votes, coupled with the votes that the Constitution Union Party would receive, to stave off Breckinridge. Asked in Virginia if he would aid and abet secession in the event Lincoln were elected, Douglas forcefully said, "No!" After his Southern swing, Douglas headed for Pennsylvania and the Midwest. He received the disquieting news that Maine and Vermont, which at that time cast their votes in September, had gone Republican. Even more disheartening was the opinion of his running mate that he had little chance of carrying a single Southern state. A frantic movement to stop Lincoln began, with Douglas and Bell trying to get together on the same ballot. The "Little Giant" traveled to Chicago and then to the Northwest, supposedly the source of his strength, but the tide, he could tell, had swung to Lincoln. Weary and hoarse, the Illinois orator continued on, draining himself of all physical strength in his quest to be the nation's Chief Executive. A second trip was made to the Southland, where he hoped to eradicate any support for Breckinridge. He was happy to have Alexander

Stephens introduce him to Atlanta. Speaking trips were made to Montgomery and Norfolk, where he stated emphatically that he would accept no Cabinet position under either Lincoln or Breckinridge, and that he would not be a candidate if the election were thrown into the House of Representatives, because he would not serve as a minority President. As the campaign neared the home stretch, smears became commonplace. Douglas was lambasted for taking an election trip to his Mother's home. He was charged with being a Catholic, since his wife was Roman Catholic and since his sons attended private Catholic schools. He was accused of plagiarizing legislation originated by John C. Calhoun. The campaign drained available funds, but enough money was raked together for pamphlets and a political biography of the candidate.

Losing was not easy, but the results of 1860 must have been dismal indeed for the Democrat who had hoped to unite North and South. There was very little consolation in blocking Breckinridge or in Lincoln winning without a popular majority; getting so few Southern votes must have been almost as hard as losing his beloved Illinois. Douglas received twenty-nine percent of the popular vote but only twelve electoral votes. His defeat, he knew, was complete. He would have to hope that he still maintained the leadership of the Democratic Party so that he could play a central role in the conflict to come.

Following the election of Lincoln, the South became hysterical about secession. A move similar to Henry Clay's Compromise of 1850 was made to keep the South in the Union, but that failed. Douglas himself offered a compromise, which, among other things, would colonize freed Negroes in either South America or Africa. Buchanan would not act to preserve the Union, claiming it was unconstitutional for the South to secede but also for him to do anything about it. In the tense Senate debates of late 1860 and early 1861, Douglas reluctantly concluded that the South was acting in bad faith. Douglas now adamantly asserted that the Union should be preserved, even if it meant a million men were required to die to keep one state in the fold. The Republicans knew that conflict was inevitable, and Lincoln indicated that it was best to get the war on and over with. The South would go through the motions of a Peace Conference chaired by former President John Tyler, but it would not be satisfied until it seceded.

The new President had asked for and received the counsel of Senator Douglas, and the two were very cordial and warm to each other. Douglas promised to respect the President personally, though he would oppose policies on principle. During Lincoln's inaugural address, Douglas held the new President's hat and then heartily commended him on his remarks. As secession began, Douglas intensified his efforts against disunion, and his speeches had much to do with border states remaining in the Union. In fact, some people began to speak of a Union Party for 1864 with **Stephen Douglas** at its head. When war erupted, Douglas counseled the President to call for 200,000 volunteers rather than the 75,000 proposed. Saying he would stand by the President, he evoked great feelings of unselfish patriotism and fidelity for the Union cause, especially in border states, where undecided citizens made their decisions based on Douglas' remarks. Southerners, on the other hand, felt that Douglas had become their arch-enemy.

EARLY DEATH

Douglas had returned to Illinois to attend political gatherings and make patriotic speeches of support for the Union when he became ill in early May of 1861. His condition deteriorated rapidly, and he was diagnosed as having acute rheumatism, which was worsened by the physical and emotional fatigue from the events of the past year (and lifetime). After several weeks of recuperation, he went outside, only to become more severely ill the following day. Typhoid fever seemed to set it, accompanied by liver problems and constipation. The effects of smoking cigars and drinking heavily for so many years now demanded their toll. Physicians were brought from Washington, but he did not improve. His wife, a faithful Catholic, asked that a Bishop visit him. Douglas received the prelate but sternly denied to be baptized; he also forbade a Catholic Mass upon his death. Asked shortly before his death if he had any last messages for his sons, he replied, "Tell them to obey the laws and support the Constitution of the United States." He died on June 3, 1861.

His passing greatly shocked people throughout the United States, who felt the forty-eight year old Senator was robust and who did not know the physical and mental strain he had been suffering. In Chicago, bells tolled and flags flew at half mast upon the announcement of his demise. In Washington, government buildings were draped with black bunting and banks closed. Military units were ordered to observe a period of mourning. Grief stricken, Mrs. Douglas wanted to have her husband buried in Washington, but a host of Illinois leaders, both friend and foe, prevailed on her to bury the Senator in his adopted state. She consented to this but insisted on a Catholic burial service. The Masons, to which Douglas belonged, then conducted their own private rituals. Douglas' funeral cortege was impressive: he was accompanied to a resting place overlooking Lake Michigan by sixty-four pallbearers, sixteen companies of soldiers, and five thousand mourners. It was a fitting final tribute for the "Little Giant" who had started with so little and gone so far in American politics.

George B. McClellan
The Election of 1864

Stephen W. Sears, McClellan's biographer, described his subject as "The Young Napolean." In his own day, his soldiers referred to their General as "Little Mac." The latter description perhaps better fits the feisty military leader, whose paranoia and procrastination during battle campaigns cost him not only his command as General-in-Chief of the Union armies but probably the Presidency of the United States.

SON OF A PHILADELPHIA DOCTOR

Of Scotch descent, George Brinton McClellan was born on December 3, 1826, to one of the more prominent social families of the Quaker City. His forbearers included a Revolutionary War Brigadier General. His father, a graduate of both Yale and the University of Pennsylvania, was a prominent physician, and his mother was from a leading Philadelphia family. The McClellan family were among the social elite of Philadelphia.

Young George was from his very earliest days prepared well for a life of leadership. At the age of five he attended an infant school and then spent four years in a private school tutored by a Harvard graduate. At age ten, George received tutoring in the classics, Latin and French. This sojourn was followed by enrollment in the University of Pennsylvania at the tender age of thirteen. The youthful scholar at first thought he would be a lawyer, but after two years of college he decided that a military career was the life he wanted. Therefore, he applied for admission to West Point at the age of fifteen. There was some delay in his acceptance because of his age, but a few "strings" were pulled by his prominent father, who wrote President John Tyler, among others, and George McClellan was granted admission in the summer of 1842. West Point authorities still had some reservations about accepting the fifteen year old boy, but his academic skills and natural military bearing convinced them to waive the sixteen year old minimum requirement and accept him as a Plebe.

WEST POINT AND THE ARMY

Cadet McClellan found himself among one of the most distinguished groups of cadets in the history of West Point. Perhaps only the class of 1914, which produced Eisenhower, Omar Bradley and so many other Generals that it received the nickname "The Class the Stars Fell On," can claim a better reputation. Among McClellan's classmates were A.P. Hill, Joseph Johnston, Winfield Hancock, Ambrose Burnside, John Gibbon and "Stonewall" Jackson. Although physically small, Mac drilled hard and quickly came to like the field training at the Point. Academically, the well-trained Cadet had no problem whatsoever. He ranked third in his first-year class and sometimes did not do as well as he could purely because of overconfidence.

An extremely able scholar who studied in detail not only academic subjects but military science as well, McClellan studied under the fabled Dennis Hart Mahan. He was elected President of the Dialectic Society, which was composed of West Point's most elite students. Though much younger than most of his classmates, McClellan ranked second in his graduating class (he thought he deserved first) and easily received his choice of an assignment in the coveted Corps of Engineers.

The War with Mexico awaited West Point's Class of 1846, and Lt. George McClellan, just twenty years of age, was anxious to receive his baptism to combat. But first, he was assigned to West Point to train a crack company of engineers. After teaching and learning the fundamentals of drill and building bridges and fortifications, McClellan armed himself with a double-barreled shotgun, two pistols, a saber, a dress sword and a bowie knife and took his company south to Mexico, where he was placed under the command of the General-in-Chief of the Army, Winfield Scott.

Although he suffered from malaria and dysentery while in Mexico, he did not suffer from a lack of action. "Old Fuss and Feathers" embarked upon the conquest of Vera Cruz and then headed for Mexico City, cutting all communications and supplies behind him. With no choice but to fight, the Americans headed for Mexico City. Engineers played an important role in Scott's attacks, and McClellan, finding himself in the company of such officers as P.G.T. Beauregard and Robert E. Lee, helped gather intelligence and construct batteries. At the Mexican stronghold of Conteras, two horses were shot from under Lt. McClellan, and "grapeshot" shrapnel exploded next to him, but fortunately the hilt of his sword protected him from being wounded. At Mexico City, Gen. Santa Anna's force of over twenty thousand was nearly double the American forces, but the U.S. forces, with such other officers as future Presidents Franklin Pierce and Ulysses S. Grant on hand, engaged in daring and brave maneuvers, and within two days Santa Anna evacuated the city. Cited for bravery, McClellan was content with his role in the war. After spending additional time as an occupation soldier, he was assigned again to West Point as a military instructor.

At West Point McClellan trained his units hard and pushed for the adoption of new tactics and standards for Engineers. He published his first work, *Bayonette Exercise,* and became a member of Dennis Hart Mahan's Napolean Club, a group of West Point faculty members and officers who met to discuss Bonaparte's campaigns. After West Point, the twenty-five year old officer served stints at Fort Delaware, where a masonry dam was being constructed, and at Fort Smith, Arkansas, where he acted as engineer, commissary, quartermaster and second-in-command of a unit exploring the Red River. Assigned next to the military department of Texas, McClellan was directed to map the rivers and harbors of the Texas coast.

In 1853 McClellan was ordered to Washington Territory to assist in the survey of a Pacific Railroad route. Traveling to the western territory by way of the Isthmus of Panama, he explored passes along the Colombia River at the 49th parallel. He depended on Indian guides for reconnaissance, and this proved to be fateful: he found two deep passes but failed to recommend them because of deep snows; and he did not find a route later used by the railroad. The newly promoted First Lieutenant became embroiled in a dispute with Isaac Stevens, the territorial Governor and a fellow officer in the Mexican War, over the wisdom of further exploration. It would not be the last time that McClellan would dispute his superiors.

Lt. McClellan's next assignments were directly for the Secretary of War, Jefferson Davis, who took a deep interest in McClellan. The young Lieutenant surveyed the fortifications of the Dominican Republic for Davis and found that the island could be easily taken as an American naval base, if necessary, in order to thwart British interests in the Caribbean. McClellan then made a survey of railroads for the Secretary of War. Soon, McClellan was rewarded for his services with a promotion to Captain. Receiving this rank at such an early age and with such little active service meant that George McClellan had been picked to go to the top of the Army.

This view was substantiated even further when the Captain was selected to be one of three members of a military commission created to study the latest military affairs in Europe, including the Crimean War. Moving throughout the continent, the armies of England, France, Prussia, Austria and Russia were studied by the commissioners. However, attempts to study Crimean embattlements were stymied by both the French and the Russians, neither of which would grant permission to the members to study first one side and then pass through friendly lines into enemy lines. A study of the site of the Charge of the Light Brigade was made, however, as well as various siege and fortifications of the combatant armies. McClellan, who was to use the information gathered later during the Civil War, returned and wrote the Commission's report for the Army, a clear signal that the young officer's rise was imminent. Therefore, there was general shock throughout the Army when the thirty-one year old Captain announced in 1857 that he was resigning his commission to go into the railroad business.

RAILROAD EXECUTIVE

Some of McClellan's former army comrades had left the service for the railroad business, and it was through one of them that contact was made to secure a position with the Illinois and Central line. Beginning as Chief Engineer at a salary of $3,000 annually, he adapted quickly to his new station and within a year was promoted to Vice President with annual earnings of $5,000. The former army officer was somewhat bored with his job, even though his financial status was three times what it was while in the service, and, as usual, he felt that his superiors could not lead as he could. He thought of returning to active duty, but a financial panic in 1857 put this plan in abeyance.

The Illinois and Central, solvent but cash poor, had to file for bankruptcy in order to maintain operations. A team of officers and directors was formed to deal with creditors, and McClellan was named chairman of this group. He refused to accept any salary for himself while the crisis was underway, but he vigorously objected to an attempt by the company's management to cut the pay of laborers below $1 per day. This and other disputes had him ready to resign and either accept a position with another company or return to the Army, but the bank's directors assured him they would not allow a resignation.

It was while a civilian that McClellan wed his wife. During his southwest assignments McClellan had made the acquaintance of Randolph Marcy, a career Army officer who would serve with and under McClellan through the Civil War. Marcy had a beautiful daughter, Ellen, who was at the time away to school in Connecticut. After his Northwest assignment ended in 1854, George and Ellen were introduced, and George immediately tried to woo her into marriage. She would resist his proposals time after time, preferring the hand of A.P. Hill, but her parents, who suspected that Hill had a venereal disease, vehemently opposed that union. Finally, in 1860, six years after initial introductions, she agreed to George's proposal. George in turn accepted her fundamental Presbyterian faith as his. The couple had a son and a daughter and would remain close confidants until his death in 1885.

It was also as a civilian that George McClellan witnessed the 1858 Lincoln-Douglas debates. The former officer was a Democrat who thought very little of Lincoln's abilities either as a politician or as a lawyer representing the interests of the Illinois and Central Railroad. McClellan feared that war would come between the North and the South and that he would have to fight against many of his former comrades from the South. Like many Northern Democrats, McClellan did not feel that the freedom of slaves was worth civil unrest, and he favored an accommodation with the South. Yet, he strongly disagreed with those who felt the South had the right to secede over slavery or any issue. After Lincoln was elected in 1860 and more ominous tones were heard, he knew that it was just a matter of time before war would begin. When Ft. Sumter was attacked, he prepared himself to immediately re-enter the Army.

CIVIL WAR GENERAL

With his West Point education, Mexican War combat experience, peace-time service and railroad executive background, George McClellan was in immediate demand by various states and the federal government as a top officer. There were cries from leading citizens in Cincinnati, his current home, to make him commanding officer of the Ohio militia. An offer was also made by his home state, Pennsylvania, to make him Chief Engineer of that state's militia. McClellan accepted the Ohio offer and began his Civil War service as a Brigadier General of Volunteers in the west.

Using his extraordinary organizational skills, McClellan promptly and diligently mobilized, housed, fed and trained the 30,000 troops initially assigned to him. Exhibiting a trait that he would practice throughout the war, the General inspected his troops often, showing a sincere care for his men, and addressing them with spirited words that inspired them to do their best not only for the country but for him as well. His respect for some others was not as considerate. When an obscure former officer arrived from Illinois to seek a position, McClellan refused to see him; after two days of waiting, Sam Grant returned to Illinois and finally secured a position there.

The major action at the beginning of the war was just south of Washington, at Bull Run. The South scored a major victory, with many in the Union capital fearing an overrun of the city by the Rebels. President Lincoln and General-in-Chief Winfield Scott were sorely distressed with the military leadership displayed by the Union generals in this battle and began looking around for a new leader. McClellan would be the commander Lincoln would select. The young Brigadier General had probed into western

Virginia and scored victories that had insured the separation of that area from Mother Virginia. Even though McClellan had procrastinated in mounting his drives and had issued a proclamation which said, contrary to Lincoln's views, that slave holders who cooperated with the Union could keep their property, he, as the North's only military hero, was the only General the President could summon to defend the Capital.

As McClellan traveled by train to Washington, he was hailed at each stop along the way by large groups of citizens. Arriving in the Capital, the President and General Scott informed him that he would be commander of the Army of the Potomac and Washington's defense forces. McClellan set about his tasks tirelessly and in his usual methodical way. His first problem was to restore morale, and he did this by immediately conducting a series of detailed inspections, visiting every encampment in his command and conversing with his soldiers in his earnest fashion. Often he would address a group in an imploring tone, charging them to train hard for the trials at hand. His men affectionately referred to him as "Little Mac," and they often cheered him as he made his rounds.

The President and General Scott pushed McClellan from the beginning of his command to take on Gen. Lee's forces and relieve the pressure on the Capital, hopefully making inroads also toward the defeat of the Army of Northern Virginia. However, McClellan resisted their pressures, believing that his army with its inexperienced officers was ill-prepared for a major campaign. McClellan also resisted because his intelligence led him to believe that the enemy's forces were far greater than his. In this he was wrong, and Gen. Scott, who disbelieved McClellan's intelligence estimates, pressed the young General to take the initiative. McClellan's response was to ignore the General-in-Chief, questioning whether he was a "dotard or a traitor." It was unfortunate that McClellan resorted to bad estimates of enemy strength; it was even worse that, when questioned by superiors, he would withdraw from their counsel but yet assert that if an operation went bad, the fault would be the superiors and not his. His name calling was not limited to Gen. Scott: later, when he came at odds with the President, he would refer to his Commander in Chief as a "gorilla." On another occasion he went to bed rather than meet with the President, who had come to his headquarters late in the evening for a conference.

Gen. Scott, whose health was failing, continued to press Gen. McClellan for action. Soon, there were various factions around Washington advertising the differences of the two. The President finally decided to make a change in command, but he did not dispose of his young Brigadier. Instead, he replaced the General-in-Chief, Winfield Scott, a hero of both the War of

1812 and the Mexican War. In his place, he chose the thirty-five year old commander of the Army of the Potomac, George B. McClellan, to be the new General-in-Chief.

President Lincoln felt that McClellan should relinquish command of his Army of the Potomac and direct overall strategy, but the new commanding general assured him he could do both jobs. Lincoln was wanting a fighting general, and in this he was to be sorely displeased, for McClellan would continue to argue that his officers and troops needed more combat experience, that the enemy outnumbered him, and that all available troops — in many cases even troops committed to other action — should be put in reserve for his use. Even an objective questioning of his planning would bring a sharp retort that he could not be held responsible for what happened if he could not have what he wanted. This policy soon led to much discontent with various Cabinet members, particularly Secretary of War Stanton, and with the President himself. The General held all who opposed his views in disdain: on one occasion, when the President visited McClellan's headquarters and maps were being reviewed, McClellan nodded and grinned in assent all the way through the conversation, only to poke fun at the President's lack of understanding on military matters as soon as the Commander in Chief left.

McClellan assumed command of the entire Army in November of 1861. The Army of the Potomac engaged in only minor actions in northern Virginia during the winter. In other theatres, commanders such as Brig. Gen. U.S. Grant were scoring decisive victories with fewer troops and resources. Pressure in the Capital mounted for McClellan to do the same, but he continued to delay any movements. When no substantive action came about, the President in March 1862 removed McClellan from his position as General-in-Chief but left him in command of the Army of the Potomac, insisting that action be initiated against Lee. McClellan finally undertook the *Peninsular Campaign*, a move down Virginia's Chesapeake Bay coast line with a thrust hopefully aimed at Richmond, but he continued to act slowly and insisted upon all the reserves he could get against what he considered to be a greater force. He was also terrified that the *Merrimac* would come up one of the many rivers in this area and divide his forces. At Yorktown, McClellan encircled a huge Southern force and laid a siege. No attack was undertaken, though, and after thirty days, the Southern force escaped with little harassment by the North. Many in the North were upset and became even more so after a major confrontation occurred at Harrisonville, just a short distance from the Rebel Capital. McClellan's forces had scored well on the Army of Northern Virginia and gained an advantage. Most combatants, including Lee, felt that McClellan would press on the next day.

However, Lee had left his defeated troops in place, and McClellan, once again using faulty intelligence, felt that not only had the South won the battle but that they had a much larger force in place than was the case. The Union General thus retreated from a victorious battlefield. This was too much for Lincoln, who decided it might be best to transfer most of McClellan's troops to Gen. Pope's Army of Virginia, which was about to engage Lee at the Second Battle of Bull Run (Manassas). When the Union suffered another loss at Bull Run, with most officials believing that Gen. Pope was totally responsible. Lincoln decided to move McClellan's troops back to "Little Mac." Gen. Pope was ultimately assigned to Indian duty in the Northwest.

ANTIETAM

McClellan had the opportunity to retrieve his military reputation at Antietam Creek in Maryland when Gen. Lee began his first invasion of the North. Ever cautious, and fearing that he was outnumbered, McClellan delayed taking any initial action against any of the individual bodies of troops first encountered. When he was finally ready to move, Lee's entire army was opposite his own. A major engagement finally occurred at Harrison Creek Bridge, and McClellan defeated Lee's forces and checked the invasion to the North. Unfortunately for McClellan, however, he refused to follow up his victory with another attack the next day, claiming that his troops needed rest, and Lee used the time granted him to retreat to the South and reassemble his forces.

Lincoln, members of his Cabinet, Congressional leaders, newspaper editors and the general public were astonished and upset that McClellan had not taken advantage of his victory. The President, who had in the past uttered words to the effect that McClellan had the largest personal body-guard in the Union Army, concluded once and for all that McClellan must go. Secretary Stanton, who was assigned to take care of the details, relieved the General of his active command and ordered him to Trenton, New Jersey. George McClellan, who had become General-in-Chief at age thirty-five and had been heralded as the "Young Napolean," was without a command at age thirty-six. He would not return to military command again.

INTO POLITICS

McClellan was granted permission by the War Department to stay in New York while writing a report on his commands. There he was greeted as a conquering hero. Trips to other parts of the Northeast found him being treated likewise, especially in Boston, where a crowd of 10,000 hailed him. His personal life found him attending the theatre and opera. His political life found him making no public statements, but his associates were conservative Democrats who had designs on his future. Some talk arose from time to time that Lincoln might reinstate him to keep him from running for the Chief Executive's office in 1864, but "old Abe" preferred not to have the problems of dealing with McClellan, who would have jumped at the opportunity to return to command. McClellan privately wrote articles for *The Round Table* explaining the battles of the war.

Since before the Civil War, McClellan had expressed a preference for the Democratic Party. During the War, he issued proclamations and tried to formulate policies that closely resembled the politics of the Democrats rather than the Republicans who were in power. The young General was not interested in abolition but rather in preserving the Union, even if that meant slavery, and he had openly used this policy when taking his troops through Southern lands. It was no secret that McClellan had disdain for Lincoln's policies, and this apparently filtered down through the ranks to subordinate officers who often made comments to the effect that if McClellan were relieved of command and wanted to resist, or that if McClellan chose to try to effect a peace based on a reunion with slavery, these officers could be depended on to support their army commander over their civilian Commander in Chief. Toward the end of his command, McClellan, who knew the power of political pressure, called upon a conference of Governors for support, but he was rebuffed when they called for his ouster rather than giving him a vote of confidence.

RUNNING FOR PRESIDENT

Once out of his army command, leading Democrats at once began to tout him as a possible candidate for President in 1864, some two years away. It was reasoned that a man popular with his troops — as McClellan was — and that a "Copperhead" Democrat in favor of peace over abolition — as McClellan seemed to be — was the ideal candidate to take on Abraham Lincoln, whose Republican principles made abolition more important than either victory or the Union. Yet McClellan, perhaps fearing that he would lose his military pay if he did not stay non-partisan, avoided the political battlefield as long as possible. When he was solicited to run for Governor in Ohio, he refused. He also refused to preside at a political meeting in New York City called to defame the President. He finally made a political statement, though, when in 1863 he endorsed the Democratic nominee for Governor of Pennsylvania after party leaders there advised him that he must do so in order to gain support for the Presidential nomination in 1864. From then on, most observers felt that McClellan would be an active candidate for the nomination and the likely nominee.

As the Democrat's convention in Chicago approached, McClellan resisted normal campaign practices of making partisan speeches to elicit support. Instead, he relied on an address he delivered at West Point and a report he gave to the Congress on the conduct of his campaigns as his personal platform for the campaign. Except for Gov. Horatio Seymour of New York (who was to be the 1868 nominee), who indicated he would accept a draft, he had only token opposition, and his star seemed to be rising, while Lincoln's was fading, due to the deteriorating war record of the Union. When the convention convened, extreme peace elements of his party seized control of the convention and pushed through a plank proclaiming that under a Democratic administration the war would be unilaterally and immediately stopped, with talks held to reunify the country. After this action, the convention nominated McClellan, thought of nationally as a war candidate, on the first ballot by acclamation and then proceeded in the name of unity to name for Vice President Sen. George H. Pendleton of Ohio, an avowed peace candidate. The combination of a "peace at any price" plank, which called for no enforcement if the South chose not to rejoin the Union, a "war" Presidential candidate, and a "peace" Vice Presidential candidate would prove to be a painful burden for McClellan to carry throughout the campaign.

The nominee accepted his party's nod by rejecting the "peace at any price" plank, but now his party was torn asunder. To add to his political woes, the North's military record, with U.S. Grant as General-in-Chief, was faring much better. Sherman took Atlanta, Farragut took Mobile Bay and advances were being made in Virginia and elsewhere. Still, the Republicans and Lincoln were concerned, and a close election was predicted. State elections held in September and October generally went Republican, but McClellan's advisors still felt he would win because of the vote of the soldiers, who had always revered and cheered their General. But this proved to be a fatal assumption. The soldiers saw the peace plank of the Chicago convention as a surrender plank, and Republican campaigners were quick to point out that Democratic posters advertised that a peace man would be the Secretary of War in the "Copperhead" administration. When the votes were counted on election day, the vote was surprising. Abraham Lincoln, considered an easy victim of George McClellan just a few months earlier, had defeated his former General-in-Chief handily, carrying all but three states, receiving 55 percent of the popular votes to McClellan's 45 percent, and receiving 212 electoral votes to the General's mere 21. To add insult to injury, the man to whom McClellan had referred to as a "gorilla," and whom he felt had little knowledge of military tactics, received 78 percent of the soldier's vote.

TRAVELER, RAILROADER AND ADVISOR

McClellan had resigned his commission the day before the election, and, since he was only thirty-nine, needed to find a position to support his family. An overture was made for him to become President of the New Jersey Morris & Essex Railroad, but the line's directors thought better of this when it was learned that the government under the Republicans might not do business with them. McClellan decided to go to Europe, where the cost of living was less than in the states. For the next four years, he traveled around the continent, visiting military and political dignitaries, and doing little work except for unsuccessfully trying to sell a war ship of an American entrepreneur to European governments. His support during this period came from rental income from a home given to him by friends in appreciation of his war service and from income from the sale of stocks and investments also acquired through the efforts of friends in gratitude for his service. He also wrote articles for various periodicals from time to time.

As the election of 1868 approached, his name was once more mentioned as a possible nominee, but seasoned Democrats knew that he, as the man who did not take Richmond, would be easy prey to Grant, the man who did take the Southern Capital. He supported New York Gov. Horatio Seymour, who fared better in 1868 than McClellan had done in 1864. When the election of 1872 came about, McClellan refused to support Horace Greeley, the liberal editor of the New York *Herald Tribune*, who had criticized his performance during the war.

Refusing an offer to become President of the University of California, McClellan in 1870 accepted a position as Chief Engineer of Docks for New York City. In 1872 he became a trustee and then President of the Atlantic and Great Western Railroad at a beginning salary of $15,000. He considered but refused on the advice of close friends an offer to become Comptroller of New York City following the expose of Tweed Ring. In 1873, the former General formed Geo. B. McClellan Consulting Engineers & Accountants to represent European investors in American railroads. The successful businessman then took his family on another tour of Europe, this time for two years, and also visited Egypt to study the ancient ruins there (the study of Egyptology was of special interest to him).

He returned to the United States in 1876 in time to enthusiastically campaign for Samuel Tilden against Rutherford B. Hayes. When Tilden won the popular vote but began to lose the Electoral College through the machinations of corrupt Republicans, McClellan offered to organize former soldiers into Democratic political clubs which he would lead to Washington to install Tilden, but this offer was not accepted.

GOVERNOR OF NEW JERSEY

In 1877 McClellan unexpectedly received the Democratic nomination for Governor of New Jersey and won election to that position for a three year term of office. The Governor proved to be a fiscal conservative, reducing expenditures and state debt by 23 percent. The job apparently did not require much of his energies, for he was able to fulfill his duties with only one day of work per week. The Governorship of New Jersey was the only elective office McClellan ever won.

LAST DAYS

After his term of office ended in 1881, McClellan decided to take another trip to Europe, this time just for several months. He returned to find that while he was away a warehouse storing his goods had burned. Unfortunately, among these goods were his *Memoirs*. Disheartened, he at first said that he would not expend the effort to redo them, but he soon changed his mind and started to work on rewriting his autobiography.

McClellan strongly supported Grover Cleveland in 1884 and believed that the new President would tap him for Secretary of War. But factional party infighting in New Jersey forced Cleveland to select no Cabinet member from that state, dealing McClellan a bitter blow.

As time passed by, McClellan was feted time and again for his efforts in the Civil War. He was particularly pleased in 1885 to pay his first visit to the Antietam battlefield since the war ended for a celebration of his victory. He was also delighted to again visit with his father-in-law the Red River area of Texas that he had explored some thirty years before.

In early October of 1885 McClellan suffered an attack of angina pectoris. Following doctors' orders, he rested and seemed to be making a recovery when another severe attack struck him on October 28. The next morning he passed away at age fifty-eight.

Immediately an outpouring of sympathy was heard from around the nation. A simple funeral was conducted at Madison Square Presbyterian Church in New York City, with friends, including the 1880 Presidential candidate, Gen. Winfield Scott Hancock, acting as honorary pallbearers and accompanying the body to its burial in Trenton, New Jersey. The young General-in-Chief, who had led Union forces in some of the most horrible actions of the War Between the States and who as the youngest major Presidential candidate in the nation's history had sought to end the conflict between the North and the South, was now himself at peace.

Horatio Seymour
The Election of 1868

Democrats in New York from time to time bestow the Horatio Seymour Award to a party member who is loyal and unselfish. These traits were especially true of the intermittent politician who rarely sought an office but who campaigned so hard for others. Drafted against his wishes, he would have been, had he won, probably the one President in American history who could have said that he did not in any way ask for the job.

BORN INTO A NEW YORK POLITICAL FAMILY

Horatio Seymour entered life on May 31, 1810, at Pompey Hill, New York. He was the second of six children born to Henry Seymour, who had taken as his bride in 1807 Miss Mary Forman, the daughter of a Revolutionary War Colonel and New York farmer. Henry Seymour had a distinguished lineage; his Dutch forbearers had also served in the Revolution and in the New York legislature. Henry Seymour's brother, after whom Horatio was named, was a United States Senator from Connecticut for twelve years. Horatio's father was a successful businessman and banker who became involved in politics. He established close ties with Martin Van Buren and eventually became a Canal Commissioner for New York. As such, he led the second phase of the development of the Erie Canal. Unfortunately, the financial Panic of 1837, just after Van Buren had become President, caused some severe setbacks for Henry Seymour, and he became so depressed that he committed suicide.

By the time of this unfortunate event, Horatio Seymour was well along the path of his personal success. He attended school — along with a family slave — at Pompey Hill until he was ten years of age, and then, after his father became Canal Commissioner, he attended Oxford Academy in Utica, where the family had moved. At Oxford, the young Horatio particularly enjoyed history and geography, and he ultimately became a renowned authority on the geography and geology of New York. From 1822-24 Horatio attended Geneva Academy (now Hobart College), but no record of his academic achievement exists. Seymour then enrolled in a Connecticut military boarding school for two years, and his formal education was completed with this experience. In 1827, Horatio began a legal apprenticeship; five years later, he was admitted to the bar of New York at the age of twenty-two.

AID TO NEW YORK'S GOVERNOR

Because of his father's political connections, Horatio was chosen the following year to become the military secretary to William L. Marcy, the newly elected Governor of New York, and a man who would for years to come be influential at the state and national level. Marcy became Secretary of War in the administration of James K. Polk and Secretary of State under Franklin Pierce, and he was influential enough that he was in the running for the Democratic Presidential nomination in 1852. Horatio occupied his influential position under Marcy for six years, learning the intricacies of government and politics, and making friends with many of New York's future leaders. While in Albany, Horatio found another lifelong friend, Mary Bleeker, the daughter of a very rich Dutch land owner. The two were wed on Horatio's twenty-fifth birthday, and their marriage lasted for over fifty years. The couple never had any children.

LEGISLATOR AND MAYOR

In late 1838, as the national economy under President Van Buren collapsed, Gov. Marcy was defeated in his bid to win a fourth consecutive term as the state's Chief Executive. Horatio Seymour returned to Utica to attend to family business matters. He was placed in charge of the affairs of his late father's estate as well as some of the Bleeker properties in Utica. In 1841, Seymour ran for and was elected to the New York State Assembly, and in 1842, he was elected Mayor of Utica by a majority of 130 votes. During his tenure he tried to solve Utica's financial problems by raising taxes; this maneuver led to his defeat for re-election the following year by sixteen votes.

Seymour was a very active legislator. The Democratic Party was divided into two groups, the conservatives, or "Hunkers," made up of businessmen and bankers, and the "Radicals" or "Barnburners," who were composed primarily of small farmers. Political squabbles between the Hunkers and the Barnburners were often so vicious that the Democratic Party in New York split completely, causing state and national elections to be lost. Seymour was a Hunker conservative, but for the most part he was a composed and courteous legislator who tried to conciliate differences. These traits would fare well for him in later years.

Elected to a second term, Seymour was considered for but not nominated by his party to run for Speaker of the House. In a pivotal move for his future, he became Chairman of the Canal Committee. One of the most pressing problems for state government, in a time of economic crisis, was how to handle excess revenues from the canals. One group of the Democratic Party proposed that any revenues from the canals be used to retire the state debt. Seymour argued that the revenues should be used to complete the Erie Canal, maintaining that such a move would create economic growth that would generate the very tax revenue that his opponents were trying to take from the canal system. Skillfully forging an alliance with Whigs, Seymour guided the bill through the state House and the Senate, and it was enacted into law. Subsequent history proved that his foresight was correct; it also installed Seymour as the successor to DeWitt Clinton as the protector of the Erie Canal.

SPEAKER OF THE HOUSE

Seymour was elected to the state House again in the fall of 1844, the only Democrat to be returned. His party still maintained the majority, and he was elected Speaker of the House, due to his experience as well as his conciliatory nature. The House over which he presided, however, did not lend itself to conciliation. Disputes erupted over the elections of United States Senators, over the canal system and over the state constitution itself, which was in need of revision. The latter issue found certain legislators voting against constitutional amendments so that a state constitutional convention would be called. This strategy, which Speaker Seymour condemned, was successful, and New York held a convention. Seymour was thoroughly disenchanted with his tenure as Speaker. He chose not to run for re-election, and he did not hold elective office again for eight years.

POLITICAL INTERLUDE (1845-1853)

For the next few years after he left the legislature at Albany, Seymour tried to conciliate many of the differences among the divisions of his party. Martin Van Buren was still trying to regain the White House, and he exercised immeasurable invective against any who did not support his goal. The slavery issue was now also dividing the New York Democracy, and old economic issues were still creating painful splits. Horatio Seymour in 1848 held a meeting with John Van Buren, the former President's son, to heal party differences and help his party gain control of both Albany and Washington, D.C. This meeting resulted in the dissolution of the Hunkers and the Barnburners but new coalitions of "Softs," or conservatives, and "Hards," who were recalcitrant Barnburners, wanting no compromise on anything, were formed to replace the existing factions. Seymour's standing in the party was enhanced, however. In 1850 he was nominated to run for Governor of New York.

The election of 1850 had few issues. Both Seymour and his opponent, Washington Hunt, refused to attack each other personally. A faction of "anti-renters" provided an endorsement for Hunt that proved crucial, for on election day Hunt received 214,614 votes to Seymour's 214,352, a difference of only 262 voters. Since the Whigs had been in control of the Governorship for some time, and since Seymour had run far ahead of other members of his ticket in many parts of the state, prominent Democrats throughout the state felt that Seymour could be a formidable candidate in the future. Indeed the forty year old Seymour still had quite a career ahead of himself.

In 1852 Seymour attended the Democratic National Convention at Baltimore as Chairman of a New York delegation that was divided, as usual, because of the divisions of either Hunkers and Barnburners or Softs and Hards. Seymour was supporting his old friend, William L. Marcy, for the nomination, and Marcy's chances were good except for New York itself, where Sen. Daniel Dickinson, one of the few personal enemies of Seymour, was supporting Lewis Cass but hoping that the convention would deadlock and eventually swing to the Senator himself. The first ballot strength of Marcy was only 27 delegates, but his count steadily grew until on the forty-fifth ballot he had 97 of 188 needed votes need for nomination. At this point "dark-horse" Franklin Pierce's name gained momentum, and he was drafted as the Democratic nominee.

Following the national convention Democrats in New York assembled and once again nominated Seymour for Governor to oppose Washington Hunt, the Whig incumbent. As in 1850, Seymour and Hunt refused to attack each other, and there were few hot issues on which to campaign. The Whigs were disadvantaged by the Compromise of 1850 and the growing national dissension. Prohibition and temperance were becoming an issue in New York, but both Seymour and Hunt refused to take a stand on the issue. Fortunately for Seymour, the "anti-renters" did not oppose him, and on election day, the forty-three year old protege of William L. Marcy eked out a narrow majority to become New York's Governor in 1853.

GOVERNOR OF NEW YORK

One of the first people to greet Seymour upon his inauguration was his cousin, Thomas Hart Seymour, the Governor of Connecticut. This cordial greeting and the selection of his friend Marcy, as the new Secretary of State under President Pierce (other patronage requests were for the most part ignored by Pierce), were two of the few pleasures he enjoyed as Governor in the turbulent times leading up to the War Between the States. New York's finances were again in disarray, so much so that Seymour proposed a tax increase. He then had to call a special session of the Legislature to deal with the Erie Canal. The new Governor proposed a loan to be paid off over nine years to carry on the work of the Erie Canal, a measure which ultimately proved that Seymour possessed outstanding foresight with respect to the Canal. Ironically, Seymour, thought of as the Canal's best friend at this time, signed a bill that allowed the merger of a number of railroads into the New York Central system. This group would eventually be swallowed up by Cornelius Vanderbilt and supply much of the competition that caused the decline of the Erie Canal.

The Democratic Party continued its internal squabblings, and the Whigs gained a majority during his second year of office, with much controversy ensuing. When the Governor suggested that the Legislature look into Prohibition laws, the Whigs quickly acceded and passed such a measure. Seymour, however, then created a row when he decided to veto the measure as being unconstitutional. Ironically, angry opponents said that the Governor, a teetotaler, was an alcoholic. Another row was created when Seymour invited a delegate of the Pope together with other Protestant clergymen to a gathering at his home.

Seymour, thoroughly upset with the handling of party affairs in New York by President Pierce, did not want to seek re-election in 1855. Some of his friends, it is said, were so concerned that he would send a telegram to the state convention announcing his disavowal that they actually cut telegraph lines. The Softs endorsed Seymour and a platform calling for Temperance, Free Soil and Nativism, and he was renominated to remain the state's Chief Executive The campaign that followed was bitter, with the Whigs and Know-Nothings, along with Sen. Dickinson of the Hards, attacking Seymour for catering to the liquor interests. Governor Seymour campaigned willingly on the issues, but found personal attacks distasteful. He was once again defeated by a narrow margin, receiving 156,495 votes to the Whig candidate's 156,804, a difference of only 309 votes.

POLITICAL INTERLUDE (1856-1862)

The former New York Governor wanted to stay active in party affairs but genuinely intended to refrain from seeking future elective office, including the Presidency, the idea for which by this time had been implanted in his mind. He was passed over by President Pierce as Ambassador to England and declined an appointment as one of two Commissioners to resolve the disputes of "bloody" Kansas. For the next several years, he was involved in the development of a canal in Wisconsin, serving as President of the

Green Bay and Mississippi Canal Company. This venture was appealing to the Canal Builder Seymour, but it was a source of constant problems and ultimately was a disappointing investment.

Seymour attended the 1856 Democratic Convention at Cincinnati which nominated James Buchanan and then campaigned actively for his party's choice, making a speech at Springfield, Massachusetts which was one of the most significant policy statements of his entire career. Seymour, who felt that arguments over slavery were more of the reason for discord than slavery itself, began his remarks by proclaiming the old Jeffersonian premise that that government governs best which governs least, and averred that local jurisdictions should resolve problems first. He noted the differences of the North and the South but proclaimed that they were secondary to the Union. Summarizing the history of the slave problem, he stated that the South had made more concessions in the formation of new territories and states than the North. He felt that slavery would fail because it was a bad economic system and that Northerners should be patient in waiting for its end. He concluded by declaring that people of the North should examine their own hearts before passing judgement on the South. The policy expressed in Seymour's speech adequately reflected his party's position, and Buchanan claimed victory in November as a Northerner with a Southerner's heart, as had Franklin Pierce before him. When the Dredd Scott decision was rendered by the Supreme Court shortly after his inauguration, the new President stood by the South in its claim for enforcement of laws favorable to slavery.

WAR GOVERNOR

Seymour supported the unsuccessful candidacy of Stephen A. Douglas in 1860, even attempting to put together, with Whig Washington Hunt, a "fusion" ticket of Douglas and Union Party candidate John Bell of Tennessee. When Abraham Lincoln was declared the winner and secession loomed over the South, Seymour called the "Tweedle Hall" Convention in Albany in early 1861. At this conclave, attended by such personages as Horace Greeley, Seymour called for the North to use persuasion rather than military power to suppress the already seceding states, and to put to a public vote the question of what should be done about the Union and slavery. The Republicans, who were now in power, wanted no such vote, however, and Seymour's convention achieved no success in avoiding secession or war.

Shortly afterwards, Seymour became the Democratic candidate for United States Senator. The Republicans were in control of the Legislature, and the Democratic candidate lost this election. He decided to go to Wisconsin and check on his canal project, and while enroute, he received word that Fort Sumter had been fire upon. Seymour immediately made a speech calling for total support of the Lincoln government. Upon arriving at Green Bay, he helped raise a company of artillery for the Union cause. Returning to New York, he made numerous speeches in support of the Union, and raised money and men to fight the South. He himself never served in the Army — a fact that was used against him later — perhaps because he was not always in the best of health, having often to take to a sick bed for days at a time. He did offer his services at one point when there was fear that the British would join with the Confederacy and attack New York from Canada.

Overtures were extended by the Republicans to form a fusion ticket for the gubernatorial election of 1861, but Democrats scoffed at this idea. When their convention was held, they once again nominated their famous "Conciliator," Horatio Seymour, and adopted a platform calling for the constitution and slavery to be left in its present condition and for the Union to be preserved by any "legitimate" means. The Republicans nominated Gen. James Wadsworth to run against Seymour, but he could not campaign actively because he was leading troops at the front. Seymour received help in one of his campaign addresses from Samuel Tilden, who would be the 1876 Democratic nominee for President, who drafted a message to the South warning, first of all, that while Northern Democrats were sympathetic to the Southern cause, they could not be expected to turn their backs on the Union and that, secondly, the South itself must stop the conflict and return to the Union. Such statesmanlike declarations together with the ineptitude of the Union army to have any notable combat successes provided Seymour with the favorable feelings of New Yorkers. On election day he scored a close but spectacular victory for the Democrats, gathering 306,649 votes to Wadsworth's 295,897, a margin of 10,752.

The newly returned Governor had hoped that his election would signal to the South a message for a negotiated peace, but Abraham Lincoln favored total victory so that the evils of slavery could be eliminated. The President was promoting policies, such as the issuance of an Emancipation Proclamation and the suspension of Habeus Corpus, that were difficult for Seymour to embrace. New York Republicans, in charge of the Legislature, passed a law that was also hard for him to embrace, a bill allowing soldiers the right to an absentee ballot. Gov. Seymour, wary that Democrats might lose future elections, vetoed this measure, but it was subsequently adopted by a constitutional convention. Seymour at times had the distasteful distinction of being called a "Copperhead" and other unsavory names, all implying disloyalty for the practices he conducted.

The New York Governor continued to raise men and money for the Northern cause. When Lee attacked at Gettysburg, Seymour rushed all available troops at his disposal to Gen. Meade, a move critical to the North's success in that critical battle in July of 1863. Seymour spoke at the same ceremony where Lincoln became immortal for his "Gettysburg Address." Unfortunately, a week later the draft riots of New York City erupted in protest of the nation's first draft laws, which allowed for substitutes to be used for a payment of $300 (a young Buffalo Democrat named Grover Cleveland used this method to avoid the draft), and angry mobs took to the streets, building barricades in streets, disrupting traffic, raiding stores, burning a colored orphanage and beating blacks — whom they were blaming for the war — and creating so much dissension that scores of people were killed with hundreds more being injured. Gov. Seymour, who had himself always opposed the "Enactment Laws" as being unconstitutional and unwise, was in New Jersey at the time but returned to New York City to take charge of the situation. A crowd called for him to speak, and he did so, telling the group that he would appeal to Washington to postpone the draft. He stated that, irregardless of the outcome of the law, people and property must be protected; yet, if the law were enacted against his wishes, he would do everything in his power to see that the law was administered fairly, meaning that he opposed the use of money to buy substitutes. During this speech, which was impromptu, reference to "My Friends" was reported by a hostile press, and the impression was given that Seymour was sympathetic to the rioters. This was to cost him dearly in the years ahead.

Gov. Seymour, by now a nationally influential Democrat, opposed the selection of George McClellan as the party nominee in 1864. He was permanent chairman of the 1864 Chicago convention that nominated the General and adopted a platform which in effect called for surrender to end the war. Lincoln, aided by the victories of Grant, captured his party's nomination and became the first President since Jackson to win two terms. Against his will, Seymour was named by the New York convention to run for Governor again, and he reluctantly consented to do so. He was opposed by Republican Reuben Fenton, who was able to benefit from Seymour's "My Friends" speech to the New York City rioters as well as the recent Northern victories and an economic situation where Greenbacks rather than gold were being used to finance New York policies. Seymour once again went down to defeat, garnering 361,264 votes to Fenton's 368,557. As usual, a Seymour election had been determined by a small margin.

PRESIDENTIAL CANDIDATE

The former Governor once again desired to retire from holding public office. The end of the War Between the States found the Republican

Radicals in control of much of the nation's government machinery, and as a national leader, Seymour was compelled to speak on the issues of the day. He was not biding his time to seek office, however. As the 1868 election approached, he conferred with Samuel Tilden, the Chairman of the New York delegation, and indicated his preference for the Democratic nomination to be either Chief Justice Salmon P. Chase, who received overtures from both parties, or Indiana Senator Thomas Hendricks.

The convention was held in the new facilities of Tammany Hall in New York City, and Seymour was once again named permanent chairman of the assembly. The Democrats adopted a platform denouncing reconstruction and opposing passage of the Fourteenth and Fifteenth Amendments without the seating of Congressmen from all states, including those of the former Confederacy. The major candidates for the nomination were President Johnson, elected as a Union candidate with Lincoln in 1864 but actually a Democrat; Gen. Winfield Scott Hancock, whose chances were considered by Democrats as limited since another general, Ulysses S. Grant, was running; Indiana Sen. Thomas Hendricks; and Sen. George H. Pendleton of Ohio. When balloting began, Pendleton was in the lead and Johnson second; as more votes were taken, Hancock seized the lead; still others bolted into contention as more votes were taken. On the ninth ballot, North Carolina abruptly cast its votes for Seymour, who promptly announced that he was not a candidate and begged not to be considered. Seymour and Tilden had planned to wait for an opportune moment to submit Chase's name, and that opportunity appeared to have come after the twenty-first roll call, but Tilden hesitated to push Chase, perhaps biding his time to submit the name of Horatio Seymour. On the twenty-second ballot, Ohio suddenly cast its votes for the convention chairman, who protested once again that he did not seek the nod, but a stampede to him occurred, helped along in no small way by the New York City galleries which had reacted to the votes for Seymour with a feverish display of emotion and affection. One state after another agreed with a declaration from the floor that only Seymour could unite both North and South. Tradition has it that Seymour was in tears begging that he not be accorded the nomination, but the convention now would have no other choice, and he was declared the nominee by acclamation. Tragically for the Democrats, Francis Blair, a plain speaking, heavy drinker who said that the Democrat's main purpose in 1868 was to overthrow the Radical Republicans plan for reconstruction in the South, was nominated for Vice President.

The Republicans made the Democratic platform and Francis Blair major issues in the 1868 campaign. Innuendo was widespread, and remarks questioning the loyalty of Democrats were published throughout the land. Their candidate, Gen. Grant, was a genuine war hero who was more popular than any soldier since George Washington. Seymour's campaign was a commendable one, and although he lost, it was in part because the Radicals controlled the votes of the South, which had some questionable tallies and which favored Grant as a whole over Seymour. The General received 3,012,833 popular votes to Seymour's 2,703,249. In the Electoral College, the margin was wider with Grant obtaining 204 votes to the Democratic nominee's 80. Seymour carried his home state despite an onslaught of campaigning by the Republicans, including his brother-in-law, Sen. Roscoe Conkling, whose defeat for the Congress in 1862 had made him a fierce opponent of Seymour.

TITULAR LEADER AND ELDER STATESMAN

Seymour, now fifty-eight, returned to his Utica home, named "Marysland" after his wife, again seeking political retirement. However, he maintained close contacts with political leaders and intended to exert influence whenever possible. When the Erie Canal's operations were brought under question in 1870, he proposed lower tolls, a measure that was adopted and which aided the development of the waterway's commerce. He joined Samuel Tilden in fighting Tammany Hall, the New York City Democratic organization controlled by Boss Tweed and which was bereft with graft and corruption. At the 1870 state convention, Seymour refused to serve as its Chairman rather than be associated with the shameful organization. Tilden became Governor and exposed the graft of Tweed and Tammany; this event propelled him to the Democratic nomination for President in 1876. Seymour reluctantly supported Horace Greeley when the somewhat mad newspaperman captured the Democratic nomination in 1872, but he did not campaign for him actively.

In 1875 Seymour refused to run for U.S. Senator when he could have won election. The following year the state convention nominated him by acclamation to run for Governor, but he resisted all pressures and declined the honor. He did work for the election of Tilden as President in 1876 and was deeply angered and disturbed when his protege was robbed of victory, but he cautioned Democrats not to resort to violence. He was asked to run for Governor again in 1879, and in 1880 he was seriously considered again for the Presidential nomination. Old, tired, and often sick, Seymour dismissed all such overtures.

Seymour received appointment as "Path-master" for his home town of Utica in 1876, the only post he ever requested. The job required him to see after the town's roads, and while doing so during the summer of 1876, he suffered a sun stroke. This marked the beginning of the decline of his health.

He apparently also suffered from a liver disorder, and other infirmities of old age, such as losing his hearing, poor eyesight which required wearing glasses, and using a cane, all of which showed the effects of time on his body. A cold in early 1880 put him to bed for a considerable period of time with disabling effects, and then the vigorous campaigning he conducted for the election of Winfield Hancock for President later in 1880 so exhausted him that his health suffered another setback from which he never really recovered. He continued to nurture other Democrats, however, and one of them, Grover Cleveland, became Governor of New York and then President of the United States in 1885, the first Democrat to hold the position since James Buchanan in 1861.

Fittingly, his last public function was to attend a canal convention in 1885, which honored the heir to DeWitt Clinton and Henry Seymour by electing him its Chairman. In early 1886 his wife became ill, and the couple that had been wed for fifty years moved into the house of his sister, the wife of Republican Sen. Roscoe Conkling. Unfortunately, the stress of dealing with his wife's illness, coupled with his own illnesses, led to his own passing on February 12, 1886, at the age of seventy-six.

After his body lay in state at the Conkling home, services were conducted at Trinity Church in Utica, and his body was buried at Utica, to be joined less than a month later by his wife. No sooner had be been buried than some old antagonists tried to charge that he had been disloyal to the Union during the Civil War. Such rash charges were both false and unfitting, particularly so for the man who had tried so hard all of his life to conciliate differences and to promote peace throughout his native New York state and the entire Union.

Horace Greeley

The Election of 1872

Surely no man who ever ran for the American Presidency was as eccentric as Horace Greeley. He became famous for saying "Go West, Young Man, Go West!" but he himself as a young man went east to become famous. All his political life he supported the conservative Whigs and Republicans only to accept the nomination of the Liberal Democrats to run for President. Unpredictable, tempestuous and sometimes bordering on the insane, Greeley is nonetheless still remembered both as a great newspaperman and as a fighter for the causes of the oppressed and downtrodden.

GETTING ESTABLISHED

Greeley was born February 3, 1811 on a family farm near Amherst, New Hampshire. His father's family was of English descent and had been in America for some two hundred years. His mother, of a Scotch-Irish background, was of much greater influence on him than his father, who was only mediocre in his pursuits as a farmer, and who was said to drink a bit too much. The family had to move west to try and better its situation, moving once to Vermont (to escape the local sheriff) and then on to Pennsylvania. The family's existence was, in fact, a very poor and miserable one.

So sickly in his youth that he had the nickname "The Ghost," Greeley began school at age three, was winning spelling bees at four, and reading the Bible fluently at five. At age nine a group of men offered to pay his way to Exeter Academy, but his mother was too attached to him to let him go. Then at age fifteen, when his father was ready to move west to Pennsylvania, Greeley on his own applied for and received an apprenticeship as a printer with the *Northern Spectator* in East Poultey, Vermont. It was his first, but not his last, venture in journalism.

Greeley's tenure with the *Northern Spectator* did not last the intended time. Shortly before he was expected to complete his apprenticeship at age twenty, the paper bankrupted. Greeley, too poor to afford even meager clothing, returned to his parents' home in Pennsylvania in a donated overcoat. But he did not go back to Pennsylvania with a poor spirit, for Greeley had mastered many elementary skills of his trade, some fundamental political philosophy (he had supported John Quincy Adams and opposed Jackson), and had developed a strenuous hatred of alcohol and tobacco, going so far as to help organize a local temperance society in East Poultey. He had also left East Poultey with the friendship of a young man working there for another newspaper. This man was George Jones, who was later to be the co-founder and Publisher of Greeley's main competition, the New York *Times.*

Now twenty and on the family farm in Pennsylvania, the discontented Greeley pondered his future. He tried to secure a permanent job in Erie County, Pennsylvania, but was unsuccessful. He worked for the Erie *Gazette* but was laid off. From his salary of $15 per month with the *Gazette,* however, he had saved $25. He gave half to his father and then headed for New York City with only the remaining $12.50 in his pocket.

GETTING INTO THE NEWSPAPER BUSINESS

He arrived in New York after a harsh journey that had included walking, boating, ferrying and hitch-hiking. Getting board for $2.50 a week, he sought employment, finding a position for $6 a week setting type for a firm printing pocket-size New Testaments. When this work played out, Greeley worked at a number of odd jobs before going to work for a weekly entitled the *Spirit of the Times.* This publication failed after Greeley had been there a only few months. Greeley began to have a future when he formed a printing partnership with Francis V. Story, who had been a foreman at the *Spirit of the Times.* The enterprise of Greeley and Story was organized for general printing. Shortly thereafter, Greeley and Story met H.D. Shepherd, who joined the two to form the *Morning Post.* The idea of this daily was to publish a one penny paper that would appeal to the poor, especially to immigrants. Shepherd introduced a novel idea to American journalism: newsboys would be employed to "hawk" the sales of the papers. Unfortunately, the paper did not succeed. Greeley then came into contact with Benjamin Day, who added to the ideas of the *Morning Post* the additional idea of sensationalism in reporting. The resulting publication, the *Sun,* left no stone unturned to report every scandal, every murder, every miracle and every ghost story. Editorials were without mercy for the reputable. While Greeley was repulsed by these tactics, he at least for the first time was with a successful business; the *Sun* was an instant success.

Greeley, with $1,500 in savings, had in the meantime decided to start his own weekly, the *New Yorker.* This publication was intended not only to publish articles of quality but to refrain from some of the more odious practices of the journalism of the day, without any "humbug," it said in its first issue on March 22, 1834. Greeley, who was enthralled by the hustle and bustle of New York — its gaiety, its theatres, its constant commercial expansion, its literary talent, and, in general, its entire culture — did not entirely appreciate the New York newspaper practices, though he himself would quickly learn and soon apply the craftier editorial practices of the day. Greeley had a new partner in the _New Yorker_, a printer named Jonas Winchester, who was brought into partnership after Story had drowned while swimming in the East River.

New York's newspaper talent of Greeley's time included many of the future barons of the industry. Because of the size of the population of the city, papers faced with stiff competition would stop at no trick or scheme to control the market. More often than not this led to bitter rivalries, with editors often meeting in the street to cane each other if their pens had offended a competitor. Even with names such as William Cullen Bryant, William L. Stone, Park Benjamin, William Leggett, and Col. James Watson Webb dominating the newspaper scene, the New York publishing business was not reputable with the public, which was seeking a publication that chiefly had literary appeal, rather than vindictiveness for the world in general and other papers in particular, as its primary goals.

Greeley was beginning to prosper and now entertained the thoughts of marriage. He had met at his vegetarian boarding house Mary Cheney, a schoolteacher who loved poetry, and who adhered to many of the same codes as did Greeley. When she took a teaching position in North Carolina, Greeley could not stand to be without her and went there to propose marriage. Their marriage was not a happy one. Their first two children died in infancy and two miscarriages followed. A son, "Pickie," was then born, and he was the apple of Horace Greeley's eye, but unfortunately he died at an early age. A daughter and another son followed, but the marriage became neither stable nor affectionate. Mrs. Greeley suffered from a variety of physical and nervous disorders. She and Horace sought refuge in many ways, among them the use of a spiritualist who would conduct "rap" sessions for communication with their lost "Pickie." Greeley at first did all he personally could to take care of his ailing wife, but as he became completely involved in the newspaper business and accompanying lecture circuit, he hired help to stay with Mrs. Greeley, staying in bachelor's quarters near his office while in town, and coming home only on weekends, if time then permitted. The marriage more and more seemed to be a union of convenience, and there is reason to believe that Greeley was later involved in an extra-marital affair.

WHIGGISM AND SOCIALISM

Perhaps seeing his own success as a product of the American experience, Greeley was drawn to the philosophy of Henry Clay, whose "American System," complete with its system of canals and roads, it seemed to Greeley, could only lead to wealth for the entire country. Very soon Greeley was writing editorials that were decidedly Whig, and his political roots were starting to grow. Greeley at this time was not the "Crusader" for which he was to be later known but rather a conservative editor, not involving himself in the social issue of slavery but rather choosing such items as Irish Tammany rioters in 1834 and hunger rioters who invaded flour warehouses in 1836 as areas of concentration for his newspaper. Greeley looked with pleasure upon the success of land speculators and bankers, whom he thought were leading the nation to financial wealth. While some editors, such as William Cullen Bryant, warned of impending danger, Greeley continued to endorse the policies in effect, even though they were Jacksonian Democratic rather than Whig, because the whole country, including himself, was prospering.

His views were to change suddenly and drastically. Shortly after Van Buren assumed the Presidency in 1837, a depression swept the land. Greeley himself, who had labored hard to achieve financial security, was threatened with ruin. But this was not all that troubled him. In his ramblings about New York City, he could see the distress of the unemployed, the hungry and the sick. It sickened him to see the plight of so many while the government took no action to alleviate their misfortunes. It was during this period that he wrote the famous "Go West!" clarion, desperately hoping that many of the unemployed of New York City could find a better way of life elsewhere. It was also during this period of time that Horace Greeley slowly but surely developed the fundamental tenets of a new political philosophy that would one future day serve as the cornerstone of his political platform for the Presidency: Socialism!

Greeley did not yet fully realize the leanings he had taken. He was to become be a major leader in the affairs of the Whig Party, first, and then the Republican Party, secondly, before publicly pronouncing his socialist views. He was induced to serve the Whigs by a fellow newspaperman named Thurlow Weed. Greeley had known and respected Weed for a number of years, though not necessarily agreeing with his personal habits. Yet Greeley realized that Weed possessed the ability to attain and use political power, and Weed proposed to have Greeley in on the move to capture the state of New York and then the entire county for the Whigs.

Weed offered Greeley the position of editor for a new state Whig publication. Greeley accepted, naming the new weekly the _Jeffersonian_ so that it could hopefully have greater popular appeal. That this was a Whig venture was to be kept as secret as possible, and the first few issues did not even mention the word Whig, but soon news was out that it was a Whig work, especially when Greeley's virulent anti-Democratic essays and editorials were read. But subscriptions rose and the paper flourished. This was indeed fortunate for Greeley, whose _New Yorker_ was suffering vast losses, and who badly needed the extra revenue he was being paid by the Whigs.

It was during this period of time that Greeley became closely associated with an upcoming young politician being sponsored by Weed, William L. Seward. Seward was running for Governor, and he, Weed and Greeley formed an alliance of political thought and action that was to be formidable for some time to come. With Weed's political organization and Greeley's zealous penmanship Seward became the first non-Democrat to win the Albany statehouse in over forty years. Horace Greeley's ability to sway voters through the newspapers was recognized as one of the best in the land.

After this election in 1838, Greeley, just twenty-seven years old, returned full time to the _New Yorker._ Though he had employed Parks Benjamin, a New Englander formerly with the _Atlantic Monthly_, as literary editor so that he himself could devote more time to political essays and editorials, the _New Yorker_ continued to flounder. He thus had to take fill-in jobs with a host of eastern papers just to make personal ends meet. This was humiliating to the man who had made Seward Governor, and a state job would have been appreciated, but it was not offered. It was a great relief, therefore, to find that Weed wanted him to be editor for a national publication of the Whigs for the Presidential campaign of 1840.

Greeley had long been a disciple of Henry Clay, whose American System and banking principles held special appeal to him. Weed, to Greeley's chagrin, felt differently about the "Gallant Harry of the West.". Weed felt that Clay's personality was too strong for the Whigs, that Clay would want to control the party and that his strong and forcible leadership would spell defeat for the Whigs. Weed commissioned Greeley to relate this message, but Greeley demurred at the last moment. One reason was that Weed was supporting General Winfield Scott, and the pacifist Greeley did not feel a military man was right for the country. Nonetheless, Greeley did finally join in supporting an anti-Clay candidate, William Henry Harrison, even though he was a military man.

In the campaign of 1840, the organ set up by the national Whigs to popularize Harrison was called, appropriately enough, the *Log Cabin*. Greeley displayed a masterly knack for getting out the vote. Time and time again he used the popular slogans of the day to entice voters to support "Tippacanoe and Tyler too!" or "Harrison, two dollars a day, and roast beef." The rhetoric increased as the campaign progressed, with Greeley reporting every mass rally, every torchlight parade, every Democratic setback. As circulation reached eighty-thousand, Greeley's exuberance was uncontrollable, and he proclaimed a host of declarations: "The Harrison Tornado is sweeping over Indiana and Kentucky;" "Rhode Island is True;" "Georgia Falls into Line;" "New Jersey Avenged;" etc...

Of course Harrison prevailed. Greeley was ecstatic and hoped for the cabinet position of Postmaster General as just reward for his invaluable talents, but he was overlooked. Needing to establish himself more securely, he set about looking for a new venture. The new venture he founded was ... The New York *Tribune*.

Using borrowed money, Greeley formed a publication, he said, that would be "a New Morning Journal of Politics, Literature and General Intelligence," that would "advance the interests of the people, and promote their Moral, Political and Social well-being," and not engage in the degrading advertising of other periodicals. Of course the paper would be a Whig publication editorially. Greeley had a simple idea for selling papers: he would dispatch messengers to the most distant places to get the news back to the *Tribune* first, and he would sell this first news cheapest, at $4.00 annually. The paper struggled at first but gradually built up its circulation and financial stability. By employing correspondents in far away places such as San Francisco and London, Greeley was able to give his readers exciting news, and his circulation rose to 50,000 by 1850. He was always especially excited to discover that he had beat a rival paper with the first coverage of some newsworthy event. He remained editorially in favor of the Whigs, especially his hero Clay, but more and more socialist tendencies could be detected on issues such as land reform and redistribution of wealth.

Greeley's paper had many notable correspondents. One close associate was Schyler Colfax, editor of the *St. Joseph Valley Register* in South Bend, Indiana, and later the somewhat corrupt first term Vice President of U.S. Grant. Other newspaper and literary giants would be associated over the years, men such as Henry Raymond, who would desert to become editor of the *Times*; Whitelaw Reid, who succeeded him as editor of the *Tribune*; Charles A. Dana, who was befriended during utopian days and would work for Greeley before becoming Assistant Secretary of War under Lincoln and then editor of the New York *Sun;* and John Hay, Lincoln's private secretary, to name a few. Another associate, recruited by Charles Dana, was a contributing editor named Karl Marx! Such associates led to the *Tribune* becoming not only New York City's leading daily but America's most widely read weekly. Newspaperman Bayard Taylor, speaking of the *Tribune's* influence with the American people, said that it "...comes next to the Bible."

The financial panic of 1837 had already seriously altered Greeley's views of the role of government. About 1840 Greeley read a book by Albert Brisbane entitled *The Social Destiny of Man*. This work electrified Greeley and instantaneously transformed him into an activist for the causes of socialism. His subsequent activities brought him into intimate contact with some of America's most prolific social thinkers of the day: the likes of Ralph Waldo Emerson, Henry David Thoreau, William Loyd Garrison, James Russell Lowell and Nathaniel Hawthorne. He would also be associated with the social "utopias" of the day: Brook Farm, Rugby and Lowell. Equally important, he would mold and have burning inside him many social issues: agrarian reform; the firm establishment of labor unions (he, not Ronald Reagan, would become the first union president to become a major party candidate for President when he became President of the New York Printers' Union); the elimination of poverty and the vices which bred it; and more so than ever, the redistribution of wealth. He freely loaned or gave of his own funds to utopian experiments and experimenters. As time passed, he began to see that the means being used to bring about a new social order were not succeeding. Though it was somewhat surprising to his newfound friends that he had endorsed a Whig (his old hero Clay) for President in 1844, he had not forgotten his new cause when he resumed full time activities with the *Tribune*.

CONGRESSMAN

Back in the mainstream, Greeley was soon working with Weed and Seward on Whig political schemes. But his Whig leanings were beginning to wane for a number of reasons. First, there was the matter of his new socialist feelings. Then, there was a rebuff by Weed for Greeley, who wanted to run for Senator, to hold any high public office. Then wanting to be Governor, but being coy about announcing this desire to Weed, he was instead offered the opportunity to run for Lieutenant Governor, but he declined this. To mollify Greeley, Weed arranged his election to Congress for a period of ninety days to fill the unexpired term of a corrupt Democrat. Once installed, Greeley was a great embarrassment. He immediately began to speak loudly for reform on various social issues or any cause that he felt needed reform. Land reform was chief among his causes, but he could gather no support for any of his measures. One item he questioned extensively was the travel expenses of Congressmen, citing especially an Illinois Representative named Lincoln, but he was ignored on this also. The louder and louder he railed the more and more he was avoided by members of the House.

In the Presidential Election of 1848 he did not want Zachary Taylor as the Whig nominee, but after the Whig convention he did support the Mexican War hero. He thought he might be appointed Postmaster General or an Ambassador by the new President, but he was conveniently overlooked.

BECOMING REPUBLICAN

The issue that finally made Greeley break with the Whigs was slavery. He had personally witnessed the "Great Debate" of Clay, Webster and Calhoun and thought the delicate issue could be resolved. But when, after the deaths of the "Great Triumvirate," Stephen Douglas rose to the forefront of power and the Kansas-Nebraska bill was enacted into law, Greeley realized that a complete new party was needed. Probably adding to this realization was the establishment in New York City, with the blessings of Whigs Weed and Seward, a new daily, the New York *Times*. The competition from and the loss of advertising to the *Times*, created in no small part by the Whig state administration, greatly irritated Greeley, who also saw some of his key people desert, at the secret bidding of the *Times* owners, to the new daily. Greeley's editorial comments against the *Times* were at times vehement, and he moved further away from the Whigs. Now that Clay was dead, he had no spiritual connection with that political party.

Horace Greeley had much to do with the success of the Republican Party in general and Abraham Lincoln in particular. After his decision to break with the Whigs had been made, he became an apostle for the Republican cause. His writings and lectures were at first a call to a new order. He supported the unsuccessful campaign of John C. Fremont in 1856, though he realized the Pathfinder was lackluster and ineffective. However, Republicans made gains in Congress, and together with other minorities in the House, a chance for power was at hand. Therefore, Greeley himself decided to go to Washington and lead a fight for Republican strength. Greeley lobbied hard and effectively to see that a Republican was elected Speaker of the House in 1855. He used his *Tribune* to make scathing attacks on either Democrats or Republicans who balked at his attempts for power. One attack went a bit too far; an Arkansas Democrat who resented Greeley's editorials floored him with a punch to the face. The *Tribune's* circulation continued to increase as Republican popularity increased, however.

During this period Greeley's wife decided to take a vacation in Europe, and Greeley joined her in London. While in Paris, he was arrested in connection with a debt owed a French investor in the Crystal Palace in New York City, in which he had also invested. Ever the newspaperman sensing good copy, Greeley daily reported his mistreatment by the French to his American readers, and he was soon released, while his circulation soared. With his heart in the politics of the United States, he let his wife continue her European travels while he returned home to continue his crusade for the Republican Party.

HELPING MAKE LINCOLN PRESIDENT

Greeley had his paper cover the Lincoln-Douglas Senate debates in Illinois and, after hearing Lincoln's famous "Coopers Union" speech in New York, realized that Lincoln should be the Republican candidate for President in 1860. To assist Lincoln, Greeley engineered one of the most successful schemes in the annals of American politics. First, to the anger of many Republicans but in order to divide the Democrats, he promoted Stephen Douglas favorably in his *Tribune*. Second, knowing that in 1860 the Republicans would need ideas and a candidate not from the east nor too established on the slavery issue to keep the Republicans from being outright rejected, he had the *Tribune* promote an obscure former Whig, Edward Bates, rather than his former Whig partners — Weed and Seward, with whom he had a score to settle — so that no one would go into the Chicago Republican convention with the momentum to win. Then Greeley, who was unable to be seated as a New York delegate to the convention, gained a seat from Oregon so that he could conduct instrumental maneuvers both on and off the convention floor for Lincoln's success. Greeley maintained that Seward, who was leading on each ballot, was not electable. The wily publisher then struck a major deal: the powerful Simon Cameron of Pennsylvania would be a Cabinet Member in exchange for shifting his support to Lincoln. This carried Lincoln, and Greeley was exuberant, having repaid some "debts" to Seward. He then traveled widely for Lincoln while his paper with its large circulation did everything possible to support Lincoln's successful cause.

Never dreaming that Lincoln would resort to picking Seward for Secretary of State, he had misgivings about Lincoln's Cabinet as a whole, but for the most part he kept his feelings to himself. Seward got some measure of revenge when he successfully led the opposition to Greeley's attempt to become Senator from New York. Greeley wanted Lincoln, whom he intercepted on the way to Washington for his inauguration, to intercede for him, but the beholden President-Elect refused, probably remembering Greeley's tenure as a Congressman and being afraid of what he could stir up in the Senate.

Known to be a pacifist, Greeley now led a chorus calling for force to confront the Southern states that started seceding after Lincoln was elected. "NO COMPROMISE!" and "NO CONCESSIONS TO TRAITORS!" were rather typical headlines of the *Tribune*. When action seemed imminent, he called for the North to meet Lincoln's request for 75,000 volunteers and be in Richmond by July 20, never dreaming that a gory struggle would ensue for four long years. The first battle of Bull Run left him in a panic, and he tottered on his total support from time to time. Not until Grant was appointed General-in-Chief with the North winning major battles did he become convinced of the necessity of Lincoln's re-election. His full support came after Sherman burned Atlanta and after the politically astute Lincoln wrote some glowing words about him, which were conveniently put in his hands, through the maneuverings of Lincoln, by an ally of the President.

Lincoln and Greeley kept a continuous correspondence over the years. Neither man exactly liked the other, but each was accommodating. After the Emancipation Proclamation was issued, the Tribune had as its lead headline "GOD BLESS ABRAHAM LINCOLN." Later, Greeley's support of. Lincoln almost cost him his life when the draft riots erupted in New York City. His office was attacked, and he stayed out of sight until he secured two escorts to accompany his through an angry mob.

Greeley was one of the first to grasp the significance of Grant's gestures to the South at Appomatox, with the *Tribune* proclaiming "MAGNANIM-ITY IN TRIUMPH." He had high hopes for a successful reunion; the news of Lincoln's assassination was doubly saddening when both Lincoln and the dream of peaceful reconciliation were lost.

AGAINST THE RADICAL REPUBLICANS AND JOHNSON, TOO

During the War Between the States, Greeley had often clashed with the Lincoln administration on the conduct of the war. He had been warm to the election of Gen. McClellan until the victories of Grant and Sherman and until Lincoln had extended personal overtures. After the war, Greeley, the former war hawk, was perceived by northern Radical Republicans to be pursuing his typical eccentric policies. During the war Greeley had pushed for a meeting between Northern and Southern leaders to negotiate peace; after the war, he wanted a reconstruction program much like Lincoln's, especially desiring that the bitter disunion stop. To this end he went so far as to post bail for Jefferson Davis after he was captured by Union forces! Greeley had a hard time adjusting to the ill-bred, uneducated, brash Andrew Johnson. For some time he held his criticism, but when Johnson continually opposed legislation for black suffrage, the new President received Greeley's editorial wrath. Off on a western lecture circuit when Johnson was impeached, he did not object to the *Tribune's* endorsement of the proceedings. When U.S. Grant ran for President in 1868, he received only lukewarm support from Greeley. The newspaper magnate was pleased, though, when his old comrade, House Speaker Schyler Colfax, became Vice President.

BOLTING THE PARTY

Greeley was incensed when he discovered the depths of "Grantism": of Indian trading post irregularities; of the "Credit Mobilier" and the Union Pacific; of military connections and family nepotism. Greeley came to feel that corruption was rampant in both political parties and for a while felt that he had no political forum to support. He openly criticized men of both parties (including the young leader of the New York Democratic Party, Samuel Tilden, who was considered impeccable) for political misdeeds.

As the election of 1872 neared, a growing number of liberal Republicans felt that something had to be done to turn around the debacle of Grant. Among those who sought change were Charles Francis Adams, Senator Carl Schurz, Lyman Trumbull (the future mentor of William Jennings Bryan), and Senator Charles Sumner. They asked the already indignant Greeley to consider jumping ship with them to form a third party, and he consented.

A national convention of Liberal Republicans meeting in Cincinnati decided to nominate Greeley to run against Grant. Not immodest about the opportunity to run, Greeley won the nod over the likes of Charles Adams because of his better organization and political skill. For Vice President the Liberals nominated Governor Benjamin Gartz-Brown of Missouri. The Democrats, at this point almost a broken party, decided to cast their lot with the Liberal Republicans, making Greeley a two party candidate rather than a minority candidate.

Greeley was finished before he started. Not only was he opposing a truly popular military hero who, despite his shortcomings, would be beloved by most Northerners until his death, but he was drawing opposition from his closest allies: from other Liberal Republican leaders who sensed he was out of tune with their thoughts and the American people; from many Democrats, especially Southern conservatives, who thought of him as a "nigger lover;" and especially from his associates in the press, who wagered a vicious campaign against him. Especially damaging was *Harper's Weekly*, which ran a series of cartoons entitled "What I Know About Stooping to Conquer," "What I Know About Honesty" (showing Greeley shaking hands with Boss Tweed), "What I Know About Bailing Out" (bringing up old thoughts about posting bond for Jefferson Davis), "What I Know About Eating My Own Words," "What I Know About Bolting," and "What I Know About Running for the Presidency." Knowing that he was in trouble, Greeley began a tour of the country in his own behalf. His wife had returned from Europe to be with him, but she was in very poor health. As she began to fade, Greeley returned to New York and quit his traveling campaign. She died on October 30, just before the election. Then the results of the people poured in, and they were overwhelmingly for Grant, who won by about three-quarters of a million popular votes and by 286 to 63 in the electoral college.

OBITUARY

To the already downtrodden Greeley another blow was to follow. A conspiracy was organized by old friends at the *Tribune* to buy control of the paper and name former Vice President Schyler Colfax as its Editor and return it to the Republican fold. Over the years, Greeley had sold various shares of his stock and given vast sums of money to various people who favored his socialist experiments, and now he was only a minority stockholder. Greeley was utterly destroyed, both mentally and physically, by this undertaking. He sold all of his assets quickly and wrote letters to various borrowers over the years. One letter to Cornelius Vanderbilt asked him to take care of his children as repayment for loans made when Vanderbilt's father had disowned him. He made a will, declaring himself bankrupt. One of his final papers said that he had "...done more harm and wrong than any other man who ever saw the light of day. And, yet, I take God to witness that I have never intended to wrong or harm anyone..."

Sinking fast, he was taken to a private mental sanitarium at Pleasantville. The *Tribune* spoke of nervous prostration; others spoke of brain fever; still others said old Horace had just been plain crazy for years. He passed away on November 29, 1872, the only major candidate for President to die before the electoral votes were counted.

His funeral was quite a scene. One eulogy in the Unitarian service was delivered by Henry Ward Beecher. Of course his old friends and adversaries of the press were there: Charles A. Dana, now of the *Sun;* William Cullen Bryant; George Jones of the *Times;* and even a representative of *Harper's*

Weekly, which had so viciously attacked him just a short time before. The Mayor of New York attended, as did the Governors of New York, New Jersey and Connecticut; also present was the Chief Justice of the Supreme Court, Salmon P. Chase. Another conspicuous dignitary was the President-Elect of the United States, Ulysses S. Grant, who led mourners as city bells chimed and citizens of New York City lined sidewalks to pay their final respects to the "Man in the White Hat" who had always dressed so raggedly; to the eccentric vegetarian who had been Utopian and Socialist; to the reformer who fought corruption and slavery and who had been both War Hawk and Peacemaker. But mostly they paid respects to the newspaperman Horace Greeley, the *Tribune's* founder and the nation's most widely read editor and publisher for more than thirty years.

Samuel Tilden

The Election of 1876

The protege of Martin Van Buren, and probably the most outstanding Democrat from Jackson to Cleveland, Samuel Tilden was the one man in American history who rightfully deserved but was deprived of the Presidency of the United States. He was a skillful political writer and organizer and a successful and wealthy attorney, but he allowed the big prizes of his life to escape him. Thus, his legacy is now largely forgotten, though in his time he was one of the most powerful influences in the Democratic Party and the American political scene.

HUDSON VALLEY HERITAGE

Samuel Jones Tilden was born on February 9, 1814 in New Lebanon, New York, the son of Elam and Polly Jones Tilden. Tilden's ancestors came from England and settled in Connecticut; several of them, including his maternal grandfather after whom he was named, fought for the cause of freedom in the American Revolution.

Elam Tilden was a farmer turned storekeeper who was a respected member of his small community located in the Hudson Valley of New York. Mr. Tilden had been a strong admirer and supporter of Thomas Jefferson in the early 1800's and was later even a stronger proponent of a rising Democratic power, Martin Van Buren, who was both a neighbor and a friend. As a storekeeper, he was actively engaged in political discussion, on which he weaned his young son. Father and son were also very close personally. Later, when Sam would go away to college, he would be so homesick for his dad that he would come home after only one term and then wait several terms before finding another school to enter. The two maintained a close, lifelong correspondence on personal and political matters.

Sam Tilden was a sickly child who seemed to suffer one ailment after another, encountering so many illnesses that he could not enjoy the normal outdoors of childhood so common in that era. About the only outdoor activity he could enjoy was horseback riding. His young life was mainly spent indoors taking a variety of homemade remedies prepared by his father, who along with his storekeeping assumed the role of druggist. As a result of so many illnesses and medicines, Sam became a lifelong hypochondriac.

The young boy had much time for his chief pleasure, reading. He perused various books, but invariably turned to political works such as Adam Smith's *Wealth of Nations*. He received the rudiments of a basic education at home, but perhaps the educational influence at this age that was to shape him most came from his childless Aunt Polly, a staunch Jeffersonian Democrat, who provided Sam with a set of Thomas Jefferson's papers and letters as well as her strong feelings for Democratic politics.

EDUCATION AND EARLY POLITICS

At age sixteen Sam began what can at best be described as an itinerant education. Over the next seven years, from 1830 to 1837, he alternated between various institutions of learning, illnesses and political activities. His parents, desiring the best for him, sent him to a college preparatory academy in Williamstown, Massachusetts, but he withdrew after a term of three months and returned home for the next two years. In 1832 he went to New York City to live with relatives and study under tutors, but he seemed to be more interested in politics and the affairs of the bustling city than his education. He thought he wanted to study elocution seriously and enrolled in a special course but soon withdrew from this regimen and returned home again. During this leave, Sam began his active political career, campaigning for the re-election of Andrew Jackson and especially for the election of Martin Van Buren, by now also his personal friend, as Old Hickory's Vice President. He and his older brother organized a "committee of correspondence" in support of the ticket, his brother being Chairman and Sam becoming Secretary. Using this position, Sam prepared an essay to be given by him as a speech against the National Bank. The paper, masterfully written and completely logical from the Democratic viewpoint, was shown to Van Buren, who heartily endorsed it and had it published under the signatures of prominent Democrats. At age eighteen, Samuel Tilden was influencing the national politics of the United States of America.

Shortly after the Democrats won the 1832 election, Sam returned to New York to again receive college preparatory tutoring. His correspondence home revealed that he was more interested in political matters, such as the nullification issue in South Carolina, than his education. He returned home in the spring of 1833 and attended Kinderhook Academy that fall for two months but seemed to do more political writing than studying. In June of 1834, he enrolled in Yale. He compiled a 70 percent average in the classical subjects of the day, but he became ill again and, after losing ten pounds in three months, returned home. The return was just in time to participate in the fall gubernatorial election, in which he wrote pamphlets that aided in the election of the Democratic candidate. In January of 1835 he entered New

York University, where he engaged off and on in special studies for the next two years. He paid no more attention to his studies, however, than in the past, preferring politics to a degree. He especially could not contain himself during the Presidential election of 1836, when his good friend, Martin Van Buren, was the Democratic candidate. The twenty-two year old Tilden's contribution was significant: he formulated a plan, which Van Buren followed exactly, that had his candidate opposing Abolitionists to gain Southern support, opposing the National Bank to get popular support, and side-stepping Masonic issues to negate the influence of the Anti-Masonic party in the critical home state of New York.

Sam attended New York University for two more terms, and in July, 1837, he completed his work there. It is uncertain as to whether he received a degree, but after seven years of dubious effort, he was fundamentally well educated. While he was perhaps only somewhat ready to begin the endeavor of law, he was especially well qualified to begin the practice of politics.

LAW CAREER AND POLITICS

Tilden began his career in law by clerking for John W. Edmunds, a prominent Democrat and friend of Martin Van Buren. Edmunds, who later was appointed to the State Supreme Court through Tilden's influence, allowed Tilden ample time to participate in party affairs while developing as an attorney. Tilden also enrolled in the first law class of New York University, completing his requirements for a degree there, although it is again uncertain as to whether or not he actually received a diploma. While a law student, he continued to contract illnesses, which he tried to cure by bleeding, ice packs, poultices, morphine and mustard plasters. He also continued his involvement in politics, writing defenses of Van Buren after the Panic of 1837 and campaigning for Van Buren's unsuccessful re-election bid in 1840, this time making a speech on "Prices, Currency, and Wages" that was converted to a pamphlet in support of his political hero.

In May of 1841 Tilden was admitted to the bar in New York and promptly opened his own office. For the next several years he engaged in his legal practice, using his position to also be involved intimately in politics. In 1843, he successfully sought the office of Corporate Counsel of New York City, a position that paid him $2,500 annually. When the Whigs won the New York's Mayor's office the following year, he resigned rather than be discharged. His practice was interrupted often by the demands of politics. He became a member of Tammany Hall, and he organized a newspaper, the *Daily New York Morning News*, which helped the Democrats in 1844, but this publication soon became insolvent (Tilden left the enterprise before suffering any financial losses personally). Also in 1844, he was a leader to have Van Buren nominated again, writing pamphlets in the former President's behalf and attending the Baltimore convention in his support. A loyal Democrat, he supported James K. Polk, the "dark horse" who was drafted when Van Buren could not muster the necessary two-thirds to be nominated. After Polk's victory, it was Tilden who met with the new President about New York patronage matters. Polk, fearful that New York's new Governor, Silas Wright, wanted to be President in 1849, manipulated matters to hold down Wright's national influence. Tilden met with the President several times and particularly protested Polk's appointment for the Collector of the Port of New York. The young thirty-one year old New Yorker was gaining first hand experience at the highest level of government.

A schism of New York Democrats that was to have profound results soon occurred. The party split into two factions, the "Hards" and the "Softs." The Softs, to which Tilden belonged, were led by Governor Wright and would eventually include the Van Buren faction of the Party. The Softs were led by Secretary of War William Marcy, who owed allegiance to President Polk, and included Speaker of the State House and future Presidential candidate Horatio Seymour. The Marcy connection to the Southern Chief Executive eventually resulted in sides being taken over the slavery question. In 1848, both the Hards and the Softs presented slates of delegates to the national convention in Baltimore. The convention wanted to seat both slates and have harmony, but the Softs considered this an affront and left the Democratic Party to form the Free-Soil Party with Van Buren as its candidate. Tilden campaigned hard for his friend, but Van Buren ran a poor third to Zachary Taylor and Lewis Cass of Michigan. Taylor, who had New Yorker Millard Fillmore on his ticket, carried the Empire State and with it the election.

STATE LAWMAKER

The schism made Governor Wright realize that he needed friends in the state legislature, which had seriously embarrassed him by selecting two Hards to the U.S. Senate over two friendly Softs. Tilden was put forth as a candidate for the State House in 1845 and won election. Once seated, the new lawmaker proved to be a very effective leader and adept at political compromise. Tilden chaired a committee to resolve an "anti-rent war," a protest of tenant farmers against landed interests that had existed since before the Revolution. Tilden's solution provided for the landowners to retain ownership but for tenants to be given relief, a compromise acceptable to all. Tilden became know as a reformer, primarily because he sponsored a bill to end the practice of the state printer being employed by the party in power.

Yet he was involved in the patronage matters of the day, and he also made the acquaintance of many corporate leaders, particularly railroad executives, who would benefit him greatly later.

Tilden did not wish re-election to the state house, choosing to become involved in a more important matter, a new Constitution for New York. A reform movement underway for sometime created a convention in 1846, and many of the giants of New York government for years to come were delegates. Tilden was active in the work of the convention, and its work was overwhelmingly adopted by the people of New York. Tilden, now age thirty-two, was recognized as one of most able young leaders of the Democratic Party in New York and the nation. But for the next decade he was to be involved in the political arena in an advisory rather than an elective capacity.

Tilden's political service was in such areas as determining New York patronage when Franklin Pierce came to the White House in 1853. A Northern Democrat with Southern sympathies, the new President had little time for New Yorkers. Tilden, the conciliator, was selected to call on the President about appointments and to give advice on the new Cabinet. Again, in 1857 with the election of James Buchanan, it was Tilden who was called upon to discuss patronage matters with the new Chief Executive. It was becoming rather commonplace for Tilden to go to Washington and meet with Democratic Presidents.

CORPORATE LAWYER

By not serving in office, Tilden was able to develop his law practice. In the period of time from 1845 to 1860, Samuel Tilden became known as the greatest corporation lawyer in the country. This was a time when railroads were developing rapidly, and when one got into financial trouble, Tilden was called to reorganize the company or give financial advice. One reorganization, that of the Chicago & Northwestern Railroad, left Tilden with both a fortune and a reputation as *the* lawyer to consult when corporate difficulties arose. When other railroads and coal companies failed, they also came to him for rescue.

Private individuals also consulted him. His old friend, Martin Van Buren, used Tilden as his investment counselor. He represented a friend in a vote fraud case and won, dramatically showing in court to an astonished judge and jury how missing vote tallies had been altered. In another celebrated case, he proved that a woman claiming to be the wife of a murdered dentist was fraudulently seeking his estate. Tilden, the itinerant student who did not seem to have everything together during his college years, was now at the top of his profession.

With his financial success assured, Tilden was free to pursue social and recreation callings — and a wife. While he had many flirtations, he apparently was never seriously in love with anything but his law practice and politics and never married. He stayed active in Tammany Hall, and he joined various clubs, but these too were secondary except as they related to his true loves.

In 1855 Tilden was induced to run on for Attorney General of New York on a reform ticket. He did not really care to run since he had such a successful law practice, but he finally agreed and campaigned as hard as possible. This ticket went down to defeat by a landslide. As the War Between the States approached, he seemed not to be as strongly against slavery as in favor of the Democratic Party healing its wounds and re-gaining the Governor's seat. The Hards and the Softs were still holding separate conventions and losing elections. Despite his efforts for a reconciliation, a reunification was not to come until some time later.

WAR BETWEEN THE STATES

Since the enactment of the Kansas-Nebraska Act, Tilden had felt that a civil revolution was inevitable. His attitude had been somewhat like that of Lincoln — he favored union over all else. Thus, he had made many statements, and was to make others after the War, that sounded as if he had sympathy for slavery, when in fact he was trying to have the Democratic Party unified. For this reason he had in 1852 supported Pierce, who was definitely sympathetic to the South, and in 1857 the inept Buchanan, not because either was his preference but rather because he was trying to achieve party harmony. As war became more and more imminent, Tilden was among a group of Northerners who called for meetings with Southerners to avoid conflict. Even as South Carolina seceded, Tilden was corresponding with Van Buren about ways to effect a compromise — even if it meant the maintenance of slavery — to avert war.

But when war broke out, Tilden assumed an exemplary, even statesman-like role. He had already pledged to "sustain President Lincoln ...[as] I would do to sustain Andrew Jackson, if he were President." "We cannot afford to have two wars at once," said Tilden after the war broke out, refusing to criticize Lincoln or his administration on personal terms, though he often offered constructive criticism on policy matters. He felt the number of volunteers Lincoln called for was totally inadequate, for example, and also felt the way the war was being financed would later create financial panic. Tilden lent his name to a number of causes supporting the war effort and personally contributed and raised thousands of dollars for various regiments and other military organizations. More noticeably, he agreed to serve on a committee whose purpose was to unite Republicans and Democrats in a Union Party dedicated to preserving the republic.

A turning point in Tilden's political career occurred in 1862 when an old Democratic adversary, Horatio Seymour, received the Democratic nomination for Governor. Seymour had been Speaker of the State House when the schism of Hards and Softs had occurred, and Tilden's opposition to him had not been forgotten. But this same schism had been the cause of many losses for the Democrats, and Tilden, anxious to have harmony for the sake of a Democratic Governor, threw his whole-hearted support behind Seymour, speaking publicly for the nominee and, perhaps more importantly, writing a position paper for the Democrats explaining that the Party wanted restoration of the Union and could never tolerate dissolving the federal government. The campaign proved to be close, but Seymour prevailed, an important victory for Democrats in this period of the nation's history. Following the election Tilden, who had served as a "Sachem" of Tammany Hall, was selected Chairman of the Democratic Party of New York and put in a position to profoundly affect the future of both New York and the nation as a whole.

During 1863, the people of New York City began to react to the draft imposed during the Lincoln administration. Governor Seymour addressed a large New York rally against conscription, and a week later riots erupted. Fortunately, they subsided without spreading to other areas. Tilden had been a sponsor of the rally at which Seymour spoke, but he probably did not support the riots. Afterwards, though, a federal Marshal claimed he had held a warrant, issued by Lincoln's administration, for Tilden's arrest had matters worsened, but the warrant was never served.

Tilden took what today would be classified a racist attitude with respect to the black population. He was for the Union first — but he was willing for slavery to be maintained to have union. At one point, he advised that the Negro question not be "agitated." Even before war began, he had urged a Constitutional Convention to have amendments passed that would accommodate the South. The election of 1864 found Tilden vigorously supporting Gen. George McClellan against Lincoln. This ticket, doomed by the selection of a military man for President together with a pacifist for Vice President, was based on a platform of peace, the only condition being reunification, and the implication being that slavery could be maintained.

McClellan lost the Presidency, and Seymour lost his position as Governor. In 1867 and 1868, Tilden served as a delegate to another state Constitutional Convention and was very disappointed when a proposal for Negro suffrage was packaged so that it could not be voted on separately and thus defeated. After the War, he complained that the election of Republican black Senators and Representatives from Southern states was leading to imbalance and "...Negro supremacy..."

The death of Lincoln and the subsequent trials of Andrew Johnson found Tilden, as Chairman of the state party, making unusual moves.   He corresponded often with the President, praising the Southern Democrat for his stand for "constitutional democracy" and extending overtures for him to be the *Democratic* nominee in 1868. But in the end Tilden played a coy game of politics with the entire '68 nominating process, hoping to gather the nomination either for himself or Salmon Chase, the former Lincoln Cabinet member from New York. Several prominent Democrats had indicated to Tilden, the astute politician and successful lawyer and businessman, that he could lead the country. As state Chairman, Tilden controlled his large delegation and had votes shifted to and from leading candidates, thinking that either he or Chase could be summoned as a compromise candidate at the appropriate time. After several days of balloting, an Ohio delegate suddenly proposed Seymour as the candidate, and the nomination spread like wildfire among the delegates. Tilden had unwittingly allowed himself to be out-maneuvered.

CAMPAIGN MANAGER AGAINST U.S. GRANT

Seymour appointed Tilden his campaign manager, and an admirable campaign was waged against war hero Gen. Ulysses Grant. Grant polled 53 percent of the vote to Seymour's 47 percent, but had the Negro vote not been in effect or if the Southern white vote had been allowed, the popular war hero would probably have lost the vote of the people, though he still probably would have won the Electoral College. Tilden's political and management skills were apparent to all Democrats, and he had certainly endeared himself to Seymour and other leading Democrats for the future.

REFORMER

The event that turned Tilden into a compelling candidate for high office was the exposure of the "Boss Tweed Ring" in New York. Tweed began his rise to power in 1857 by becoming a member of a bipartisan board of supervisors under a state legislative act designed, of all things, to reform local government. The unscrupulous Boss soon had enlisted not only

Democrats but also willing Republicans to create the most corrupt city and state political machine in the history of the country. His plan was brutally simple: have the city of New York award contracts to friendly contractors who would add certain sums to their prices which would then be "kicked back" to Tweed's ring; use part of the kickbacks to buy favors from influential judges, elected and appointed officials, and law enforcement personnel; and use other kickback funds to buy votes on election day to stay in power. Soon Tweed, a Grand Sachem of Tammany Hall, had complete control of city hall and much of the state government at Albany. Initially having contractors add ten percent to their bills, he had them adding, before he was exposed, 35 to 55 percent to their invoices. As a result government costs soared. The County Courthouse, which was by law supposed to cost only $250,000, had a final cost to the taxpayers of over $14,000,000. The city had over $5,000,000 in printing bills alone and spent enormous sums on the rental of public halls for government events. When an audit of city finances was ordered, the investigation was rigged so that $4,000,000 could taken by the corrupt group. Taxes during this period increased from $10,000,000 to $30,000,000, and the public debt tripled.

Tweed simultaneously bribed judges, mayors, governors, legislators and even railroads. Democrats and Republicans were enlisted, along with attorneys, to protect his legal interests so that he could maintain his scheme. He became so powerful that he openly scorned criticism, asking a detractor when exposure of the ring occurred, "What are you going to do about it?"

Never very close to Democratic Tammany Sachem Tweed, although he had cooperated in political campaigns with him, Tilden became involved in the exposure after the New York _Times_ had investigated the ring and begun printing articles and publishing some very funny — but nasty — cartoons of Tweed. Tweed offered the _Times_ $5,000,000 to call off the investigation, but this highly respected paper wanted no part of corrupt money. Tweed then tried to have the _Times_ building confiscated on a trumped-up delinquent tax charge, but this also failed. As state party chairman, Tilden wanted to move slowly and cautiously so that his beloved party would not be damaged by the powerful Tammany Hall Sachem's corrupt ring, but as the corruption became more apparent, Tilden called meetings and conventions where he gave speeches against the corrupt alliance and exerted his influence to have reforms made. He became a member of a Committee of Seventy, whose purpose was to thwart corrupt influences in government, and then he ran for and was elected to the State House once again as a reformer. Tweed tried to crush him, but Tilden gained more influence and power. Finally, Tilden became actively involved in an investigation that clearly showed the corruption of the Tweed ring, and he leaked the information to the press. This information brought the public up in arms, and soon most members of the Tweed ring were voted out of office, though Tweed himself retained his State Senate seat. Soon, however, Tweed and his entire ring were indicted. Samuel Tilden was a star witness in the trial, which saw one corrupt official after another turn on each other to keep from going to jail. Tweed himself was indicted on 120 counts and fled the country to avoid jail. But upon the request of Tilden while running for President in 1876, Tweed was extradited and ultimately found guilty. Imprisoned, he said shortly before he died, "I guess Tilden and Fairchild have killed me at last. I hope they will be satisfied now." It is estimated that the Tweed ring bilked the City of New York of as much as $200,000,000. For his part in exposing this, Samuel Tilden was to become Governor of New York and, after more reforms from that platform, a candidate for President of the United States.

GOVERNOR OF NEW YORK

Tilden had little trouble garnering the Democratic nomination for Governor at the convention held in Syracuse in 1874. Some elements, including Whitlaw Reid of the *Tribune*, indicated that Tilden had become reform minded a bit too late, but the large majority of Democrats wanted Tilden. The Republicans renominated the incumbent Governor, George Dix, an old friend of Tilden's. The Democratic nominee took charge of his own political organization, enlisting party workers to get out the good word on Tilden, writing pamphlets and having them distributed by the same workers, and, making few speeches upon the advice of former Gov. Seymour. The results were decisive: Tilden had a plurality of over 50,000; the New York Congressional delegation to Washington was Democratic; and the State House was also Democratic, although the State Senate was Republican. With a victory such as this there was soon talk that Tilden would be swept to the White House in 1876.

Hardly had Tilden settled into office than he began a movement to reform the laws that had fostered the Tweed ring in New York City. The Governor had long wanted repeal of a law engendering the system, and what he now proposed and pushed through the Legislature was a series of laws making it unlawful for officials to pay false claims or receive stolen items. More importantly, the Governor was given the power to suspend from office indicted officials until they stood trial.

No sooner had Tilden completed his task with local governments than he took on another group of corrupt officials, the so-called "Canal Ring". This was a group of Democrats and Republicans, some also members of the

Legislature, who were involved with the Erie Canal and getting kickbacks from contractors, lawyers and employees. This ring had been awarding contracts through a guise of competitive bidding by allowing friendly contractors to bid low on base bids and then receive exorbitant "extras." Over $11,000,000 was believed to have been stolen from 1870-75 through this medium. Some members of the Canal ring had supported him in the general election, but Tilden had no mercy on them. Indeed, by exposing to the general public not only that the stealing was taking place but how it was taking place, the new Governor became a sensational hero to the public-at-large. He was able to thwart the efforts of certain legislators who wanted to block his reforms, taking to the road to make a number of speeches on the situation to the people of the state. A series of measures were enacted to have independent state inspectors verify quantities and quality of work on state canals. Corrupt officials were removed from office and went to jail with crooked contractors.

Tilden easily recaptured his party's nomination, but during the general election claims were made that he had personal "conflicts of interest." In particular, it was claimed that this railroad attorney had signed legislation favorable to the New York Elevated Railway Company even though he knew that legislators, including Republicans, had had their votes bought. This was hard for the reform Governor to explain, especially since he had said he considered the act unconstitutional. Yet the reform Governor was able to withstand the claims that he was corrupt and easily won re-election to another two-year term. His victory led to the nationwide feeling that he would easily win the Democratic nomination for President of the United States in 1876.

One area of service that Tilden provided magnificently was tax reform. He had argued during his 1873 campaign that he could lower taxes, and he did. This shrewd corporate attorney and investment advisor was able to cut state taxes in half, substantiating his belief in sinking funds to cover deficits and in hard currency to satisfy everyday needs of the people.

PRESIDENTIAL CANDIDATE IN 1876

The New York State Democratic Committee started the bandwagon for Tilden by proposing him in June, 1876, for the nation's highest office. There was some state opposition with certain delegates going to the St. Louis convention in favor of Sen. Thomas Hendricks of Indiana. But when Tilden's name was presented to the convention, a great celebration erupted, and while the New York Governor did not get the necessary two-thirds necessary for nomination on the first ballot, he easily captured a second ballot victory. Pandemonium erupted on the convention floor, the delegates believing the popular reformer would easily win. Senator Hendricks was chosen as Tilden's running mate. The Republicans passed over James G. Blaine, who was perceived to have several problems with his integrity and probably would have had a difficult time against the reform minded Tilden, and nominated instead Rutherford B. Hayes, a Civil War General and the current Governor of Ohio, for President, with William A. Wheeler of Maine for Vice President.

The Election of 1876 is now remembered as the one election in American history where a candidate was robbed of the Presidency. The chief issues of this especially dirty campaign were reform and reunification. The Republicans assailed Tilden for cheating on income taxes, for not serving in the army during the War Between the States and for favoring unification with the South. Tilden, managing his own campaign, made few speeches, building an organization to manage the vote and striking back through pamphlets. The Democrats were especially well financed and spent money liberally and somewhat questionably to insure that certain officials in critical states would insure a safe vote. Tilden, the national figure, expected victory from a base of strength from his native state, the South and Western areas also favoring reform.

The initial results on election day were favorable to Tilden. He had won a majority of the popular vote, and in the all important electoral vote, he appeared also to have a decisive majority. The New York Governor went to bed on election night thinking he would be the next President of the United States. But as he slept, radical Republican forces began a devious campaign to deprive him of his office. Led by Whitelaw Reid of the New York *Times*, these people saw that by challenging the votes in certain precincts of various states and having these precincts not counted, Hayes could keep the Presidency in Republican hands. Immediately, Republican papers put out a cry of foul in South Carolina, Louisiana and Florida, and President Grant dispatched federal troops under General William Tecumseh Sherman to supposedly maintain order and insure fairness. The honest intentions of Grant were soon turned to the Republican's advantage, however. Republicans in those states and Oregon sent electoral certificates in favor of Hayes to challenge those sent in favor of Tilden. Tilden clearly had 184 electoral votes of 185 necessary for victory and Hayes 165. The remaining votes were claimed by both sides...a constitutional crisis was at hand!

As Democrats nationwide saw Tilden being robbed, many were ready to bear arms and seize the Presidency for their hero. To his credit, Tilden, remembering the civil strife of just fifteen years before, used his influence to avoid this. Many other Democrats thought, as did many Republicans, that the Presidency was for sale, and apparently thousands of dollars were spent on potential Democratic and Republican electors and other officials with the influence to gain a vote(s) in the Electoral College. Tilden felt that there were only three courses to pursue: fight, surrender or negotiate. The latter posture ultimately led to the creation of the now famous Electoral Commission, composed of five Representatives, five Senators, and five Supreme Court Justices. The House, being Democratic, and the Senate, being Republican, were expected to offset each other. The Justices were expected to select two Democratic and two Republican Justices, who in turn would select an Independent Justice who was on the bench. Unfortunately for Tilden, the Independent resigned and was replaced by a Republican, and his chances for a negotiated Presidency were lost forever. On every vote taken affecting electors, eight Republicans voted in favor of Hayes and seven for Tilden. Most historians feel that Tilden was cheated of the Presidency. He himself felt so, but refrained, as did Richard Nixon eighty years later when there were indications of possible vote fraud in Illinois and Texas, from instigating a constitutional crisis. President Grant, known for personal integrity himself although his administration is remembered otherwise, was unsure as to whether Hayes was the legitimate President. In any event, Tilden bowed to the dictates of the Electoral Commission, whose mission he had feared from its beginning, and was relegated to a minor role in American history books. The South, whose cause Tilden had championed, became the big winner in the Election of 1876 by insisting on a pledge that self-government be restored in exchange for Hayes' election. President Hayes, himself an upright man, had no problem fulfilling this pledge.

SAGE OF GRAYSTONE

The strain of the 1876 election aftermath left Tilden in a state of broken health. He apparently suffered a stroke during the proceedings and thereafter suffered from palsy, dragging one leg as he walked. An abscess over his left eye also made that eyelid droop, and his physical appearance became haggard. Ever a hypochondriac, Tilden was to resort to various home remedies over the years, even resorting to electric shock, before finally consulting licensed physicians on a regular basis. Still mentally sharp, he continued to write on the various political subjects of the day and exert influence over the New York and national Democratic Party, but before long his declining health forbade him from speaking.

After the election of 1876, a Congressional committee had subpoenaed him to testify over charges that Tilden had used "Cipher" telegrams to communicate with his lieutenants in the Southern states where electors were being sought for money. While defending himself and proving that he was beyond reproach, his Republican adversaries continued to charge that the reformist Governor had various character flaws. New charges arose that Tilden had not paid his fair share of income taxes during the War Between the States, and an investigation and lawsuit found Tilden vigorously defending himself against this action, which was the first of its type in the history of the nation. He finally made an expensive out of court settlement in this matter.

He thought seriously of running for President in 1880, but when he could not actively participate in the defense of a lawsuit, he realized that he must decline the Democratic nomination that was his for the asking. He was thereafter the senior statesman of the Party, but his participation was limited. He did not become intimate with Gov. Grover Cleveland, who did not consult him very much either on policy or patronage, but he was pleased nonetheless to see the reform minded New York Democratic Governor go to the White House in 1885.

Active to the end of his days, Tilden nonetheless was slowed by his ailments. In 1879 he had bought an estate in Yonkers which he called Graystone (he himself became known immediately as the "Sage of Graystone") at a total cost with improvements of nearly $400,000. He became a country squire, entertaining guests with exquisite foods and fine wines. He especially enjoyed raising and selling horses. From time to time, rumors started that Tilden was getting married, but he remained a bachelor to the end of his days. He traveled abroad, visiting ancestral sights and meeting many European leaders of the day. He continued to accumulate a vast fortune, being known for his exacting business acumen and for making generous contributions to many worthwhile causes.

Sensing that his days were numbered, Tilden labored to complete certain tasks, such as publishing his memoirs. But the march of time and a lifelong rigorous agenda were taking their toll. He became known as "Whispering Sammy" because he often lost his voice from bronchitis, and his haggard appearance was maintained due to his prolonged bad health. Tilden passed away at his beloved Graystone on August 4, 1886.

Word quickly spread throughout the nation of the beloved Democratic leader's death. No area was more remorseful than New York; flags flew at half-mast in New York City and tributes were given at the state capitol in Albany. The remains of Tilden, the simple Democrat who rose to the heights of his party, were memorialized at the New York City Presbyterian Church that he did not often attend in life. He was then returned to New Lebanon for final services and burial in the area where he was first stirred by Martin Van Buren and where his father had weaned him on Democratic politics.

BROKEN WILL

Ironically, Tilden was to lose one final battle, this time after his death. The great corporate lawyer who amassed a fortune of over $5,000,000 had had other attorneys prepare a will in which he not only left substantial sums to family members and close friends but also to various charitable institutions, most notably the Yonker's Library. But two nephews, both in financial trouble, challenged the will, and prevailed on a legal technicality. Yet, even after the nephews prevailed, there were enough funds from a "Tilden" trust to be combined with the Astor and Lenox libraries and form the New York Public Library, a fitting tribute to an itinerant student who yet had a love of books and the ability to write great political pamphlets and communicate well with the people of New York and the nation.

Winfield Scott Hancock

The Election of 1880

The Democratic Party has nominated several career generals[1] for President, but only the first, Andrew Jackson — more politician than general — was successful in getting elected. Winfield Scott Hancock, nominated over a hundred years ago, is today remembered more for his military feats than his political success. While the nation was fortunate to have the gallant Hancock as a soldier, it did not choose to accept him as President, refusing to understand how a Civil War general could be a Democrat.

VALLEY FORGE INFLUENCE

Winfield Scott Hancock was born February 14, 1824, while the nation still had vivid memories of its second war with Great Britain. His ancestry was of Revolutionary War stock and had been settled in Montgomery County, Pennsylvania for several generations. Hancock's birthplace was but a few miles from Valley Forge, and his father, Benjamin Franklin Hancock, who had given up the Quaker faith to become a deacon in the Baptist Church, was constantly reminding his sons of their heritage.

Hancock was a twin (his brother became a prominent Minnesota attorney) and was named for Winfield Scott, famous at the time for having been wounded in a battle against the British during the War of 1812, and later famous as a Mexican War hero and as the unsuccessful 1852 Whig Presidential candidate. Perhaps quickly identifying himself with Scott, young Hancock early decided to go to West Point and pursue a military career.

Hancock's father was both a schoolteacher and an attorney. Though never pursuing office for himself, he was prominent in the Democratic Party, and when Winfield, after receiving a basic education in Pennsylvania, turned sixteen, Benjamin Franklin Hancock persuaded Congressman John Fourney, a friend, to nominate Winfield for an appointment to West Point. The young Hancock was accepted in the Corps of Cadets and quickly adapted to the rigors of cadet training, graduating from the academy in 1844.

MILITARY CAREER

Commissioned a Second Lieutenant, Hancock was immediately dispatched to the Texas frontier where war with Mexico was imminent. When hostilities erupted, the young officer was in the middle of action, serving under General Winfield Scott and participating in the battle of Vera Cruz and in the capture of Mexico City. He undoubtedly had contact with other rising officers such as Robert E. Lee, Jefferson Davis and Ulysses Grant.

Having distinguished himself in Mexico, Hancock was then assigned to a series of frontier assignments, as was the requirement for a young military officer of the time. While stationed in St. Louis, he met and married, in 1850, Almira Russell, the daughter of a prominent St. Louis physician. The Hancocks in time became parents of a boy and a girl, but unfortunately the daughter died in her early years.

Hancock rose to the rank of Captain in the early 1850's, and after service in Florida he was sent to California in 1856 as chief quartermaster. He remained in California until 1861, when the War Between the States beckoned him to combat once again.

CIVIL WAR GENERAL

While promotions in the frontier army were slow, the War Between the States found young officers rapidly advancing. Hancock was promptly breveted to Brigadier General (Volunteers) and transferred from Los Angeles to Washington, where he served under another future Presidential candidate, Gen. George McClellan. Hancock was soon moved from quartermaster duties to the command of combat troops and saw some of the bloodiest action of the war. His service found him active in Virginia during the Peninsular Campaign, in the battles of Fredricksburg and Chancellorsville, and in many other skirmishes. He was a dashing officer who would ride back and forth in front of his troops and exhort them to victory, and in doing, his horse was shot from under him several times.

Hancock's major effort to the Northern cause was his valiant leadership and determination to hold the Southern forces at Gettysburg. Robert E. Lee had hoped by attacking Pennsylvania that he could in one swoop take Philadelphia, move to Baltimore and cut off Washington from the North, then move to take New York City, and thus force the North into a negotiated settlement with the Confederacy. As the two armies were maneuvering in Pennsylvania, Hancock urged the Yankee commander, Gen. Meade, to make his stand at the small village of Gettysburg. When hostilities commenced on July 1, 1863, the Northern corps commander at the center of battle — Cemetery Ridge — was killed, and Hancock was dispatched to replace him. The 6'-2" dashing Hancock arrived just in time to restore order in the Yankee lines and repulse the initial first-day Confederate assaults. On the days that followed, Hancock rallied his troops time and time again to defend the central defensive position, and he as well personally led his forces in the relief of other beleaguered Yankee lines. When Lee on July 3 began his all-out offense to take Cemetery Ridge, Hancock was at the top, riding back and forth among his troops and encouraging them to hold steady, as 125 heavy Southern cannon continually blasted the Northern fortifications, trying both to batter and demoralize the entrenched Yankees. It was at Hancock's position that "Longstreet's Charge" was directed, and the resulting scene, one of the most ghastly battle scenes in the history of warfare, left the stench of death at Gettysburg for weeks. That action went on all day long, and Gen. Hancock was himself shot, suffering a groin wound which at first appeared to be fatal. But faced even with such a wound, he stayed at the scene of battle until victory for the North was assured.

General U.S. Grant later said that Hancock was the ablest Northern General not to command an army. That Hancock, now a war hero who was regarded by both North and South as one of the decisive factors of Gettysburg and thus the War itself, had rendered invaluable services to the Union was indisputable. He went to his Pennsylvania birthplace to recover from his injuries, remaining there for some six months. In December, though not fully recovered, he was attached to the Army of the Potomac as it began its "Wilderness Campaign," the final conquest of Lee's Army of Northern Virginia. Here Hancock, now a Brigadier General in the Regular Army, associated with many legendary American military figures: Grant, Sheridan, Meade and Burnside for the North; and Lee, Johnston and Breckinridge (who had been James Buchanan's Vice President) for the South. Hancock during this campaign would have himself transported to battle after battle in an ambulance and then mount his horse to ride back and forth among his troops and perform his familiar exhortations. His contributions continued to advance the Union cause.

In late 1864, President Lincoln ordered Hancock back to Washington to recruit and train more volunteers for the Union cause. Hancock was successful in this endeavor, and was standing by to take his newly trained troops either to the command of Grant in Virginia or Sherman in the South when Lee finally surrendered.

AFTER THE WAR

The untimely assassination of Abraham Lincoln, whom Hancock had come to know quite well personally during the war, had a profound effect upon the Pennsylvania General, a military man who had kept silent on political matters, although as a Northern Democrat he, like Lincoln, desired reunification. Before the war, this military officer who had served with Southerners in Mexico and at other outposts had made speeches at various military gatherings leaving no doubt that he was loyal to the Union, though not desiring conflict among the states. At the time of Lincoln's murder, Hancock was the commanding military officer of Washington, D.C. To him fell the grizzly duty of hanging Mrs. Surratt, the woman conspirator in the Lincoln murder circle. Not caring for this assignment, he nonetheless carried out his orders.

In 1867, following a year of duty fighting Indians in Missouri, Major General Hancock was assigned to succeed Gen. Phil Sheridan as Commander in Chief of one of the five military districts — Texas and Louisiana — established by the post-war Radical Republicans. His rule was efficient, fair and sympathetic. Challenged by the Radical Republican Governor of Texas with respect to not being strict enough on the recently rebellious population, Hancock replied in a lengthy and scholarly memorandum that as a military man his duty was to enforce rather than to establish policies. But he also made it quite clear that he felt the Radicals were going too far in their quest for punishment, and that reunification, which he strongly desired, required efforts on the part of the victors as well as the losers. Such a policy by Hancock was not very well accepted in the Radical Republican Congress, and, Hancock, sensing dissatisfaction among that body, requested and was granted transfer to another post of duty. In 1868 he was assigned to command the Atlantic division of the Army for a year and then given a post, in 1869, as an army commander in the Dakotas.

Hancock's emergence into politics was quite natural considering that he was both a Democrat by birth and a war hero-General. He additionally believed, as was the principal policy of Northern Democrats, in reunification. Thus, his name was placed in nomination as a candidate for President at the 1868 Democratic National Convention. He received some votes, but Gov. Horatio Seymour of New York was named the Democratic nominee. Hancock continued to serve in the military, keeping a low political profile. The Democratic Party in 1872 was in total disarray and resorted to endorsing Horace Greeley for President, who promptly took the fortunes of the Democrats lower than ever before. In 1876, after scandals such as *Credit Mobilier* had embarrassed the administration of Grant and reform was wanted by the people, the Democratic chances for winning the White House appeared to be very high for the first time in twenty years.

Placed in nomination once again, the non-political Hancock was submerged this time by the reform Governor of New York, Samuel Tilden. Remaining as non-political as possible because of his military post, Hancock still hoped that Tilden would win. When Tilden was robbed of the Presidency and rebellion was being talked of openly by Democrats, it was rumored that Hancock would be commander of an army to install Tilden, but Tilden himself, as did Hancock, abhorred the thoughts of another rebellion, and no such army was formed. Hancock was very much in favor of having the House, which was Democratic, decide the 1876 Presidential election, but he did not expound this view publicly.

Hancock's military career continued to rise. In 1872, he was reassigned to Governor's Island, New York, as Commander-in-Chief of the Military Division of the Atlantic. This command, second only to that of Army General-in-Chief William Tecumseh Sherman, included a territory from Minnesota to Texas and from Maine to Florida. His administrative skills were superb, and he continued to inspire those who served under him.

NOMINATED FOR PRESIDENT

In 1880, the Democratic nomination was Samuel Tilden's for the asking, but the aging "Sage of Graystone" declined to run again. The convention at Cincinnati was an open one, and nominations were being placed almost at random by each state. A delegate from Pennsylvania made a rousing nominating speech in favor of Hancock, and the convention gave the General a commanding, though not decisive, first ballot lead. With momentum building for Hancock, the convention adjourned for the evening, and when it met on the next day, a huge majority of delegates had swung to him, and he was nominated. For Vice President, the convention chose W.H. English, a prominent Indiana banker who had formerly served as a Congressman. The Democratic team would oppose James A. Garfield, the rabid Ohio Congressman and former Civil War General (also running for Senator), and Chester A. Arthur, whose tenure as Collector of the Port of New York was under question for corruption.

With a thirty-six year military career behind him, Hancock was not too adept at politics. He revived charges of corruption against the Republicans and called for lower tariffs, but when pressed for an explanation of his proposed tariff policy, he stated that tariffs were a matter for local rather than federal consideration. The entrenched Republicans, perhaps a little cleaner after the Hayes administration, attacked Hancock as merely a soldier and not an administrator. Furthermore, Garfield supporters pulled out the "bloody shirt," a Republican practice where Northern voters were incited to question the loyalty of Northern Democrats who favored reunification. The popular election in November of 1880 was extremely close, with Garfield collecting 4,454,416 to Hancock's 4,444,952, a margin of less than 10,000! But the Electoral College gave Garfield a decided edge of 214 to 155. Hancock's undistinguished political career was quickly completed.

TAPS

Just as Winfield Scott was allowed to continue his military career by the opposing administration after he lost the Presidency, so was Winfield Scott Hancock. He resumed his command of the Atlantic Division in an era of relative peace. One of his last official duties was to preside over the military funeral of the Army's most revered soldier, former President Ulysses S. Grant, in August of 1885.

In later years Hancock lost his lean, dashing look and became rather portly. His health declined, and he suddenly died at his military headquarters at Governor's Island in New York City on February 9, 1886. Tributes were immediately given from throughout the land. Though not acclaimed as a Grant or a Sherman, the army General turned politician was recognized for significant services, especially at Gettysburg, that were of lasting importance to the survival of the United States of America.

James G. Blaine

The Election of 1884

The presidential election campaign of 1884 was surely one of the most distasteful in American history. New York Governor Grover Cleveland was opposed by James Gillespie Blaine, an extraordinary politician and government official who was known for his ability to attack an opponent unmercifully. In a close election, one that could have been decided differently by a switch of some 600 voters in New York, the Presidency eluded Blaine because of campaign tactics which backfired. The distinguished "Plumed Knight" from Maine was thus relegated to an obscure place in American history, although his service and achievements warranted him a much more favorable treatment.

PENNSYLVANIA FARM BOY

Of an Irish lineage that had seen his ancestors fight in the Revolution, James G. Blaine was born January 31, 1830, in Washington County, Pennsylvania, in the western section of the state. Blaine's father, a farmer, was a Whig and admirer of Henry Clay and was elected to the position of county Prothonotary (chief clerk). He was Presbyterian while James' mother was a Catholic; all of the Blaine children became Catholic except for James, who alone followed his father and became Presbyterian. Yet Blaine had a deep attachment to his mother, who, he later said, was responsible for his moral character.

While James grew up on a farm, he was never known for the mischievousness or athletic prowess of so many other famous boys. From an early age he was inclined to studious endeavors. His home was situated on the Cumberland Road, then a famous and well used highway by such notables as Jackson, Clay and James K. Polk. The young Blaine probably saw these famous leaders as they traveled to their duties in Washington, D.C. and perhaps had dreams of one day fulfilling a similar occupation.

At age thirteen, James was enrolled at the local Washington College (named after the first President). His curriculum was traditional, and James graduated as one of the top three students in his class four years later. His father had hoped that James would be a lawyer, but funds were not available for him to pursue this course of study. James therefore decided to take a teaching position and save his earnings so that he could later take up the study of law.

Blaine obtained a position in a Lexington, Kentucky military preparatory school and proved to be a popular and effective teacher. While there, he met and soon married Harriet Stanwood, also a teacher, who had migrated to Kentucky from Augusta, Maine. Blaine also had the opportunity while in Lexington to hear the eminent Henry Clay speak. The "Great Commoner" became Blaine's political hero, and Blaine is supposed to have boasted while in Lexington that he himself would one day be Speaker of the House.

Blaine eventually became a teacher of the blind in Philadelphia. He had been diligent in saving his money, and the new location afforded him the opportunity to enroll in the study of law while simultaneously teaching. He and his wife were looking forward to his career as an attorney and rearing a family.

RELOCATING TO MAINE

An unfortunate family disaster altered Blaine's life. His first child died suddenly in 1854, and a decision was made to bury the child in Augusta. It was his first trip to Maine, and he found his wife's home state to his liking. He was able to meet many leading citizens of Augusta, and some were impressed by the young schoolteacher. On the return train trip to Philadelphia, Blaine was offered a position with an August weekly Whig newspaper, the *Kennebec Journal.* With little hesitation, Blaine, who had no formal training in newspaper work, accepted the position and gave up his study of the law.

The *Journal* was not a national newspaper but rather a typical rural American newspaper of the day which specialized as much in human interest articles as the news. Blaine displayed a natural ability for writing articles that were readable and interesting as well as factual. After a series of ownership changes at the beginning of this career, Blaine became a partner in the enterprise with John Stevens, who was to be Chairman of the Maine Republican Party and Ambassador to Paraguay, Norway, Sweden and Hawaii. The publication prospered with the help of Blaine's pen, and a contract was secured from the Republican state legislature for the publication of state advertisements. A rough and tumble battle ensued over the advertisement contract between the *Journal* and the Augusta *Age*, a Democratic paper. The editor of the *Age* was Melville Fuller, later Chief Justice of the United States Supreme Court.

Blaine's abilities soon led him to the position of editor of the *Journal*, and he began writing about political issues more and more. Coupled with his political writings were essays on a variety of general subjects, such as the Crimean War and Christian creeds. In his spare time, Blaine engrossed himself in a rigorous study of the history of Maine. The combined effect of his abilities and studies culminated in the production of a newspaper that soon made Blaine prominent widely in the traditionally Democratic state. His influence became more and more pronounced as dissension over slavery issues increased between Northern and Southern states and he was able to express the sentiments of his constituents. Especially appreciated by his readers was an article condemning President Franklin Pierce, the Northern Democrat with Southern sympathies.

INTO POLITICS

Blaine's entry into politics began when he was chosen to be a delegate to the first Republican Convention in 1856. He did not support John C. Fremont for the nomination, but he campaigned heartily for "The Pathfinder" in the general election. During this campaign he made his first public political speeches and found that they went over well when he introduced them with an anecdote or story. This became a custom of his speaking style.

In 1857 Blaine was appointed by the Governor to serve as Commissioner of an investigation into the prison system of Maine. Blaine's questioning of many corrupt practices led to reforms, and his reputation was enhanced by his impartial conduct. In 1858, only four years after moving to Maine, Blaine was elected to the state House of Representatives. His service and leadership there found him being elected Speaker in 1861.

Blaine by this time had established himself in national Republican circles. In 1860 he boldly endorsed Abraham Lincoln and worked hard for him at the Chicago convention, though he was not a delegate. He was, however, influential enough to be made a member of the committee that went to Springfield to officially offer Lincoln the nomination. Hannibal Hamlin from Maine was chosen as the Vice Presidential candidate. The stage was being set for Blaine himself to enter the national political scene.

The outbreak of the War Between the States upon the election of Lincoln found Blaine called upon to render many duties. As an editor, he cried fervently for the rebellion to be put down. As a legislator and Speaker, he pushed for legislation to help the war effort and strongly favored the use of Negroes as soldiers. As a Republican political leader in the state of which it was said, "As Maine goes, so goes the nation," Blaine organized the 1862 campaign with all diligence so that the military set backs in the early part of the war would not erode national Republican leadership. Early victories in Maine helped maintain Lincoln's effectiveness.

Blaine was drafted but paid for a substitute to take his place in battle. When he ran for office some twenty years later, he would not be able to raise this issue against his opponent, Grover Cleveland, who had done likewise. Like Cleveland, he would find throughout his life that his refusal to serve would bring forth detractors.

ELECTED TO THE HOUSE

Blaine's national political career commenced with his election to Congress for the term beginning in 1863. His service in this body was to be during some of the most perilous and controversial periods in American history: the War Between the States, the impeachment of Andrew Johnson, Reconstruction, the Teapot Dome scandals, and the Presidential Election of 1876.

While his political career advanced quickly, Blaine made political enemies which probably later cost him the Presidency. His conflicts with the pompous Thaddeus Stevens, for example, were numerous. He had a bitter confrontation with Arthur Conkling, later a prominent Senator, over a military bill. Their debates were so bitter, with Blaine attacking Conkling on the House floor so sarcastically that he himself was later remorseful, that they never spoke to each other again. President Grant and Blaine also had a bitter conflict, and Grant refused to speak to Blaine while he was President, though the two did reconcile years later.

Blaine was instrumental in seeing that Reconstruction legislation passed the House. He favored Lincoln's plan, but when Lincoln was assassinated, the radicals took control as Southern states refused to admit fault and accept re-admission on the terms offered by Lincoln. Blaine himself was not as vengeful or as interested in imposing harsh Reconstruction measures as most Northerners, but he wanted guarantees that the South would not rebel again. Then Thaddeus Stevens precipitated harsh feeling when he proposed that no members of Congress from the Confederate states be allowed to sit in the national legislature until the Reconstruction acts were decided. The subsequent news from the South that former Confederate officers were being elected to state legislatures and attending sessions in Confederate uniforms created an uproar in Congress that soon led to the Reconstruction Act and the Thirteenth and Fourteenth Amendments being enacted. Blaine guided the Fourteenth Amendment to passage but was not as deeply involved in other Reconstruction legislation.

President Johnson's impeachment was not favored by Blaine. Initial resolutions found that the Maine Congressman voted against such a move. Even when Secretary of War Stanton was removed, Blaine was opposed to impeachment on the grounds that Lincoln, not Johnson, had appointed the Secretary of War, and thus only Lincoln could be tried under the *Tenure of Office Act*. Blaine even attempted at one point the parliamentary maneuver of having the House adjourn until November so that the House would not be present to impeach. When impeachment articles were presented, Blaine did not participate in any debate, but he did finally follow party lines and vote for impeachment.

SPEAKER OF THE HOUSE

When Schuyler Colfax was elected Vice President in 1868, Blaine became a candidate to succeed him as House Speaker. He was opposed in the Republican caucus at first, but that opposition was withdrawn, and Blaine then was elected Speaker, a position he held until 1875. These years were probably the happiest and most productive of Blaine's life. He purchased a home in Washington so that his family could be with him. His new position was one which he enjoyed and mastered. It was also one for which he gained a reputation of fair play. At one point, Blaine left a formal dinner to rush to the House and preside over an uproarious session that was created when Northern Democrats and Southerners were filibustering over a bill introduced by a young Congressman named James A. Garfield. Blaine presided from 7:30 p.m. until 4:00 p.m. the next day, patiently but fairly hearing and ruling on all objections. Such moves greatly enhanced his prestige.

However, Blaine became involved in the scandals of the Grant administration, and, although never indicted or found guilty of any actions, he was to always suffer politically. The initials of Blaine and many other Congressmen were found beside dividend entries in a notebook of Oakes Ames, a Massachusetts Congressman who headed the Credit Mobilier construction company. Allegations were soon rampant that various Congressmen had received stock free or at nominal values. Blaine and many Congressmen did not deny this and were never indicted; those who did deny the allegations, however, generally were indicted and convicted. Blaine used his position as Speaker to have an investigation made which completely exonerated him of any wrongdoing in this matter.

More damaging to Blaine, though, were the "Mulligan Letters," which came forth in 1875 after the Democrats had gained control of the House and Blaine was the Minority Leader and the leading candidate for the Republican nomination to succeed President Grant. These letters, presented by a disgruntled former aide to Blaine's brother-in-law, insinuated that Blaine, while Speaker, had arranged for the Union Pacific Railroad to purchase some bonds he owned in an Arkansas railroad that was in financial difficulty. A long and agonizing period for Blaine followed. An investigation was held by the House, and Blaine, in a moment of high drama, forcefully and emotionally presented a defense of his actions that saw him exonerated him by his fellow Congressmen — but not by the professional politicians or the people. The 1876 Presidential nomination that had been his for the asking was now gone. To be sure, he tried to gain the favor of his party, but a deadlocked convention turned away from Blaine to Governor Rutherford B. Hayes , the deciding factor being the transfer of New York delegates from its favorite son, Senator Arthur Conkling (who had been insulted by Blaine years before), to the Ohio "dark horse." It would not be the last time that a former adversary would stop Blaine's drive to be Chief Executive.

An interesting sidelight to the 1876 campaign was an illness suffered by Blaine shortly before the convention. Going to Church the Sunday before the session began, he suffered a sunstroke. He recovered, but there was always thereafter the suspicion that Blaine had an irrecoverable sickness. This was not helped in the least by Blaine's future decisions to return home during the middle of a long train trip to recuperate from a minor illness rather than continue an important government or political function. Blaine's health was good, but he was probably a hypochondriac.

UNITED STATES SENATOR

Blaine campaigned hard for Hayes in 1876, and many expected a Cabinet appointment to be tendered, but it was not. Instead Hayes appointed a Maine Senator as Secretary of the Treasury, and Blaine was appointed to that Senate vacancy. Taking his seat in 1877, Blaine initially was not very active, though he did state his opposition to the Election Commission formed to resolve the disputed 1876 Presidential election, believing the move to be "extra-constitutional."

Blaine's activities in the Upper House consisted of support for "bi-metalism," or coinage of both gold and silver; of passing legislation allowing Americans to buy ships made abroad for registration in the United States; and of bringing to the attention of the American public an unfair arbitration with Britain over Canadian fisheries. He also strongly objected to the dismantling of Southern Reconstruction governments, a move that had been promised in return for Hayes' election. A movement was begun in the Democratically controlled House and Senate to allow Southern states to disenfranchise black voters. Blaine, who to his political misfortune had earlier supported repatriation of Confederate officials and soldiers *except* Jefferson Davis, now again created future political havoc for himself with eloquent speeches, full of statistics and sarcasm where necessary, in favor of Negro voting rights. He ultimately prevailed not because he could personally muster enough votes to help the Negro cause but because his opposition could not gain enough votes to pass the anti-Negro measure.

Blaine was considered again for the Presidential nomination in 1880 but was thwarted this time by former President U.S. Grant, who had just completed his world tour and was still immensely popular. But Grant no longer had total control of party machinery and also had the "third term" problems to overcome. For over thirty ballots Blaine and Grant doggedly held their delegates with the stubborn Grant, whose character prevented him from acceding to a man to whom he would not speak (Blaine had also insulted the former President on one occasion), refusing to withdraw. Grant's chief supporter, Arthur Conkling of New York, also refused to break away from Grant in favor of Blaine. Finally it was Blaine who broke, choosing to support James A. Garfield, a former General whom Grant could also support.

SECRETARY OF STATE

If disheartened, Blaine did not show it. He campaigned hard for Garfield, who appointed him Secretary of State upon his election. In return Blaine pledged and gave Garfield his true loyalty, and the two had a gratifying relationship. Blaine was with Garfield at the Pan-American Exposition in Washington in July of 1881 when an assassin struck. The new President lingered until September before dying; Blaine was in effect handling the reigns of government during this period, literally exhausting himself from the swarm of activity around himself. The new President, Chester Arthur, chosen on Garfield's ticket to keep peace with the New York Conkling Republicans and the Stalwarts, was no master for Blaine to serve. Soon after Arthur's inauguration, Blaine resigned to private life for the first time since 1863.

Of course Blaine stayed active in political affairs. When President Arthur and his new Secretary of State took a position different to that of Garfield and Blaine, Blaine spoke out. Blaine also began a book, *Twenty Years*, which was replete not only with his own accomplishments and opinions but with accurate references to the works and character of many prominent leaders from the mid-1860s to the mid-1880s. During this "retirement," Blaine also took the time to enjoy an intimate relationship with his wife and children, the first time in many years he had done so. Events would prevent any further close family relationship during his lifetime.

THE CAMPAIGN OF 1884

In late 1883 a group of prominent newspaper publishers met with Blaine in New York City and pledged their efforts to secure for him the Republican nomination and the Presidency. A reconciliation between Grant and Blaine was brought about by intermediaries, and then Blaine wrote a letter to General William Sherman asking him not to run, receiving from the General his famous reply that he "...would not run if nominated, would not serve if elected." By the time of the Chicago convention, Blaine's momentum was too strong to stop. On the fourth ballot he went over the top. His running mate was General John A. Logan of Illinois, a long time Republican Congressman and party leader.

Opposing Blaine was Grover Cleveland, the austere but sincere Governor of New York. No Democrat had won the Presidency since Buchanan, and Blaine — former editor, former state legislator and state Speaker, former Congressman and Speaker, former Senator and former Secretary of State — was the odds-on favorite to continue the Republican tradition. Blaine's past and a series of campaign blunders, however, led to his defeat.

Even before Blaine had won the nomination, a group of prominent New York Republican newspapers announced that if the reform-minded Cleveland were the Democratic candidate, they would be compelled, considering Blaine's past railroad activities, to support *this* democratic nominee. A "Committee of One Hundred" was formed to spread Blaine's past, particularly the "Mulligan Letters." With glee these opponents of Blaine entitled themselves "Mugwumps," which became a synonym of the campaign of 1884. This campaign would prove to be one of the dirtiest in American history.

After Cleveland was nominated, the Republicans struck hard at "Grover the Good." He was first of all condemned because of Tammany connections, but Cleveland's reforms against corrupt practices were his primary strength. Some ado was stirred up about Cleveland's paid substitution of another man to serve in the Civil War for himself, but Blaine also had used this practice. Then a newspaper in Cleveland's home town of Buffalo published a story that was easily the most shocking in the history of American presidential politics. Under the heading of "A Terrible Tale," the newspaper revealed that Cleveland had fathered a child out of wedlock eleven years earlier. The story was not denied by Cleveland, and Republicans began chanting:

> Blaine! Blaine! James G. Blaine!
> Plum-ed Knight from the State of Maine!

To which the Democrats retorted:

> Blaine! Blaine! James G. Blaine!
> Continental Liar from the State of Maine!

The Republicans got a little bit nastier:

> Ma! Ma! where's my Pa?
> Gone to the White House, ha, ha, ha!

Blaine tried to ignore the allegations about railroad misdealings, which he thought had been disposed of in past investigations, and began a rigorous travel schedule. He knew that the South would be solid for the Democrats, but he was confident of support in most Northern states. Four states were in doubt: New York, New Jersey, Indiana and Connecticut. Blaine could win the Presidency with either New York or with Indiana and one other state. His two-month tour solidified his support in many states, but he was still running behind in New York. His campaign leaders in that state encouraged a visit, which proved fatal. While in the state just ten days before the election, a Presbyterian Minister speaking in behalf of Blaine made the now famous "rum, Romanism and rebellion" speech. The Democrats promptly seized upon these remarks and had them printed onto flyers that were then circulated to Catholics as they attended Mass the Sunday before election day. The results were devastating: James G. Blaine, son of a Catholic and of Irish lineage, lost New York by 1,149 votes and with it the Presidency of the United States.

The popular vote was 4,874,986 to 4,851,981, while the electoral vote was 219 to 182. Blaine was not as disheartened as some of his supporters. He had reason to contest the counting of returns in New York, but he declared, magnanimously, that the nation had already been through enough of a trial in the 1876 Tilden-Hayes election and did not deserve another such episode.

SECRETARY OF STATE UNDER HARRISON

Blaine took up writing again and completed *Twenty Years*, which he had begun after resigning as Secretary of State under Arthur. He then assembled a collection of his speeches and articles, which he had published under the title of *Political Discussions: Legislative, Diplomatic and Popular.* A summer residence at Bar Harbor, Maine, was built in 1886, and he toured his native western Pennsylvania the same year.

Any talk of running again for the Presidency was disavowed by Blaine, who declared, "...having had my chance and lost [in 1884], I do not wish to appear again as a claimant with the demand 'Try me again.'" He decided to travel to Europe as the nominating convention approached, and he made many acquaintances which would be of benefit in his service under Harrison. He was with Andrew Carnegie at the steel magnate's Scottish castle when the convention deadlocked over Harrison and John Sherman of Ohio. In a coded message erroneously construed even today to be the work of Carnegie, Blaine, who had not endorsed a candidate but felt that Harrison was the stronger of the two, sent instructions for the convention to take Harrison, which it did. Harrison then proceeded to win the election *with fewer popular votes than Cleveland*, as Blaine had hoped to do four years earlier.

No one was surprised when it was announced that Blaine was Harrison's choice for Secretary of State. He quickly assumed the lead in foreign affairs, primarily being involved in bringing together nations of North and South America at an assembly named the International American Conference. Blaine was elected President of the meeting, which sought ways to peacefully resolve disputes. Blaine hailed its work as a new *Magna Carta,* but disputes arose after the conference which resulted in bloodshed. Yet some boundary disputes were resolved peacefully, and a further meeting tended to find ways to resolve matters without resorting to arms.

Blaine also negotiated with Germany and Britain over a dispute concerning Samoa, and with Britain over the commercial rights to sealing in the Bering Sea. In each case, the events probably were not of such great significance as was the acknowledgment of the emergence of the United States as a great commercial power. In the case of the Bering Sea seals, for example, a treaty was enacted calling for arbitration concerning confiscation of British cutters by the United States, which lost the arbitration. But the world was taking note that the United States was now an international power to be reckoned with.

LAST YEARS

In 1892, at age sixty-two, Blaine suddenly left a meeting of the Cabinet. Some Cabinet members thought that some remark had offended him or that he might be plotting a run for the Presidency against Harrison. But Blaine was seriously ill, the result of a weak body, long years of service and a broken personal spirit after the sudden deaths of a son and a daughter within two weeks of each other at the beginning of the year. Many friends and party leaders thought Blaine, like Henry Clay in 1852, might seek one more time to be President. But Blaine refused, saying he did not want the office. He resigned as Secretary of State in June of 1892, shortly before the Republican convention met to renominate Harrison. Then another terrible tragedy struck when he learned of the death of his last son shortly after the June convention had adjourned.

Blaine was not extremely aged, but he was suffering from exhaustion and, some said, temporary delusions. He spent the summer in his Bar Harbor, Maine summer residence but made no progress toward recovery. He published some articles and made one speech in favor of Harrison. He traveled to Whitelaw Reid's New York country home for a dinner in his honor, where everyone present noticed how much he had deteriorated. Then, weaker and more feeble than ever, he returned to Washington. He attended Church, took Holy Communion, and walked home accompanied by President Harrison.

The outing left him with a cold too severe to handle. He grew weaker and weaker, finally passing away on January 27, 1893, just four days before his sixty-third birthday. A host of reporters had been keeping a vigil outside his Washington residence, and word of his demise soon spread throughout the land. President Harrison issued a Proclamation extolling his virtues and closing the offices of government on the day of his funeral.

This service was supposed to be a private occasion, but Blaine had been on the center stage of American politics and government too long for prominent officials not to be present. There at the funeral to pay final respects to one of the masters of American politics for over thirty years were the President of the United States, Cabinet Secretaries, and most members of the House of Representatives and the Senate. While later generations might tend to forget his outstanding leadership in the government of the United States, the "Plumed Knight" was appropriately remembered and honored by both his fellow government servants and the American people of his own age.

William Jennings Bryan
The Elections of 1896, 1900 and 1908

Like Henry Clay of a generation before, William Jennings Bryan was a formidable force on the American political scene, three times running for the Presidency but, like Clay, three times losing. A man who dominated the "Party of the People" by the sheer power of his oratory and command, he played the political game, also like Clay, a bit too much. In the beginning he suffered defeat because of inexperience and youthful zeal. In the end defeat occurred because of too much political experience and too many dogmatic stances. Ultimately, his defeats were the trappings of his own words and workings.

BORN A DEMOCRAT

Bryan was born the son of Silas and Mary Baird Bryan on March 19, 1860, in Salem, Illinois. Silas Bryan traced his roots to Revolutionary America and was himself into politics, a loyal Democrat who was a state Senator and knew the likes of Stephen A. Douglas and Abraham Lincoln. During William's infancy, Silas Bryan campaigned for the election of Douglas as President. After Lincoln's election and the start of the War Between the States, Mr. Bryan, a "copperhead" Democrat, was arrested and held without benefit of a trial for three months before being set free. He stayed in politics, though, later becoming a Circuit Court Judge.

William Jennings Bryan was raised on a 488 acre farm outside Salem in a strict Christian atmosphere. He was surrounded primarily by his devout mother and other womenfolk, his father being constantly on the circuit, and he was therefore especially pleased when his father heard local cases so that he could accompany him to court. He took great pleasure in hearing his father speak in court and at special rallies such as the annual Fourth of July picnic.

At age 10 Willy's formal schooling began when was sent to "the Old College" school at Salem. Tradition has it that Bryan indicated, upon questioning from his teacher, that his ambition was to someday be President of the United States. He not only received the rudiments available in *McGuffey's Reader* but fundamental religious instruction as well. The foundation of faith that was to be such an integral part of his political life began to be solidly laid at this age.

Another foundation — this one political — was laid when Willy was twelve. His father received the Democratic nomination for Congress and was considered a sure winner, especially when he received the Greenback party nomination as well. A popular tale is that William Jennings Bryan's first political speech was made in this campaign on behalf of his father, being so effective that he was carried from the platform on the shoulders of supporters. Unfortunately Silas Bryan did not play — or pay — the right politics in this election. He refused to pay a $500 party fee for the nomination and was upset by a renegade Democrat who just a decade before had been a supporter of Jefferson Davis. Young Will Bryan loathed the idea that his father had not been elected because of corrupt practices that needed reform. It was a cause he would carry throughout his life.

For the next couple of years Will continued his farm boy growth. His main hobby, it is said, was meeting in the barn with his friends and participating in mock debates. William Jennings Bryan took the role of a Democratic Senator from Illinois. During this period of time, Will decided to break from his Methodist background, joining the Cumberland Presbyterian Church. When he reached age fifteen, Will was sent to Whipple Academy, a preparatory school for Illinois College, at Jacksonville. Whipple had only seventy-eight pupils, and the college had only sixty students with a faculty of but eight. It was steeped in religious fundamentalism, and his course of instruction was rather classical with very little science. Byran's scholastic standing at Whipple was mediocre, but he was very active in Sigma Pi, the debating society, and finished third in the memorized recitation of a poem.

After two years, Bryan advanced to Illinois College, where his course of instruction was similar to Whipple, though more advanced. He took courses in geology and science but much preferred courses in American Government and moral philosophy, scoring 100 percent in each, and ultimately becoming Valedictorian of his class. His main interest was debate. He was Vice President of the Interstate Oratorical Society, associate editor of the school paper, and chaplain of Sigma Pi—but never President of any, which, especially in the case of Sigma Pi, he coveted.

Bryan was busy in the study of American politics. Very possibly he had already decided upon a political career. In the campaign of 1876, Bryan was witness to a trainload of New York "Tammany" officials visiting Illinois on their way to the convention in St. Louis. An Illinois Senator prevailed upon the Easterners to consider the plight of the Western farmer, reminding them that Easterners had been nominated by the Democratic Party in the last three elections — only to lose all three. Along with the farmers sixteen year old

Will Bryan cheered lustily. Yet another Easterner, Samuel Tilden, won the nomination in 1876. In 1880 Bryan took great pain to study the nomination procedures of both the Republicans and Democrats. At home on college break, he was asked by local Democrats if he might like to make some remarks at a local Salem rally. The young Bryan accepted and upon delivering his speech realized that he could be very effective as a political orator.

The year 1880 was important to Bryan in two other respects. At Illinois College he had met a remarkable young lady interested in, of all things, politics, especially the future politics of Will Bryan. Later to gain a law degree herself, Mary Baird was to be the major political confidant and plotter of her future husband. They were engaged to be married, agreeing that the union would take place as soon as Will's future was secure. The year 1880 also marked the year Bryan was to graduate from college and begin a career that was to be directed in but one path — toward the White House. He was only twenty and not even eligible to vote; yet his ambition was set. Sixteen years later he would be the nominee of his party for President of the United States.

LAW SCHOOL

Bryan's path to success first led to Chicago, the heart of the midwest, a place of opportunity and growth. His family urged him to go to his father's law school and return to Salem to practice. Bryan did go to Union College (later incorporated into Northwestern), but he did not plan to return to Salem. He was already plotting his future.

He went to Chicago and arranged a position in the firm of Lyman Trumbull, an illustrious lawyer who had been a Justice of the Illinois Supreme Court, a Congressman, a Senator, a Gubernatorial candidate and considered seriously as a Cabinet member and Minister to the Court of St. James. A close friend of Abraham Lincoln, he authored the Thirteenth Amendment, the Freedmen's Bureau Legislation, and the Civil Rights Bill of 1866. He had also been one of seven Republicans to vote "not guilty" for the impeachment of Andrew Johnson. Trumbull had been proposed for President on the 1872 Democratic ticket by Silas Bryan when he was running for Congress. No doubt this played a key role in young William securing a position in Trumbull's prestigious firm. Another reason may have been that Trumbull's son, Henry, who had not done well at Yale and was back home also studying at Union, might perhaps be favorably influenced by the religiously devout Bryan.

To save money, Bryan walked four miles each day each way to school. For breakfast it is said that he walked three blocks to get three buns — rather than the usual two — for ten cents. Bryan's course of study lasted two years. He was not well liked because his fellow students felt that he used his courses to learn to debate rather than study the law. He was also resented because he would not participate in the college beer drinking rituals of the day. Some students thought his dress, manners and speech closely resembled one of Chicago's and the country's greatest speakers of the day, evangelist Dwight Moody. His primary extracurricular participation was in the Debating Society, and though he might have resembled an evangelist, these class-mates surely knew that Bryan was not headed for the Ministry. When Bryan's study of law was completed, its content and substance consisted not so much of the principles of Blackstone as of the ideas of what human and moral justice should be. All the time Bryan was at Union he was also with Lyman Trumbull, discovering the evils of monopolies and wealth — what he would later call plutocracy — and formulating the themes of future political campaigns.

It would have been useful for a future politician to be able to say that he had been Valedictorian of both his college and law school. Successful at Illinois College, Bryan tried also at Union. He lost by one vote and demanded a recount. He lost again. It was a pattern that was to haunt him throughout his political career.

EARLY CAREER

After graduating from Union in 1881, Bryan returned to his college town of Jacksonville to begin the practice of law. His first case was to defend a horse thief. He lost the case, though he thought it commendable that his client received a sentence of only seven years rather than the usual ten. He joined various Church groups and, of course, participated actively in Democratic politics. In 1884 both the Republicans and Democrats met in Chicago, and Bryan spent all available time studying the political move-ments of the political leaders of the day. He managed to get tickets to the Democratic convention and was enthralled as he watched the speeches and maneuvers on the convention floor. On the train back from Chicago, Bryan decided it was time to put his career on a more direct path. First of all, he thought it was time to marry Mary Baird. Their ceremony was performed on October 1, 1884, with Bryan presenting a wedding ring to his new wife which was engraved "Won 1880. One 1884." After a short honeymoon to St. Louis, Bryan began making campaign speeches for Grover Cleveland. Now in his twenty-seventh year, he also decided it was time to move away from his rural beginnings to a new stage that would afford him an opportunity to achieve his innermost ambition.

Bryan sought a number of positions outside his native Salem. First, he tried to secure the position of Assistant U.S. District Attorney at Springfield but was unsuccessful. He then sought to be Recorder of Deeds for Washington, D.C. but was unsuccessful in this pursuit as well. Shortly thereafter, Bryan had to go to Kansas on some legal matters and stopped at Lincoln, Nebraska to visit an old friend who was an attorney for a railroad. Conversations between the two led the young attorney from Illinois to consider moving to Lincoln, where his talents might be more useful and where he might rise to the top of a somewhat obscure local Democratic Party more rapidly. Bryan kept his silence before leaving Jacksonville because he was running for Chancellor Commander of the Knights of Pythias and felt this position on his political resume might be helpful in the future and also provide him a proper introduction to the lodge in Lincoln. After staying in Jacksonville long enough to win the position, he resigned and moved to Lincoln.

He sat up offices in the same building as Charles G. Dawes, a young Republican attorney who became a close friend. Dawes would serve as Vice President from 1925-29 under Calvin Coolidge. His legal practice was but a front for his political hopes. Within two weeks of arrival, Bryan looked up J. Sterling Morton, a perennial Democratic contender for a variety of offices who was the state Democratic party boss. Morton took an immediate liking to the tall, muscular, good looking Bryan. This relationship was to serve Bryan well as he sprung to national prominence.

Bryan's big break in Lincoln came when a Democratic dignitary from another state failed to show up at a rally. When a volunteer to take the missing dignitary's place was called for, Bryan responded, delivering a masterly two hour oration filled with jokes, tales, gestures and power. The audience hailed him back again and again for more remarks. It was Bryan's first mastery of an audience, and he knew he must build on this beginning. The next day he sent anonymous articles to newspapers in Lincoln and Omaha explaining how a young Lincoln attorney named William Jennings Bryan had swayed a large Democratic crowd. Sterling Morton saw to it after this performance that Bryan was a delegate to the National Convention of 1888 and the State Convention of the same year. Some talk was made of nominating Bryan for Lieutenant Governor, but Bryan realized he could not win and was wise enough to decline, choosing instead to campaign for Grover Cleveland for President and Sterling Morton for Congress. Both of these gentlemen lost, but Bryan won the loyalty of many Nebraska Democrats.

In 1890 a burning issue was raging in Lincoln — Prohibition. Young Bryan, who was later to be the instrumental force in securing passage of the Constitutional Amendment on Prohibition, took a rather strange stance in this election. The incumbent Republican Congressman was assessed $1,200 by Lincoln businessmen intent on keeping the state "wet." James E. Boyd, a wealthy Democratic businessman who desired to be Governor, informed the liquor interests that he would put up the $1,200 desired in return for their support for him for Governor. Boyd was not a particularly good speaker, but he had a plan for handling this. That young, good looking orator, William Jennings Bryan, should be nominated for Congress and be the speaker for both. This was duly arranged. Bryan had only one problem: how he as a "tee-totaler" could be politically "wet." His adroitly handled the matter by stating, "I want you to understand thoroughly my position on prohibition. Although I do not touch liquor myself, I do not endorse the prohibition amendment." Another problem Bryan faced was the emergence of the Populist Party. This he handled by telling the farmers that although he was a Democrat, he felt that there was little difference in the platforms of the two parties. In a predominantly Republican state and district, he won the election with relative ease.

CONGRESS

Not only was Bryan one of the youngest members of the Congress convening in 1891, he was one of the most ambitious, and his every move was calculated to build his future. In Nebraska he toured the state speaking for other Democrats. He was, according to the Lincoln *Herald*, "able, brilliant, young, magnetic, hopeful, candid, honest, and poor." He was also downright political. He had abandoned his first Nebraska mentor, Sterling Morton, to run with James Boyd. Throughout his travels Bryan found again and again that the farmers were overwhelmingly Populist. To maintain his position in Congress, Bryan knew that he must be more Populist himself, and he did so by taking up the cause of quick and easy money. He now abandoned James Boyd and formed a machine with Nebraska Supreme Court Judge James Broady, whom Bryan had nominated for the court position at the state convention. At this same convention Bryan made his first speech on "free coinage of silver." He was, to be sure, in direct opposition to Grover Cleveland, but he decided that his future justified his stance.

It is interesting to note that Bryan was not the father of free coinage. That distinction belonged to a former Ohio Congressman by the name of William McKinley, who lost his seat after the tariff bearing his name became law and the country suffered great financial distress. Bryan was to be returned to the

House for one term, while McKinley was to become Governor of Ohio and then face the "Boy Orator of the Platte" for the Presidency.

In Washington Bryan turned every stone to advance his future. He campaigned for an old Jacksonville friend to be Speaker of the House. He openly solicited and received a position on the House Ways and Means Committee. He continued to speak around the country for Democrats. Knowing that to be re-elected he must be Populist as well as Democrat, he also spoke widely in favor of free coinage. On March 16, 1892, Bryan, just in Congress over three months, made the speech that secured him lasting national prominence. Only thirty-two years of age, Bryan spoke for some three hours on tariffs and economic issues. Democrats sat breathlessly and with hearts fluttering. By the sheer power of his oratory, William Jennings Bryan in one speech became a national leader of the Democratic Party. His fellow House Democrats exploded into a display that had not been witnessed since the days of Henry Clay. Predictions were made that he would obtain the next Vice Presidential nomination until it was learned he was too young to constitutionally qualify.

Bryan's bid for re-election in 1892 was to be tough. Fortunately he had played the Populist cause well and was considered by all in Nebraska to be a national leader of the Democratic party. But Nebraska was Republican, and a strong race was mounted to unseat Bryan. He thought he might lose, but he won re-election in a squeaker — by only 140 votes. Sterling Morton, running again for Governor, this time on the "gold standard," lost by over 5,000 votes.

Because Bryan had won in predominantly Republican Nebraska, he was immediately summoned by Democratic organizations throughout the country to make speeches. He realized his opportunity to be President was getting closer and closer. His Populist views were particularly popular in the South where he was building a strong political base. But Bryan's actions were dividing the Democratic Party deeply. President Cleveland was not for silver, and he found the upstart Congressman an embarrassment. Accordingly, instructions were issued through Sterling Morton, now Cleveland's Secretary of Agriculture, to see that Bryan did not return to Washington. Morton saw to it that Bryan was not renominated for Congress. Cleveland, very sick from cancer, did not realize that this was not the end of Bryan. Nor did he realize that the leader of the Democrats was now William Jennings Bryan.

Bryan took his defeat without complaining too much. Being out of Congress was probably somewhat of a blessing, for Bryan was now free to travel the country, making speeches against the gold standard, for tariff reform, for the direct income tax and for the common man as opposed to Wall Street. Until his term in Congress expired, he would use this forum carefully. In August he spoke extemporaneously to Congress on his free coinage ideas and was received again like a Henry Clay. He made one final speech before he left in December, 1894. In it he said, "I shall not help crucify mankind upon a cross of gold. I shall not aid in pressing down upon the bleeding brow of labor this crown of thorns."

THE ELECTION OF 1896

Without an office to serve as a base of power for running for President, Bryan nonetheless carefully plotted his course for 1896. Being rather poor, he needed a means of supporting his family. This was provided, along with the means of expanding his political horizons, when some wealthy silver miners backed the financially plagued Omaha *World-Herald* and installed Bryan as its Editor at the salary of $30.00 per week, plus expenses. Bryan immediately began to travel widely, especially in the West and South. He attained a constituency of some twenty million people in a very short time, a formidable force to be reckoned with at the Chicago convention.

Bryan envisioned himself somewhat like Lincoln, who had migrated from his native state, had elevated himself from humble origins to an attorney, was a Congressman, and had been rejected by his state legislature for the Senate, only to be elected President two years later. His primary obstacle to overcome was President Grover Cleveland — a gold standard man who was in charge of the party machinery. Bryan's plan to gain the nomination was simple. He intended to lead a rival, "free coinage" delegation to Chicago and seek to unseat the regular Nebraska delegation. The credentials fight that would result would allow him to appear before the convention, where he knew his masterly oratorical powers would sway the delegates to give him the nomination. This is exactly what happened, with Bryan's performance so persuasive and masterly that he was carried from the podium on the shoulders of delegates with an hour long demonstration following! Bryan's subsequent nomination so alienated Grover Cleveland, however, that the President made a deal that, should William McKinley adopt the gold standard, the support of the regular Democrats would not go to Bryan.

The resulting campaign was bitter. McKinley ran his "front porch" campaign, being both a "tariff man" and in favor of the gold standard. The Silver Knight traveled extensively, making over 600 speeches and shaking, some said, five million hands. He was endorsed by the Populist Party and had two running mates: Arthur Sewell of Maine was his Democratic counterpart, while Thomas Watson of Georgia was the Populist nominee for the second spot. Only thirty-six years of age, the "Boy Orator" was no match for the campaign put together by Mark Hanna, McKinley's campaign manager. Negroes were imported wholesale to the North to carry critical states. And warnings were issued by manufacturers that jobs would be lost if Bryan won, while insurance companies spoke of mortgages that might be extended for five years if McKinley were elected, or perhaps cancelled if the Democrats won. McKinley won by 600,000 popular votes, and by 271 to 176 in the Electoral College. But when Bryan studied the election returns, he took heart upon finding that some 14,000 votes, properly placed, could have made him President.

THE ELECTION OF 1900

The Republicans were wary of the "Boy Orator" who had polled 800,000 more votes than any previous Democrat and who was young, good looking, and certainly the greatest orator of the age. After the election of 1896, Bryan had his usual problem of how to support his family. This he solved by writing _The First Battle_, which was an immediate success and provided him with some financial security for the first time in his life. When war with Spain erupted, he enlisted in the army as a Private but was soon commissioned a Colonel in the Nebraska Guards, for which he raised a regiment. But because he was such a popular Democrat, the Republican administration saw to it that he got no closer to the action than Florida. The hero of this war was to be a Republican — Theodore Roosevelt — rather than Democrat Bryan.

Bryan was now in total control of the Democratic Party. No real opponent was available to oppose him. Of course, McKinley would be renominated and his campaign again managed by Hanna. McKinley would run on the record of the war successes with Spain, America's new international prominence and "Four More Years of the Full Dinner Pail." Bryan, who had used his influence to see the peace treaty with Spain ratified, now was campaigning on an anti-imperialism plank as well as his traditional free coinage plank. His running mate was Adlai Stevenson, former Vice President under Cleveland, and the grandfather of future two-time nominee Adlai Stevenson II. The tide of the country, of course, was Republican, with Americans being proud of their newfound international respect. Bryan in 1900 received fewer votes than in 1896, losing by some 800,000 popular votes and in the electoral college by 292 to 155. This time he even lost Nebraska.

INTERIM PERIOD (1900 TO 1908)

Bryan was deeply disappointed by his defeat. Being only forty and not wealthy, he had to consider his future. He turned down several offers to be editor for other papers and became Publisher and Editor of his own paper, *The Commoner*. Shortly he was wealthy in his own right. Still discontented, he decided to travel, going first to Cuba and then to Europe, where he met the Pope, the Czar and Count Tolstoy.

Although Bryan returned home in triumph in 1903, he soon learned that the Democratic sentiment in 1904 was to "Bury Bryan." Bryan did not plot a path for the nomination as he had in the past. He was alarmed to find that newspaper magnate William Randolph Hearst had enlisted his campaign manager of 1896 and 1900 and might be carrying the Silver Knight's cause. But he was more alarmed that party regulars were so desirous of victory that they were rallying around conservative Alton B. Parker, who endorsed the gold standard, as the candidate to bring victory. Bryan made a desperate appeal to the delegates at the St. Louis convention to seat delegates favorable to Hearst, but this time his oratory could not work the wonders of the past. Parker became the nominee, only to suffer defeat to Theodore Roosevelt by 2,500,000 popular votes.

Bryan resumed his world travels, going to Japan, where he met Admiral Togo; to China; to Russia, to India; to Turkey; to the Holy Land; to Egypt, where he viewed the Sphinx; to England, where he met King Edward VII; and to other European ports. His dispatches to *The Commoner* kept his name before the public, as did the favorable receptions received during his foreign calls. As he sailed home to America, he plotted once again a race for the Presidency. Knowing that he would be speaking at a welcoming rally at Madison Square Garden, he prepared a speech to launch him toward his third nomination. Warmed by a glowing reception, he launched into one of his oratorical masterpieces but then startled Eastern Democrats by calling for government ownership of railroads. Though he would get the nomination, the results of the 1908 election were already sealed.

Running against Bryan was William Howard Taft, Secretary of War and former Philippines Governor, hand picked by Teddy Roosevelt. Bryan had swept the Democratic nomination on the first ballot and began his typical whirlwind campaigning. Senator John Kern of Indiana was Bryan's running mate. But the endorsement of Roosevelt, whose policies in many respects were similar to Bryan's, was too much for Bryan to overcome. This time Bryan lost by one and one-quarter million popular votes and in the electoral college by 321 to 162.

SUPPORTER OF OTHER CAUSES AND CANDIDATES

Forty-eight years old but finished as a candidate for President, Bryan resolved to lead an active life and work for the many causes in which he believed. The first cause was Prohibition, and now he would not have to skirt this issue because of personal political considerations, as he had done when running for Congress in 1890. The cause started in Nebraska when an old friend did not support "county option," which would have allowed each county to vote down liquor sales. Bryan then went on the stump against an old ally running for Governor, and the former partisan lost decisively. Bryan's prominence and endorsement were instrumental in the eventual passage of the Prohibition Amendment. In Bryan's travels he found another cause to support. On a trip to Jamaica, his ship went aground. To his astonishment, he found that ships only had one wireless operator on board for twenty-four hours of duty. His lobbying led to passage of an act requiring two operators on board at all times. Bryan also voiced his opposition to the Payne-Aldrich higher tariff bill, but it was enacted. In still another major position which was to be eventually adopted, Bryan favored universal suffrage for women. A Populist at heart, Bryan also favored the recall, the referendum, and the initiative, as well as the direct election of Senators.

The election of 1912 found Bryan in the position of President maker. The normally cool Republicans were hotly divided. Theodore Roosevelt wanted his old job back, but William Howard Taft and the regular party machinery were retaining control. Bryan sensed victory for the Democrats and decided to support Woodrow Wilson over Speaker of the House Champ Clark, although Wilson had refused to support the Democratic ticket in 1896, had refused to run as Vice President on the 1908 ticket, and had on one occasion hoped to "knock Bryan once and for all into a cocked hat." Yet Bryan admired the way Wilson had repelled New Jersey political bosses and felt that a progressive Democrat had the best chance of winning the Presidency. When he learned that Alton B. Parker was to be temporary chairman of the Convention, he ran in opposition, losing by less than 100 votes. Later, however, he out-maneuvered the conservatives when he introduced a resolution stating "...we hereby declare ourselves opposed to the nomination of any candidate for President who is the representative of or under any obligation to J. Pierpoint Morgan, Thomas F. Ryan, August Belmont, or any other member of the privilege-hunting and favor-seeking class." From this position, which was overwhelmingly adopted, Bryan maneuvered the nomination of Wilson. Wilson was able to defeat Roosevelt and Taft, and he named William Jennings Bryan as his Secretary of State.

SECRETARY OF STATE

Though inexperienced in foreign affairs, Bryan's tenure was to be relatively successful. He and the new President were very cordial. Unfortunately, his friendship with Speaker Champ Clark waned. The new President
allowed Bryan to use his conscience about drinking at state affairs, and the
"tee-totaler" did refuse to drink at state dinners. Bryan negotiated a host of
treaties, especially with Latin and South American countries. When
Mexican authorities stirred up trouble in 1913, Bryan was in the lead to see
that American honor was preserved. Of course a break between Wilson and
Bryan occurred over the impending war with Germany. When the *Lusitania*
was sunk, Bryan felt that the United States knew that contraband was being
shipped and that the United States should have expected Germany to protect
its interests in the way it did. He could not endorse Wilson's stern messages
and resigned as Secretary of State in 1915. Even after resigning, though,
Wilson and Bryan remained extremely cordial for some period of time.
Bryan seriously fell out with the President, though, over the Versailles
Treaty. While in favor of the League of Nations, he saw the futility of
Wilson's intransigence and refusal to compromise. After the Democrats
lost in 1920, a campaign in which he refused to speak for his party, he called
upon Wilson to resign and allow Vice President Marshall to succeed. He
then wanted "President Marshall" to appoint Warren Harding Secretary of
State and then resign, letting Harding assume the Presidency and satisfy the
mandate of the people at once.

DEATH OF A CRUSADER

Bryan's wife was beginning to become very frail, and the couple moved
to Florida in 1921. There he speculated in real estate and was retained to
speak in the interests of Florida Realtors, increasing his wealth. He was
pleased that his three children were achieving successful marriages (one
daughter had remarried after a bitter first marriage). He continued to speak
on temperance and other issues of the day, and he represented for a fee many
varied interests.

The convention of 1924 was to be the last for the man whose oratory had
inspired and galvanized so many past Democratic conclaves. It also offered
some deep embarrassment. Woodrow Wilson's son-in-law, William
McAdoo, was the leading candidate. Bryan initially withheld his support
but then swung to McAdoo, who had three important bases of support:
Bryan, the dries and the Ku Klux Klan! Unfortunately Bryan took to the
podium one last time to debate a major measure, but when he tried to explain
that the words "Ku Klux Klan" were of no significance to the platform, he

— the Eloquent Boy Orator of the Platte, the Silver Knight, the Great Commoner, three times the party candidate — was hissed. The convention swung to John W. Davis of West Virginia and then, perhaps as a gesture of conciliation to their past leader, chose Bryan's brother, Charles, as the Vice Presidential nominee. They were overwhelmingly defeated in November.

Bryan's last major act was the Scopes Monkey Trial in Dayton, Tennessee. This was the famous case where a group of merchants in the small East Tennessee community met at a corner drug store and decided that the arrest of school teacher Scopes for teaching evolution might bring prominence — and commerce — to their town. No one dreamed that it would attract William Jennings Bryan and Clarence Darrow. What followed was a classic American courtroom battle, with the fundamentalist Bryan in the midst of the Bible Belt taking on the agnostic Darrow, supported by the American Civil Liberties Union. The most dramatic point in the trial came when the clever Darrow called Bryan to the stand and subjected him to a scathing examination of his beliefs, all the time cajoling and ridiculing him, Bryan all the time verifying the childlike faith taught him by since his birth sixty-five years before. Bryan won the case, but he was subjected to a barrage of publicity that forever tarnished his historical effectiveness on the issues he had espoused: free coinage; the rights of the common laborer against the trusts; prohibition; women's suffrage; anti-imperialism; recall, referendum and the initiative; the direct election of Senators; and so many other causes...

Sadly, Bryan died unexpectedly a few days later. Dayton was to remember him by erecting Bryan College in his honor. As the train bearing his remains traveled to Washington, thousands of America's common folk came to train stations along the way to pay their respect to "The Peerless Leader." Washington remembered him with an outpouring of more than twenty thousand persons passing by his coffin, perhaps the greatest expression of sympathy since Lincoln's death. He was then buried in Arlington National Cemetery. The golden voice of William Jennings Bryan, the most eloquent of the age, forever to be remembered in American history, was now silent.

Alton Brooks Parker

The Election of 1904

Poor Alton Brooks Parker! Of all Presidential candidates, none is so obscured by the passing of time as is the 1904 Democratic nominee, who had the misfortune of being nominated by a party in disarray and then having the unenviable task of facing Teddy Roosevelt while TR was at the height of his popularity. So overwhelming was his defeat and so inglorious his memory that even today no scholar has come forward to write a definitive biography of his life.

NEW YORK FARM BOY

The ancestry of Parker can be traced to colonial Massachusetts, where his great-grandfather was a planter who took up arms and fought as a soldier under George Washington in the Revolutionary War. The descendants of this fighter for Independence subsequently moved to New York, settling in Courtland. Alton's father was himself a planter and known for being well read and concerned for his fellow citizens. He was wed to Harriet Straton, and from this union Alton Brooks Parker was born at the Courtland farm of his parents on May 14, 1852.

Young Alton performed the usual chores of a nineteenth century farm boy. He attended the Courtland village school and then the Courtland Academy. He had hoped to attend Cornell University, but the family's finances were not sufficient to permit this, and, at age sixteen, he accepted a position as a schoolmaster in Courtland at a salary of $3 per day. Tradition has it that young Alton was confronted by the school bully and thrashed him soundly in order to maintain order.

INTO LAW AND POLITICS

Unable to attend college but wanting to advance himself, the bright young schoolteacher decided to "read books" in a Kingston, New York law office. Enough income was saved from this employment for Alton to attend the Albany Law School, and he graduated from that institution in 1873. He returned to the Kingston firm which first hired him to continue reading books and to begin trying cases in court. He was soon representing Ulster County against the City of Kingston in a matter of property assessments, and when he went to court, he won nearly every contested point. Not only were county officials pleased, but so were rural residents who were obviously concerned over their tax rates.

Shortly after this, the ambitious young Parker decided to leave his firm and form a partnership with a fellow attorney. For the next twelve years he practiced in various state courts, establishing a reputation as a very able attorney. He also established a reputation as a man of exceptional principle and integrity.

In 1873 Parker took as his wife Mary Louise Schoonmaker. The couple had one daughter. They set up housekeeping in Courtland, but as Parker prospered, they purchased three farms, the favorite being at Esopus on the Hudson River. Parker was an avid horseman and farmer, often assisting in the planting and cultivation of crops.

Parker entered politics quite by chance. One of the partners in his old law firm had been attacked by political opponents, and Parker decided to come to his assistance. A long fight ensued over the matter, and Parker ultimately prevailed. In the meantime he was recognized as one who understood the makeup of political organizations. The Democratic Party in Ulster County recognized him as its best organizer, and Gov. Samuel Tilden regarded Parker as his chief lieutenant in the area.

In 1877 Parker engaged in his first race for public office, winning the post of County Surrogate. The twenty-five year old attorney apparently performed his duties well, for he was re-elected in 1883 with no Republican opposition.

STATE SUPREME COURT JUSTICE

Parker attended the 1884 Democratic National Convention as a delegate from New York pledged to New York Governor Grover Cleveland. When Cleveland won the Presidency, he offered Parker the position of First Assistant Postmaster General, but Parker declined the appointment, considering it too political. However, he accepted the position of Chairman of the Democratic State Executive Committee and then managed the successful 1885 campaign of David Hill to become Governor of the Empire State. Soon after Hill was inaugurated, a vacancy due to the death of a judge occurred on the State Supreme Court, and the new Governor named Alton Brooks Parker to the state's highest judicial body. Parker was only thirty-three at the time of his appointment.

Parker's work on the court was recognized by other judges and lawyers practicing before the court as outstanding. He was appointed again to the high court in 1889, 1892 and 1896. His decisions while on the bench tended to be liberal. For example, in one celebrated case, he found that unions had the right to strike to obtain a closed shop *(National Protective Steamfitters vs. Cumming)*. In another, he ruled constitutional a provision limiting the amount of work in a bakery to sixty hours per week *(The People vs. Lochner)*. While these cases had a liberal strain, he also believed strongly in using common law as a basis for judicial decisions but did not believe the courts should interpret legislative acts unless they were specifically unconstitutional.

In 1897 Parker was nominated by the Democratic Party to run for Chief Justice of the New York Court of Appeals. This was but one year after the 1897 national election year that had pitted William McKinley against the young William Jennings Bryan over the issue of gold or silver coinage, with the nation overwhelmingly rejecting Bryan and other Democratic candidates and leaving Eastern states practically void of either Democratic Senators or Governors. Thus, when Alton B. Parker won his 1897 statewide judge's race by the significant margin of more than 60,000 votes, he was immediately regarded as a formidable future candidate for higher office and was immediately thrust into the limelight of national politics. He was suddenly deluged with requests from both Tammany and anti-Tammany Democrats to run for Governor of New York, but as a man of strong-willed principle who believed in the independence of the Judiciary, he declined all offers.

DEMOCRATIC NOMINEE FOR PRESIDENT

Bryan received the Democratic nomination again in 1900 but was again defeated by an overwhelming majority, and Democratic candidates for high offices in traditionally Democratic states again suffered inglorious defeats. As the election of 1904 approached, it was the consensus feeling of influential Democrats that a conservative candidate who favored the gold standard might be more palatable to the national corporations which had been the object of trust proceedings by the administration of Theodore Roosevelt. The same influential party leaders felt that their nominee should be from the East, and, although only a State Chief Justice, Alton Parker was one of the highest ranking officials in that area that had won a statewide election.

A movement was begun to bring about his nomination, but Parker refused to sanction it, stating, despite the urgings of both friend and foe, his long established belief that members of the Judiciary should remain free of political maneuverings and not make political statements. David Hill, the former New York Governor whose campaign Parker had managed in 1885, led the fight at the St. Louis convention in behalf of the New York jurist. Parker received the nomination of the convention but then, in one of the strangest actions of any national party meeting, sent a telegram frankly stating his support of the gold standard and allowing the nominating body to withdraw his name if it did not understand his position. Such a move in the face of the still powerful influence of William Jennings Bryan, the nominee in 1896 and 1900 who favored the silver standard, was an action of principle. The delegates voted by a larger margin than it had in granting him the nomination that this presented no problem to the Democratic Party. The convention then chose Henry G. Davis of West Virginia as its Vice Presidential nominee.

While party leaders may have intuitively felt that the choice of an Eastern conservative was the way to victory, they could not have been more wrong. Theodore Roosevelt, the hero of San Juan Hill who had impressively presided over the nation after the assassination of William McKinley and then taken on the giants of American business in various trust actions, was in full command of the political scene. Parker chose to conduct a front porch campaign and make few speeches, which were regarded as sincere but lacking motivation. Toward the end of the campaign the Democratic nominee charged that Roosevelt was accepting huge corporate donations, a charge that later was proven to be true, but a charge that Parker would not verify when questioned by the press because he had received the information in confidence.

The election of 1904 was the most one-sided landslide in the popular vote in the history of the country. While Parker carried the solid South, Roosevelt swept the rest of the nation, gathering 60 percent of the popular vote, winning by a margin of over 2,500,000 out of 12,500,000 votes cast, and winning in the Electoral College by 336 to 140.

PROMINENT LAWYER

After the election, Parker resumed his law practice and became one of the nation's leading labor lawyers. He joined in partnership with E.W. Hatch and William F. Sheehan, and this firm was succeeded by the firm of Parker, Auchincloss and Marshall, with offices on Broadway Avenue. He represented the American Federation of Labor in many actions, including those in which the famed labor leader, Samuel Gompers, was tried in contempt proceedings. The former Chief Justice was also selected to be the prosecuting attorney in the impeachment proceedings of New York Governor William Sulzer. In 1912 Parker was selected to be the temporary Chairman of the Democratic National Convention in Baltimore. He opposed the nomination of Woodrow Wilson but supported him in the general election. (Wilson never really liked the 1904 candidate). Parker, an eminent attorney, served as President of the New York Bar Association and the American Bar Association. He was also President of the National Civic Federation.

In 1917 Parker's wife of forty-four years passed away. He took a second wife, Amelia Day Campbell of New York City, in 1923. This wife and his daughter by his first marriage survived him when he passed away in New York City on May 10, 1926, after suffering a heart attack while being chauffeured through Central Park on the way to his Esopus farm to recuperate from bronchial pneumonia. A memorial service was conducted at St. Thomas Episcopal Church in New York City, and then his body was returned to his native Kingston for interment. Condolences were received by the survivors from President Calvin Coolidge, Charles Evans Hughes, James M. Cox, John W. Davis and a host of other prominent Americans, who paused at that time to remember the contributions of a man who was valuable to the Democratic traditions of his country, though today he is practically forgotten.

Charles Evans Hughes
The Election of 1916

The two leading statesmen of their time were Woodrow Wilson and Charles Evans Hughes, and they faced each other in the 1916 Presidential election. Hughes went to bed thinking that he had scored an upset, but when he awoke the next morning, he found that the voters of California had cast their lot with President Wilson, allowing the incumbent to retain the Chief Magistracy by a narrow margin.

It is unfortunate that Hughes is so scantily remembered today, for he made outstanding contributions to the nation and the world community. A man of unusual legal and administrative abilities, he was blessed with little political skill. This weakness cost him the singular office so many men have sought and so few have gained.

SON OF A NEW YORK PREACHER

Charles Evans Hughes's father was a Welshman who immigrated to the United States in 1855 as a Methodist minister. After pastoring Methodist congregations in New York for several years, David Hughes met a teacher named Mary Connelly, of American lineage for several generations, and a Baptist. Mary's parents were not eager to see the two wed, but Rev. Hughes overcame obstacles by converting to the Baptist faith. He married Mary in 1860. Their only child was born on April 11, 1862 in Glen Falls, New York.

The young Hughes boy belonged to parents who moved about quite often as the Rev. Hughes served one congregation and then another. Formal schooling for Charles in his younger years was avoided not only because of the transient nature of his father's position but because Charles was an exceptionally bright boy who learned to read in his home by age three-and-a-half and was reading the Bible and Shakespeare by age eight. He persuaded his parents to allow him to study privately at home rather than in the confines of schools. At age nine he entered public schools in New York City; he graduated from high school at age fifteen as Salutatorian of P.S. 35.

Charles then entered Madison University (later named Colgate), and for a time it appeared that he would follow his parents wishes of becoming a Baptist minister like his father. Soon, however, Hughes wanted to escape the rigors of the Baptist Seminary. He convinced his parents to let his enroll in Brown University. There, Hughes was a rather active student, participating in many student organizations. Though somewhat of a loner, he was respected for his scholarly abilities. He was elected to Phi Beta Kappa, and he delivered a commencement address on "The First Appearance of Sophocles." Hughes had been greatly influenced by his liberal arts professors at Brown and by their methods of instructions. His inquiring mind did not lead him to question the beliefs of his parents, but he was nearing that point in life where he would pursue the vocation of law rather than the Baptist ministry that they desired for him.

The final decision to study for the bar came while Hughes taught mathematics at a high school academy shortly after graduating from Brown. He enrolled in Columbia Law School and received a conservative indoctrination of legal theory and proceedings that was to guide his entire law career. Yet he also received somewhat of a liberal, humanitarian outlook that was to have a pronounced influence on his later years as a progressive politician and statesman. Graduating from Columbia in 1884, Hughes took the New York bar exam, passing with the extraordinarily high score of 99 1/2. At age twenty-two, he was admitted to the practice of law.

LAWYER AND CIVIC MINDED CITIZEN

For the next twenty years Hughes was to be a model lawyer and citizen. He was fortunate enough to become a member of the prestigious firm of Chamberlain, Carter & Hornblower, for whom he had worked part-time while attending college. He quickly adapted to the legal profession and was soon handling clients such as Joseph Pulitzer and prominent railroads. His ability and legal scholarship were such that when a reorganization of his firm became necessary in 1887 due to the resignations of Chamberlain and Hornblower, he was made a full partner in the firm. Hughes was only twenty-five years of age.

Hughes had met Netty Carter, daughter of the managing partner, shortly after joining the firm but did not have the nerve to court her until he became a full partner. Now he began to see her regularly, and they were married in 1888. Their marriage was ideal for his career. She was Republican, but more than that, she knew, due to being an attorney's daughter, the rigors that her husband faced daily. She did much to shield him from the pressures of home life, and she encouraged him in his profession. The couple had one son and three daughters.

A Republican and a Baptist by birth, Hughes joined the New York Republican Club and the Fifth Avenue Baptist Church. He was active in his congregation, serving on the Board of Trustees with John D. Rockefeller,

Sr. and teaching a Sunday School Class attended by and later taught by John D. Rockefeller, Jr. He was elected head of the New York Baptist Social Union and President of the Northern Baptist Convention.

Continuing his highly successful commercial practice, Hughes was brought into public life quite by accident. A scandal was rocking the gas utility industry, and a special counsel was needed to investigate improprieties. Hughes was selected over the protest of certain papers who felt that his connection with the Rockefellers would create a "white wash," but his "model inquiry," which revealed numerous illegal actions by the Consolidated Gas Company, made him a highly respected individual.

Next, Hughes was asked by the New York legislature to act as special counsel in investigating improprieties in the insurance industry. Hughes again undertook a formidable task with excellent investigative results. His findings indicated that Mutual Life, New York Life, a partner of J.P. Morgan, a state Senator who was Republican boss of New York, and U.S. Senator Chaucey DePew were all involved in stock manipulations that were defrauding policyholders through the purchase of political influence by extremely large contributions to the Republican Party.

Though a Republican, Hughes had investigated and reported truthful findings that were extremely embarrassing to his party. This was at a time that the extremely popular President Teddy Roosevelt, former Governor of New York, was at the peak of his political influence. One piece of information Hughes had discovered was that a contribution of $49,000 had been made by New York Life to the Republican National Committee during Roosevelt's campaign of 1904.

Despite the embarrassment caused Roosevelt, the sitting President thought the Party would be wise to nominate the reform minded Hughes for Governor of New York. Though Hughes was not seeking the position, word from Roosevelt led to a unanimous nomination that he could not decline.

He was matched in the race against the crafty William Randolph Hearst, a New York Democratic fixture for several decades. With little political experience, especially as it related to extolling appeals to ethnic groups, Hughes nonetheless waged a successful campaign, defeating Hearst by some 58,000 votes. At age forty-five, Hughes had in his first political campaign been elected Governor of New York.

GOVERNOR OF NEW YORK

The office of Governor of New York has always been one of the strongest political positions in the country, often serving as a springboard to the Presidency. In the early 1900's, it was a position also to bring about great social changes. Theodore Roosevelt, Charles Evans Hughes, Alfred E. Smith and Franklin D. Roosevelt would all be remembered for their innovative techniques to bring about change from this forum.

No sooner had he become Governor than did Hughes press for changes in New York. Under his administration came regulations for railroads, an eight-hour workday for certain railwaymen, and countless safety reforms. Also, the nation's first workman's compensation law were passed in New York during Hughes' administration.

But at times Hughes was a recalcitrant politician who was not easy to move on certain issues. He would not approve a measure to grant equal pay to women teachers, and he would not appoint a member of labor to the Public Service Commission simply because he was a labor union member. Hughes also simply did not see the necessity of providing political favors, making appointments on merit without first consulting political leaders. Soon he had Republican leaders talking of running him for Vice President (as they had done for Teddy Roosevelt in 1900) to get him out of the way, even though he had gained the support of countless "Good Government" groups.

To his aid came once again the President himself. TR summoned New York Republican leaders to Washington and laid down the law — Hughes would be supported by the Party. To show he meant business, TR dismissed an opponent of Hughes as the Collector of Customs at Rochester with a comment to reporters that he was strengthening Hughes's position. Hughes then made perhaps the biggest political blunder of his career. He told a reporter that he "...had known nothing about it [the removal] until it was publicly announced."

The President was furious. Immediately the Republican controlled New York State Senate voted to override a dismissal that Hughes sought. Roosevelt in the months and years to come would speak of the "colossal ingratitude" of Hughes, sometimes referring to him as a "cold fish." And while TR would support Hughes for re-election as Governor in 1908, he would throw the Presidential nomination the same year to William Howard Taft, though there was much national sentiment already for Hughes. TR put on the finishing touches to the demise of Hughes in 1908 after The New York City Republican Club had endorsed the Governor for President and was holding a banquet for the President to announce his support in the Governor's race. As the chief speaker, Roosevelt used the occasion to call for tariff revisions and a strengthening of the Sherman Anti-Trust Law. He also made a blistering attack on the Congress. But TR's real purpose with this address was to deny publicity for Hughes. "If he is going to play the game," said the President, "he must learn the tricks."

Hughes managed even after the split with TR to attain certain goals by bypassing New York Republican leaders and taking some issues (such as the creation of the Public Service Commission and a move against race track betting) directly to the people. After Taft won on the first ballot, an offer was made for Hughes to receive the Vice Presidential nomination, but he declined the overture. Hughes was undecided as to whether or not to run for a second term as Governor but finally consented to do so. Roosevelt, fearful that the Republicans might lose, came to the aid of Hughes, saying privately, "Hughes is not a man I care for;...but he is a financially honest man and one of much ability..." On election day Hughes was returned by 69,000 votes.

Hughes plunged once again into fights for reforms, especially one for primary elections. He was constantly at odds with the legislature and was growing weary of his office. In March of 1910, President Taft visited Albany and stayed at the Governor's mansion. The two Republican leaders had the opportunity to talk and become intimate. Before he left Albany, Taft promised Hughes that if the position of Chief Justice became vacant while he was President, he would appoint Hughes. Just a few days later, an Associate Justice died, and Taft offered the appointment to Hughes, with the promise that he would later appoint Hughes Chief Justice if that vacancy occurred. In 1910, at age forty-eight, after only three years as Governor, and with no other political offices behind him, Charles Evans Hughes was going to Washington as one of the top nine judicial officials in the land.

SUPREME COURT JUSTICE

The Supreme Court was a medium in which Charles Evans Hughes was comfortable. He was able in part to be an advocate for the social issues that he desired to be implemented, and he was also able to employ the rigorous discipline imparted through his childhood, his formative college years, his years studying at Columbia, his two decades of legal work and his tenure as a special counsel and as Governor.

The Court Hughes joined was an elderly one, but it was composed of some distinguished Justices, including Oliver Wendell Holmes. The elderly Chief Justice soon assigned some of the more laborious research work to the forty-eight year old Hughes, who responded in a scholarly fashion. On one occasion a fellow Justice said that an opinion that Hughes was rendering was "...as able and important an opinion as any ever delivered from this Bench..."

Hughes played a major role in many decisions. He supported the right of the Interstate Commerce Commission to intervene in the setting of interstate rates. And he held generally a favorable attitude toward labor, being against "yellow-dog" contracts, and holding also that aliens working in Arizona were entitled to equal access under the law. He also voted to uphold child labor laws. Civil rights questions received mixed opinions. An Alabama case requiring compulsory "peonage" of a black man for debts was overridden. But another case, in which equal railway dining car facilities in Oklahoma had not been provided, was dismissed due to a lack of proper legal work by the minority attorneys. A Georgia case involving the intimidation of a jury to convict a black man for murder was also overridden by the Court on which Hughes served.

In but six short years, Hughes made a powerful imprint upon the Supreme Court. He was genuinely respected by his colleagues. He was also respected by many Republican leaders who thought he should serve in a higher position, President of the United States of America.

CANDIDATE FOR PRESIDENT IN 1916

When Hughes accepted the appointment to the bench in 1910, most people felt that his partisan political career was finished. Never before had a Justice run for the Presidency. Additionally, Hughes did not appear to have the proper demeanor for politics and had alienated some Republican leaders, particularly Teddy Roosevelt.

But the political blood bath of 1912 involving Taft and Roosevelt found a Democrat now occupying the White House. Woodrow Wilson, a reformist who had adopted many of the policies put forth by Hughes when he was Governor of New York, had taken advantage of the Republican rift to win the Presidency.

There had been talk of nominating Hughes in 1912, but he flatly refused to be considered because of the possible damage that could be done to the Supreme Court. As 1916 approached, a more serious consideration of Hughes began since he had not been involved in the bitter melee of 1912 and since he was both experienced and well known nationally. Still Hughes refused to either publicly or privately allow his name to be used, forbidding, for example, the entrance of his name in the Nebraska primary.

But as the Convention in Chicago approached, some adept political bosses maneuvered him into the position of considering being nominated. On the third ballot he achieved the necessary two-thirds to be selected. He had apparently considered his chances for nomination good and he also apparently wanted to get on the campaign trail quickly, for as soon as he received a telegram notifying him of his nomination, he immediately wired President Wilson, "... I hereby resign the office of Associate Justice of the Supreme Court of the United States." Then he sent a telegram accepting the Republican nomination.

A supporter said that Hughes "would be strongest on the day he was nominated and weakest on election day." This proved to be precisely the case for the politically inept Hughes. The first mistake that Hughes made was to appoint an incompetent man to chair the Republican National Committee. Next, he failed to identify issues properly and made speeches that may have appeared scholarly on paper but which lacked political charisma. He also failed to appeal to the minority and ethnic groups essential for election.

Teddy Roosevelt agreed to campaign for the temerous Hughes, but his efforts probably hurt the candidate when he called for the Republican Party to get prepared for the upcoming war. Wilson's placid theme, "He kept us out of War," seemed to be much more appealing to the American public.

But perhaps the biggest campaign mistake was made in California, where a campaign between the Progressive Hiram Johnson and a conservative Republican was heated. When Hughes visited the state, he refused to take sides, and this angered Johnson, who had been Teddy Roosevelt's running mate on the 1912 "Bull Moose" ticket. While Hughes made other mistakes, such as attending a banquet in a California hotel under strike, the Johnson rebuff probably cost him the election.

The November 1912 returns were the tightest since the Hayes-Tilden election in 1876. Hughes carried almost all of the industrial East and midwestern states, while Wilson won the Solid South and most of the Western states. Several combinations could have made Hughes President, but his biggest loss came in California, where the reform minded Johnson won by over 300,000 votes and where Hughes lost by 3,000. Hughes also lost New Hampshire by less than 100 votes and North Dakota by less than 2,000. Several small shifts could have changed the fate of the country, but Wilson prevailed, winning the Electoral College by 277 to 254.

PRIVATE CITIZEN

Unhappy at losing, Hughes did not, however, wallow in a period of moroseness. He resumed his practice of law, becoming so successful that his income would reach $400,000 per year. His practice bordered on the spectacular, as he defended Michigan Sen. Travis Newberry on corruption charges, and as he took on the case of five Socialist members of the New York Assembly who were expelled by Republican leaders because they were opposed to American involvement in World War I. The case involving the Socialists was a bitter and divisive one for the Republican Party. Hughes managed to get the New York City Bar to call for justice in the matter but the Republican controlled Assembly rebuffed Hughes by passing a law outlawing the Socialist Party. The titular head of the national Party was still lacking control of his own state's party machinery.

When war came, Hughes made no statement claiming that if he had been elected the conflict would have been avoided. Instead, he called for public support of President Wilson's actions and served as Chairman of the New York Draft Appeals Board. Later, he headed an investigation into the delays of the aircraft industry in getting war planes to the Army.

Of course, Hughes came to disagree violently with President Wilson upon the terms of settlement of the Great War. Wilson had made the mistake of visiting Paris and acting as his own Secretary of State, thus offering himself to the Republicans for open criticism. He probably aggravated the problem by not having a Republican as a member of his negotiating team. The ensuing battle over the Versailles Treaty was largely along political lines. The President would make no compromise, though Hughes made a strong appeal for him to do so. Wilson destroyed his own personal health as he fought stubbornly for his ideals and refused to conciliate. He also destroyed the chances of victory for his party in the 1920 election.

That election pitted Warren G. Harding and Calvin Coolidge against the Democratic team of Gov. James Cox of Ohio for President, and the Assistant Secretary of the Navy, Franklin Delano Roosevelt, for Vice President. Hughes had shown no interest in the nomination and received no serious consideration. Harding, who had been chosen as a compromise candidate because he looked like a President was supposed to, won by a landslide.

SECRETARY OF STATE

Harding is vilified as one of the nation's worst Presidents, and certainly his administration was filled with corruption. Yet he did make several noteworthy appointments. For Chief Justice he selected former President William Howard Taft, who performed much better in that role than as President. For Secretary of Commerce he chose an experienced administrator who had been a successful mining engineer and the distributor of food to the world's needy, and who would in 1929 become President of the United States, Herbert Hoover. Another noteworthy appointment was that of Charles Evans Hughes as Secretary of State.

The placid new President made it clear that he would not conduct his own foreign affairs. He also made it clear that he would not oppose isolationist Republican Senators who were violently opposed to Wilson's dream for a League of Nations. While Hughes entertained some hopes for such an organization, he soon found that it would be fruitless to pursue such a goal, and he arranged a separate peace with Germany.

Hughes was very effective in several causes. He took the lead in having the United States join the World Court, which came about only by his patient efforts. His largest contributions, however, came in his actions to control the arms race after World War I.

This was probably the only bright historical spot of the Harding Administration. While the nation languished in charges of graft and corruption, Hughes in 1921 called the Washington Conference on the Limitation of Arms. As Chairman he called for "...a practical program which shall at once be put into execution." The conference adopted several treaties, the most important of which was the Five-Power Treaty. This agreement among Great Britain, France, Italy, Japan and the United States called for a substantial scrapping of war vessels and for a "holiday" in the construction of new warships. The conference also took action to outlaw poisonous gas in war, to keep the "open door" policy in China, and to resolve future disputes over Pacific Islands by negotiations rather than conflict.

In retrospect, Hughes's efforts have been condemned because the actual production of war-making vessels did not decline. Within a decade, Germany, Italy and Japan would be pursuing goals of war rather than peace. Some critics would later claim that the Japanese secretly sought revenge against the United States because of an unfair formula put forth by Hughes for deleting tonnages. Hughes efforts were earnest endeavors that did not sense the deviousness of warmongers. The culmination of his efforts was the Brian-Kellogg Peace Pact of 1928, to which over sixty nations eventually affixed signatures of peace. Hughes, having just witnessed the ravages of World War I, was earnestly working for a solution to the disputes of nations other than war.

It was his fervent desire to avoid war that caused Hughes to negotiate gross reductions in the amounts of war loans made to allies and to also allow the new negotiated balances to be paid over periods of time of up to sixty-two years, with interest rates no higher than three per cent. Many Americans now feel that the United States was humiliated by this policy since, one by one, all allies except Finland refused to make repayment.

Hughes rejected the idea of granting diplomatic recognition to the Soviet Union. The memory of the Czar's murder and the "Red Scare" of the 1920's were probably the reasons Hughes sought no friendship with the new communist state. In Latin American affairs, he was stern in warning other world powers that the Monroe Doctrine was still the policy of the United States.

After four years in office, Hughes decided to resign and return to the practice of law. Not since William Seward or perhaps James G. Blaine (another unsuccessful candidate for the Presidency) had there been such a forceful and effective leader of foreign policy. Unlike many an unsuccessful candidate for President, Hughes is remembered today, but it is more so for his accomplishments as Secretary of State than as a Presidential candidate.

CHIEF JUSTICE

For three years Hughes practiced law, accumulating a sizable fortune. He also engaged in public service when possible, serving upon the request of Gov. Alfred E. Smith, for example, as Chairman of a Commission for the Reorganization of the Government of New York State . Additionally, he began to write some scholarly pieces on his life's work and on the institutions he had served. His works included *The Pathway to Peace* and *The Supreme Court of the United States,* among other works.

In 1928 he was called again into public service. The World Court, for which Hughes had secured the affiliation of the United States, now had a vacancy, and President Coolidge appointed Hughes to the position. Hughes held this position for only two years and then was appointed the eleventh Chief Justice of the Supreme Court when William Howard Taft, only a month away from death, resigned. The choice was a sound one by President Hoover but not necessarily, during the Depression, a politically good one. A Senate floor fight ensued, with twenty-six dissenting votes out of a total of seventy-eight being cast against the nominee. The Senate did ratify his appointment, though, and Charles Evans Hughes was returning to the medium which he thoroughly enjoyed and where he could be most effective in his lifelong pursuit of social reform.

For fourteen years he occupied the position of Chief Justice. At the time the Court was known for its conservative opinions while the nation under FDR was clamoring for dramatic change. Hughes himself was regarded as an arch-conservative in his opinions, but he was in fact still a social minded reformer, casting votes, for example, in favor of the right of railway workers to organize and in favor of the Tennessee Valley Authority to construct dams. He fell into disfavor with the New Deal when he joined other Justices in declaring the National Recovery Act unconstitutional. However, it was Hughes who led the Court into broad new areas of judicial authority, asserting time and time again that "due process under the law" and "equal protection under the law," were the law of the land. The Hughes Court was a scholarly, if rigid, one, that upon reflection seems to have been the precursor of the Warren Court a generation later.

The same Court under Hughes that ruled against the NRA also used a broad construal of the "general welfare" clause of the Preamble to the Constitution to allow the Agricultural Adjustment Act. Hughes was with the Court Majority in declaring unconstitutional an Oklahoma act requiring a license for selling ice, but he was with the majority in allowing New York to fix milk prices. In a paradox, he voted at first to disallow a minimum wage for women in New York, only to change his position in a Washington case one year later because "economic circumstances had supervened."

Activity in the Hughes Court was constant. The Court ruled the Governor of Texas was violating "due process" when he tried to fix oil production during a period of martial law. The Court also took a rather strong position on Civil Rights, dismissing an Alabama case against the "Scottsboro [black] boys," who had been denied proper counsel in the rape trial of a white girl. A Missouri case found the Court ruling that a black should be admitted to the university law school because there were not "separate but equal facilities." A series of decisions under the Hughes Court disallowed certain voting laws, including the "grandfather" acts against blacks. A final case found a Georgia Negro who was a Communist acquitted of charges that he had violated a pre-Civil War statute to incite revolution.

It was during the Hughes Court that a number of religious freedom cases were heard. In one celebrated case an immigrant Yale theology professor was denied citizenship when he said he would not fight in a war he could not conscientiously support. Hughes joined the majority in another case which allowed members of the Jehovah's Witnesses to distribute literature without a permit on, the grounds that it was a violation of freedom of religion.

In a celebrated freedom of press case, a suit for slander involving sensational reporting against public officials alleged to be involved in bootlegging and racketeering was denied by the Hughes Court.

The Hughes Court on the whole, though, is most remembered for the scheme of President Franklin Delano Roosevelt to add more members to the top judicial body. The Democratic leader was not happy with many decisions of the Court, especially the one to outlaw the NRA. After an overwhelming re-election in 1936, FDR attempted his "packing" scheme, but this was rejected by the Congress. Hughes was at one point prepared to testify before a Congressional committee on the matter, but he was persuaded by Justice Brandeis, a liberal whom he greatly respected, not to appear but give a written statement instead. Hughes's letter was a masterful defense of the Court's procedures and efficiency and helped convince the Democratic Congress to rebuff the Democratic President.

Nonetheless, it is believed that the measure so frightened some members of the Supreme Court that ways were found to be more conciliatory to New Deal legislation. The Wagner Labor Relations Act was approved, for example, with the Chief Justice casting the deciding vote in a five to four decision. The Court also upheld the Holding Companies Act and a measure to devalue the gold standard by almost 50 percent. And a minimum wage law was not repudiated when it later came before the top judicial body.

Hughes provided perhaps his greatest service to the Court and the entire federal judiciary system by being the most responsible Chief Administrator in some time. He persuaded the Court to approve new rules of civil procedure, and he expedited the work of lower courts. Attuned to the increasing necessity for litigation in the judiciary system, he made earnest efforts to streamline a legal system growing more cumbersome by the day.

RETIREMENT

In 1941, after eleven years as the eleventh Chief Justice, Hughes tendered his resignation to President Roosevelt. He was now seventy-nine years of age and knew, as his earlier writings about the Court indicated, that Justices often served beyond the time of their effective capability. The tenor of the Court had changed to a distinctly more liberal one than the one he had joined, but he realized that he probably would not survive until a Republican President was in office and could appoint a Chief Justice with views similar to his own.

His performance as a Chief Justice ranks among the highest of all who have held that post. Friend and foe alike issued statements of praise for his dignified service. A mellowed President Roosevelt did not appoint a true radical, but rather Harlan Stone, who had been appointed an Associate Justice by Calvin Coolidge, to replace Hughes.

Retirement was not all rest. He found time in 1945 to write one more scholarly piece, *Nations United for Peace.* He spent more time with his family, as the ravages of age closed in upon him and his wife. He had already lost a daughter in 1919 to tuberculosis. In December of 1945, his wife of fifty-seven years passed away. He took great pride in his namesake, Charles Evans Hughes, Jr., who was quite successful in his own right, having served for a time as Solicitor General of the United States, while the Sr. Hughes was Chief Justice. The Chief Justice, of course, recused himself from cases his son argued before the high court.

Death came to Charles Evans Hughes in 1948, during his eighty-sixth year. Tributes flowed from throughout the land, but perhaps the most fitting expressions were two sessions before the Supreme Court. One was *Proceedings of the Bar and Officers of the Supreme Court of the United States, November 4, 1949* and the other *Proceedings before the Supreme Court, May 8, 1950, In Memory of Charles Evans Hughes.* In the Court Room where he had administered justice for so long came extended and worthy tributes to one of the greatest statesmen and citizens of his age. The former Governor of New York, Secretary of State, Associate and Chief Justice of the Supreme Court, and unsuccessful candidate for President was appropriately honored and remembered for his great abilities as well as his many services to the nation.

James Cox
The Election of 1920

Today James Cox is primarily remembered as the running mate of Franklin Delano Roosevelt — when the latter ran for the Vice Presidency. In his time, Cox was regarded as a formidable politician and as a capable government leader. Unfortunately, his try for the Presidency came when a change from his party's domination was inevitable, and the true contributions he made to his country are today largely forgotten.

AN UNHAPPY BOYHOOD

Born on an Ohio farm near Dayton on March 31, 1870, Cox was descended from a rather undistinguished lineage that had migrated from New York to Ohio after the War of 1812. Cox himself was the seventh child of an unhappy marriage; his parents divorced when he was quite young, with his mother moving out of the household and his father retaining custody of the children. The young boy did not have an affectionate bond for his father, who looked upon his children as a source of labor to boost the family's farm income. Young Jimmy was required to be up before daybreak and in the field plowing until dark. He was also denied the opportunity to have a decent formal education because of his father's need to have the boy's hands working rather than his mind developed.

What education Cox obtained was through sparse sessions in the local one-room schoolhouse, where he read *McGuffey's Reader* and *Venable's History of the United States.* At age sixteen, the young farm boy decided to leave his father and moved from his birthplace of Jacksonburg to Middleton, also near Dayton, to be with his mother and married sister. At Middleton, Cox was tutored by his brother-in-law to become a schoolteacher, and after passing the Ohio exam, he was, at age seventeen, granted a two year's certificate.

SCHOOLTEACHER AND NEWSPAPERMAN

Cox settled into his teaching position and soon advanced to become director of the local night school that taught adults basic skills. He also a became a close friend to a local businessman, Paul J. Sorg, who was the town's leading Democrat and the publisher of a local newspaper, the *Middleton Daily Signal.* On Saturdays and Sundays Cox delivered the local newspaper for extra income and then began working in the paper's print shop. Before long, the newspaper business was in his blood and he decided that someday he would be in the publishing industry himself.

When the young reporter received an opportunity to move to Cincinnati and become the railroad reporter for the *Enquirer*, he quickly accepted and began covering railway expansions from Cincinnati to Chicago in the West and to Chattanooga in the South. Cox enjoyed the travel associated with his position as well as the opportunity to learn of the major commercial ventures of Cincinnati. But when he reported that the president of a large railroad was manipulating stock transactions, his position with his paper was soon in jeopardy. Fortunately, his old mentor, Paul J. Sorg, had been elected Congressman and needed a secretary. He selected his young news friend for the post, and James Cox was now involved both in government and politics.

Cox spent only about two years (from 1894 to 1896) in the nation's Capital, but they were useful years in terms of learning the inner workings of government, the personalities of various political leaders and the practical aspects of elections. In 1894, for example, Cox lined up the votes of Civil War Veterans, an idea unheard of for Democratic candidates. By doing so, his boss won re-election by the slim margin of 202 votes. Cox never forgot that Veterans could make a difference in elections.

In 1896, Congressman Sorg decided not to seek re-election, and Cox was once again seeking employment. With a love for newspapering still in his blood, he decided to purchase a daily in Dayton. To finance this, he borrowed $6,000 from Congressman Sorg and issued $20,000 of stock. At age twenty-six, James Cox was on the way to a successful business and political career.

The newspaper Cox purchased, the *Dayton Daily News*, was an old Democratic daily without much reputation or financial success. Cox quickly proved himself an astute and aggressive publisher. He introduced a woman editor, added a society section, published "neighbors" news, added magazine supplements, used the *Associated Press* wire service to get news faster, and promoted a metropolitan concept for Dayton. He also secured printing equipment that would get his paper to buyers, both in Dayton and in outlying small towns, faster than his competition. Advertising, at special rates to buyers, was secured on the basis that if the buyer did not make money, he did not have to pay for his ads. Within a short time competition that had predicted Cox's failure was itself folding. Within a decade, Cox was firmly entrenched in the newspaper business.

Cox gave his paper the publishing motto, *"the People's paper."* He promoted various concepts, including better parks, traffic systems (including paved roads and a bridge to expedite paper delivery), flood control, and a training school for industrial labor — all with the idea of promoting opportunity for the middle class. But when it came to the rights of minorities, Cox sounded a theme which would today be indeed strange for a Democratic candidate. Cox intimated that appeals for convicted Negro criminals should be limited and further stated that blacks were deficient because their black skulls were thicker than whites, thus leaving less room for their brains. Cox also believed that labor strikes, which he tolerated but did not prefer, should be resolved by arbitration rather than strikes. (He himself once arbitrated a strike at the National Cash Register Company.) When it came to freedom of the press, however, Cox stood firm. He exposed, in a series of articles, the misuse of power in getting a road right-of-way through a residential section, and his paper was hit with a criminal libel suit and the newspaper's doors were padlocked by the sheriff. Some papers predicted Cox's downfall, but soon Cox made bail, won the suit, and saw his circulation dramatically increase. He always bragged thereafter that this was the incident that finally made his paper show some profit.

CONGRESSMAN

Cox's position in the Democratic party and the Dayton area-at-large grew considerably in the decade from 1898 to 1908. His paper became the leading Dayton daily and as its circulation increased from 2,600 to over 35,000. When the traditionally dominant Republican Party had a split in 1908, Cox seized a golden opportunity to become personally involved in politics himself. He received the Democratic nomination for Congress without opposition and then waged a vigorous campaign against a Republican and an Independent. William Jennings Bryan, the three-time Democratic nominee, was brought to Dayton to speak for him. Cox himself traveled the countryside outside Dayton and sounded a populist cry for sound money and banks and better roads and schools, while in the cities he announced his support for a Department of Labor. The three man race benefited Cox, especially since the Republican vote was split, and the Democratic nominee eked out a victory with 49.8 percent of the vote. The thirty-eight year old newspaperman would soon be publishing his views in Washington, D.C.

An active first term Representative, Cox was quick to serve his District. He skillfully maneuvered a bill through the House which brought a new Post Office to Dayton rather than renovate an undersized existing facility. Realizing the political value to him of Veterans, he introduced over 800 individual pension bills. He also introduced a bill calling for subsistence for Soldiers Homes across the nation, a bill of some importance to him personally since one of these Homes, with some 3,000 votes, existed in Dayton. He was named to the House Committee on the District of Columbia (an appointment he did not particularly care for) and successfully introduced legislation to streamline traffic facilities in the nation's Capital. However, efforts to establish a minimum wage for Washington failed. Cox qualified as a Progressive not only because of his anti-trust demeanor but also because he was willing to join other Progressives in challenging the power of the Speaker of the House, Joe Cannon, in making committee assignments. His first term efforts would lead to the election of a new Speaker in 1910.

Cox had little trouble winning re-election, gaining 56 percent of the vote, a record for his District. The Democrats won control of Congress, and a new Speaker, Champ Clark, was named. An assignment to the Appropriations Committee now made the second term Dayton Congressman important, though perhaps not all that powerful. He supported regulation of public works projects financed by the federal government and supported a Children's Bureau for underprivileged youngsters. He also sponsored legislation which gave financial assistance to local governments for the maintenance of local roads. His support in favor of funds to create an air mail postal service, however, was fruitless.

GOVERNOR OF OHIO

Cox, who had outpolled all other Democrats in his District in the 1910 election, was now a popular figure in Ohio. When the Democratic Governor of Ohio, Judson Harmon, decided to give up his Governorship to seek the Presidency in 1912, he asked Cox to be his Congressional representative. The Governor was unsuccessful, of course, but political pundits saw his selection of Cox to an important campaign post as a signal that Cox would be the next Democratic nominee for Governor.

The three term Congressman returned from Washington to indeed announce his candidacy, based upon his experience in government and his support for reforms to the state constitution. Initially, he had some opposition for the nomination, but by the time of the state nominating convention, this opposition had so dissipated that he received the nomination by acclamation. A state constitutional convention had just adjourned after proposing some forty revisions to the state Constitution. These provisions were designed to reform Ohio's agrarian laws by making changes that were more attuned Ohio's new industrial makeup. By endorsing these changes, Cox was able to secure the support of the Progressive wing of his party. Fortunately, a split, as was the case in his first Congressional race, occurred in the Republican Party, and the Progressives fielded a candidate, making the race a three man heat. National assistance to his candidacy came when Woodrow Wilson came to speak in behalf of himself and Cox. When the returns were counted on election day, the forty-two year old Cox was elected Governor of Ohio with a plurality of 41.5 percent of the vote, outpolling his closest rival by 167,000 votes.

Saying in his inaugural address that "civilization was simply a relay race," the progressive but pragmatic new Ohio Governor administered an efficient state government. Himself an experienced legislator, he skillfully guided his programs through the state legislature, soon gaining from the press the title "Boss Cox." A host of new laws were enacted, including a "blue sky" statute to protect investors from fraudulent national securities houses, a bill to put banks under state regulation, a reorganization of the Public Utilities Commission which required municipalities furnishing power to abide by the same regulations as private firms, and the creation of the Ohio Industrial Commission, a three man board empowered to administer workman's compensation laws, safety, working hours for women and children, state unemployment offices, and laws to arbitrate labor disputes. True to his progressive belief, Gov. Cox pushed for an increased workman's compensation benefit, and although the bill was compromised due to the efforts of business, a bill to his satisfaction was enacted.

In addition to being a Progressive in favor of traditional themes such as the initiative and the referendum, Gov. Cox also promoted "scientific management" in government, in which he tried to make objective decisions based on political surveys. This sometimes got him into hot water politically, as when he accepted a maximum nine-hour workday rather than the eight-hour day labor wanted, or when he as a "wet" Governor skirted a new constitutional amendment by having local boards established to regulate taverns rather than doing this politically unsavory task himself. Race matters did not seem to be a part of his progressive agenda, but prison reform was. The Governor often visited state penitentiaries to explain reforms and paroles; on occasion he was cheered by the inmates.

The Progressive Governor's major first term contributions, however, were in the area of state government reorganization. He fought for and won various reform measures, including giving the Governor the power to appoint all state officials except the Governor, Lt. Governor and Supreme Court Justices; granting local governments "home rule" by streamlining procedures for receiving state charters; bringing tax assessment under unified state rather than local control; creating a Civil Service Commission; and reorganizing the education systems, including rural ones, into a modern system that emphasized the industrial development of Ohio. Not all of the new acts were successful, and they were soon to be a political problem for him, but they did show that the new Governor was sensitive to the needs of a new era.

By far the one single event of his administration that displayed his ability as Governor was a flood that struck his state in March of 1913. After eleven inches of rain in five days created $300 million of economic damage and leveled whole towns, disrupting the home life of thousands, Cox responded by declaring martial law and taking control of railroads to distribute food and medical supplies to destitute citizens. Effectively mobilizing public support by giving news stories each day to the newspapers in exchange for publishing urgent requests for food and medical supplies, the Governor soon raised over $250,000 of relief for victims. He also received help from the War Department in his relief effort. Then, as people began digging out of the mud, Cox provide new assistance through the creation of an Ohio Flood Relief Commission and the transfer of state funds to building and loan companies located in the disaster areas. When a bank foreclosed on a mortgage, Cox vented his wrath, causing a reversal and enhancing his image with the flood's victims. For his decisive leadership, Cox was praised in editorials across the nation and received the Red Cross Medal of Merit.

Despite his successes, Cox was defeated in his bid for re-election in 1914. His tax reform measure, which had the state rather than local governments receiving revenues, had proved to be an impossible system for effective collections. Additionally, insurance and business interests mobilized to counteract the effects of the new workman's compensation laws. The race was a bitter one with Democrats making both Anti-Catholic and racial slurs. A divided Democratic Party and the votes of Anti-Saloonists saw Cox lose the election by some 30,000 votes out of slightly more than a million cast. This same 1914 Ohio election produced a new Senator from Ohio — Warren G. Harding.

After six years of service at the federal and state levels, Cox returned to the publishing business and began re-adjusting to private life. Just as when he started his publishing business, Cox devised innovative techniques, such as the use of wire services and weekly magazines, to generate sales. A prominent publisher and former Governor, he decided to build a mansion of Georgian architectural design, which he named "Trailsend," outside Dayton and took up the life of a country squire, constantly entertaining people who could be of future political assistance. Unfortunately, Cox was alone at his mansion insofar as family was concerned; he and his wife had divorced in 1912 after seventeen years of marriage, and he was without a helpmate until 1917, when he married again.

Finding that the newspaper business was not in his blood nearly so much as politics, Cox yearned to return to government and knew that he would be running for Governor again in 1916. Support soon emerged for him, and he received the Democratic nomination with virtually no opposition. Cox campaigned on a platform of honest government and averred that the programs begun under him in 1912 should be completed under him. He also campaigned on the theme that he was helping Woodrow Wilson win Ohio in his bid to win re-election to the White House in 1916. When the returns were tabulated, Cox had barely won, with a plurality of 48.4 percent of the votes and a margin of only 6,600 votes out of nearly 1.2 million cast. President Woodrow Wilson, for whom Cox had said he was campaigning, had carried Ohio by 89,000 votes; the President's coattails had carried Cox rather than Cox carrying the President.

Cox began his second term by again promoting his Progressive reforms, but soon his impetus swung to the defense efforts being requested by President Wilson in anticipation of World War I. The Ohio Governor supported moves to strengthen reserve forces and also favored efforts to control, rather than regulate, the coal and railway industries. Under Cox, Ohio adopted a plan to resolve labor disputes through government arbitration. A plan was also developed to mobilize farm labor into industrial labor if required. Since Ohio was a major food producer for the war effort, a secondary plan was formulated to have students work on farms to take the place of farm workers who would be industrial workers. Cox also instituted measures to increase farm production and to have city dwellers plant home gardens, thereby increasing goods available for the soldiers overseas.

When war was declared, Cox organized efforts to promote patriotism, creating a speakers' bureau that tapped famous personalities, industrial leaders, teachers and government officials to promote the American cause. Cox also took a strong position against strikes, and when a railroad strike seemed imminent, he threatened martial law. The strike was averted, but the Ohio Chief Executive still had national guardsmen posted at strategic points in the state to prevent sabotage.

1918 was a banner year for Republicans over all the nation — except for Ohio, the state of Presidents. There James Cox won re-election by a slim majority of some 10,000 votes. By doing so, the Progressive Democrat who had refused to campaign for his own re-election except in connection with promoting the U.S. position in World War I, became a leading candidate for the Democratic Presidential nomination in 1920.

Cox spent most of his third term concentrating on post-war problems. He saw that legislation was passed that banned the teaching of German in elementary schools. (In 1918 a large Ohio German population had largely supported the Republicans.) As inflation increased, labor demands and strikes became stronger. When violence became imminent in Canton and the Mayor would not take action, Cox suspended him and intervened to have calm prevail; the strikers then went back to work. The Governor supported funding a black school, Wilberforce University, so that it could train its students to migrate back to the farms, thereby relieving industrial tensions in the cities. When the Prohibition amendment came before the Ohio legislature for approval, the Governor sided with the "wets," claiming a corruption greater than before the amendment would result.

As unemployment rose, Cox called for a road program that would repair highways and streets and simultaneously put men to work. He also called for President Wilson to stimulate the economy, to investigate inflated prices in the building industry, and to publish fair price guides. He joined New York Governor Al Smith in calling for rent controls to curb inflation, and he supported collective bargaining as a means of peacefully and fairly resolving labor disputes. In Ohio, he arbitrated a miner's dispute that gave increases of 18-25 percent to labor.

Cox had strongly supported President Wilson's war program, and he just as strongly supported the President's efforts for the League of Nations. Serving as chairman of the Ohio League to Enforce Peace, the Governor claimed the League of Nations would guarantee peace and prosperity while promoting security. In January, 1920, Cox was invited to be the speaker at the annual Jackson Dinner in Washington. While there, he persuaded Senate Democrats that they must make a stand with Wilson. In his speech at the dinner meeting, he defended Wilson's policies and assailed the Republicans, predicting revolution if the problems of labor and capital were not resolved. This speech verified what everyone knew: the Ohio Governor was seriously considering a run for the Presidency. This proved to be true some three weeks later when he formally announced his candidacy.

RUNNING FOR THE PRESIDENCY

The major contenders for the Democratic nomination in 1920, besides Cox, were Attorney General Mitchell Palmer and Treasury Secretary William G. McAdoo, the son-in-law of President Wilson. The President himself indicated he might be a candidate for a third term, especially if a third term would assure passage of the Versailles Treaty. Because Wilson would not disavow a possible bid for the nomination, Palmer and McAdoo refrained from actively campaigning. Wilson's lack of action divided the McAdoo and Palmer camps and afforded Cox the ability to build strength. Momentum for Cox greatly increased when a group of urban Democrats opposed to Prohibition and in control of enough votes to block the nomination of Wilson or his "dry" son-in-law met with Cox, who favored legalization of light wines and beers, and assured him of their steadfast support.

The San Francisco nominating convention was a divisive conclave, with party disputes erupting over the League of Nations and Prohibition. The platform finally adopted was one of the longest such documents in history, but it was a platform with which Cox was comfortable. Numerous ballots for the presidential nomination were taken, with strength alternating among Cox, Palmer and McAdoo. On the twenty-second ballot, Wilson received two votes, and McAdoo sensed his defeat. On the thirty-seventh ballot, Palmer's delegates started to desert, and he withdrew. Cox began to gain, but McAdoo refused to withdraw. Finally, on the forty-fourth roll call, James M. Cox was declared the Democratic nominee. For Vice President the convention chose a young Wilsonian who offered the hope of carrying Eastern states such as New York. He had served as Assistant Secretary of the Navy during Wilson's war administration and was considered a rising star in the Democratic Party. He was Franklin Delano Roosevelt, destined to serve longer as President of the United States than any other person in its history.

Cox and Roosevelt had little chance to win the 1920 election. The Democratic Party, in power for eight years and in favor of the Versailles Treaty, was held in disfavor by the American people, who were ready for change. The Republicans, with Ohio Senator Warren G. Harding as their nominee, pointed out the difficulties with the Democratic economic policies and the League of Nations. While Harding conducted a "front porch" campaign, doing little more than to call for a "return to Normalcy," Cox traveled widely and made almost 400 speeches. Upon the advice of his advisors, he spoke little of the League and concentrated on his Progressive ideas. But as the November election date neared and he realized that his campaign was not exciting Democrats in favor of the Treaty, he finally came out soundly in favor of Wilson's position. By this time, however, it was too late to create any interest in his campaign. Cox suffered a complete loss: Harding received over 16,000,000 votes to his 8,000,000, with an electoral margin of 404 votes to 127. Ohio would put another son into the White House, but that son would be Warren G. Harding.

NEWSPAPER BARON AND POLITICAL ADVISOR

Cox did not drop out of politics after his defeat in 1920, but he never sought public office again. His name would be mentioned as a possible candidate in 1924, but, knowing his chances of being either nominated or elected were limited, he chose to play the role of Democrat Party statesman and hoped to create a harmonious party. He mediated a dispute between the "wets," headed by Al Smith, and the "drys," headed by William Jennings Bryan. He continued to insist on the adoption of the Versailles Treaty. As in the past, he took no strong position on racial matters. Alas, there were too many party divisions for democratic harmony in 1924: the League, Prohibition and the Ku Klux Klan (the Democratic Party refused to condemn this group, Bryan arguing that it would be politically inexpedient to do so) were issues choking the Democratic Party, and its failure to resolve these issues found the Republicans under Calvin Coolidge winning another landslide victory.

Cox had moved to Miami, Florida in 1923 and purchased another daily, naming it the Miami *Daily News*. He was in the process of creating a newspaper empire. The Canton, Ohio *Daily News* became his in 1928. He next acquired the Springfield *Sun* in Springfield, Ohio, which was located near Dayton. Some two decades later in 1949 he purchased the Dayton *Journal* and the Dayton *Herald*, and thereafter enjoyed a virtual monopoly in his home area. In 1939, Cox Industries purchases the Atlanta *Journal,* and then in 1950 it acquired the Atlanta *Constitution,* also enjoying a virtual monopoly in that area. From this empire emerged an even greater empire that included a nationwide network of television stations, Cox Communications.

The former Presidential candidate used his power to promote communities and causes. He boosted Miami as a center of commerce and used his editorials and money to promote candidates who did likewise. In Ohio, his editors were instructed to promote business expansion and to expose crime elements, for which a *Pulitzer Prize* was awarded in 1928. Perhaps his greatest influence was in Atlanta, where his papers openly sided with a reform candidate to attempt to squelch the influence of the Talmadge family, and where Ralph McGill, who was named publisher in 1950, waged an unending fight for civil rights, a change from Cox's attitude in the 1910's.

When his former running mate sought the Democratic nomination in 1932, Cox joined a "Stop Roosevelt" movement, supporting instead fellow Buckeye Newton Baker, Secretary of War under Wilson, for the nod. Roosevelt received Cox's support during the general election, but the two never really developed a warm relationship. Cox was offered an Ambassadorship and the Chairmanship of the Federal Reserve Board, but he refused all offers in FDR's administration other than advisory posts. In such a capacity, he served as a delegate to the London Economic Conference, a meeting of world economic powers to stabilize world and domestic prices, during the famous "First Hundred Days" of FDR's first term. As time went by, Cox expressed displeasure with many of Roosevelt's economic acts, including the Wagner Act and public relief bills, but overall he supported Roosevelt and felt the New Deal actions were needed to prevent chaos in the American society. He remained active politically into his seventies, praising FDR for his buildup of American forces to deter the forces of fascism in Europe. He also was a stalwart of support for a fourth term for Roosevelt in 1944.

DEATH AT "TRAILSEND"

Remaining active in his newspaper business, Cox also found time to write an autobiography of sorts, *Journey Through My Years,* in which he narrated various events in his career. He kept a pragmatic view of how government should be run but remained a liberal and progressive ideologue for the middle class. But in his personal affairs, he was all business, amassing a fortune of some $10 million through his various acquisitions and enterprises.

In July of 1957, at age eighty-seven, Cox succumbed to heart failure while at his "Trailsend." His will dispensed to his surviving wife, two sons and two daughters the various necessary provisions for the distribution of his wealth. But it also charged his survivors to "...have devotion to the best interests of the communities wherein my papers are located," "...to recognize [their] debt... [to the working people]....," and to remain "champions of the rights of the weak."

Such was the life of James Middleton Cox.

John W. Davis
The Election of 1924

Regarded as the most outstanding Solicitor General in the history of the United States, considered the ablest US Ambassador ever to Great Britain, and known as the best lawyer — the "Lawyer's Lawyer" — in the country, John W. Davis was indeed a leading figure of his age. Chosen to lead a party bereft with divisions, he was in an unenviable position, much as Barry Goldwater was forty years later when another Vice President had assumed office and was perceived by the people to be doing a good job. His overwhelming loss relegated him a rather minor position in his nation's history, but the story of his life is yet another of the fascinating success stories so common to the American scene.

WEST VIRGINIA POLITICAL HERITAGE

John W. Davis was born in West Virginia on April 13, 1873, the fifth of six children and the only son born to John J. and Anna Kennedy Davis. The senior Davis, of Scottish and Irish ancestry, was a prominent Clarksburg lawyer and Jeffersonian Democrat who was deeply involved in politics. At the age of twenty-five he served as a delegate to the Virginia General Assembly of 1860-61 and bitterly condemned Southern leaders calling for secession. When the War Between the States erupted, John J. Davis joined other western Virginians to help form a new state — West Virginia. He served in that state's legislature, supporting the Union but opposing the immediate ending of slavery. After the War, he supported the Fourteenth and Fifteenth Amendments but opposed other measures for Negro equality. Elected to the U.S. House of Representatives, he voted for a 50 percent pay raise for Congressmen and suffered defeat when running for re-election. Later he ran for the Senate but lost that bid for higher office.

Anna Kennedy Davis was one of the first female college graduates in the country. From a Quaker background, she attended the Presbyterian Church with her husband but refused to accept the "Virgin birth" of Christ. She was well read and dedicated to intellectual pursuits, and she taught her only son to read before he started school.

At age ten John was enrolled in courses with much older students studying for state teachers examinations. Two years later, much to his personal regret, he attended an all-girls school; yet his grades were all A's. In 1887, the fourteen year old lad was sent to preparatory school at Charlottesville, adapting easily to being away from home and again doing well in school. By age sixteen, his preparation was sufficient for him to begin college at Washington and Lee University, where a fellow student was Newton Baker, later to be Secretary of War and a contender for the Presidency. There John won honors in English and geology, joined Phi Kappa Psi, played intramurals and sang in the glee club as well as the Presbyterian choir. During his college years, Davis discovered that he was diabetic; his self-discipline allowed him for the most part to adapt to this handicap without too many problems. He graduated with a bachelor's degree in 1892.

The young scholar wanted to begin law school in 1892, but family finances would not allow this. He took a teaching position in Charles Town, West Virginia at a salary of $300 and board for nine months. Davis worked so hard that he became depressed with teaching. He was deeply lonely until he became acquainted with the school master's daughter. He soon fell in love with Julia McDonald, later to be his wife.

In 1893, Davis returned to Clarksburg to begin "reading books" in the law offices of his father. He engaged in many of the functions of the firm but after fourteen months realized that he needed formal training to get ahead in the legal profession. After persuading his father to co-sign a note for $300, he headed back to Washington and Lee. Because of the lack of money, he decided to "double-up" on his classes and compete his regimen in one year — half the normal time. Despite this restriction, Davis still ranked fifth in his graduating class and was selected by his fellow students to be Class Orator at Commencement exercises.

LAWYER AND COLLEGE PROFESSOR

Upon graduation John J. Davis was granted a license to practice law in West Virginia and then joined his father as a partner in Davis and Davis. His first cases were rather mediocre, and the young Davis, displaying a habit that would be with him throughout his life, toiled hard into the night to be adequately prepared, often working himself into a nervous fervor for fear of embarrassing himself in a courtroom appearance. With fees not coming up to expectations, the fledgling young attorney decided to return to Washington and Lee as an assistant Professor of Law at a salary of $1,000 annually. Here Davis once again worked himself to the bone and let his fear of failure create undue nervous tension for him. Despite being a satisfactory professor and being offered a full Professorship at $3,000 per year, Davis decided to return to the full time practice of law, where he hoped he could do better financially and where he felt his real talents lay.

In June of 1899 Davis took as his wife Julia McDonald, the daughter of the school master he had been in love with since 1892. He had delayed marriage for fear of not being financially secure, but his practice had prospered somewhat. The young couple seemed well suited for each other and were elated when they found they were to be parents the following July. Unfortunately, Julia McDonald Davis died of complications from the delivery of their child a month after the birth. John Davis was crushed and mourned his wife's death for many years. Because of the tragedy, he was for many years quite distant from the daughter who survived her mother.

WEST VIRGINIA PRACTICE

As the twentieth century began, a period of prosperity was sweeping across the West Virginia mine fields. The commerce of the state created opportunities not only for businessmen but for attorneys. John W. Davis received many opportunities and made the most of them. While he took on all types of cases, including one notable one where he kept some unruly union members from serving long terms in jail, he was for the most part an attorney for business interests. He became the counsel for railroads and coal companies and began to bring in so much business to Davis and Davis that he became an equal partner with his father. His thorough preparation and courteous demeanor impressed most clients, judges and opposing attorneys. On occasion, however, he lost his temper; once, he threw an ink well at an opposing attorney; later, he took a whip to a Republican editor who had made some disparaging statements about his father.

Soon he was recognized as one of the outstanding young lawyers in the state and was selected County Attorney. Realizing that civic endeavors would help his legal practice, Davis joined the Elks and the Masons. In 1906, at age thirty-three, he served as president of the West Virginia Bar Association. With a flourishing practice and good civic reputation, Democrats, against his wishes, drafted him to run for the state legislature. He reluctantly consented to run but then campaigned hard and won the election.

STATE ASSEMBLYMAN AND U.S. CONGRESSMAN

In the House of Delegates, Davis became both Democratic Floor Leader and Chairman of the Judiciary Committee, though he was only thirty-five years of age. Considered to have one of the sharpest legal minds in the whole body, other legislators looked to him for leadership on legal matters. He fought for revision of the West Virginia Code of laws, had a measure passed allowing public schools to establish kindergartens, voted for a bill to enforce better safety inspections of mines, and worked to ban the use of child labor in dangerous occupations. He also supported a resolution which declared that West Virginia was not responsible for any debt of Virginia due to the former association of the two.

Davis' law practice became more and more lucrative. By 1910 he was earning $10,000 annually in fees, and he began to invest in various gas and oil companies. His financial success was assured, and he began to dress and act as the very successful attorney he was. His reputation was now spreading beyond Clarksburg, and Democrats in his district decided that he should run for Congress. Once again Davis, against his own wishes and his father's, was drafted to run. Though the Republican Party had held the seat he was seeking for the past sixteen years, Davis, after a hard fought campaign, won rather easily, with 20,370 votes to his opponent's 16,962. Thirty-seven year old John W. Davis was heading to Washington, D.C. as a new member of the House of Representatives.

John W. Davis came to Washington with a reputation as an outstanding young lawyer, and he quickly proved this reputation to be true. He became a member of the Judiciary Committee and provided invaluable assistance in drafting new bills. Soon the young Congressman was being hailed as the ablest attorney in the Congress. Although he had a business background, his efforts were surprisingly strong in behalf of labor interests. He pushed through the House a compromise to limit the use of injunctions in curbing disputes and worked in behalf of the first federal workman's compensation laws. Davis, showing a Progressive leaning, supported the direct primary and the popular election of Senators. However, he did not support women's suffrage, and he endorsed literacy tests to limit immigration.

Davis ran for re-election to the House in 1912, the same year that a three-man Presidential race was taking place among William Howard Taft, Theodore Roosevelt and Woodrow Wilson. Davis had been a popular Congressman, but his Republican opponent made an issue of Davis' support for a low tariff bill, and the Bull Moose Progressives tended not to support him. In a very close race, Davis won re-election, but only by the scant margin of 148 votes.

Before resuming the duties of a second term, Davis decided to take a second wife, Nell Bassell, the daughter of a leading rival attorney. Nell had been married before, and John's mother opposed the union, but Davis went ahead with the marriage and enjoyed the company of his wife for many years. She was quite interested in his advancement and over the years encouraged him to take many positions that he might not have taken without her insistence. The couple never had children.

Davis was bored with the duties of his second Congressional term. He participated in the prosecution, before the Senate, of an impeached federal judge and later developed language which led to the arrest, trial and conviction (the punishment was a public rebuke in the "well" of the House) of a Washington banker who had verbally and physically accosted a Congressman while the House was in session. For some time Davis had been disenchanted with Southern members of the House who had been routinely re-elected and who resisted any changes in election laws, Negro rights or trade policy because of the fear of upsetting the status-quo and losing their seats. Davis also considered the process of patronage distasteful and could not stomach the endless numbers of job and favor seekers. For these reasons, and perhaps since he had won his last election by such a small margin, he was eager to leave Congress, and he openly solicited appointment to a vacancy on the Fourth Circuit Court of Appeals. He received the endorsements of bar associations, judges, Congressmen and Senators, but President Wilson, who over the years displayed an uncanny disrespect for Davis, nominated another man instead. Later, fellow House members, among them James Cox, a good friend of Davis who would be the 1920 Democratic nominee, moved to create a new judgeship with the understanding that Davis would be the nominee, but Wilson stalled any appointment to a Judgeship. In August of 1913, a position became open for which Davis was imminently qualified and which he accepted at once. John W. Davis was selected by President Woodrow Wilson to be Solicitor General of the United States.

SOLICITOR GENERAL

Approaching his new responsibility from the position that the government was his client, Davis discharged his duties not with respect to his personal philosophy but with regard to the wishes of his government. He appeared in person before the Supreme Court as the government's advocate more often than any other Solicitor General in U.S. history, arguing many of the more important cases to come before the Court during the Progressive era. Both his oral arguments and written briefs were a welcome relief to a Supreme Court often bored by less entertaining attorneys. He was not always successful in his arguments. For example, his advocacy to have U.S. Steel dissolved was rejected by the Court, and his arguments in behalf of new child labor laws were dismissed as unconstitutional. But he also won some important decisions, such as having Standard Oil pipelines classified as a monopoly practice, allowing Congress the right to regulate the hours of railroaders, and also allowing Congress the right to establish the Selective Service Act at the outbreak of World War I. The Solicitor General also had success in civil rights matters. He argued successfully against an Oklahoma "grandfather" clause that required literacy tests for Negroes, and he was also instrumental in the overturning the practice in Alabama of "peony," where Negroes who were arrested were required to make bond and then work on plantations until the bond was released.

As in earlier days, Davis often felt ill-prepared before a court appearance and would completely exhaust himself working around the clock so that he would not embarrass himself. So impressive were his presentations that nearly all the Justices he practiced before hoped that someday he would be appointed to serve on the Supreme Court. He was disappointed when President Wilson did not appoint him to be Attorney General when a vacancy occurred. Later, he turned down the opportunity to be Counselor to the State Department, which was headed by Robert Lansing, a close personal friend. In 1918, after having achieved the reputation of being the greatest Solicitor General in the nation's history, Davis resigned to again resume private practice.

AMBASSADOR TO GREAT BRITAIN

President Wilson soon called Davis back to duty, asking him to serve as a delegate to a Prisoners of War Conference while the war was still active. Journeying to Berne, Switzerland, he participated in negotiations over the treatment of captured soldiers on both sides, which were completed only two days before the end of the war. While in Europe, Davis received word that President Wilson, acting upon the advice of Secretary of State Robert Lansing, had selected him to become Ambassador to the Court of St. James in England. After returning to the U.S. and receiving Senate confirmation, Davis sailed to France with the President to participate in the Peace Conference at Paris. He then traveled to London and, dressed in frock coat and silk stockings, presented his credentials to King George V.

Relations between the United States and England were at times strained following World War I. England feared that demands from the U.S. to have a large navy might lead to future problems. Many English leaders also felt that President Wilson had been rude during a visit and were further offended when Gen. John J. Pershing had implied that the U.S. alone had won the war. Davis realized the damage done by such actions, and he set about repairing the damage. Without apologizing, he made a series of speeches praising British actions and sacrifices. His delivery and use of the English language charmed his hosts, who were delighted when Davis' name started being mentioned for the Presidential nomination in 1920. Davis became close to the King, the Prince of Wales and Prime Minister Lloyd George, and he also came to know other dignitaries, including Winston Churchill, quite well.

Davis worked behind the scenes to have tensions between Ireland and England eased. He also warned that England was trying to seize all the oil fields of the Mideast, but felt that she had a role to play in settling the problems there. When President Wilson sought and got the resignation of Robert Lansing as Secretary of State, Davis, tired of the bickerings involved in the Ambassadorship, decided to resign himself. Many English notables, including the King, asked him to reconsider, but he was firm in his decision. When he sailed for home, the British Navy "passed in review," its sailors cheering, as his homeward bound ship steamed by. John W. Davis was the only American Ambassador ever so honored by the British government.

PRIVATE PRACTICE

Before he had resigned as Ambassador, Davis' name was put forth by some West Virginians as a possible nominee for President in 1920. Because he earnestly wanted to return to private practice and also because he did not desire to run, Davis delayed his resignation, for fear that his leaving would fuel speculation that he was indeed a candidate. As the convention deadlocked and the number of ballots went on and on, many felt that Davis was certain to be the nominee. However, on the forty-fourth roll call, James M. Cox received the nomination. Davis was delighted to campaign for Cox and the youthful Franklin Delano Roosevelt in the fall of 1920.

A campaign among leading legal firms of Washington and New York was waged for the services of the renowned former Solicitor General and Ambassador, and from a choice number of Washington and New York law firms he entered, with the encouragement of J.P. Morgan and other leading businessmen, the firm of Stetson, Jennings & Russell as a Senior Partner. Always in the past concerned about his financial security, Davis' worries were now over. He began with a minimum guaranty of $50,000 annually and 15 percent of the net profits; within a decade he would be making hundreds of thousands yearly. Davis had spent the previous quarter-century in law and politics. Except for his sojourn into politics to run for the Presidency in 1924, Davis would spend the rest of his days — some thirty years — as the leading lawyer of his age.

His new found affluence also found him with an affluent life style. He and his wife acquired a small estate on Long Island, which they named "Mattapan," used primarily for weekends. They also owned a fashionable Manhattan apartment, from which he commuted to his offices each day. Davis also purchased a country home (Yeamans Hall) in South Carolina, where he spent as much time as possible fishing, his one sporting passion. He often played golf with his new rich friends, but that sport interested him very little; he preferred instead to read, acquiring an extensive library on the classics, English literature, and religions of the world. He and his wife took long cruises to Europe, and he would often stop in England, where he especially enjoyed renewing his London acquaintances.

Davis occupied the same office that Grover Cleveland had occupied when he returned to the practice of law after leaving public life. Many of his new partners were expecting of Davis merely the business that he would attract, and they were pleasantly astonished to find that he worked long hours in the legal end of the business as well as in public relations. His gifted legal abilities would soon be known throughout the business world, and the fact that John W. Davis was available to be personally involved in a case brought the firm more and more business. He came to enjoy the practice and benefits of his partnership so much that he turned down overtures to be a Justice of the U.S. Supreme Court. He was dedicated to the principles and canons of the American Bar Association, which he served as its national president in 1923.

DEMOCRATIC NOMINEE

As the 1924 Presidential Elections approached, there was a groundswell of support for the former Ambassador known to have one of the finest legal minds in the country. Davis did not covet the nomination and made statements designed to kill any hopes for getting it, but in June he indicated he would accept a draft. New York Gov. Al Smith and former Treasury Secretary William McAdoo, the son-in-law of the late Woodrow Wilson, were the chief contenders for the party's nod at Madison Square Garden in New York City, but they were hopelessly deadlocked. Bitterly divided on a number of issues — prohibition, the Ku Klux Klan, the League of Nations and progressive economics — neither would release his delegates for fear of having to support the other. The two men finally agreed after ninety-three ballots to withdraw, and then support for Davis began to increase. On the 103rd ballot he was still far from being named when the Texas delegation unexpectedly switched to Davis. The convention then stampeded to his name, and he was declared the nominee by acclamation. After a number of men, including his old classmate Newton Baker, declined the opportunity to run for the Vice Presidency, Nebraska Governor Charles Bryan, the brother of William Jennings, was nominated for the second post.

What chances Davis had against Calvin Coolidge were destroyed by the New York convention, the longest and most divisive in Democratic history. The party's refusal to condemn the Ku Klux Klan or take a stand against Prohibition greatly weakened his chances from the beginning. Soon another blow struck when the Progressive Sen. Robert LaFollette of Wisconsin entered the race as a third party candidate, receiving the endorsement of many labor leaders and draining away from Davis many traditional Democratic voters. While the Republicans had given the nation a big dose of corruption, Calvin Coolidge had not been tainted; as the campaign progressed, Davis, the Wall Street lawyer with connections to the House of Morgan, was suspected by the public of being more corrupt than the sitting Chief Executive.

Davis waged a tiresome campaign, traveling throughout the country. He boldly condemned the Klan and tried to draw Coolidge out into the open, but the President, who believed that he could not get into trouble if he did not say anything, kept his silence. On election day, the voters were not silent for Coolidge. The President won overwhelmingly, with 15,718,211 votes to Davis' 8,385,283 and LaFollette's 4,831,289. In many states Davis trailed LaFollette; in others he received less than 10 percent of the vote. Only the South and border states cast electoral votes for the Democratic nominee — even his beloved West Virginia had gone for Coolidge.

AMERICA'S LEADING LAWYER

Davis was fifty-one when the election was over. While his name was mentioned from time to time for a public office, particularly a Supreme Court appointment, he never sought a government position again. Instead, he settled into the life of corporate New York lawyer, arguing more important cases in the highest court of the land than any other attorney in the twentieth century. His clients were a "Who's Who" of American business, and he sat on the Boards of many of America's giant corporations, including US Rubber, AT & T, the National Bank of Commerce, the Topeka & Santa Fe Railroad, and other national firms, He also joined several exclusive country and city clubs and became a Director of the Carnegie Endowment, the Rockefeller Foundation and the influential Business Round Table.

A client which brought much notoriety to Davis was the House of Morgan, which in 1933 was investigated by Congress on allegations of using its influence to manipulate stock prices for its own members and close friends, while letting the general public suffer gigantic losses. Davis strongly felt that government was intruding on the privacy of corporations, and during the proceedings he often advised Morgan officials not to release information that they were willing to make public because he felt the government was going beyond its constitutional bounds. Davis coached Morgan officials, particularly J.P. Morgan, on their conduct before the investigating body, and this counseling was so effective that the Committee never discovered any legal wrongdoing on the part of the House of Morgan, although the junior partner (and son) of the managing partner had some irregularities and had to pay some tax penalty. Later in the proceedings, it was discovered that J.P. Morgan had only paid $48,000 in income taxes in 1930 on an income of millions, and this information instantly became sensational news. Davis and the House of Morgan had relied upon the fact that its partners, who had suffered millions in losses and thus had no significant tax liability, were legally without fault to hold down the public's concern, but in this they were badly mistaken.

So devoted to big business had Davis become that he had an open split with Franklin Roosevelt when the new President took office in 1933. Davis had supported FDR but not to the same degree as he had in 1928 for Al Smith, for whom he vigorously campaigned, condemning religious bigotry, and for whom he had high regard for his government philosophy. Ever the Jeffersonian who believed in limited government with a constitution that promoted "states rights" and required a "strict construction" in its interpretation, the 1924 nominee felt that liberals were delving into areas far beyond that permitted by the Constitution. To Davis the New Deal was an attack on property rights, which were in his mind fundamental to American society. Additionally, Davis never quite trusted Roosevelt, and when the New Deal programs were instituted calling for a variety of "alphabet" agencies that many felt were bordering on communism, John W. Davis rose to oppose the Democratic administration. In court, he argued against new laws radically altering holding companies and labor policies, and he signed *amicus curiae* briefs (as a friend of the court) on other suits seeking to have many New Deal programs declared unconstitutional. As a private citizen, he joined with Al Smith and a number of corporate giants to form the American Liberty League, an organization whose specific purposes were to oppose the domestic programs of the New Deal and Franklin Delano Roosevelt. FDR's invective against Davis was often bitter, especially after Davis commented on one occasion that he would spank Eleanor Roosevelt if she were his wife. Davis never voted for a Democrat for President again, supporting Alf Landon, Wendell Willkie, Thomas Dewey and Dwight Eisenhower rather than FDR, Harry Truman or Adlai Stevenson.

Davis, with his Ambassadorial background, was not an isolationist and his views therefore often coincided with FDR on foreign policy matters. The 1924 candidate had supported the League and the World Court, and he had served as a Director of the Carnegie Endowment, the American Foundation, the League of Nations Association, and as President of the Council on Foreign Relations. When war loomed in Europe, Davis approved of the moves of FDR in support of England, and he joined the Committee to

Defend America by Aiding the Allies. The former Ambassador feared Germany more than Russia, but after the war he favored re-arming the former Nazi state to help contain communism in Greece and Turkey.

For a while after Harry Truman succeeded FDR, it appeared as though Davis would come back to the Democratic fold, but Truman's liberal policies were too much for the conservative, Jeffersonian Davis. In 1951, Davis represented the steel industry when Truman nationalized it after a satisfactory wage pact with the United Steel Workers could not be negotiated. Deeply disturbed by this trend in government, Davis personally argued the cause of the steel corporations before the Supreme Court. At age seventy-eight his bearing in court was one of dignity, and his arguments were well reasoned and backed by legal precedents. The Court ruled in favor of Davis' clients; the "lawyer's lawyer" had won once again.

While Davis was thought of as a corporate lawyer, he also took cases, often without fee, that were constitutional in nature. In 1928, he took a case of a Canadian who was denied US citizenship because he was a conscientious objector. Davis argued the case all the way to the Supreme Court — and lost, to him a very bitter decision. However, in 1946 the Court reversed itself and upheld Davis' arguments.

Davis also became involved in matters affecting the conduct of members of the bar. He represented a New York federal Judge undergoing impeachment proceedings in the House and, using his legal standing to make points with the Congressmen, showed the House committee holding hearings that the Judge was not guilty of violating legal canons. He also defended a leading opposing trial lawyer who was charged with perjury. The lawyer in question had been representing the Bank of the United States, which had bankrupted in 1930, and Davis strongly felt that his client was being wrongly charged for the actions of its officers, who were guilty. The case from beginning to end was long and arduous, involving a mistrial and two other jury trials, a bribed juryman and appeals. Davis was particularly offended when the trial Judge delivered a nine-hour charge to the jury; Davis used this, along with other irregularities, to make an appeal. In 1935, the case was overturned.

Although a conservative, Davis personally came to the defense of Alger Hiss, one of the formulators of the United Nations and President of the Carnegie Endowment, who was charged with and ultimately convicted of perjury, after he had at first denied — but later admitted — an affiliation with the Communist party. Davis testified as a character witness at Hiss' trials and always felt that justice was improper in this matter. In another celebrated case, Davis represented J. Robert Oppenheimer, who had worked on the "Manhattan" atomic bomb project and who was a member of the Atomic Energy Commission, when his security clearance was lifted because of associations with known communists in the 1930's. At age eighty-one, Davis agreed to take the case provided the government would allow hearings in New York. Davis, however, was rebuffed in this request but then decided nonetheless to make the trips to Washington in defense of Oppenheimer before the Army's Personnel Security Board. Davis convinced the Board that Oppenheimer had not been disloyal and that no secrets had been transmitted to foreign powers. Yet, in the age of McCarthyism, Oppenheimer was still found to be a possible security risk and his work with the government was stopped. Davis, highly upset by the ruling, was vindicated after his death when Oppenheimer was presented the Enrico Fermi award, together with a $50,000 prize; this announcement, made nine years after the ruling, was given by the White House on the morning of November 22, 1963 — the date that John F. Kennedy died in Dallas.

Davis' last case before the Supreme Court involved the desegregation suit of *Brown vs. Plessy* in 1954. Although the case originated in Kansas, Davis represented South Carolina, which had become involved under a broad case that the Court wanted to decide jointly. All his life, Davis had believed in the Jeffersonian principles of limited government and states' rights, and this case so appalled his basic instincts that he took it without fee. When the case was argued before the nation's highest tribunal, Davis was opposed by Thurgood Marshall — later to become the first black Justice in the nation — who shocked the normally placid Davis, a strong believer in the principle of legal precedent, when he used sociological testimony to argue in favor of desegregation. Davis was even more dismayed when the Court ruled 9-0 against his arguments.

LAST DAYS

By his eightieth year in 1953, Davis could look back upon a life of resplendent accomplishment. He had been the most outstanding Solicitor General and the most outstanding Ambassador to Great Britain in his nation's history. He was also considered the foremost lawyer of his age. Honors had been bestowed upon him from all quarters: Oxford had granted him an honorary degree, as had many American universities; Queen Elizabeth had awarded him the Honorary Knight Grand Cross of the Order (the highest civilian award a foreigner could receive); the New York bar had presented him with a Gold Medal for distinguished service at the bar and had also placed his bronze bust in its headquarters; the Harrison County Bar placed a similar bust in the county courthouse at Clarksburg; and Washington and Lee had named a dormitory after its distinguished alumnus. The only thing of distinction John W. Davis did not achieve during his entire career was the Presidency in 1924, but that failure was more because of divisive elements in his party than of his own talents.

His second wife had died in 1943, and Davis had finally begun to develope a close, warm relationship with his daughter Julia, which had been missing since the death of his first wife. He also began to shower affections on close relatives and friends, often making monetary gifts such as paying for the tuition of the child of a close friend. He reduced his percentage of take from his firm and showed an interest in the advancement of junior partners and associates, while professionally insisting upon stricter qualifications for admittance to law schools and the bar.

In 1955 Davis was visibly weak from the rigors of old age, diabetes, and the illnesses of the past decade. He had been hospitalized four times in seven years, and he had become so feeble that he could no longer climb up and down river banks to enjoy his passion for fishing. He went to Yeamans Hall in South Carolina for recuperation, knowing that his days were numbered. In February he was hospitalized once again with pneumonia. He spent the next few weeks both reminiscing and lingering. Then on March 24, 1955, John W. Davis suffered a heart attack, went into a coma and soon passed away.

Tributes naturally arrived from all over the country, as well as England, extolling his long and useful life. His body was taken to New York for a service at the Brick Presbyterian Church and for burial beside his second wife. At his memorial service a minister prayed, "For the dignity and integrity which he brought to the practice of law, the service of his country, the cause of international friendship and peace, and every relationship of life, we give Thee thanks."

The prayer was an apt one from all the people of the United States.

Alfred E. Smith
The Election of 1928

A poor Irish boy who grew up to be Governor of his state, candidate for President and head of the Empire State Building, Al Smith was almost a mystical character. His was the Horatio Alger story come true — of an American lad born with nothing who, acquiring but an eighth grade education, could use his wit and determination to rise to the top. He was coarse in mannerisms and speech; he was also colorful, known for his brown bowler hat and a cigar stump jutting out of the corner of his mouth. Dubbed "The Happy Warrior" by none other than Franklin D. Roosevelt, Smith left a large imprint on the nation, even though he lost his Presidential campaign by an overwhelming margin. It is a tribute to this gruff campaigner that he maintained his religious faith despite the fact that it cost him the Presidency he dearly wanted.

PRODUCT OF NEW YORK CITY

It was in the lower East Side of New York City on the last day of the year, 1873, that Alfred Emmanuel Smith, Jr. was born. His father, whose heritage is not clear, provided for the family by handling a team of horses on a milk route. His mother, of Irish descent, worked in an umbrella factory along with keeping the household. She also provided most of the family discipline as well as its inspiration — inspiration based on the sacred teachings of the Catholic Church.

Smith's father died when young Al was only thirteen. At this impressionable period in his life, the Church came to his need; a parish Priest organized a youth club, called St. Jame's Union, which required good behavior and character to remain a member. Smith met the prerequisites to keep his membership and always remembered the value of this aid. He completed his formal education when he graduated from the eighth grade of the parish school.

To assist the family's needs, Smith during his teenage years held a variety of jobs, including newspaper delivery boy, "chaser" and "handy boy" for truckers, and other odd jobs as they became available. These experiences as a young man were to profoundly influence his later political philosophy. At age nineteen, Smith became an assistant bookkeeper at the Fulton Fish

Market. This position required not only tabulating accounts but hawking business on the open dock much like a modern commodity salesman might do in a closed exchange. His pay was $12 per week plus all the fish he needed for family usage. His hours were long and his spare time limited, but the Fulton Fish Market would sharpen Smith's human understanding, allowing him to view with disgust the working conditions forced on the working man but simultaneously to develop a personable and humorous outlook on the situation of mankind. Years later Smith would say, with a tongue-in-cheek reference to his harsh days on the dock, that his alma mater was FFM (Fulton Fish Market).

What spare time he had Smith spent running with his friends in his neighborhood and enjoying the pastimes of the day. One especially alluring attraction at that time was the Theatre. Smith joined various productions and, with his coarse but deep-carrying voice, was often a member of some cast involved in either a dramatic or humorous play. It was while considering the Theatre as a career that he met a dapper character named Jimmy Walker, who would be deeply involved in his future political career.

INFLUENCED BY TAMMANY HALL

Tammany Hall had been established under the influence of Aaron Burr as a means of opposing the Society of Cincinnati, which was established for Officers of the Revolution and their heirs. Other early Tammany members had also included DeWitt Clinton and even George Washington, who obligingly joined while residing as Chief Executive in New York City. Down through the years, however, the Society became almost exclusively an Irish society for the benefit of Irish politicians.

By the close of the nineteenth century, Tammany was controlled in large part by the Irish saloon keepers of New York City. As a group they would gather and distribute patronage and select candidates for office. All too often a "Grand Sachem" (the Indian nickname given to the leader of the Society) would be indicted and led off to jail, only to be replaced by another Sachem, whose fate was all too often the same. Occasionally, however, there would be a genuine reform movement within Tammany itself. Young Al Smith became part of such a movement.

A new saloon keeper and pretender to Tammany power moved into Al Smith's home Fourth Ward. A rapport grew quickly between the two, with Al joining the Seymour Club (named after the first Democratic nominee to oppose U.S. Grant) and joining in bar room debates and festivities. He began to also speak outside the saloon and on street corners for Democratic candidates and causes, and soon the word was out that young Al Smith, not even twenty-one, was a powerful and effective speaker. For his efforts he received an appointment to serve jury summonses in New York County at a salary of $800 annually. He kept this position until his late twenties, when Tammany, faced with charges of corruption from the Catholic Church, saw fit to find younger candidates who might be reform minded.

STATE ASSEMBLYMAN AND SPEAKER OF THE HOUSE

The position to which the young orator was nominated was State Assemblyman from the Fourth Ward. His personable manner and intimate knowledge of the people and problems of this area easily gained him a landslide victory in his first race, collecting over seventy-five per cent of the vote. He headed to the state capital, Albany, in 1904 at age thirty-one without the educational background of many of his peers. But Smith studied hard and worked even harder, mastering the intricacies of government and gaining the respect of members of both parties. He was re-elected term after term, eventually becoming the Majority Leader for the Democrats and then Speaker in the state Assembly.

Social reform caused Al Smith's star to soar. In 1911, a fire hit a garment workers' factory on the Lower East Side with 146 people being killed and scores more injured. Smith was outraged. With this single event, Smith began to generate a following as a social reformer. Time and time again over the years, he would push for changes in the civil liability laws relating to the rights of workers. He was appointed to a select committee to investigate the 1911 fire, serving with the likes of Henry Stimson, Henry Morganthau, Sr., State Senator (and future U.S. Senator) Robert Wagner, Sr. and labor leader Samuel Gompers. During the course of the investigation Smith also became an associate of a young social reformer destined to fame as the first female Federal Cabinet member, Frances Perkins. From the Commission's report several major pieces of reform legislation resulted which were generally adopted later not only by New York State but also most other states and the Federal Government. They included Fire Protection Bureaus, Workmen's Compensation Acts, Widows' Pensions Acts, Social Welfare Laws and Departments of Labor. The foundations of the New Deal in many respects lay with the early work of Al Smith.

To keep pace with the soaring social changes of the early twentieth century, liberal reformers in New York State called for a new Constitutional Convention. Smith was elected a delegate to the 1915 meeting, and continued to fight for the causes he espoused. Tammany Hall officials often expressed concern about the outspoken Smith, but his gilded, raspy voice would sternly rebuke those who dared question the wisdom of his actions. His stamp of leadership was all over the Constitutional Convention that concluded its business in 1915, the same year that Al Smith, after twelve years service, retired from the Assembly for a more financially rewarding position.

SHERIFF OF NEW YORK AND BOARD OF ALDERMEN

Shortly before being elected to the State Assembly, Smith had married Catherine Dunn, a Bronx Catholic girl of a somewhat more refined background than he. They had been courting for over six years, and his election to the State Assembly was to their good fortune, for the position paid $1,500 annually, almost twice what he had made as a server of summonses. After his distinguished service in the Assembly and in the Constitutional Convention, Tammany Hall decided that Smith was properly groomed for a prized reward, Sheriff of New York County. The nomination was readily and happily accepted by Smith, for, if he were elected, he would be paid an annual salary of $12,000 — plus 50 percent of all fees collected, with his total earnings in the neighborhood of $50,000 to $55,000 per year! The campaign that followed was another landslide for Smith, who beat his Republican opponent by the measure of 113,791 to 72,590. He had campaigned in his easy style of meeting people in a friendly way. Practically all the newspapers endorsed him.

Becoming Sheriff in 1914 election provided a happy situation in life for Smith. His duties were not burdensome, and the money was useful, allowing him to buy his first car and enjoy some financial security for the first time in his life. Tammany Hall was indeed pleased with its new star and decided to run him in 1917 for an even sweeter reward, President of the Board of Aldermen of New York City. This position was second in importance only to the Mayor of New York.

Challenged during a debate in this race by his Republican opponent to give his qualifications, Smith showed how his political invective could destroy an opponent in one swoop. "My qualifications are twelve years as a member of the New York Legislature and four years Democratic Floor Leader there. I was for one year Speaker of the Assembly ...I was vice-chairman of the committee which obtained enactment of our existing excellent fire protection laws. I was a member of all the important committees of the last Constitutional Convention. If there is any man in the city with the same legislative experience, let him speak. I will be glad to surrender my nomination to him and go back to the Fulton Fish Market." It was not only another easy victory for Smith but a campaign style that was to gain him both favor and disdain in the future.

TAMMANY NOMINEE FOR GOVERNOR

Tammany Hall decided that Smith should bypass any other lesser offices and vie directly for the Governorship. There was, to be sure, some friction in Tammany for the nomination of the man known for his reform ideas. Fortunately, Smith had during his Assembly days gathered the favor of upstate Democrats by treating them courteously, and he made an excellent statewide Democratic nominee. He was opposing in the General Election the Republican incumbent, Charles S. Whitman, whose forces were hitting hard at Smith's anti-Prohibition stance and at his Catholicism. The election was felt to be extremely close. Then, in the closing days of the campaign another disaster hit New York which offered Smith a clear opportunity for victory. A transit line car crashed, killing 90 victims, and Smith immediately lambasted the Administration for having appointed officials based on favoritism rather than merit. When the counting was all over, Alfred E. Smith at age forty-five had been elected Governor of New York by a margin of 15,000 votes.

GOVERNOR (1919-21 AND 1923-29) AND NATIONAL NOMINEE

Smith's tenure as Governor was not always tranquil. He began his term by having Frances Perkins moderate a long strike at the Rome Brass and Copper Company. He also moved to have qualified applicants rather than political cronies appointed to the Public Service Commission. Stating, "Democracy does not mean merely periodical elections. It means a government held accountable to the people between elections ....," Smith proposed the enlargement of state unemployment offices, of compulsory public education and new housing.

A strange conflict erupted between Gov. Smith and publishing magnate William Randolph Hearst about four months after Smith's inauguration. Hearst suddenly charged that Smith was responsible for the high price of milk in New York City and began a long and vicious attack upon Smith's conduct and character. Behind the matter actually lay Smith's refusal to accept a Hearst ally for a judgeship and Smith's further refusal to endorse Hearst as a future candidate for Governor or Senator, even though Hearst had supported Smith in 1919. Smith hoped the whole affair would blow over, but when the attack continued and Smith's mother, who was deliriously ill, said, "My son did not kill the babies," Smith went on the attack. He challenged Hearst to a debate at Carnegie Hall, but the sly Hearst, knowing that he was no match for the invective and crowd appeal of Smith, declined. Smith went ahead and held an open meeting at Carnegie, and the outcome for Hearst was devastating.

Like an evangelist before a Baptist gathering, Smith went about his work. "I am going to ask for your absolute silence and attention..., Smith began. "...he [Hearst] flares out a headline that Smith appointed a representative of the milk trust to office. That is a lie...I am not a czar, I am not a despot; I am just a plain ordinary man [in contrast to the rich Hearst, away at the time in his California mansion]...," continued the Governor in his raspy voice. "He [Hearst] doesn't spend any time in New York; he is in Palm Beach all winter, and in California all summer... What can it be? It has got to be envy, it has got to be hatred...," said Smith, who, before setting down, called on the people to "...get rid of this pestilence that walks in the darkness." Smith knew he had humiliated Hearst but not to what extent. Over the next decade or so, they would continue to fight bitterly, with Smith winning most of the battles; in 1932 Hearst would get a measure of revenge by helping FDR gain the Presidential nomination over Smith. Then, oddly, the two would join together to fight FDR and the New Deal.

The election of 1920 was one of the most difficult experiences in Smith's life. He felt that he had done a good job in Albany and knew that his name was even being considered for the Presidential nomination. (His name was actually placed in nomination as a "Favorite Son" at San Francisco.) Thus he was dismayed to find that the nation was swinging back to the "Normalcy" of Warren Harding rather than to the "reforms" of Democratic nominees James M. Cox and Franklin D. Roosevelt. Smith had opposed some of the "red scare" tactics of Attorney General Mitchell Palmer and had vetoed certain measures against communists, though as a loyal Catholic he had no use for Moscow. But the Republicans in New York made mincemeat of the Democrats over the Versailles Treaty, and Smith went down to defeat by 75,000 votes. He threatened to get out of politics permanently and accepted a position as Chairman of the Board of United States Trucking Company at a salary of $50,000 per year. He would work at this occupation until the gubernatorial election in 1922.

Smith's background in acting was put to one of the most effective tests in the American political arena ever during the 1922 election. As the election approached everyone knew that Smith wanted the nomination again. But there was a paramount reason for Smith deciding to hold his announcement for running. William Randolph Hearst wanted to make a bid for the Senate and create for himself a springboard to the Presidency. Smith balked at running on a ticket with Hearst, painfully remembering the vicious attacks made by Hearst just two years earlier. Various representatives from Tammany called on Smith to agree to a fusion ticket, but Smith would refuse to commit to such an arrangement. Four weeks before the convention Smith was asked to run with Hearst, but he remained silent. With only two weeks to go, he exchanged "open" letters with Franklin Roosevelt, and in reply to a plea by the young FDR that he should consider running on a joint Democratic ticket with Hearst, Smith only replied that he would heed the call of his party, while still tactfully refraining from agreeing to run with Hearst. In the final two days before the convention began, a swarm of party and Tammany officials urged him to run on a joint ticket, but Smith would not budge. Finally the Grand Sachem of Tammany himself made a plea for unity, but Smith roared, "The answer is no! No, no, no!..." Soon the word came from New York City that William Randolph Hearst was backing off and did not desire to be considered further for the Senatorial nomination. Al Smith had stuck to his instincts and won his battle, resisting even the advances of Tammany Hall.

Returning to Albany in 1923, where he would stay until 1929, Smith continued the social reforms begun in the Assembly. His lieutenants in his many causes included many names that would be leaders and supporters of the New Deal: Sen. Wagner, Henry Morganthau, Jr., Adolf A. Berle, Jr., Herbert Lehman, Frances Perkins, Charles A. Beard and Harry Hopkins, among others. The forty-eight hour work week for women and children came about during this period. There was also a program of low-cost housing and legislation dealing with Black Lung disease.

Having attained national fame, Smith was being prominently considered for the Democratic nomination in 1924. His chief opponent was William G. McAdoo, son-in-law of former President Woodrow Wilson. McAdoo was a "dry" and a strong Protestant, reason enough for many voters to favor him over Smith. The Madison Square convention meeting in New York in 1924 was the longest in Democratic Party history. First, a controversial Ku Klux Klan resolution was debated, with Smith furiously denouncing it but McAdoo keeping silent. Former standard bearer William Jennings Bryan was stating that "...it takes more courage to fight the Republican party than it does to fight the Ku Klux Klan." A resolution in favor of the Klan was approved by 3.3 votes out of 1,098 cast. Then nominations for President were offered.

Franklin D. Roosevelt, still recuperating from his polio attack, nominated "the Happy Warrior of the Battlefield," while the Garden, filled with Tammany boosters, gave an uproarious demonstration. But for ballot after ballot, neither Smith nor McAdoo could get anywhere close to the two-thirds needed for nomination. After ten days of balloting, the two camps saw that it would be fruitless for any man to try further, and a deal was made for each to withdraw in the interest of party harmony. Soon, John W. Davis, a West Virginian who had served as Ambassador to England and was currently one of Wall Street's outstanding lawyers, was nominated. Charles W. Bryan, brother of the "Great Commoner," was named for Vice President. They suffered an overwhelming defeat that November.

Smith was offered the opportunity to address the convention after he withdrew his candidacy. He called for party unity, but everyone knew that his sights were on the 1928 nomination. To this end he devoted himself tirelessly. First, he secured his New York political base through the leadership of Tammany Hall. When the Grand Sachem of Tammany had died in 1924, Smith did what few non-saloon owners could: he took virtual control of Tammany, though he did not become Grand Sachem himself, and became the dispenser of patronage. One of his more unfortunate favors was given to State Senator Jimmy Walker — playboy, heavy drinker, social fop and insincere leader — whom he made Mayor of New York to even a score with an old enemy.

The Governor also put together, under the leadership of Franklin Roosevelt and New York State Democratic Chairman George McNamee, an effective, smooth running national organization to make sure his efforts at the 1928 Houston convention would not fail. He had been the front runner since the Republican victory of 1924 and had had no problems with the 1928 primaries, but he still had the same two serious problems as in 1924, Prohibition and Catholicism. Smith deeply resented having to defend his position on either issue. Everyone knew that he drank in spite of the law of the land, and he did not go out of his way to keep it a secret, although he did not advertise it, either. In Smith's homespun way of understanding the matter, he felt that the issue should be left alone. His advisers acquiesced somewhat to this, but they insisted that he not let the religious issue hound him as it had in the past. Tradition has it that a Protestant adviser urged Smith to defend charges against his Catholicism made by an Episcopalian clergyman, and that Smith used the advice of a Jewish attorney to answer the charges. Many felt that one of Smith's frontal verbal assaults would have served him better.

The Houston convention was a point of high political drama throughout the land. Radio was just coming into its own, and the nation's listeners sat by their crystal sets with headsets fastened to ears, straining through the crackling static of each evening to hear the outcome. In Albany, the Smith family gathered with close associates to monitor the proceedings, smiling happily to learn each evening of continuing harmony and increasing strength. The dramatic point of the convention was, of course, Franklin Roosevelt's great speech nominating Smith as "...one who has the will to win — who not only deserves success but commands it. Victory is his habit

— the happy warrior!" A great demonstration ensued and Smith won a first ballot victory. Sen. Joseph T. Robinson of Arkansas was chosen as his running mate to give regional balance and to moderate claims of Smith's "wet" reputation and his Catholicism.

The high point of Smith's life was but short-lived. Another poor boy who had done well had been nominated by the Republicans, and he was Protestant. Furthermore, the nation was in a boom period, unaware of impending economic disaster. Herbert Hoover could remain quiet on Smith's weaknesses, while the Protestant clergy attacked on every corner, frantically pointing out that Smith had imbibed and that he had kneeled to a bishop of Rome. Some publications feared the persecutions of the Middle ages; others said Smith would end public education in favor of Catholic parochial teaching; and various fliers warned that all Protestants would be faced with living in adultery since the Roman Church did not sanction Protestant marriages.

Smith's approach to these charges was to use the same, friendly manner of campaigning he had developed in the Fourth Ward, to go meet the people publicly and win their confidence with his big smile, his coarse but eloquent speech and his friendly handshake. He went on a series of train tours, and made a point of traveling throughout the midwest heartland where his opposition was heaviest. But everywhere he went he encountered placards and verbal barrages about his religion and drinking. Finally he decided he must make a stand, similar to how he took on Hearst. He chose Oklahoma City as his forum, and proclaimed, "I shall speak openly on the things which people have been whispering to you." He thundered his position in plain words, but, alas, the message was not understood. As his train progressed to other stops, it was not uncommon for Smith to see a KKK cross burning in the center of a track or on an approaching hilltop. His defeat at the hands of Hoover was complete; he carried only 41 percent of the popular vote, losing in the Electoral College by 444 to 87.

EMPIRE STATE BUILDING

Smith had known his defeat was coming, but he still was depressed for an extended period of time. He received much consolation from his family and close friends. In a strange twist, he was kept at a distance by the new New York Governor, Franklin Roosevelt, whose nomination he had controlled. FDR did not seek Smith's advice on matters, and he also used his influence to keep Smith out of the limelight that he himself was enjoying and managing. After a while Smith left Albany, vowing to never run for office again. He had no employment, but some of his old friends had a position worthy of his background — President of the Empire State Building.

This was a position Smith was to hold until his death. Started shortly before the depression hit, the building was to be symbolic of New York's economic strength and spirit. The driving personality of Smith was to be used to see the building through its initial period of setbacks; he was the public relations master who conducted "VIP's" on guided tours. Until the policy of charging visitors for viewing from the Observatory was implemented to help the project become economically successful, the skyscraper was known as the "Empty State Building" or as "Smith's Folly." Smith kept an office at the building which he visited daily. He also found time to write a memoir entitled *Up To Now.* Another enterprise which demanded his attention was the County Trust Company Bank, which had been started by Irish Tammany affiliates. The bank President committed suicide during a financial crisis, and Smith was summoned to lend the prestige of his name to save the bank. This move was successful, with the Irish bank surviving while many others failed.

Smith's family also finally received more of his time, as did the Church, to which he become more devout as he aged. Another activity on which he spent more time was the zoo. All his life Smith had been fond of animals, always keeping pets. Now he found more time than ever before to visit the zoo and see the members of the animal kingdom.

THE ELECTIONS OF 1932, '36 AND '40

While Smith was leading a public relations campaign for the Empire State Building, Franklin Roosevelt was methodically building a following. Smith was still being snubbed by his successor as Governor, and the proud Irishman was offended more and more by this indifference. Smith's standing in the Party and the nation was strong, especially after the catastrophic depression under Hoover. He decided to stand once again for the Democratic nomination.

When he got to the 1932 Chicago convention, he found Roosevelt in a commanding but not overwhelming lead. Smith won several platform issues, notably the call for an outright repeal of Prohibition and the refusal to have Presidential candidates selected by majority rather than two-thirds of the ballots. But after the adoption of the platform came the nominations, and Roosevelt's strength was strong — though not strong enough for the two-thirds majority to receive the nomination. After three ballots Roosevelt's forces, frantic that their delegates might be slipping to Smith, went to William Randolph Hearst for aid. The old newspaper magnate, who controlled critical delegates from Texas and California, got his revenge for Smith's scurrilous attack during the milk issue a decade earlier. Roosevelt, considered an upstart by the least three Democratic nominees (James Cox, John Davis and Al Smith) had wrested control of the Party from the old guard regulars, who were so embittered that they would not appear on the platform with the nominee in a show of unity.

Smith grudgingly gave an endorsement to FDR for the '32 election but grew more embittered when a call for his services was never issued. When the New Deal President called for a series of new social programs that shocked even the reform minded Smith, the former Fulton Fish Market graduate now turned businessman began a vicious attack upon the new policies. He published a number of articles in *New Outlook*, asking "Does the Star Spangled Banner still wave?", "Where Are We Going?" and "Is the Constitution Still There?" Smith was against FDR's fiscal policies and used his biting invective to attack "alphabet soup" labels attached to the many new programs. He thought the National Recovery Act unconstitutional and feared that Roosevelt might try to pack the Supreme Court.

New York politics made the Smith-Roosevelt schism even greater. FDR, to his credit, had not been fooled by the clever cover-ups of New York City Mayor Jimmy Walker; FDR probably also had not forgotten that when the New York delegation had been polled at the '32 convention, Walker had voted for Smith. Walker's indigressions were many, but when it was time for him to go, it was Smith who told him so. Thus a long but rocky relationship was at an end, Smith losing a supporter and Walker traveling to Europe to continue his bawdy chases. Symbolic also of Smith's problems was that Tammany Hall, whose dispensation of patronage was once controlled by him, now was in the firm control of FDR.

Smith joined an organization called the Liberty League, which had the purpose of opposing Roosevelt's New Deal. An attempt to persuade the '36 Democratic convention to repudiate Roosevelt resulted in FDR's nomination by acclamation. Smith's only place to now go was to ... the Republican Party. This he did, supporting Gov. Landon of Kansas. But the nation was by now devoted to FDR, and he was overwhelmingly re-elected.

1940 found Smith still warning of the dangers of FDR, especially now that he was seeking a third term. Smith gave the same diatribes that he had been making since 1933, but Roosevelt was still in control, winning a third term by a wide margin over Wendell Willkie.

FINAL YEARS

Smith became less attuned to politics and closer to his inner circle of friends and his family. He celebrated his seventieth birthday in 1943 with a large party at his Fifth Avenue apartment, and received greetings from both old allies and enemies (including FDR). He and his wife were now both in ill health. She died in early 1944, and his family knew that his time was limited. Admitted to the hospital, he finally called for an old friend, Father John Healy, to visit him.

"Am I dying, Father?"

"Yes."

"Start the Act of Contrition."

Al Smith, the "Happy Warrior," died on October 4, 1944. He was not forgotten by his fellow New Yorkers, who knew of his rise from obscurity to the heights of greatness. Over 200,000 people passed his coffin in final tribute. Millions of others have wondered what would have been the outcome if he had been elected President of the United States in 1928.

Alfred M. Landon

The Election of 1936

A fiscal conservative who was successful in meeting the financial woes of Kansas during the dark days of the Great Depression of the 1930's and one of the few Republicans able to win a prominent office during that era, Alf Landon was thought by the leaders of his party to have the best opportunity to unseat Franklin Roosevelt after one term in office. Landon was no match for FDR, however, and he suffered one of the most humiliating defeats in the history of presidential politics. His contributions to government — especially to fiscal conservatism — are noteworthy, and his life in general is a tribute to the system of government he tried to lead.

BORN IN PENNSYLVANIA

Alfred Mossman Landon became famous as the Governor of Kansas, but his life began in West Middlesex, Pennsylvania, where he was born on September 9, 1887, the son of John M. and Ann Mossman Landon. His father's roots could be traced to England, and ancestors fought in both the Revolutionary War and the War of 1812. His mother was of French descent; one of her forbearers was a French officer who had come to the United States with LaFayette and stayed. Also mixed into Landon's heritage was some Dutch, so much so that he was said at times to be either "Pennsylvania Dutch" or "Dutch stubborn."

John Landon, Alf's father, was to influence him greatly during his formative years. He was a hard working oil man whose employment required that he travel from field to field and state to state. He was working in Ohio when his son was born back home in Pennsylvania; soon the entire family was united at Elba, Ohio. Alf had one sister who died in childhood, so he was reared an only child. The family was not wealthy, and the young boy grew up knowing the rigors of hard work.

Much of his basic education was bestowed by his parents, who decided to further his basic upbringing through their summer vacations at the famous Chautauqua camp in New York, which emphasized both religious and secular instruction. Alf heard many nationally known religious and political leaders at the revival meetings. Alf's high school training was at the Marion (Ohio) Academy, where he was only an average student scholastically. His education continued at the University of Kansas after his father moved the family west, first to Oklahoma and then to the Jayhawk state, to get into the oil business himself. Alf took a year of liberal arts courses at Kansas, not faring too well academically, as he failed physics, hygiene, and physical training, although he made A's in history and English. Rather than get an undergraduate degree, he followed his father's wishes and enrolled in the school's law program. While only an average student scholastically in this area of study, making mostly B's and C's with a few A's, his hard work in his legal studies did get him elected to Phi Delta Phi, the national legal fraternity. At Kansas, Alf showed early signs of sociability, being elected president of Phi Gamma Delta social fraternity, and acquiring both the reputation of a "hell-raiser" and the nickname "Fox."

Landon's intention was not to engage in the active practice of law but to go into banking. Upon graduation, he secured a position with an Independence, Kansas bank as a bookkeeper, staying in the banking industry for three years and acquiring knowledge of sound credit and oil leases. From his $75 per month income he saved $2,000 and eventually decided to pursue the oil business, as his father had before him, by becoming an independent producer and leasing sections of farm lands. The work was hard and demanding, with Landon often working from dawn to midnight, but his business prospered, and soon he was wealthy, although not rich. During this period of time he tried to form a partnership with a college fraternity brother, Henry Sinclair, later the founder of the Sinclair Oil Company, one of the dominant oil producers of the twentieth century, but this attempt did not come to fruition.

Alf Landon was more or less born a Republican. As an eleven year old boy, he had idolized Teddy Roosevelt of San Juan Hill fame. His father later became a political disciple of TR, the "trust-buster" who would take on Standard Oil, a concern which had little use for small independent oil producers. The elder Landon was a delegate to the 1912 Republican National Convention, and Alf also attended the conclave as a spectator. This was the famous convention where Roosevelt, denied the nomination by the forces of the incumbent William Howard Taft, bolted the Republicans and formed the Bull Moose Party. John Landon went with TR, and so did his twenty-five year old son, who became the organizer for Roosevelt in Montgomery County, Kansas, which went for TR, although the state went for Woodrow Wilson, with Taft coming in third. In this election young Landon had proven his ability to organize. He also made some valuable political connections within the state. These would eventually come in handy to Alf, who had made up his mind to become actively involved in politics and perhaps someday run for high office himself.

In 1914 Alf took a bride, Margaret Fleming, whom he had known since his childhood in Pennsylvania. His wife joined Alf in Kansas, and a son was born to the newly wed couple in 1916, but it died shortly after birth. In 1917 a healthy daughter arrived. Then tragedy struck Landon again in 1918 when his wife died of meningitis. Because he was an only parent, Alf was declared not eligible for the draft after the eruption World War I, but he bypassed his deferment and joined the Chemical Warfare Service, receiving a Lieutenant's commission. He arrived in Europe just as the war was ending and thus saw no combat. After the war, he settled back into the oil business and Kansas politics. In 1929, he was married a second time, to Theo Cobb, the daughter of a Topeka banker. Alf and Theo had a son and daughter of their own. The daughter, Nancy Kassebaum, became a U.S. Senator in 1978.

In 1922, Alf became executive secretary to Kansas Governor Harry White, but left the position after only three months due to the petty political bickering incumbent with the position. Soon afterwards he was appointed county committeeman for his party. Maintaining an active interest in Republican affairs, he was elected State Executive Committee chairman in 1928. Alf was gaining more and more influence, counting among his close acquaintances Congressmen, Senators, Governors — even the Vice President of the United States, Charles Curtis, the Kansan who was elected with Herbert Hoover in 1928. But Alf supported the wrong candidate for the Republican gubernatorial nomination in 1930 and was ousted from his post.

The young Republican leader was also active in many civic endeavors. He was an Elk, belonged to the Izaak Walton League (a conservationist group), led a drive for the Red Cross, was active in the Chamber of Commerce, belonged to the American Legion, was a Director of the Mid-Continent Oil and Gas Association, and was selected to the national committee of Phi Gamma Delta. His business, political, social and civic contacts were gaining him more and more influence in Kansas.

Shortly after losing the chairmanship of the Republican State Committee, Alf was selected as one of a committee of three persons to protest an effort by major oil companies, which controlled the pipe lines that small "stripper" producers had to use to send their product to refineries, to cut off the independent oil producers in the Kansas area. The resourceful Alf applied to Washington for help but was refused. He then organized a boycott of Standard Oil products; this measure was so successful that the oil giant soon had a representative in Topeka negotiating with Landon on ways to rectify misunderstandings. This incident established the Republican political leader as a folk hero of sorts in Kansas, and was useful when he later decided to seek office.

Landon surprised most of the Kansas political experts when he announced in January of 1932 that he would be seeking the Republican nomination for Governor. He was not considered a good speaker or to be that well known politically. Moreover, the Republican party was in debacles after the Great Depression had begun under Herbert Hoover's tenure in 1929. The plain spoken candidate developed a charisma, though, by making the people he met on long drives across his state feel as though he were one of them and cared for them. In his campaign speeches he pledged to cut state spending and to eliminate delinquent taxes on the property taxes of farmers, who were strapped for cash in depression times. He also promised to slow down building programs until revenues were available to pay for them and to eliminate the ages-old practice of collecting five percent of each state employee's wages to finance an incumbent governor's campaign. Alf received an overwhelming popular vote victory in the state primary and obtained the Republican nomination with little problem. He then had to face not only the incumbent Democratic governor but also a maverick, independent "quack" doctor who was well financed and possessed outstanding speaking ability. Though Vice President Curtis was a Kansan campaigning for re-election, his chances did not appear good with Herbert Hoover heading the national ticket. Yet Landon campaigned tirelessly and won the three man race by a plurality of 6,000 out of nearly 800,000 cast. Though he received only 35 percent of the vote, his victory brought instant notoriety, for Landon had won in Kansas while most other Republicans nationwide were being decimated. National leaders decided in November of 1932 to keep an eye on the new Kansas Chief Executive.

GOVERNOR OF KANSAS

Taking office during troubled times, the forty-six year old Landon was true to his word on his campaign pledges. He immediately lobbied the Legislature to pass a "cash basis" law, which required state and local officials to have a line-by-line budget with both revenues and expenditures explained in advance, and to publish statements of financial condition to the public. To adjust the state's system of inequitable taxes, the new Governor simultaneously proposed an income tax together with cuts in the sales tax, gasoline levies and vehicle fees. To show his personal sincerity, the Governor took a voluntary 25 percent cut in his $5,000 annual salary (other state officials, particularly judges, followed suit). Having pledged governmental reform, the Governor delivered, soliciting an engineer, rather than the state party chairman, as was the custom, to run the highway department in a businesslike manner.

Landon's personal demeanor as Governor surprised many. He remained a plain-spoken man and encouraged thrift in all government and personal actions. He adopted an "open door" policy at the statehouse, so that anyone could walk into his office at practically any time for a conversation. But his plain manners belied his intellect, for he enlisted some able scholars from Eastern universities to advise him on state problems, particularly economic ones. Landon was opposed to state relief, feeling it was the responsibility of local governments to provide welfare assistance, but Kansas did receive much federal relief and public works money during the "New Deal," so much so that some referred to him as a New Deal governor. However, he surprised everyone when he opposed the Kiro Dam project, a massive program designed to create a lake along the Kaw River in Kansas for the use of military biplanes, because he felt it would add to flooding and erosion, destroy farmlands and railroads, and, of course, cost too much money. Public opposition was at first against the Governor, but when he explained his position, the people sided with him and the project was cancelled. Not just a critic, the Governor then urged the creation of ponds, with tax exempt status, to control erosion. Landon also used his influence to have utility rates reduced, advising corporations to make reductions along with everyone else.

A crisis for the entire state arose in 1933 when it was revealed that a Kansas businessman with considerable political connections had penetrated the state Treasurer's office and used the state seal to forge illegal bonds. Landon immediately instituted an investigation and cooperated with all agencies so that a clear accounting could be made, even though he had himself received contributions from the bond manipulator. Landon closed the treasurer's office over the protests of state bankers and amidst allegations by some that he had personally benefited from the corrupt operation. The kidnapping of his daughter was threatened, and he had to resort to the use of security guards to protect his family. When the investigation was complete, the state Treasurer was committed to jail and the bond manipulator committed suicide. Landon's reputation, however, was untarnished, primarily because of his forthrightness in the matter. He had also saved the state from a sizable fraudulent loss of revenues.

Landon was easily renominated for a second two-year term as Governor, and he coasted to an easy victory, receiving a plurality of 62,000 out of some 750,000 votes cast. He maintained his program of reform, instituting a measure (much in the same spirit of Teddy Roosevelt) to regulate corporations, while making sure that government agencies stayed within their means. Many had expected that the Governor would be swallowed up by the New Deal in 1934, but instead he had emerged from the election as the only notable Republican governor in power with any standing whatsoever. He wrote a brief book entitled *America at the Crossroads*, which had as one of its chapters the title "The New Frontier," a topic that was later copied by a liberal Democrat, John F. Kennedy. Many influential Kansas political leaders and some newspapers (including the Hearst chain) felt that Landon was the man to take on Franklin Roosevelt in 1936. Landon for President clubs were quickly formed throughout the country, and public opinion polls indicated that the Kansas Governor who could balance budgets was the leading candidate for the next Republican nomination.

RUNNING FOR PRESIDENT

Although former President Hoover wanted the nomination, the party did not want him. The initial opposition to Landon came from Senators Arthur Vandenburg of Michigan and Charles McNary of Oregon, but neither could muster any real support. Col. Frank Knox, the *Chicago Daily News* publisher, entered the race, as did, at the last minute, the famous progressive Nebraska Senator, W.E. Borah. Landon, however, with his winning record, a business (oil) background, a tie to the Progressive wing of the party dating back to TR's day, and a record for reducing the size of government spending and reducing taxes, was clearly the front runner for the nomination. Landon entered several primaries and did well overall in those races. He was careful not to alienate different factions of the party, and this wise move fostered much good will for him among party regulars. The Republican convention met in Cleveland and denounced the "alphabet soup" programs of the New Deal, claiming that the nation was "in peril," and also charging that there was a close tie with the New Deal and communism. These charges were not just idle Republican charges, for to the Republican dais came none other than Al Smith, the former Governor of New York and Democratic candidate for President in 1928 — whose nominating speech had been delivered by none other than Franklin Roosevelt — to condemn the New Deal programs. The 1924 Democratic nominee, John W. Davis, also condemned FDR, as did Woodrow Wilson's Secretary of State, Bainbridge Colby.

The forty-nine year old Landon received a first ballot nomination and accepted the Republican platform, which, in addition to condemning the New Deal, called for the gold standard to return, the removal of government controls of private enterprise so that employment would increase, placing relief at local levels, using old-age pensions in lieu of Social Security, enacting a protective tariff, following an isolationist foreign policy, and condemning the World Court. The new Presidential candidate had some difficulty in selecting a running mate but resolved this by asking the convention to make its own selection. Col. Knox was then chosen by acclamation, and the Republicans, aided by a $9 million dollar campaign chest, (the largest in history at that time), had high hopes for a November victory. The GOP gained more confidence when _Literary Digest_ polls showed a two-to-one edge for Landon. But Alf Landon had little chance of unseating the popular and wily Roosevelt, who had been renominated along with Vice President Garner on the first ballot of the Democratic convention at Philadelphia. The nation was united under FDR's leadership and reinforced by his indomitable spirit to overcome a national handicap, as he had overcome a personal one. Moreover, he significantly upstaged Landon during a midwest drought crisis: the President made a visit to Des Moines, Iowa, and state delegations, including the Kansas delegation headed by Landon, went _to_ the President almost as supplicants. When the votes were tabulated in November, FDR had scored a landslide victory of major proportions, carrying forty-six states (all but Maine and Vermont), receiving 60.2 percent of the popular vote and a plurality of almost eleven million votes. Landon, suffering the humiliation of not even carrying his home state of Kansas, lost in the Electoral College by the vote of 523 to 8.

A LONG, LONG POLITICAL RETIREMENT

Landon took defeat well personally. He visited the President at the White House, and the two were extremely cordial to each other. At the annual Gridiron Club dinner, the affable Kansan impressed the media with his sense of wit and magnanimity toward FDR. Completing his term of office as Governor in 1937, he assumed the role of "titular head" of the Republican Party and led the loyal opposition against FDR's attempt to pack the Supreme Court. He refused to run for any political office ever again, though maintaining that he had not retired from politics, and traveled widely, speaking on the various issues of the day. He also refused, though he did consider, an appointment to FDR's cabinet; his former running mate, Col. Frank Knox, accepted a Cabinet position as Secretary of the Navy.

When former President Hoover, whom Landon never really liked, made an attempt to have a mid-term national convention in 1938, Landon successfully thwarted the move, realizing that the former President was attempting to restore the "old guard" of the Republican Party to power. Landon, ever the Progressive, was working for a both a modern and a unified party. On the third ballot of the 1940 Republican Convention, Landon personally announced that all eighteen votes of the Kansas delegation were being cast for Wendell Willkie, who went on to win the nomination and run Roosevelt a good race, though the Republicans still could not capture the White House.

As World War II loomed, Landon envisioned an internationalist rather than an isolationist position for his party and the country. However, he thought FDR was out of order in calling for the "lend-lease" program for England. Even so, he did support the measure to reinstitute the draft, and his support was surely helpful, for the bill passed the House by the bare margin of one vote. When war came, the former candidate supported the moves to bring victory, but he clung tenaciously to the belief that partisan politics should be practiced even in time of war, announcing that this freedom was the cornerstone of American government. He was a leading campaigner in the 1942 off-year elections and rejoiced when the Republicans made gains in the House, the Senate and several statehouses.

In 1944 Landon led the movement to stop Willkie for a second nomination, believing that his statements and actions were too rash for election. He was not particularly fond of Thomas E. Dewey, but he did campaign widely for him and was disappointed that Roosevelt had been elected to a fourth term. When FDR died in 1945, Landon felt more comfortable with midwesterner Harry Truman, who held friendly meetings with the 1936 candidate. Landon supported the new President in his attempts to organize the United Nations, an agency which drew the earnest support of the former Republican nominee the rest of his life.

The 1948 election year found Landon in a familiar pattern — not supporting the previous nominee but trying to find a new candidate with the charisma to bring victory to the party. He tried to enlist Gen. Dwight Eisenhower to run, but Ike declined, choosing to become President of Colombia University. When Dewey was nominated, Landon supported him, but once again he saw his party lose the Presidency. The 1948 elections also saw the former Kansas Governor lose his base of power to conduct a national forum. Since the mid-1930's, "Landon's machine" had controlled Kansas politics, and Alf Landon had decided the fate of Kansas. But enemies had been made, and a party squabble in 1948 found Landon's progressive wing of the party losing control of Kansas. From then on, he was snubbed politically at state and the national levels. In 1952, he spoke against Eisenhower, whom he wanted drafted in 1948, and tried to get the Kansas delegation to support Ohio Senator Robert Taft, but again he was on the losing side. His efforts to be recruited to speak in favor of Ike were brusquely declined. After the election, the White House did not call him for advice.

In 1956, after Ike's illnesses, he declared that the President should not seek re-election and felt that Vice President Nixon was an acceptable candidate. In 1960, he favored New York Governor Nelson Rockefeller over Nixon.

His opinion of the 1964 Republican nominee, Barry Goldwater, was not at all high, but he continued to support the nominees of his party at both state and national levels.

He also continued to speak out on the issues of the day. He supported the Truman Doctrine in Turkey and Greece and the Marshall Plan in Europe. He also approved of Truman's use of the United Nations as a "police action" in Korea. He chastised Republicans for not endorsing free trade and for supporting protectionist policies. He applauded the work of the House Un-American Activities Committee but was critical of "McCarthyism" and its leader, who had after all defeated Robert LaFollette, the epitome of Progressivism in the United States. In 1958 he called for Ike's Secretary of State, John Foster Dulles, to resign, and in 1960, he appeared with Eleanor Roosevelt, Walter Reuther and Socialist Norman Thomas at a rally sponsored by the Committee for a Sane Nuclear Policy and spoke of the perils of nuclear war. Often sympathetic to causes of labor, he opposed right-to-work laws. He felt that John Kennedy was too young to handle the problems of the Presidency and was critical of Kennedy's mishandling of the Bay of Pigs. He also strongly disapproved of Kennedy's proposal to have the Executive Branch empowered to adjust tax rates without the approval of Congress, as well as JFK's later proposal to stimulate the economy through a tax cut. Through all of his public utterances, Alf Landon above all called for a balanced budget at any level of government.

After his fall from influence in 1948, Landon spent more time at his Topeka home, a 170 acre farm capped with a handsome Georgian colonial house. He continued to speculate in oil leases, which had provided him with a tidy return during World War II. He spent a good deal of time enjoying his favorite pastimes of riding his horses on his farm or hunting. Deciding to diversify his interests, he purchased several radio stations in Kansas and Colorado. He almost secured Denver's first television station but declined the opportunity to invest there, saying that the profit of margin was too low. With some insight he predicted the coming political influence of this medium, stating that future candidates would be have to be "telegenic" and have Hollywood "it" to be elected.

In 1958 progressive Republicans again gained control of the Kansas Republican Party and the Kansas statehouse, and Landon was restored somewhat to his former power. He was more in demand as a speaker and as a leader of civic causes. He became influential in the National Council of Christians and Jews, supported CARE, and raised funds for the Boys Clubs of America.

From time to time newspapers across the nation would carry articles about the 1936 nominee, who, though having suffered defeat overwhelmingly, was regarded with fondness by the American people. He kept his sense of humor over the years, once remarking that he was "...an oilman who never made a million, a lawyer who never tried a case, and a politician who carried only Maine and Vermont..."

Active to the end of his days, Landon kept fit by walking a quarter a mile a day. He maintained active political dialogue in Kansas and was pleased when his daughter, Nancy Kassebaum, was elected a United States Senator from Kansas in 1978. She was re-elected in 1984 and 1990.

Three days before his one-hundredth birthday, Air Force One made a stop in Kansas so that the President of the United States, Ronald Reagan, could join millions of Americans in congratulating the former Kansas Governor and Presidential candidate on this milestone. Shortly afterwards, Landon was hospitalized for gallstone problems and bronchitis. He returned to the nursing home where he was staying for recuperation, but he passed away just a little over a month after the visit of the President, who had led millions of Americans in a proper tribute for one who had made so many contributions to Kansas and the nation.

Wendell Willkie

The Election of 1940

Few people have catapulted to the top of American politics as did Wendell Willkie, the Democratic businessman and attorney who was drafted by the Republicans in 1940. Forceful and dynamic, he was also far-reaching in his imagination and appeal. While losing to the popular Franklin Roosevelt is in retrospect understandable, his political biography should not be so easily forgotten.

INDIANA FARM BOY

Born in Elwood, Indiana, on February 18, 1892, Lewis Wendell Willkie was the fourth child of Herman Francis and Henrietta Trisch Willkie. Of German lineage, Willkie's father had been a schoolteacher and was also an attorney. He was a strict but sensitive parent who saw that his children received a good education and the proper civic outlook on life. A Democrat, he was a friend of "The Great Commoner," William Jennings Bryan, and Woodrow Wilson's Vice President, Thomas R. Marshall, each of whom he invited to speak to his Methodist Sunday School class. Willkie's mother was also a former schoolteacher turned attorney, a highly unlikely position for a lady at the turn of the twentieth century. Not as sensitive to her children as her husband, she was equivalent, more or less, to a modern day feminist.

Willkie graduated from Elwood High School, serving as President of his senior class, and then attended Indiana University, where he showed a proclivity to debating. He was a member of the school's Booster Club and served as a director of the Jackson Club, an undergraduate Democratic organization. At first he disavowed fraternities, but in his senior year he was inducted into Beta Theta Pi, perhaps because of a girlfriend who had already persuaded him to join the Episcopal Church. To help pay for his college tuition, Willkie worked a number of part-time odd jobs and summer jobs, including vegetable picker in South Dakota, a wheat harvester in Wyoming, and an oil field laborer in Texas.

Upon graduation from Indiana in 1913, Willkie accepted a position as a history teacher and coach of track, basketball and debate at a high school in Kansas City to earn money to attend law school. After one term of teaching, he moved to Puerto Rico and became a laboratory assistant at a sugar company where his brother was head chemist. An event that was to sear Willkie's memory for life occurred while he was there. During a strike of the plantation's employees, the young Indianian accompanied the plantation manager on a horseback ride. Suddenly a native striker sprang out of some bushes. The manager, taking no chances, swung his cane knife and nearly severed the possible attacker's arm at the shoulder, never stopping his ride to show any concern for the native. Such indifference became a life-long concern of Willkie's.

After saving enough money, Willkie returned to Indiana University for the study of law. An outstanding student who ranked at the top of his class, he was chosen as a speaker at the 1916 commencement. However, his message was such an attack upon the Indiana state constitution that the law faculty refused at first to grant him his degree, but it was conferred several days later. At age twenty-five, Willkie was ready to begin his practice of law.

He joined his parents' firm, Willkie and Willkie, but before he could develop a significant practice World War I erupted. Willkie joined the Army and was commissioned a Second Lieutenant. He became an artillery officer and was sent to Europe. However, the war ended before he could see combat action. He spent the rest of his time as a successful defense attorney in rather minor court-martial cases, such as AWOL. He left the Army with the rank of Captain.

During a leave, Willkie had taken as his wife Edith Wilk, an Indiana lass whom he had met at the wedding of a friend. Theirs was to be a long and faithful marriage. The couple had one son, born in 1919, and she was to be a business and political confidant over the years.

In 1919 Willkie was solicited by some Elwood area friends to run for Congress — as a Democrat. Having served as an officer in the war and dedicated to the progressive policies, including the League of Nations of Woodrow Wilson, he was tempted to run. However, a friend persuaded him not to do so, arguing that he might win the current election, only to go down to defeat in traditionally Republican Indiana the next election, thence to serve an obscure politician's existence.

CORPORATE LAWYER IN OHIO

The same friend suggested that Willkie apply for a position with an entrepreneur named Harvey Firestone in the newly created rubber tire business in Akron, Ohio. Firestone hired Willkie, paying him $175 per month, for the purpose of giving free legal advice and services to his employees. Willkie's services must have been good, for his salary advanced to $5,000 annually within two years. When Willkie told Firestone that he wished to enter private practice, Firestone first offered to double his earnings. However, Willkie declined this offer. Firestone then told him he would never amount to much because he was a Democrat.

When Willkie left Firestone in 1921, his career began to blossom. Within three years he became a partner in Mather, Nesbitt and Willkie, not only becoming an outstanding trial lawyer (many saying he was the best in Akron) but also becoming an astute negotiator for utility companies. He was active in civic affairs, organizing an American Legion Post and serving as its commander, successfully leading a movement to oust avowed members of the Ku Klux Klan who were on the local school board, and serving as President of the Akron Bar in 1925. In addition, he was in constant demand as an after-dinner speaker for Kiwanis, Rotary, Boy Scouts and other civic groups.

One event at which Willkie spoke was a 1920 campaign rally for Ohio Gov. James M. Cox, the Democratic nominee for President. Willkie confided to Cox that he was a confirmed liberal. He must have been active in party matters, for he was a delegate to the Democratic National Conventions in 1924 and 1932. At the '24 Convention, he supported moves to banish the Klan and keep the League of Nations.

While a liberal progressive in political matters, Willkie was becoming a respected member of the business community. His practice was lucrative, and he joined a country club. He was elected a Director of the Ohio State Bank and the Northern Ohio Power and Light Company. When the utility industry was under consideration for investigation by the Senate in the 1920's, he who was chosen to go to Washington and lobby for utility interests.

NEW YORK UTILITY EXECUTIVE

Willkie's stature and ability were so great that soon other people in other areas were watching and wanting him. In 1929, after ten happy and successful years in Akron, the Indiana native was asked to move to New York City and join in the legal representation of a giant new holding company in the electrical utility field at the commanding salary of $36,000 per year. Only thirty-seven, Willkie was about to become one of the nation's leading business barons.

Weadock and Willkie was general counsel for the Commonwealth and Southern Company, a holding company with ties to J.P. Morgan and with over $1 billion in assets in power companies such as the Tennessee-Electric Power Company, Georgia Power, Alabama Power, Mississippi Power, Gulf Power, Central Illinois Light Company, Southern Indiana Gas and Electric Company, Ohio Edison, Pennsylvania Power and Consumers Power Company of Michigan. C & S, along with numerous other holding companies, was under investigation for corrupt pyramid schemes in corporate organization and finance, and considerable pressure was being applied by New York Gov. Al Smith, among others, for their breakup.

Against this backdrop, Willkie proposed some dramatic changes for holding companies. Only day-to-day managers, he averred, should be Directors, and banking control of utilities should be eliminated. Furthermore, holding companies should be self-regulated to prevent internal corrupt practices (Willkie implemented this policy within eighteen months after taking control of C & S). While this position was a refreshing change in some quarters, it was not enough to satisfy the reform movement, which ironically had been given sustenance by Willkie as a liberal progressive. Other liberals had views different from Willkie. One was Franklin Roosevelt, who took office as the new President in March, 1933, just a few months after Wendell Willkie had become President of C & S. Very soon the government of the New Deal and the holding company of utility interests would be in a bitter legal and philosophical battle, a battle that would be one of the chief legal-business encounters of the century. And the chief executives of each entity — Franklin Roosevelt and Wendell Willkie — would also become involved in a bitter philosophical and political battle, one that would move from the courtroom to the American living room in 1940.

Willkie, at age forty-two the youngest chief executive of a utility company in the nation, was an effective chief executive for C & S. Besides removing the outside Directors, he also removed lawyers in local utility areas who were given bonds or stock in return for not only representing C & S but for on occasion not suing the holding company. He also simplified corporate structure, reducing overhead costs and adopting an aggressive rate schedule. Willkie himself engaged in a gigantic public relations campaign. Often he would take whirlwind tours of Southern cities, making speeches and visiting with newspaper editors. In addition to this, he promoted the sale of appliances so that more power would be required and sold by his companies. Willkie showed a shrewd banker's skill in this area: he devised a program whereby the utility companies would allow customers to buy appliances and have them financed by increased monthly payments on their utility bills. Soon banks saw the wisdom of this procedure and adopted it; Willkie later withdrew his creative technique, but many Americans still enjoy comforts and pleasures because of his innovative financial thought. The financial results of Willkie's leadership were excellent, considering the Great Depression. Profits dropped somewhat, with a loss occurring for two years, but then his conglomerate rebounded and was in the black once again.

TAKING ON THE NEW DEAL

Despite Willkie's sincere efforts to clean up his holding company, FDR's New Deal still wanted the elimination of such corporations and enacted two programs that were to be the death knell of C & S and the entire public utility holding interests. One, in the form of the Wheeler-Rayburn Act, called for the regulation of holding companies as well as the rates they charged. The other, in the form of the TVA act, called for competition with private companies in the Tennessee Valley region, most of which were controlled by Willkie's own C & S holding company.

Willkie was cautious at first in attacking TVA, claiming only that the government had no need to produce power when it was already being adequately produced by private companies. A deal was struck between C & S and TVA in 1934 in which the utility sold TVA distribution line systems for a profit and in which C & S and TVA agreed that neither would sell power in the same territories. This arrangement worked well for C & S, since some subsidiaries were selling power at thirty times cost. But then TVA began selling its power at much lower rates, and the Tennessee Valley public clamored for the government power agency to sell at low rates in all areas. A crisis for the future of privately owned utilities erupted when TVA said it would start negotiating with municipalities to distribute power. Willkie, who became the leader for the cause of private enterprise, mounted an attack on the New Deal on two fronts. One was a public relations assault. In a series of public appearances, Willkie claimed the New Deal proposals to compete with private utility companies were based on improper capitalization methods and that TVA was an experiment in socialism. However, Willkie was careful not to attack New Deal leaders personally; indeed, his relations were so cordial with New Dealers that he was invited to the White House on several occasions to discuss matters with FDR.

The other action that Willkie and others conducted was a legal one: the utility and holding company interests filed suit on the grounds that the TVA Act and certain others were unconstitutional. The holding companies were hopeful that they could prevail in court, since several key pieces of New Deal legislation, especially the National Recovery Act, had been declared unconstitutional. But as time went by, the Courts became more favorable to the New Deal, and when the time came for the TVA Act to be ruled on, the Supreme Court refused to rule on the TVA's constitutionality, instead directing that TVA could sell its surplus power to various distributing companies. Soon TVA and C & S were in direct competition, with TVA losing C & S as its biggest customer and each party criss-crossing each other's distribution lines throughout the Tennessee Valley. More legislation challenging TVA's constitutionality was filed, but now, with a series of dams in place, TVA was in the position of power. Willkie realized this, and arrangements were made for TVA and C & S to negotiate concerning the sell of C & S's assets in the Tennessee Valley to TVA. After several years of intricate bargaining, TVA purchased the C & S holdings for $78,600,000. Upon receiving a check from TVA Chairman David Lilienthal, the affable Willkie remarked, "This is a lot of money for a couple of Indiana farm boys to be kicking around..." Willkie, one of the two Indiana farm boys, would soon be getting kicked around in another area: the Supreme Court would rule that holding companies must register with the Securities and Exchange Commission and reveal their assets and methods of operating.

Willkie had always considered himself a Democrat — a liberal progressive Democrat at that. He had registered as such when he first came of age, had considered running for Congress as one after World War I, had attended national conventions in 1924 and 1932, had been a member of the New York County Executive Committee, had been elected to Tammany Hall and had even made a $150 contribution to FDR. As late as 1938, he was still registered as a Democrat. But his involvement in the utility struggles and other New Deal proposals had found him honestly questioning the direction of the Democratic Party, especially as it embraced the New Deal.

RUNNING FOR PRESIDENT

The Republican Party, bereft with an image of being only for the rich and with being responsible for the Great Depression, was in disarray in the late 30's. Herbert Hoover, the sitting President in 1932, had been turned out by a resounding vote, and the ever popular FDR had easily turned back the challenge of Kansas Governor Alf Landon in 1936. Roosevelt, a remarkable orator and experienced administrator, had his way both in government and politics for the most part. The only hope for the Republicans to oust FDR, should he seek a third term, was to nominate a man with a forceful demeanor, a dynamic personality, and an indomitable spirit to battle the President and the New Deal. Wendell Willkie would soon be looked upon by the

Republican Party as the man to take on the President in 1940.

Willkie had received enormous attention from his battle with the New Deal. In court he would often receive the attention of the media, and his views were published throughout the nation's journals. He would often speak on nationwide radio shows, during radio's "golden age" of popularity. He wrote articles for leading weekly magazines, including the *Saturday Evening Post*, the *Atlantic Monthly* and *Life*, in which he charged that government controls were leading to government ownership. In addition, Willkie went on extended tours, speaking to civic clubs throughout the nation and warning of the dangers of big government, which he said had "...succeeded big business as the chief threat to the liberal tradition..." Willkie also received enormous public attention by serving as president of the New York Economic Club, a powerful group whose leader was required to speak and be interviewed often. With a raspy but sincere voice coupled with oratorical gestures that were compelling, the Hoosier who had gone to the top at Wall Street and taken on the New Deal toe-to-toe was being mentioned as early as 1937 as one who should be considered to run for President.

Though he had never run for public office, Willkie had considerable political experience from his many trips to Washington to lobby and testify for utility interests. His trips to the Democratic conventions and his service in various Democratic positions had also given him some political experience. But how he obtained the Republican nomination was a novelty in American politics. Beginning with favorable articles by certain columnists in periodicals, the whole Luce publishing organization ended up endorsing him. Soon, over two-thousand nationwide requests were issued for the six-foot, 220 pounder to speak to various groups. Willkie accepted many of them, telling one crowd as he felt out whether or not he should run, "If you want to vote for me, fine. If you don't, go jump in the lake and I'm still for you." Such talk caught fire, as did "Win with Willkie" clubs, which were an overnight sensation. Russell Davenport, the managing editor of *Fortune* magazine, resigned, against Willkie's advice, to act as a campaign manager of sorts. Other volunteers signed petitions urging Willkie to run in 1940.

However, Willkie did not choose to run in any of the Republican primaries or engage in any bantering or debate with life-long party members who were seeking the nomination in the established pattern. To be sure, there were several men interested in the nomination, including Sen. Arthur Vandenburg, Sen. Robert Taft and the front runner, New York District Attorney Thomas E. Dewey. Dewey had won most of the primaries that he had entered and had polls at one point showing him favored by 67 percent of Republican voters. Undaunted, Willkie supporters in the press pushed him so fast and so far that he had increased from 3 to 29 percent by the time of the late June convention in Philadelphia, at the expense of Dewey, who had dropped to 47 percent in the polls. This drop certainly damaged Dewey, whom columnists now claimed was fading in favor of their choice - Wendell Willkie.

With no staff and no campaign organization, Willkie, a Democrat less than two years before, went to Philadelphia with momentum in his favor. Many well known Governors and Senators were joining his team, and his opposition seemed helpless to stop him. A million letters and telegrams were sent to convention delegates urging Willkie's nomination. The galleries were packed with partisans who shouted down the nominations of Dewey and others, giving the convention the impression that Willkie was the choice of rank and file members of the party. Minnesota Gov. Harold Stassen, the convention "Keynote" speaker, became Willkie's floor manager after delivering his address, and soon the votes for Willkie began to increase. Starting in third place on the first ballot, his totals gradually increased at the expense of Dewey. On the fourth ballot, Alf Landon, the '36 nominee, personally announced that Kansas would shift its votes to Willkie. A motion to adjourn the convention was denied and other states flooded to Willkie's camp. A last minute attempt to forge a Taft-Dewey ticket failed and Willkie became the Republican nominee on the sixth ballot. So new to the Republican Party was Wendell Willkie that Charles McNary, the Republican Senate leader who in twenty - five years in the Senate had never made a speech (boasting that one could not get into trouble if he didn't say too much), was chosen as the Vice Presidential nominee, even though the two had never met.

Now the Republican nominee, the forty-eight year old Willkie registered as a member of that party. He resigned his $75,000 per year job, put his personal and business affairs in order, and began waging one of the most vigorous campaigns in American political history. Delivering his official acceptance speech in his Elwood, Indiana home town, Willkie reminded his audience of 250,000 of his humble beginnings and appealed to voters to elect as President one who had risen to great heights in the business community. His campaign was upbeat and sensing victory as the *Willkie Special*, his chartered train, then set out on a grueling schedule of nearly 19,000 miles. His hoarse Indiana voice charged his audiences with electricity as he called for a "Crusade for Liberty" that would end the New Deal's government controls. Speaking so often (he gave 560 separate addresses) required that a doctor be kept on his train to constantly treat his throat and allow him to continue his hectic schedule.

The campaign did have some unsavory moments. FDR was discovered to be using some of Wilikie's speech materials; they had been supplied by a lady reporter traveling on Willkie's train. Objects were hurled at Willkie, and a frozen egg once struck him in the eye. Perhaps the most distasteful act was an attempt, through the Colored Division of the Democratic National Committee, to tie Willkie's German heritage to Adolph Hitler. Unsigned leaflets were circulated alleging Willkie's sister had married a German Naval Officer, who in fact was the U.S. Naval Attache to Berlin. Willkie, for his part, stated that he wanted no part of that type of campaign and refused to use some sensitive material gathered on Henry Wallace, the Democratic Vice Presidential candidate. He did, however, as his election hopes dimmed, charge that the United States would be in war if Roosevelt were elected to a third term. To his credit, Willkie, at FDR's request, endorsed two key foreign policy provisions, the sale of war goods to Great Britain and the Selective Service System, and did not make a political issue of these items.

War, a third term for FDR, and the New Deal government controls were the issues Willkie presented to the American people. The President was concerned about his Republican opponent, but he steadfastly refused to mention Willkie's name in his speeches or to reply to any of the charges that Willkie asserted. Try as he might, Willkie could not rid himself of being an "economic royalist" from Wall Street rather than an Indiana farm boy made good. And Willkie, an inexperienced politician, did not realize how big of a mistake he made when he attacked FDR's Secretary of Labor, Frances Perkins, for not only making bad policy but for being a woman, too. Roosevelt, the consummate politician, relied on his record of leading the nation out of the Great Depression for victory in 1940. When war in Europe erupted during the campaign, Roosevelt was able to convey to the American people the wisdom of not changing horses in the middle of the stream. On election day, Willkie suffered an overwhelming defeat, with Roosevelt gathering 27,243,466 popular votes to Willkie's 22,304,755, and with FDR winning the electoral vote, 449 to 82.

ONE WORLD

Willkie gave Roosevelt the hardest of the four battles for the White House that FDR made, but his hard attack of FDR's policies during the battle did not continue after the election. Indeed, Willkie began to espouse ideas that would ultimately estrange him from the Republican Party. Republican leadership at the time was in favor of winning the war but opposed to the emerging talk of world government. Willkie, for his part, embraced the idea. He had favored the League after World War I and felt the lack of its creation had led to World War II.

Willkie also supported FDR's "Lend-Lease" program for Great Britain. Soon he was visiting London and delivering a letter from FDR to England's Prime Minister, Winston Churchill. He also visited the King and Queen of England and then visited the heads of states in other European countries. While this trip built up Willkie's foreign policy credentials and endeared him to many liberal news commentators, "old-guard" party leaders saw it as a surrender of Republican principles. When Willkie wrote articles for periodicals and made various speeches around the country not just supporting the war effort but calling for unified world leadership for peace after the war, these leaders became more wary. And when Willkie agreed to serve as counsel without fee for a communist faced with losing his citizenship, Republican leaders were not only alarmed but outraged. Willkie's supporters encouraged him to run for public office, but positions that were open, such as Congressman, did not appeal to him. He continued his practice of law as much as he could and continued to speak often and contribute articles to periodicals. He also found time to serve on various committees dedicated to human and civil rights and became somewhat a champion of such causes, receiving many awards for his efforts.

The 1940 Presidential candidate maintained close relations with President Roosevelt, whom he admired but did not trust, because of FDR's political cunning and manipulation. When the President offered to allow Willkie the use of military aircraft and facilities to travel around the world and visit various allied leaders in support his views on a world governing body, Willkie readily accepted. In a grueling trip of over 31,000 miles over fifty days, Willkie circumnavigated the globe by first going to South America, then to North Africa, to Egypt, the Middle East, to Moscow, China, Siberia, Alaska and then back to the United States. Willkie conversed with army privates and heads of state, including Joseph Stalin and Chiang Kai-shek. Roosevelt had agreed that Willkie could speak his own piece, and Willkie often did, brusquely calling for a second front in Europe, as Stalin desired, and also stating, to the mortification of England, that the war should put an end to empires. When he returned to the United States, Willkie wrote a book, *One World*, in which he postulated his theories for a peaceful world after World War II. It was clear from this book that Willkie would favor the creation of a body such as the United Nations.

One World, which Willkie was to say as the highest satisfaction of his life, even over the nomination of 1940, was an immediate best seller, reaching the 1,000,000 mark almost overnight. Subsequent editions and Book-of-the-Month selections added to its popularity. Sales were also popular in Europe; after the war had ended, it even became a best seller in Germany, where just a few years before Willkie had been feared by Propaganda Minister Joseph Goebbels as perhaps a harder leader to deal with than FDR. *One World* also placed Wendell Willkie in the forefront of consideration for the Republican nomination in 1944.

New York Gov. Thomas Dewey, as in 1940, was the front runner for the Republican nod, but Willkie hoped to make an appeal through the news media to garner the necessary support for victory. However, his closest advisers convinced him that in order to do so, he must enter the primaries, something he had not done in 1940. Willkie wanted to enter the California primary, which he thought best suited to his views, but Gov. Earl Warren was entering that primary as a "favorite son." Willkie decided, therefore, to enter other primaries that might not be as favorable as he had anticipated California to be. The first was New Hampshire, and he won six of eleven delegates from that state. But the next primary, Wisconsin — a state where he had done well in the 1944 election — proved to be Willkie's downfall. All the established Republican leadership was now opposed to the liberal who was too much akin to FDR. When the ballots were counted, Willkie did not receive enough votes to win even one delegate to the national convention. The next day he withdrew as a candidate for the Republican nomination in 1944.

That Willkie had lost was not too great of a surprise to seasoned political observers, for Willkie was a liberal progressive before he was a Republican. As time went by in 1944, he bided his time on endorsing a Republican for the nomination and did not formally endorse the candidacy of Dewey once he was nominated (Willkie did not speak nor was he a delegate to the Republican convention). In the meantime, his old adversary, Franklin Delano Roosevelt, courted Willkie consistently and graciously. From time to time, rumors had it that Willkie would take a post in the FDR administration, such as Secretary of the Navy. Another rumor held that FDR wanted civilian control over the Army in Europe, and that Willkie was his choice for this post, if it were created. Finally, there is some evidence to support a rumor that FDR wanted Willkie as his running mate in 1944!. The President apparently wanted a realignment of parties, with the unification of liberal Democrats and Republicans opposed to the conservatives in both parties. He also felt that the selection of the 1940 Republican nominee would be a signal to the world that the United States was united in its war effort. But just as established Republican leaders did not want Willkie, neither did Democratic leaders. In the final analysis, FDR's Vice Presidential running mate and successor would be Harry Truman.

UNEXPECTED DEATH

Wendell Willkie would not have succeeded FDR had he been selected to run with him. In September, the ever hard-driving crusader suffered a major heart attack. He tried to keep from the public the seriousness of his illness, still hoping for a future try for the Presidency. Over the next thirty days, thirteen more attacks would strike the man who seemed hardy but who had refused to take care of himself over the years. Yet even on his deathbed, he continued to work, answering letters, granting interviews and giving political advice to those who would listen. Then on October 8, 1944, he suffered three final heart attacks and passed away.

Tributes from President Roosevelt, Gov. Dewey, former President Hoover, Winston Churchill, Joseph Stalin, Chiang Kai-shek and a host of other national and world leaders were immediately given to the unsuccessful 1940 candidate and author of *One World*. Thirty-five thousand mourners waited outside the Fifth Avenue Presbyterian Church in New York to pay final respects; inside six thousand more — family, friends, national and international political leaders — attended a memorial service before his body was returned to his native Indiana for burial. Though of diverse philosophies, they had all gathered to pay their final respects to the Indiana Hoosier who had risen from obscure beginnings to the top of the legal, business, and political life of the United States.

Thomas E. Dewey
The Elections of 1944 and 1948

Thomas E. Dewey dashed across the pages of American history in a blaze of glory only to be denied the ultimate American political prize: the Presidency of the United States. He was an honest man and an able administrator. He was also very practical and pragmatic, so much so that one advisor said of his common sense that "...he was born with it to an uncommon degree..." More than any political figure of his age, he was the subject of numerous movies, being emulated over and over again as the "gang buster" who showed that crime did not pay. Though twice losing the Presidency, he still made many valuable contributions to the nation, keeping the two party system intact and allowing future Republican contenders to gain the coveted office.

MICHIGAN FARM BOY

"A ten-pound Republican voter was born last evening...," read the local newspaper on the occasion of Thomas E. Deweys's birth on March 24, 1902. He was born in Owosso, Michigan, of conservative, hard-working parents, and was descended from French Protestants who had migrated to the New World before the Revolution, in which they fought. His father alternated between publishing a newspaper, farming and working for merchants before becoming a Republican Postmaster under Harding, while his mother helped provide for the family by teaching piano lessons. All of the Dewey children were expected to work, and years later Dewey would remember, not altogether fondly, how hard he had had to labor as a child.

He attended grammar and high school at Owosso and graduated at the top of his class. He had earned enough money selling magazines, sweeping floors in drugstores, and working in a poultry plant plucking chickens to pay his tuition to the University of Michigan at Ann Arbor. There he became a reporter for the *Michigan Daily* campus paper, joined a social fraternity and entered into much of the social life of the campus. His course of study centered on liberal arts and literature, with his scholastic average a B-plus. He was called home at one point in his college career to run the family newspaper, but this work did not appeal to him, and the family soon sold the paper, allowing Tom to continue his college education.

Dewey showed little interest in political science or history but was quite interested in Opera. He performed in several school productions, won a state Voice contest and then placed third in a national contest conducted in North Carolina. Encouraged by this, Dewey decided to pursue his musical study further. His midwest pragmatism, however, dictated that he also have an alternate acceptable avocation; this he provided by enrolling in the full-time study of law at the University of Michigan while studying Voice part-time. In 1923 Tom received an offer to leave Ann Arbor and go to Chicago to take a refresher course in Music from a New York singing coach. Tom spent a summer in Chicago (a city he hated), and then decided to pursue his musical talents further in New York City, moving into Greenwich Village. Soon he had a solo role in an off-Broadway performance. Unfortunately, he came down with a case of laryngitis and lost control of his voice during the show. Reviews were bad, and his musical career was finished.

Fortunately, Tom was able to pursue his second career choice, the law, in which he had been taking further courses at Colombia. Able to put the failure of his musical career behind him, he now plunged himself totally into his legal studies, at which he excelled. One of his fellow students was William O. Douglas, future Supreme Court Justice and almost the nominee for Vice President with Franklin Roosevelt in 1944. If he had been selected in 1944, he would probably have faced Dewey for President in 1948. Dewey completed his Columbia studies in 1924, traveled in Europe with some friends that summer, and began the practice of law in New York City the same year.

During his summer in Chicago, Tom had become acquainted with Frances Hughes, the secretary of his music coach. He had renewed this acquaintance upon coming to New York, and they grew closer and closer. In 1928, the two were married in an Episcopal service. They would have a long and close marriage, becoming the parents of two sons. During his 1924 summer trip to Europe Tom had grown a mustache which Frances admired. All through his political career cartoonists poked fun of his Charlie Chaplin appearance, and advisors tried to get Dewey to shave it off, but he steadfastly refused to do so because his wife liked it.

INTO LAW AND ASSISTANT DISTRICT ATTORNEY

Becoming established as a lawyer in New York in the 1920's was not easy. Dewey shared an office with several associates, all of whom were on probation. A dispute between Dewey and a senior associate resulted in his dismissal, but he joined a smaller firm through which his diligent efforts gained him a more secure future.

Tom and Frances settled into their new life with a love of New York that few natives possessed. The stage and theatre offered them the entertainment they desired. They also had a love of the sea, which could be satisfied nearby. And Tom's career could be advanced further and faster in New York than perhaps anywhere else. Additionally, the midwesterner enjoyed participating in Republican Party affairs at a time when Republicans were rather scarce.

While working on a rather large civil suit, Dewey acquired the services of an experienced attorney to assist him. George Medalie was not only a good attorney but a Republican leader who would later run unsuccessfully for the Senate. When President Hoover appointed Medalie to be U.S. Attorney for the Southern District of New York, Medalie persuaded the twenty-eight year old Dewey to join his staff. It was to be an appointment that changed Dewey's life and eventually put him into the national political arena.

Appointed to a staff position, Dewey immediately showed administrative skills that would be a trademark of his career. He was a hard-driving superior who demanded perfection of subordinates. Soon he would advance from administration to the courtroom, where he would in time become known as the nation's premier gang buster. Perhaps because of his love of drama, theatre and Opera, Dewey was an ideal prosecutor. Over the next decade he would rise time and time again in open court before a jury and dramatically cry, "Convict him in the name of justice!..." as the final line of a summation against an individual of the elements of New York City organized crime. For a young assistant DA, his record was impressive; he sent hoodlums and unscrupulous police and government officials to prison, and he broke up fraudulent insurance schemes as well.

SPECIAL PROSECUTOR AND DISTRICT ATTORNEY

When Franklin Roosevelt became President, Dewey, who was by that time quite active in Republican circles, resigned his position to resume private practice. He had achieved a tremendous following, having spoken on nationwide radio and having been seen on numerous movie newsreels. He was the man who had taken on New York mobsters during Prohibition and sent them to jail. As he left the DA's office, he told friends privately that he wanted to head a private practice and "...make a hell of a lot of money."

Then, unbelievably, some private citizens took action that led to Dewey's appointment as a Special Prosecutor. A grand jury was investigating mob actions and charged that the present DA was not fulfilling his duty. Soon a cry was being heard from other private citizens, the press and then other government officials that someone be picked for the state position that would do the job. In short order the press picked up on the name of Thomas E. Dewey and began promoting him for the position. This presented a dilemma to Gov. Herman Lehman and other New Deal Democrats (including FDR), but they relented to the appointment of the Republican "Baby Prosecutor."

Dewey's performance in his new office was astounding. Using superior organization and such tactics as wire tapping, he took on a mighty array of name figures such as Johnny Dio, Jimmy Doyle, Dutch Schultz and Lucky Luciano. So relentless was Dewey's pursuit of these mobsters and their activities that gang wars broke out when Dewey was not sending them to jail, the racketeers believing that they were "squealing" on each other. A significant slowdown of the numbers rackets, prostitution and murder was evident. Corrupt officials were sent to prison also. The ultimate conviction was that of Luciano, the gangland boss thought to be above the law. He was found guilty on 558 counts of illegal activity.

The Special Prosecutors's tough reputation was now nationwide. He solidified his support in Democratic New York when he went on the air to make a radio reports somewhat in the style of FDR. "Tonight," he said in a voice so calm that many thought he had ice water in his veins, "I am going to talk with you about murder." In later speeches he would talk "...about the alliance between crime and politics..." or "..about a politician, a political ally of thieves, pick-pockets, thugs, dope peddlers, and big-shot racketeers..." By using such a format and continuing to prosecute illegal union activities, the rackets and corrupt officials, he built confidence with the people of New York. When the election for District Attorney came about in 1937, Dewey was an overwhelming choice of the voters to hold the office in his own right. It was Dewey's first electoral victory and doubly important because he outpolled all Republican candidates, including the feisty Mayor of New York City, Fiorella LaGuardia. Thomas E. Dewey at age thirty-five was being considered for Governor of New York and possibly President of the United States.

As the elected District Attorney, Dewey concentrated on the prosecution of more organized crime figures. But he also went after the rich, embarrassing FDR when Richard Whitney, Harvard educated and the SEC buddy of William O. Douglas, was indicted for violating his wife's trust fund. No one was surprised when Dewey announced that he would run for Governor in 1938 against incumbent Herman Lehman. Such a challenge would be indeed bold, for Dewey at age thirty-six would be taking on the Democrats in the home state of the New Deal and its leader, Franklin Delano Roosevelt.

In a hard hitting campaign, the young challenger struck against Lehman on unemployment compensation, housing, Civil Service, electric rates and for having ties too close to organized crime. But Lehman and the New Deal were also popular in New York, and Dewey suffered his first defeat, by 70,000 votes. Yet Thomas Dewey was not disheartened. A Gallup poll showed him as the choice of 33 percent of Republican voters to be President. And he knew that the Republican Party would probably be choosing him to run again for Governor... or possibly for President of the United States.

GOVERNOR OF NEW YORK

Dewey was a rising political star. Going into the 1940 Republican Convention in Philadelphia, he was the front runner for the nomination for President although the highest office he had held was state District Attorney. He had traveled extensively throughout the midwest, using his favorite campaign technique of citing economic statistics to show New Deal weaknesses. He had won primaries in Wisconsin and Nebraska and forced Sen. Arthur Vandenburg of Michigan out of the race. Sen. Robert Taft of Ohio had been his remaining opposition, and the "Old Guard" of the party was rallying to stop the upstart from New York. The ensuing fight was so divisive that it split the party for years. Wendell Willkie, a former Democrat who had belonged to a Tammany Hall precinct, was now a converted Republican with a businessman's reputation, and he had mounted an impressive grass roots campaign, collecting 4.5 million signatures on a petition urging the Republican Party to nominate him. When the 1940 Convention deadlocked after initially casting more votes for the District Attorney than anyone else, momentum swung to Willkie, referred to by Dewey as "my fat friend," and the former Democrat won the nomination on the sixth ballot. Dewey campaigned widely for Willkie although he did not like him personally; he did not grieve greatly when FDR disposed of him in the November general election.

The state Republican Convention that met in 1942 knew who its gubernatorial candidate would be long before it met. Thomas E. Dewey was nominated with ease, experiencing only token opposition (Wendell Willkie had himself hinted at being a candidate). The Democrats had ignored FDR and nominated the choice of Jim Farley, FDR's former Postmaster General and campaign manager who had fallen out with the President over the third term (Farley had himself wanted to be the Democratic Presidential candidate in 1940), and this Democratic divisiveness made Dewey the front runner. Since the start of World War II, Dewey had traveled around the country in support of USO clubs and had raised over $10 million for that cause. He was therefore, although not a soldier, considered a strong military supporter, and he had the liberty of attacking FDR where justified. He came out rather strongly for civil rights, suggesting that it was wrong to fight against racism abroad and tolerate it at home. When the ballots were counted in November of 1942, Dewey had won an unheard of victory. Wendell Willkie had predicted a defeat of 500,000 votes — Dewey won by 647,000! He was definitely the leading contender for the 1944 Republican nomination.

Dewey would be Governor of New York from 1943 until 1955, a longer tenure than any New York Governor since DeWitt Clinton, also a former candidate for President. While preoccupied with the campaigns of 1944 and 1948, Dewey nonetheless accumulated a formidable record as Governor. He fought for Civil Rights; fought against killer diseases such as cancer and tuberculosis; fought for fiscal responsibility (it was remarkable that he never submitted an unbalanced budget and even more remarkable that taxes actually *declined* while he was Governor); built better roads; and, of course, always fought all elements of corruption and lawlessness. Dewey in fact was a liberal Republican leader and policy maker who would be emulated by Dwight Eisenhower and others in later years.

THE CAMPAIGN OF 1944

Dewey's main opposition for the nomination in 1944 would come from the 1940 candidate, Wendell Willkie, Ohio Governor John Bricker, and General Douglas MacArthur, the Pacific hero of World War II. Early in the campaign Dewey had made the usual disclaimers about being a candidate, but various public polls and party caucuses began to produce, in effect, a draft. Herbert Hoover and Alf Landon were solidly behind him.

When the primary season opened in early 1944, Dewey proceeded to demolish his opposition. He won overwhelmingly in Wisconsin, where Willkie did not win a single delegate. Other primaries gave Dewey such a comfortable early lead that he extended overtures to Bricker to be his running mate so that conservatives would be mollified. Bricker withdrew his name at the Chicago convention, and Dewey won the nomination on the first ballot. The Vice Presidential choice of Dewey was Gov. Bricker.

In a move reminiscent of FDR, Dewey flew from Albany to Chicago and delivered an inspiring speech to the delegates. He soon attacked the "tired old men" of FDR's administration, and the stage was set for a hard-hitting, dirty campaign. But the sly and clever Roosevelt countered Dewey with some novel moves. He delivered his acceptance speech from a naval base while on an "inspection tour." He refused, until the last moment, to engage in "partisan politics" while the war was in a critical stage. And he courted prominent Republicans, among them Wendell Wilkie, to endorse him. Willkie died during the campaign without endorsing either FDR or Dewey; his failure to endorse Dewey surely hurt the Republican Party.

As the campaign progressed, Dewey spoke more and more of the necessity of planning the postwar economy. He was tempted to charge that FDR knew of the impending attack on Pearl Harbor. On this he agonized privately, calling Roosevelt a "traitor" responsible for 1,000 lost lives at Hawaii, but finally desisted for fear that the Germans and Japanese would learn that the United States had broken the enemy's secret codes. FDR, upon learning of Dewey's knowledge of the situation, was said to have suffered from depression and to have begun to genuinely hate Dewey.

The campaign must have surely agitated Roosevelt, for he began walking around the White House (with the aid of his braces) for the first time in three years. It appeared for a while as though Dewey stood a good chance of upsetting the sitting President. But in the end FDR's charm and organization won out. This was the campaign that produced the memorable "Fala" speech, in which FDR humorously counter attacked Republicans for making charges against his family and his dog. Labor PAC's on election day delivered a sizable turnout for the President, who won rather easily with a popular margin of over 3.5 million and an electoral margin of 432 to 99. But FDR, who privately referred to Dewey as a *son-of-a-bitch*, was not totally elated, since he knew that the strategic shift of some 300,000 votes could have made his opponent President. Thomas E. Dewey was also aware of this.

THE CAMPAIGN OF 1948

Dewey did not experience undue remorse following the election of 1944. Insofar as 1948 was concerned, he did not expect the Republican Party to break its tradition of never nominating a losing candidate again. He continued to control New York state politics, running for and easily winning the Governor's chair in both 1945 and 1947.

What really made Dewey a candidate in 1948 was a series of events beginning with the death of FDR at the end of World War II. Harry Truman became President, and the new Chief Executive possessed neither the political ability nor the practical tact to ward off the momentous problems following the greatest of all wars. For his part, Dewey supported the new

President on such issues as the Marshall Plan and world security. But domestic issues were another matter altogether, and the New York Governor became the chief critic of price controls and the unbridled growth of labor unions. Truman himself seemed to have little control of either his party or the nation; the Congress went Republican in 1946, and his veto of the Taft-Hartley labor reform bill was not sustained.

Dewey's re-election in 1947 by the largest margin in New York history once again made him the chief Republican contender for '48. General Dwight Eisenhower was being mentioned prominently (by both parties), but Ike assured Dewey in a private meeting that he would not be running. Dewey had made a promise in the '47 Governor's race that he would not campaign for President until the state's legislative business was transacted, and keeping that promise made him enter the '48 primaries at a late date. Harold Stassen of Minnesota had gotten an early start and defeated Dewey in both Wisconsin and Nebraska. But in Oregon a debate was held between Dewey and Stassen that was pivotal. With the subject of "coddling Communists" the main issue, Dewey claimed that Communists had rights under the Constitution and should not be driven underground to fight. The Oregon voters agreed, and Dewey then became the front runner for the nomination.

The Republican Convention in Philadelphia was an exhibition of superior organization by the Dewey forces. Opposition was provided by forces of Stassen, Senator Taft of Ohio, Senator Vandenburg, and Gov. Earl Warren of California, but all were swept aside. Dewey was nominated on the third ballot, and Warren, who was to disappoint Dewey because of his poor campaigning techniques, was chosen as the Vice Presidential nominee. The convention adjourned with harmony, and the feeling was universal that Dewey would waltz to victory over Truman in November.

The Democratic Convention was to prove to be the opposite of tranquility. A civil rights platform that was sponsored by Hubert Humphrey and would start the brash, young Mayor of Minneapolis on a climb to national prominence caused a walkout of Southern delegates, who started the Dixiecrat Party. Adding to the division was former Vice President Henry Wallace, who started his own movement, looking for better Soviet relations. No one was seriously expecting Truman to win.

But Truman was to provide the political upset of the century. The brunt of many jokes, such as "To err is Truman" and "I'm just mild about Harry," the former haberdasher came out fighting not like a distinguished President but as a gutsy "ward heeler" from Missouri. He proclaimed the Republican

Congress a "do nothing" body, and called a special session of the group to do something. He promised to give the Republicans the whipping of their lives. In his famous whistle-stop train tour, he appealed to the working man and (especially) the farmer. Unlike Dewey's sedate style, Truman lashed out hard against big interests, and on election day he scored a smashing victory. His popular margin was over 2 million votes, and he won the electoral college by a margin of 303 to 189. Truman was to have the last laugh in this campaign, broadly grinning as he displayed the front page of a newspaper saying "DEWEY DEFEATS TRUMAN," and grinning even more broadly when he appeared before the Electoral College to give his version of a radio reporter's election night remarks about how at any moment Dewey would sweep to victory over Truman.

SENIOR PARTY STATESMAN AND PRESIDENT MAKER

The pragmatic Dewey knew after 1948 that he could never be President, but he was determined to play a central role in national politics. As the economy deteriorated, fear of internal communism increased and war in Korea broke out (with no end in sight), Dewey worked behind the scenes to persuade General of the Army Dwight D. Eisenhower to become a candidate for the Republican nomination. This created a schism in Republican ranks, for Sen. Robert Taft felt that the nomination was rightly his. Senator Everett Dirksen, in presenting to the Republican Convention the argument for Taft on the seating of critical delegates, would remind that gathering and the nation that Dewey and the liberal Republicans had led the Party to defeat too often, while Dewey would shake his fist at Dirksen from the convention floor. In the end the popular General with the wide grin would sweep to the nomination and victory in 1952, providing the former standard bearer a deep measure of satisfaction.

Dewey also was a promoter of Richard Nixon. He had told the young Senator from California at a 1950 New York Republican banquet that if he would watch his weight he would someday become President. In 1952, he persuaded Nixon to support Eisenhower, and Dewey used this as a basis for persuading Eisenhower to offer the young Californian the Vice Presidential nomination. When the fund crisis arose during the '52 campaign and Eisenhower was considering dropping Nixon, Dewey provided valuable advice to the thirty-nine year old future Vice President and President, and Nixon adeptly used that advice to stay on the ticket.

Eisenhower, and later Nixon, would gladly have tendered Dewey a high position in government — either Secretary of State or Supreme Court Chief Justice — but Dewey was in no way interested in Washington life, accepting only temporary appointments to various commissions. His tenure in New York had allowed him the opportunity of finding a number of able servants who would now go to Washington, including John Foster Dulles as Secretary of State, Herbert Brownell and William Rogers as other key Cabinet members, and still many others in various top level positions.

He continued to attend Republican national and state conventions. At the 1956 San Francisco convention, he walked down the long aisle and out of the convention (temporarily and in front of national television cameras) when Everett Dirksen, who had lambasted him in 1952, was introduced to speak. He maintained a dominance of New York Republican politics and refused to encourage Nelson Rockefeller, who he said could not win dogcatcher, in his quest for Governor.

COUNSELOR TO PRESIDENTS

In 1955 Dewey retired as Governor of New York, never to seek elective office again. He became a partner in a prestigious New York law firm, where he worked actively and profitably for the firm and himself. He began leading a leisurely, plush life style and especially enjoyed his farm at Pawling (named Dapplemere) and playing golf. He did not become close to President Kennedy, whom he thought charming but ineffective as a leader, but he was a counselor to both Presidents Johnson and Nixon. He detested Bobby Kennedy and warned Johnson that the '64 Democratic convention was going to be "stampeded" by the Attorney General in order to gain the Vice Presidential nomination; Johnson promptly changed the convention agenda to avoid this. Perhaps in gratitude, Johnson later arranged for the two-time Presidential loser to sleep in the Lincoln Bedroom at the White House. Dewey found Richard Nixon as President indecisive and did not care at all for Nixon's Vice President, Spiro Agnew. However, he became a close friend of Hubert Humphrey, formerly a bitter adversary in the political arena.

In the mid-1960's, Dewey's wife contracted cancer and suffered terribly until her death in 1970. Lost at first, he began seeing Kitty Carlise Hart, an actress with Broadway connections. Dewey proposed marriage but she delayed her answer. In the meantime Dewey scheduled one of his many Florida golf trips. He had been diagnosed by his physician as having heart problems, and perhaps the trip would do him good. Unfortunately he suffered a fatal heart attack shortly before he was to return. He was sixty-eight years of age.

The nation did not shroud itself in grief, but there were many officials in government and other long-time friends who felt that the loss of Thomas E. Dewey was a loss to the nation at large. His Episcopal funeral services in New York were attended by countless state officials, by many Cabinet members, by former Vice President Humphrey (himself an unsuccessful Presidential candidate), and by the President of the United States, Richard M. Nixon. The following day Dewey was entombed beside his late wife at his beloved Dapplemere farm. The Michigan farm boy who had found his way to New York in search of an Opera career, and whose life had been so busy from the prosecution of so many criminals, from holding so long the office of New York Governor, and from running twice for the Presidency, was now at rest in quiet but dearly cherished surroundings.

Adlai Stevenson
The Elections of 1952 and 1956

Urbanely sophisticated, aristocratic, and articulate, Adlai Stevenson was the darling of the liberals of his age. The only election he ever won (Governor of Illinois) catapulted him into national prominence, but to his dismay he found that he was not acceptable to the large majority of Americans, and he twice suffered humiliating defeats. Still it was he who kept the liberal cause intact, paving the way for future Democratic victories, and with them the Democratic programs of the New Frontier of John Kennedy and the Great Society of Lyndon Johnson. Today he is remembered not by the poor or homeless whose causes he eloquently espoused but by the academic community and the media, who were more enthralled with his intellect than by his governmental abilities.

BORN INTO PROMINENCE AND THE DEMOCRATIC PARTY

Few politicians have been born into such surroundings and background as Adlai Stevenson. Since the days of the French and Indian Wars, when an ancestor was a superior to George Washington, his relatives had been prominent. They had been active in the Revolution and other government causes. He was the grandson and namesake of the Vice President of the United States under Grover Cleveland (he also ran with Bryan in 1896). His father, who took young Adlai to national conventions and introduced him to national leaders, was an heir to the dynasty and served as the Illinois Secretary of State for a period of time. His mother, whose background was Republican, had ancestors who had been connected with Abraham Lincoln. Naturally, the Stevenson family had strong social connections, and the family also had relatives in over half of the states. Among these were Vice President Alben Barkley (under Truman) and Senator Richard Russell of Georgia. It is not unlikely that when Adlai Stevenson II was born on February 5, 1900, his family expected him to carry on the family traditions already in place.

Adlai's parents were protective of him but also determined that he receive the educational and cultural backgrounds necessary to be successful. He was taken to Europe for extensive travel and training. Enrolled in schools in Normal, Illinois, he was not particularly successful, being only an average student. Indeed, after he had failed three College Board entrance exams for

Princeton, his parents decided to send the young boy who was to become known as the greatest intellectual political leader of his generation to the exclusive Choate Academy in Connecticut for more intensive schooling.

Young Stevenson's political baptism had come at age twelve, when he went to hear a speech by William Jennings Bryan. Not yet too interested in politics, he went to sleep on the platform while the Great Commoner was speaking.

Not an outstanding student at either Choate or Princeton, Stevenson still gained a repertoire of useful skills for later life. At Choate he was Vice President of his junior class and editor of the school newspaper. At Princeton, he was on the college student newspaper staff, and he was also a member of influential social groups. One of his fellow students at Princeton was John Harlan, later appointed Supreme Court Justice by President Eisenhower. Graduating from Princeton in 1918, Stevenson then attended Harvard for several semesters. He also traveled extensively in Europe, even visiting Moscow in hopes of interviewing top Kremlin officials at a time when the relations between the U.S. and U.S.S.R. were severed. He hoped to eventually be involved in the family newspaper business, but relatives with shrewd business interests had taken control of the family enterprise. It was not until he was twenty-seven that Stevenson returned to Illinois to pass the bar and take up the practice of law.

Stevenson adapted well to the Chicago legal and social scene. He joined a reputable firm, and was made a partner with an annual income of $20,000 by the age of thirty-five. He also made the right social connections, joining, for example, the Harvard-Yale-Princeton Club and serving on the boards of numerous civic enterprises. He was known as a "man about town" and a good person to have as a guest at parties because he conversed so well, especially with young ladies. During this period he met and married Ellen Borden, a socially prominent debutante nine years younger than himself. The marriage, which produced three sons, was not a happy one. Mrs. Stevenson did not care for politics, and Adlai, it would turn out, could not live without a life surrounded by others. He would, after the marriage had later failed, take up with other women, often being accompanied by his "friends" on various journeys and to political meetings. The Stevensons were divorced in 1948, after he became Governor of Illinois; this event certainly made Stevenson's quest for the Presidency an uphill battle.

ENTRANCE INTO POLITICS

FDR's New Deal attracted Adlai Stevenson to politics. Roosevelt put out a call for bright young lawyers to come to Washington, and Stevenson responded by taking a temporary position with the Agriculture Department. After a year he returned to Chicago and resumed his law practice but was discontent. He turned down offers to rejoin the government as Assistant Attorney General and as Commissioner-General of Naturalization and Immigration but served in advisory capacities to several agencies.

Stevenson's political career for all practical purposes was launched through the Council on Foreign Relations, a national organization of political, business and intellectual leaders. Stevenson had been a member of the Chicago chapter for some time before he returned to Washington, where he was elected President of this elite District of Colombia group. Within this sphere Stevenson found himself totally at ease, able to speak with his witty but refined style and to thoroughly impress his peers.

The imminence of war increased his forum and influence. While Chicago newspapers defamed him for his Council activities, Stevenson continued to support New Deal policies such as Lend Lease. In May, 1941, Stevenson became an Assistant to Secretary of the Navy Frank Knox (a 1936 Republican Vice Presidential candidate). In 1943, Stevenson was used by the Navy Department to prepare an occupation policy for Italy, where he gained renown for his field expertise.

When Secretary Knox died and was replaced by James Forrestal, Stevenson returned again to Chicago to practice law. He also tried to buy Knox's Chicago newspaper, the *Daily News*, but the $2 million he raised was not enough to fulfill his lifetime dream of being a newspaper publisher. He was called back to government service as a special assistant for public relations (and propaganda) to Secretary of State Edward L. Stettinus.

At the United Nations Conference in San Francisco, Stevenson was summoned to assist Stettinus, whose press relations were so awkward that he had come to blows with one correspondent. Here Stevenson showed a special acumen for pacifying the press — indeed, he "leaked" information so often and freely that he was dubbed "Operation Titanic." Stevenson began to be an architect of UN organization when he became head of the United States delegation to the Preparatory Commission in London after Stettinus returned to the United States because of illness. All of a sudden, Stevenson was negotiating with the top foreign ministers of England and the Soviet Union, men like Bevin and Molotov and Gromyko, and earning a reputation for not only being witty but tough. It was after this conference that Winston Churchill delivered his famous "Iron Curtain" speech.

Soon Stevenson had returned once again to his Chicago law practice, turning down offers to be a South American Ambassador or Assistant Secretary of State. Illinois Democratic leaders had taken note of Stevenson and approached him about running for Governor in 1948. With his foreign policy experience he was much more interested in running for Senator, but party leaders persuaded him to run for Governor on a ticket with Paul Douglas as the Senate candidate.

Stevenson, who knew that the national party was in serious trouble as it headed into the '48 elections, had already done some political homework by inviting nationally prominent leaders, including George C. Marshall, to speak at Chicago functions that he had organized. Knowing also that there had been only three Democratic Governors in ninety years, he joined forces with Democratic party forces that included the Cook County machine of Richard Daley. Thereafter, he was branded a machine politician, a reputation that, as an intellectual, he disdained.

The Republicans were once again fielding the incumbent Governor, Dwight Green, who as a prosecutor years earlier had convicted Al Capone. Teamed with Tom Dewey against Stevenson, Douglas and Harry Truman, Green seemed sure of victory. But 1948 was a year that confounded political experts, and the Democrats swept to victory both nationally and in Illinois. Adlai Stevenson had led Truman to victory in Illinois and soon was himself being talked of for national office.

GOVERNOR OF ILLINOIS

Stevenson became known as a hard working, fair and efficient administrator. He recruited new state workers on merit and was able to attract many bright, young attorneys — both Democrat and Republican — to state government. A state convention was held to reform the archaic Illinois constitution, and when this movement failed to redistribute taxes fairly, he sponsored an amendment to the state constitution which provided more equity in taxation. State anti-discrimination and fair housing laws similar to those of other states were enacted.

When Stevenson's wife filed for divorce in 1949, his political career seemed doomed. But Stevenson plunged himself into the work of the Governorship, resisting temptations to lash back at those who attacked his integrity and gaining the respect of the voters and party leaders for his calmness. As the 1952 Presidential election approached, President Truman, who had been involved in a great deal of controversy and was not seeking reelection, invited the Illinois Governor to the White House and offered him the Democratic nomination. To everyone's astonishment, Stevenson declined because he had promised to run for re-election as Governor. Truman tried to force the issue by announcing at the annual Jefferson-Jackson Day festivities that he would not run. Attention immediately centered on Stevenson, who still insisted he was not a candidate.

As the convention neared, Truman decided to back Vice President Barkley, but the aging Kentuckian was not acceptable to the rank and file party members or to labor. Estes Kefauver of Tennessee, the original favorite of primary voters, was suspect to Southern delegates for being too liberal; other candidates also had faults in the eyes of delegates. Volunteer "draft" committees for Stevenson had done their work well, and an outcry for the suave, candid and urbane "Man from Libertyville" found him nominated on the third ballot. For the Vice Presidential nod he selected Senator John J. Sparkman of Alabama.

The election of 1952 was a foregone conclusion against the Democrats. Poor Stevenson, who had not fought in combat in World War II, was pitted against Dwight D. Eisenhower, an authentic hero with a big smile, a campaign against "creeping socialism," and a pledge to end the unpopular Korean War that had been conducted without success by Truman. To add to Stevenson's woes, some Republicans (including Richard Nixon) had charged that the Democrats were soft on communism, and Stevenson had refused to have the Illinois government get actively involved in such matters on the grounds that this area was a federal matter.

When the votes were counted in November, Stevenson went down to a terrible defeat, losing by six million popular votes and by 442 to 89 in the Electoral College. He carried only states of the Solid South (where he had told voters that his grandfather had helped end Reconstruction) and West Virginia.

PREPARING FOR 1956

The day after the election of 1952, Stevenson held meetings with key aides concerning his future. At age fifty-two, he did not feel finished with his life's work in politics. While he was disconsolate over losing to the popular Eisenhower, he nonetheless held an optimistic outlook for the future. His political instincts simply indicated to him that with the devoted (if mixed) following of intellectuals, party bosses and party regulars who felt that his leadership was essential to the future of both the party and the nation, he had no choice but to formulate a plan to gain the nomination in 1956, which, he felt, would surely result in his election over Eisenhower or any other Republican candidate.

President Truman, who allowed Stevenson the opportunity to sleep in the Lincoln Room before Eisenhower moved in, also allowed Stevenson the opportunity to capture almost total control of party machinery when he indicated that Stevenson was to be "titular" head of the party in the interim until 1956. While there were some Democratic Senators and Congressmen who indicated that they would not be spoken for, Stevenson for the most part was the party spokesman. His intellect and manner of speaking, though without mass appeal to the American public, had a special attraction to "die-hard" Democrats. He was also endeared for his public wit after losing; indeed, a speech he made to the Washington Gridiron Club after the '52 election, in which he stated, "A funny thing happened to me on the way to the White House," became a Stevenson classic; it was a magnanimous, though light-hearted, method of accepting defeat while maintaining loyalties. "Let's talk sense to the American people" became another familiar refrain that held Stevenson in high regard among party faithful. Stevenson did not object when existing Stevenson-Sparkman Clubs or similar organizations stated they would stay intact for 1956. And Stevenson took the advice of Walter Lippman, relayed through Averill Harriman, that he correspond continuously with party leaders. Stevenson's mastery of the written language, especially his ability to flatter, was one of his strongest political assets.

Stevenson's plan of action for '56 would be governed somewhat by the necessity of providing himself with an adequate income upon relinquishing the Illinois' Governor's seat in January of 1953. A position was sought that would also allow him the time to travel, write and control party affairs at the National Committee level. The solution to this problem was provided when an agreement was reached with *Look Magazine* for Stevenson to travel around the world and publish, over a period of three years, some ten articles on various countries and world affairs and two additional articles upon subjects to be agreed upon. Stevenson obtained additional income by writing a series of books, none of which was a particularly good seller, and from investment income on his family inheritance.

The former Governor, known thereafter to intimates as "The Gov," took up residence at his Libertyville home. On the day Eisenhower was inaugurated, he took a Barbados vacation to rest and finalize his immediate plans. After this respite Stevenson left by boat for a five and one-half month world tour. His itinerary included Hawaii; Tokyo and a visit with the Emperor; South Korea and a discussion with President Syngman Rhee of continued threats from North Korean communists; Formosa to discuss with Chiang Kai-shek the aggression of Mainland Chinese communists; Hong Kong; the Philippines; South Viet Nam and North Viet Nam where he studied the emergence of Ho Chi Minh's communist guerilla movement; Cambodia; Indonesia to meet with Sukarno; Singapore; Thailand; Burma; India for sixteen days including meetings with Prime Minister Nehru and a discussion of Indo-Pakistani disputes with the Kashmir Prime Minister; Saudi Arabia; Egypt to discuss needs of the new regime which Nassar would soon lead; Syria; Jordan; Israel; Cyprus; Turkey; Yugoslavia to meet with Tito; Greece; Italy; Austria; East and West Germany; France; and England, to meet and dine with the likes of Anthony Eden, Lady Astor and Winston Churchill.

Stevenson, having been received by many of the world's greats, returned home with his prestige greatly enhanced. His foreign policy credentials were now much more substantial than before, and he was very much in demand to speak at Democratic and college functions. Some Illinois Democrats encouraged him to run against Democratic incumbent Senator Paul Douglas, but he refused. He decided instead to be a national campaigner for Democratic candidates in 1954. To this end he delivered, as head of party, a series of national television speeches, criticizing the Republican administration on foreign policy. He occasionally made remarks about other issues such as "McCarthyism" and the banning of atomic testing. One of the more significant events of this period was the collection of a staff of liberal supporters, including Arthur Schlesinger, George McGowan, John Kenneth Galbraith and Willard Wirtz, who not only provided support for Stevenson's nomination in 1956 but provided the brain power for John Kennedy's New Frontier beginning in 1961.

As the '54 off-year elections approached, Stevenson began a rigorous schedule of travel to many points throughout the land. He chastised Republican inactivity and lack of leadership, and he called upon the American people to back away from the effects of McCarthyism. In the South he shrewdly stayed away from civil rights issues, concentrating instead on the proposed Dixon-Yates contract proposal for the sale of the Tennessee Valley Authority. On election night, he was delighted to hear in his Libertyville home that the Democrats had regained control of both Houses of Congress and gained back a number of Governorships. He was clearly the man of the hour and the decided favorite for the 1956 Democratic nomination.

Stevenson formed a private law practice with future Labor Secretary Willard Wirtz and joined the Board of Directors of *Encyclopedia Brittanica*. He also spoke more and more to party and collegiate groups. He took a quick trip to Africa, and then intensely concentrated on winning the nomination and election in 1956.

THE ELECTION OF 1956

Stevenson's opposition to the nomination in 1956 came first from Senator Estes Kefauver of Tennessee, a Southern liberal with a tough reputation as a crime fighter and foe of racketeering. Kefauver began strong by winning the New Hampshire primary, which Stevenson did not enter. Stevenson had decided instead to put his talents to work in Minnesota, where Hubert Humphrey was campaigning hard for "the Guv," feeling that if Minnesota went for Stevenson, Humphrey would get the Vice Presidential nomination. Unfortunately, Republicans in Minnesota switched over by the thousands, handing Kefauver a decided victory and greatly embarrassing both Stevenson and Humphrey. Then Stevenson's luck began to change. He won unopposed in Pennsylvania and his home state of Illinois and watched Kefauver lose to a slate in New Jersey friendly to himself, while Kefauver won an uncontested match in Wisconsin.

The first real contest came in Florida where Kefauver, the Southerner, called for an end to desegregation and Stevenson, the Northerner, stayed aloof on the issue. The election was close, with Republicans switching over once again, but Stevenson pulled out the victory when a strongly segregationist area of the state voted for him. Then Stevenson took on Kefauver in a "write-in" campaign in Oregon, winning overwhelmingly. The last primary was California, where Stevenson was at his best, winning there by some 1,139,000 votes — a tremendous victory which had the effect of forcing Kefauver out of the race.

At the Chicago convention Stevenson's main opposition came from New York Gov. Averill Harriman and Texas Senator Lyndon Johnson. Harriman received the endorsement of former President Truman, but this would not deter the momentum of Stevenson. Nominated by a young Massachusetts Senator named John F. Kennedy, he swept to a first ballot victory. Then, in one of the most bizarre of political maneuvers, Stevenson left the Vice Presidential nomination to the will of the convention. A mad scramble ensued, with Kennedy only 18 1/2 votes short of the nomination before Kefauver received the support of Hubert Humphrey and others to receive the nod.

Interest in the election had intensified when President Eisenhower suffered a heart attack. Democrats suddenly were excited at the possibility of a Stevenson-Nixon match up. In what was probably a strategic blunder,

Stevenson did not make Ike's health an issue until the closing hours of the campaign, and by then it was too late to bring up the issue effectively. All through the campaign, however, he did concentrate on issues that would dominate the American political scene for years to come: a ban on nuclear testing; the reduction of armed forces and elimination of the draft; low minimum wages, low Social Security benefits, poor health insurance benefits, and poor housing; lowering women's ages for retirement from 65 to 62; medical care for the aged; the creation of new hospitals and adequately trained staff; the formation of low interest loans for education; and a general cry against Vice President Nixon, whom Stevenson attacked more and more as the campaign went along (Stevenson at the campaign's end was apparently so desperate that he predicted that Eisenhower would not live out his term and that Nixon would succeed to the Presidency).

The election of 1956 was a worse disaster for Stevenson than 1952. Vainly Stevenson labored to carry his message, but the American people saw in him none of the qualities of leadership which his faithful saw. His problems were compounded when international crises developed in Hungary, Poland and the Middle East. Eisenhower, the military hero of World War II, handled each crisis adroitly, avoiding any major conflict. Eisenhower captured 58 percent of the popular vote and all but six states of the old Confederacy and Missouri. Ike's electoral college margin was 457 to 73. Stevenson bade his followers "...good night, with a full heart and a fervent prayer that we will meet often in the liberals' everlasting battle against ignorance, poverty, misery, and war."

A HOPE FOR 1960

Stevenson resumed his law practice where he represented a number of prestigious national clients, but his actions were by now so attuned to political matters that he could not concentrate very long on legal affairs. He became a member of the newly formed Democratic Advisory Council, which was composed of most national leaders and was to serve as a forum in opposition to the Republican administration. He was in constant demand for speeches to Democratic gatherings and campuses, but he declined most. He resumed his travels, going to England (where he spoke with the likes of Harold Wilson, Harold MacMillan and Lady Astor) and to Africa. On a later trip he would visit Russia and have a long discussion with the pompous Nikita Khrushechev, who was regarded by Stevenson as a fearful, though proud, man. He was considered for but rejected because of age the Presidency of Princeton; he was also rejected as President of the University of California.

His faithful wanted him to run once more in 1960, but he continually disclaimed any desire to seek the nomination again. However, in the 1958 off-year elections, as in 1954, he once again led the Democrats to a stunning victory, with majorities increasing in the House, the Senate and Governorships. His speeches on Quemoy and his condemnation of the United States for not being first in the space race were effective, and he continued to hammer for a ban of nuclear tests. The election results gave his supporters the encouragement they needed to push him in 1960, and he could not resist the thought that he just might possibly be able to escape the William Jennings Bryan syndrome and defeat Richard Nixon. In mid 1960, after the U-2 incident which broke up an Eisenhower-Khrushechev summit, Stevenson's supporters mounted a campaign to have him drafted once again.

But Stevenson, who now was not regarded so favorably by either party bosses or intellectual leaders, was finished. John Kennedy had moved out early and scored an impressive array of primary victories, while Stevenson had not even allowed his name to be "written in" in Oregon. However, his name was put in nomination in Los Angeles with Senator Edward McCarthy crying, "Do not reject this man," and a tumultuous demonstration erupted from a packed crowd of Stevenson supporters that had stood in line for tickets wearing Kennedy buttons. But the party was no longer in his control. His generation of leadership had now been overtaken by a younger and more media conscious group, which knew how to organize campaigns and win victories. Kennedy, who had used the '56 nominating speech of Stevenson to gain national prominence, won an easy first ballot victory. Stevenson's hope for the Presidency was finished.

UNITED NATIONS AMBASSADOR (1961-65)

Stevenson supported John Kennedy vigorously with the firm belief that with his broad travels, experience and knowledge of world leaders, he would become Secretary of State if Kennedy were elected. JFK had indicated during the election that only Stevenson was qualified for the foreign policy post, but after being elected the young and politically astute President probably realized that Stevenson, the eloquent and forceful leader of Democrats for so long, would probably be an intimidating figure in the White House who could not be controlled. Kennedy instead offered Stevenson the position of Permanent Ambassador to the United Nations with Cabinet rank, the first UN Ambassador to be so designated; Stevenson refused to accept the post until Kennedy announced that he had a selection for Secretary of State. While Stevenson felt rejected, he accepted the UN post with the understanding that he would be consulted on major policy decisions.

Unfortunately, this understanding was not kept. During the Bay of Pigs fiasco, Stevenson was given false intelligence data and photos which indicated that the U.S. had not supported the anti-Castro invaders. President Kennedy admitted the U.S. involvement later, but not until Stevenson, whom the White House made inside jokes about by calling him the "official liar," suffered great embarrassment. Later, though, Stevenson was admired world-wide when, during the Cuban Missile Crisis in 1963, he confronted the Russian Ambassador before the "Court of World Opinion" and showed that the Russians were lying about missile installations; minutes later he was telling the UN Security Council that "debating points" should be dispensed with and peace talks entered into immediately. It was perhaps the finest moment of his entire career.

He was engaged in many other UN issues, including the fair payment of dues by Russian and France, the Belgian Congo crisis, the Berlin Wall, Laos, and Viet Nam, which early on he recognized as a blunder by the Kennedy administration. He urged Kennedy to consider having Communist China admitted to the United Nations, advice that was not accepted, and to enter into negotiations to ban nuclear testing, and the young President, heeding this advice, scored his most impressive foreign policy triumph when the U.S. and the U.S.S.R. signed into such a treaty.

Deeply saddened by John F. Kennedy's assassination, The UN Ambassador nonetheless had the pleasure of hearing from President Lyndon Johnson that Stevenson deserved to be in the Oval Office. Stevenson visited the White House weekly and maintained a cordial relationship at first with LBJ, even writing an introduction to a book the President authored. Later, though, differences developed between the two over Johnson's sending Marines to the Dominican Republic and Viet Nam. Johnson became infuriated with Stevenson when the Ambassador drafted a speech for Johnson to deliver at the twentieth anniversary of the UN but then, following an old custom, he "leaked" it to the press. The intellectual Stevenson regarded Johnson as a crude, Texas cowboy who wanted to resolve world affairs with conduct similar to the Battle of the Alamo.

Yet Stevenson continued to loyally represent the U.S. at the UN. He sometimes tired of the Ambassadorial routine, claiming it led to too much "alcohol, protocol and Geritol." Stevenson's weight began to be excessive, and the sixteen hour days he worked were very demanding on his body. In July of 1964, Stevenson attended an international conference in Geneva and then stopped in London to confer with Prime Minister Harold Wilson. Two days later, he was hurriedly walking the streets of London when he suddenly collapsed and died of a heart attack. He was sixty-five years of age.

President Johnson, openly crying, announced to the nation the news of Adlai Stevenson's death. Air Force One, with Vice President Humphrey at the head of a delegation, was dispatched to bring his body home, and he was received with full military honors, President Johnson personally receiving the plane carrying Stevenson's coffin. Washington funeral services were conducted at the National Cathedral, with the President, Vice President, Cabinet members, Congressional leaders and international diplomats gathered to help memorialize the fallen intellectual leader. Secretary of State Dean Rusk led a memorial service before the United Nations.

His body was then taken to Springfield, Illinois, where it rested on the same bier as had Abraham Lincoln's one-hundred years before. After further services at the state Capitol and at the Unitarian Church in Bloomington, Stevenson was buried close to his parents and his grandfather, who had served as Vice President under Cleveland. The Illinois boy who had grown up in the rural, family surroundings that were filled with the call of destiny had done much to shape the intellectual life of American government, and after an active political life on both the national and world stage, he was home again in the peaceful surroundings of Bloomington for time immemorial.

Barry Goldwater

The Election of 1964

"The official records all say Barry Goldwater, Republican candidate for the office of President of the United States in 1964, was defeated by Democrat incumbent Lyndon Baines Johnson. The truth is I lost whatever small chance I ever had to be President in San Francisco at the Republican National Convention." So spoke Barry Goldwater, in a manner so candidly reminiscent of his style of campaigning, some fifteen years after his try at the Presidency. Yet Goldwater had an even greater problem in 1964: in the most tragic national event any American could remember, young John F. Kennedy had been struck down, and Lyndon Johnson had successfully carried on the business of government. Despite the wide appeal of Goldwater's philosophy, too many Americans wanted tranquility, and there was widespread concern that Goldwater would provide the opposite. Goldwater lived to see his philosophy carried out in large part by another conservative, Ronald Reagan; indeed, Goldwater's greatest contribution was probably the introduction in 1964 of "The Great Communicator" to active politics.

EARLY LIFE AND BACKGROUND

Goldwater was the grandson of an immigrant Jewish merchant who had fled a Poland controlled by Russian Czars and eventually come to California during the Gold Rush. After attempts with his brother to establish a business were not totally successful, the Goldwater enterprise was moved to Arizona, where "overland" trail business soon made it one of the leading businesses in the territory. Goldwater's mother was descended from midwest American farmers; she had come to Arizona to recover from a lung fever. The parents of Barry Goldwater were married in 1907. Barry was born on January 1, 1909, the eldest child. A brother and a sister rounded out the family.

After attending schools in the territory and receiving much tutoring from his mother, Goldwater attended Staunton Preparatory School in Staunton, Virginia. He graduated the top student in his class and was headed for West Point until his father became ill. Goldwater returned home in 1928 to attend the University of Arizona. When the depression hit a year later, he dropped out of school to enter the family business. There he learned merchandising from the bottom up, starting as a junior clerk at $15.00 per week. The business was able to survive the difficult times.

Goldwater in 1930 took up a hobby that was for him to become a passion: flying. He began with a single engine plane and continued learning to fly other aircraft until he had flown some of the most sophisticated military aircraft afloat. His aeronautical background led to his concern for national defense and ultimately led him into the arena of national politics.

During this period of time Goldwater met Peggy Johnson, a Michigan girl whose family had leased the Arizona home of Senator Carl Hayden to see if her brother could find relief from chronic bronchitis. Her father was president of Warner Gear, which eventually merged into the highly success-ful Borg-Warner Corporation. Peggy was also being courted by another future politician, "Soapy" Williams, who was to be Governor of Michigan for six terms. Of course, Goldwater won Peggy, who was to be his helpmate for fifty-two years, until her death in 1986. Their marriage produced four children, with one son, Barry, Jr., becoming a Congressman from Califor-nia.

As war clouds began to form for World War II, Goldwater became in-volved with the Army Air Corps. An air base was located near Phoenix, and Goldwater, who had failed a physical in 1932 because of eyesight problems, was asked to become a staff officer because the Commandant needed someone who knew his way around Arizona. This was a pivotal event in Goldwater's life. Already fiercely patriotic, his subsequent service would mold his future political endeavors. Goldwater saw service in WW II in Burma and other areas of the Southeastern Asia theatre.   He tried consistently to be transferred to a Bomber command but never received his wish. He achieved the rank of Colonel before the war ended.

Returning home, he helped organize the Air National Guard of Arizona. As a member of a prominent Arizona family, he was appointed to the Colorado River Commission. He subsequently became involved in other matters and then in 1949 ran successfully for a Phoenix City Council seat as a reform candidate. When the Korean War started and President Truman did not pursue all-out victory — anything else was not in Goldwater's vocabulary — Goldwater eyed the Senate seat of Ernest McFarland. McFarland was a New Deal Democrat with power, holding the position of Senate Majority Leader. No one gave Goldwater much of a chance, but with Democratic Sen. Carl Hayden "looking the other way" and Goldwater riding the coattails of Dwight Eisenhower, a surprising upset occurred. Goldwater became the first Republican from Arizona to win a Senate seat in years. It is ironic that Goldwater's victory unseated McFarland as Majority Leader, enabling Lyndon Johnson to fill that vacancy and acquire the power that would eventually lead him to higher positions of prominence.

SENATOR (1953-65)

Goldwater's tenure in the Senate was not marked by a push for any far-reaching sociological change. Goldwater was a strict constructionist, and as such he tried to prevent abuses to the Constitution. Serving on the Labor Committee with John F. Kennedy, he opposed the extension of labor influence, once casting the only vote against a pro-union piece of legislation. President Eisenhower was irritated with Goldwater but vetoed the bill after Goldwater explained its contents. The veto was upheld.

One hot item of the times was Senator Joseph McCarthy's investigation into communist sympathizers within the government. McCarthy made such ludicrous charges that he was finally in danger of being censured by the Senate. Goldwater at one point had worked out a method for getting McCarthy out of trouble with his fellow Senators: if McCarthy would sign mild letters of retraction for certain Senators, the charges would be forgotten. Adamant, McCarthy would not, and he was censured. Goldwater voted against the measure, believing the goals, though not the methods, of McCarthy were worthy of pursuit.

Of course a strong defense was a primary goal of the new Arizona Senator. He especially supported Eisenhower's efforts to make a more effective Central Intelligence Agency. But his major efforts were aimed at overspending. He wanted foreign aid to other countries eliminated. In 1958 he attacked the budget of the Eisenhower Administration, an event that signaled the beginning of his conservative movement.

Ernest McFarland, who returned to Arizona to be elected Governor for two terms, was a decided favorite to regain his seat from Goldwater in the '58 elections. Although the nation was experiencing a serious recession and the Republicans suffered a major setback nationally, Goldwater was reelected with relative ease. The national party made him Chairman of the Republican Senatorial Campaign Committee, and Goldwater began to travel extensively around the country. While visiting South Carolina, his speech to the Republican state convention so aroused the state delegates that they pledged their national delegates to him at the 1960 national convention. Goldwater's stature with conservatives grew rapidly when his best-selling *Conscience of a Conservative* was published, quickly becoming the gospel of conservative philosophy.

Vice President Nixon was the favorite to gain the Republican nomination in 1960, but Goldwater allowed his name to stay in consideration. His home state named him its "favorite son" candidate. Goldwater's plan was to be placed into nomination and then withdraw. His ire was raised, however, when prior to the convention Nixon went to New York to visit Gov. Nelson Rockefeller, who himself badly wanted the Presidency, and accommodated the New Yorker on key platform issues. Goldwater labeled this an "American Munich," and a host of delegates from conservative states decided to cast their votes for Goldwater. After his name was placed in nomination, Goldwater gracefully withdrew and urged party unity. But he also reminded the conservatives that there would be another day for them to be heard.

THE ELECTION OF 1964

After John Kennedy defeated Richard Nixon in 1960, speculation centered on Nixon, Nelson Rockefeller and Goldwater as the Republican nominee for 1964. Kennedy's policies were not being very successful: he suffered from the ill-fated Bay of Pigs invasion; his civil rights gains were minimal; and tensions were high in the international arena from the Cuban Missile Crisis and the building of the Berlin Wall. Kennedy had been effective, however, in the expansion of the economy due to his tax cut measure. His political charisma was high except with the conservative elements in the country. He helped defeat Nixon for the Governorship of California in 1962, leaving Rockefeller and Goldwater as the frontrunners. Unsure of his re-election chances in 1964, he was on a political mending trip to Texas when he was assassinated in Dallas.

Nixon's wing of the Republican Party, which felt that a lack of effort by the liberals headed by Rockefeller had cost him the election in 1960, leaned to Goldwater rather than the New York Governor. When Rockefeller announced that he would divorce his first wife and remarry, his fate for the nomination was sealed. Unfortunately for Goldwater, a "Stop Goldwater" movement arose. Henry Cabot Lodge became a candidate in New Hampshire and won. Goldwater, however, had entered more primaries than any other candidate and won most due to better organization and lack of opposition. One by one, potential nominees appeared only to lose. Rockefeller stalled the Goldwater candidacy by winning the Oregon primary, but then Goldwater won the California primary decisively, virtually wrapping up the nomination for himself. The liberals, however, decided to make the convention in San Francisco a rallying ground for one final battle. The news media, particularly television, were present to report all the

The news media, particularly television, were present to report all the discord: Goldwater was associated with the John Birch Society and the Ku Klux Klan (even though he was half-Jewish); he was said to be willing to use nuclear weapons in Viet Nam; he was against the continuance of Social Security and the Tennessee Valley Authority; and he was generally held to be in favor of "extremism." He won the nomination easily on the first ballot but had to choose an obscure New York Congressman, William E. Miller, as his running mate when more substantial candidates shied away from the Vice Presidential nomination.

Goldwater eradicated any chances of victory with his acceptance speech. Saying that "...extremism in the defense of freedom is no vice..." and "...that moderation in the pursuit of justice is no virtue...," Goldwater in effect told his following he that did not expect those who did not believe in his philosophy to join his cause. A Republican "summit" at President Eisenhower's Gettysburg farm provided the appearance of unity, but the election was already decided. Goldwater had too many marks against him: the death of Kennedy; the success of Johnson; his vote against the Civil Rights Act of 1964; his perceived association with extremist elements; the belief that he might use nuclear weapons; and his brusque manner in speaking which, though appealing to Conservatives, was not the tenor the American people desired in 1964. Johnson, the consummate politician, orchestrated the Democratic Convention to show a high degree of calm, making the choice of the Senator Hubert Humphrey as his running mate a matter of deep suspense. He then campaigned cautiously, keeping the focus on the ills of Goldwater. The two candidates made a secret agreement not to campaign on the issues of Viet Nam and the Civil Rights Act, but this in no way affected the outcome. Johnson's victory was complete and over-whelming with over sixty-one percent of the popular vote, a margin of sixteen million popular votes, and an electoral count of 486 to 52. Goldwater carried only his native Arizona and five Southern states.

STAYING IN POLITICS

Though overwhelmingly defeated, Goldwater still had a substantial fol-lowing in the Republican Party and in Arizona. He won re-election to the Senate in 1966, 1972 and 1978. In 1968, his influence for Richard Nixon, who had been the only major Republican to campaign with sincerity for Goldwater in '64, proved significant, and Nixon easily won the Republican nomination. Of course Goldwater was especially happy to see his old liberal nemesis, Hubert Humphrey, go down to defeat.

Goldwater gradually began to be recognized as the "Senior Statesman" of

continuously against the growth of government, although he was supportive of a strong national defense. He was sought out for advice by Spiro Agnew when corruption charges were leveled against the Vice President, and Goldwater advised Agnew to take his cause to the House, but Speaker Carl Albert would not hear Agnew's pleas, and the Vice President resigned in disgrace to avoid prison. When the Watergate Crisis developed, he at first believed that Nixon was being persecuted by the news media and liberal political opponents, but when Nixon admitted to lying, Goldwater became vehemently opposed to the President. It was Goldwater who personally delivered the message to Nixon that he would be convicted by the Senate upon impeachment by the House if he did not resign. Two days later, Nixon left the White House in disgrace.

Gerald Ford and Ronald Reagan presented Goldwater with the most difficult decision of his political career when Reagan challenged the incumbent Ford for the Republican nomination in 1976. Goldwater was indebted to Reagan for his help in the '64 race, and Goldwater undoubtedly had a philosophy closer to Reagan's than Ford's. But Goldwater strongly felt that the experience of Ford plus the difficult circumstances he had faced made him worthy of his own term in office. Goldwater opted for Ford, and then was distressed when Jimmy Carter won the election.

Of course, Carter's ineptness with the economy and the Iranian hostage situation offered the Republicans an excellent opportunity for victory in 1980. This time Goldwater had no problems supporting Reagan from the beginning, and he was delighted to see Reagan not only win the Presidency but to see the Republican Party gain control of the Senate. He became Chairman of the Senate Armed Forces Committee and continued to display a deep affection for the Air Force, having retired as a Major General in the Air Force Reserve. Yet he spoke out against the abuses of excessive military spending which led to waste. He continued his writings, making *With No Apologies* a memoir of sorts and authoring numerous other books. Ever the conservative, he continued to enumerate warnings of too much government, too much spending and too much control over the life of the individual.

When the white-haired, distinguished looking Arizona Senator announced that he would retire in 1984 after spending thirty years in the Senate, a host of dignitaries spoke favorably of Goldwater's character and determination to fight for the causes, though sometimes unpopular, in which he believed. Goldwater's political world had been replete with the major figures and events of his time. He had gained his initial seat by riding on Ike's coattails. He served in the Senate with Vice Presidents Barkley, Nixon, Johnson, Humphrey, Agnew, Ford, Rockefeller, Mondale and Bush. Four of these became President and two others ran unsuccessfully for the coveted position. He also served with Senator John Kennedy, who became President, and with Senators Strom Thurmond and George McGovern, who ran unsuccessfully for Chief Magistrate. John Sparkman, Estes Kefauver, Edmond Muskie, Thomas Eagleton (a brief candidate until a history of nervous disorders was discovered) and Robert Dole were fellow Senators who ran unsuccessfully for Vice President. The brusque talking and ruggedly handsome Conservative from Arizona who so often was accused of "shooting from the hip" was among the giants of his day active in shaping the history of the nation he loved so much.

Word of his activities and personal affairs continued to reach the American public after Goldwater left the Senate. Many were genuinely concerned when he underwent "open-heart" surgery and when other ailments, including painful arthritic conditions which required hip and shoulder joint replacements, were reported, but these same supporters were delighted when the gray haired elder statesman took a second wife in 1992. Though retired from personal politics, Goldwater would not keep quiet when a controversial Republican Governor of Arizona was impeached (a move he supported). From time to time, he would grant interviews displaying a vindictiveness for Richard Nixon, who, Goldwater felt, had lied to him personally about Watergate matters. Conservatives who liked Nixon were baffled by Goldwater's criticism.

Goldwater's support was solicited by George Bush after the Vice President had lost the Iowa caucuses, the first political event of the 1988 campaign, and appeared to be losing momentum in his quest for the Presidency. Traveling to New Hampshire, the white haired Conservative appealed to his followers to support Reagan's Vice President. The momentum for the Republican nomination immediately swung to the incumbent Bush, who thereafter had no problem winning Republican primaries or the general election that November. Barry Goldwater's influence in the Republican Party and in national politics was stronger than when he ran for President himself in 1964.

Hubert Horatio Humphrey

The Election of 1968

Few men in American public life have had the profound effect of Hubert Humphrey. Flamboyant, colorful, highly intellectual, extremely imaginative; creative idealistic, loved, despised — such attributes only come to those who are not afraid to meet head-on the issues of the day. For years Humphrey was the conscience of the Democratic Party. His failure to become President after plotting so long to do so was not just his personal tragedy; it also signaled the beginning of the end of "New Deal" politics. His place in American history will remain prominent for his genius with respect to the American system of government and for his strong will to fight for the programs in which he believed.

FROM THE HEARTLAND OF AMERICA

Born May 27, 1911, "Pinky" Humphrey was the second son in an ordinary midwest American family. Hubert Humphrey, Sr., whose ancestors had lived in the United States for generations, had come to the midwest with his family from Oregon while a young man. He was a druggist by profession but also from time to time a salesman. In 1906, Hubert Humphrey, Sr. married Christine Sannes, the daughter of Lutheran Norwegian descendents who had settled in Minneapolis. She was a school teacher with a Republican background. Together the Humphreys reared four children: two sons (including Hubert, Jr.) and two daughters.

Traveling from town to town selling his wares, Pinky's father decided to settle in Doland, South Dakota and operate a drugstore. The family resided in a farm on the outskirts of town. All members of the clan joined in running the family business and were constantly admonished by their parents to work hard if they expected to succeed in life. At age 10, young Pinky was keeping ledgers in addition to running errands and sweeping floors. In school he was the leading student, graduating from high school as Valedictorian. He was a member of his high school debating team that reached the finals of the state tournament. Though his team placed second, Pinky received high plaudits from the debate judge, Karl Mundt, who was later to serve with Humphrey in the United States Senate, representing South Dakota as a Republican.

In politics Humphrey was schooled mostly by his father, whose hero was the populist "Boy Orator of the Platte," William Jennings Bryan. For some period of time the elder Humphrey was agnostic, but then he became a faithful member of the Methodist Church. The rest of the family, though baptized into the Lutheran Church, attended Methodist Churches thereafter. Highly respected, Humphrey, Sr. served as a Democratic town Councilman in a predominantly Republican area. Later he was a state Senator and considered running for Congress. In 1948 he served as a delegate to the national Democratic convention at Philadelphia where he witnessed his son's immediate rise to fame and power when the younger Humphrey pushed through the Civil Rights plank that won Truman the '48 election.

Hubert Horatio Humphrey, Jr. enrolled in the University of Minnesota at Minneapolis in the fall of 1929. He helped meet expenses by washing dishes at a campus drugstore for twenty cents an hour. Unfortunately, the depression hit the Humphrey family with full force, and Hubert, who lost $100 he had saved from earnings as a newsboy when a bank failed, had to withdraw from college after one year to help with the family drug store business, which had moved to Huron. Though the young Humphrey worked hard to satisfy the requirements of supporting his family, he missed the challenges of college life sorely and suffered fainting spells. His father insisted that he attend a two year druggist school in Denver; the energetic student completed the course in six months. Returning to Huron, Hubert became involved somewhat in civic affairs, joining in church social activities and becoming a local Scoutmaster. In 1935, Hubert took his scout troop on a trip to Washington, D.C. This trip transformed Humphrey, who then knew that he must return to college to gain the tools necessary to pursue his love of government and politics. When President Franklin Roosevelt came through Huron on a tour of the dust bowl, young Humphrey was invited with his father aboard FDR's train to shake hands with the leader of the New Deal. From that moment on Hubert Humphrey was a confirmed Democrat.

While in Huron, Hubert had dated several girls before meeting the love of his life, Muriel Buck. Together they plotted their future. Hubert finally told his father that he must break away from the family drugstore and return to college. (His fainting spells immediately stopped, never to return.) After marriage, they returned to Minneapolis where Hubert majored in Political Science at the University of Minnesota, working part-time as a druggist, while Muriel worked as a bookkeeper to help support the family. He also worked part-time as a janitor in return for a break in the rental fees of their apartment. These hard times for the Humphreys certainly had a bearing on his later political philosophy.

Deciding that teaching should be his career, Humphrey applied himself relentlessly to the pursuit of academic excellence. He was active in debating societies, touring "Big Ten" campuses as a member of a debate team proclaiming the virtues of Roosevelt and the New Deal. Along the way he made several life-long friendships, including future Minnesota Governor and Secretary of Agriculture Orville Freeman and future United Nations Ambassador Jeane Kirkpatrick. Humphrey's talents did not go unnoticed: he was graduated Phi Kappa Alpha, and he received a $450 teaching fellowship to Louisiana State University.

At LSU, the Humphreys continued to have hard times. Money was extremely scarce, with Hubert resorting to selling sandwiches that his wife had prepared to fellow students, while Muriel, who was now the mother of one child and unable to work full-time, typed term papers on the side. On one occasion the family refrigerator was sold to pay rent; more than once a friend came to their aid in the nick of time with a much needed loan.

A fellow student of Humphrey's at LSU was future Senator Huey Long, then son of the Louisiana Governor and President of the student body. It was during his Master's program that Humphrey witnessed, for the first time in his life, Southern segregation. He was particularly annoyed by separate "Colored" and "White" signs for rest rooms and drinking fountains. This experience was to profoundly affect his later political actions. By now decidedly a "New Deal Democrat," his Master's thesis was on the benefits of Roosevelt's New Deal, but it also warned of the dangers of Nazi tyranny and of the necessity of the United States arming to meet the coming war.

WORKING FOR THE NEW DEAL

Having earned his Master's Degree from LSU, Humphrey returned to the University of Minnesota in Minneapolis to teach Political Science while working toward his Doctorate. He also held a position teaching political philosophy at Macallaster College, where one of his students was Walter Mondale, like Humphrey a future Senator, Vice President and Presidential candidate. But his life-long nemesis — the lack of money — was to change him from college professor to politician. Muriel, the mother of an eighteen month old daughter, could not work to continue supporting Hubert while he was in school. While some financial aid was available, it was simply not enough to support the family. He had taught one summer for the Works Progress Administration, and he was offered the position of Minneapolis Director at a salary of $150.00 per month. He took the position and at once displayed a flair for organizing the agency into an effective New Deal program: he made disenchanted communist and socialist teachers perform, firing those who did not. He found that the Workers Education program was not working due to a lack of organization, but his energies and direction soon made it effective. Soon he was promoted to State Director of the WPA. With this influential position, he approached organized labor to establish a "Labor College." Shortly, there were more than 20,000 people enrolled in various courses.

Humphrey became active in civic, church and political circles. He became a Sunday School teacher at a Congregational Church and his "University of Life" soon became the most popular Sunday School class in the city. He continued this practice until he became a Senator in 1948. His contacts included, in addition to Orville Freeman and Jeane Kirkpatrick, newsman Eric Sevareid and Herbert McClosky. Politically, Minnesota was a Republican stronghold with Harold Stassen, the "Boy Wonder" Governor, in complete control. The Democrats were the third party, behind the Farm-Labor Party in numbers. It was Humphrey who saw the necessity of joining the Farm-Labor and Democratic parties, which he accomplished by organizing merger committees and holding rallies. At the height of the merger activities, Humphrey persuaded Vice President Henry Wallace to attend a banquet. The young activist was impressed by and devoted to Wallace, and he was bitterly disappointed at Harry Truman's selection over Wallace in 1944; upon FDR's death, Humphrey wrote the former Vice President of his deep regret that Wallace was not President.

Humphrey was tempted to run for Congress in 1942, but he realized his vulnerability as a minority candidate. In 1943, however, he was persuaded to run for Mayor, and although losing, he ran a strong second. His effective speaking and ability to organize the union vote were recognized by astute observers. In 1945, Humphrey ran again for Mayor, and this time captured the imagination of the voters. He ran on a fusion Democratic-Farm-Labor ticket, catering somewhat to radical socialists and communists, and choosing as his theme the ending of corruption in Minneapolis. So effective was Humphrey at expounding his themes and organizing the union vote, as well as the church vote (due to his "University of Life" classes), that he overwhelmed the incumbent. He took office the same year.

The early 1940's had been critical to Humphrey's emergence as a national leader. One item that was to dog him throughout his political career was his lack of military service. When war broke out, Humphrey was at first deferred because of being married with two children. Later, he tried to obtain a naval commission but was denied one for medical reasons. As his yearnings for politics increased, he was aware of the importance of any candidate having served. He tried to enlist in the Army, but he was again rejected for medical reasons. His lack of service, many believe, cost him enough votes in the '68 election to deny him the Presidency.

MAYOR OF MINNEAPOLIS

Humphrey immediately became known as a Mayor who kept his promises. Gambling and graft were immediately attacked and cleaned up. Once, the Mayor heard a noise outside his house, and as he investigated, a shot was fired at him. He was not deterred by this event, and soon Minneapolis was rid of Mafia control. Humphrey's major action as Mayor, though, was to secure passage of the nation's first municipal "Fair Housing Act." Humphrey also instituted a life-long policy of fighting for his constituents: when, for example, Northwest Airlines started to move its Minneapolis headquarters because of a lack of space for expansion, Humphrey dashed off to Washington and persuaded officials to deed Northwest some land from an air base that was to be closed. He also persuaded Gen. Omar Bradley to build a Veterans Hospital on the remaining land.

During these days Humphrey accommodated many political radicals. Soon, however, this was to permanently change. In 1946, the radicals, finding Humphrey too conservative, pulled off a coup at the state convention to rid Humphrey's faction of party control. Humphrey had been friendly to many ultra-liberals, including former Vice President Henry Wallace. It had hurt Humphrey deeply when Truman replaced Wallace and even deeper when Wallace had not succeeded FDR as President. But when Wallace made speeches condoning the Soviet Union's land grabs in Eastern Europe, Humphrey parted company. This was the issue that Humphrey used to regain control of the Democratic-Farm-Labor coalition. When he stood for re-election as Mayor in 1947, he won by the largest majority in the city's history. Humphrey's leadership was to see Minnesota eventually elect Democrats to both Senate seats, to a majority of the Congressional seats, to the Governorship, and to a majority in both Houses of the state legislature.

That same year (1947) Humphrey traveled to Washington to help organize the Americans for Democratic Action. Among the notables also present were Eleanor Roosevelt and United Auto Workers President Walter Reuther. Humphrey was chosen Vice Chairman of the group; later he also served as Chairman. This position was to often offer his political opponents the opportunity to state that Humphrey was the most liberal politician in the land.

THE CAMPAIGNS OF 1948

Humphrey wanted and received his party's nomination for Senator in 1948. Somewhat nationally prominent, there was some talk of his being a Vice Presidential nominee, but this soon faded. The election of Thomas Dewey was a foregone conclusion to almost everyone. But one person who saw a way for Harry Truman to win and for himself to simultaneously become nationally known was Hubert Horatio Humphrey. His method of doing this is well known. Humphrey attended the national convention in Philadelphia and called for a minority report on Civil Rights to be accepted. This report was indeed radical for its day, but Humphrey, who had sponsored the successful Minneapolis Fair Housing Act, pushed hard. Finally gaining the platform, he made the speech of his life, an eight minute oration charged with fact, emotional appeal, and passion. It was the last great speech to a national convention that stirred delegates to action. Like William Jennings Bryan in his "Cross of Gold" address in 1896, Humphrey changed the hearts of the delegates, who passed his measure and watched the "Dixiecrats" leave the party. But this measure in large part saved the White House for Harry Truman and gave much needed exposure back home in Minnesota for Humphrey, who then won by a landslide and became the first Democratic Senator in Minnesota history.

SENATOR (1949-65)

The bold and brazen Humphrey expected to storm into the Senate and transform it with the same success he had enjoyed as Mayor of Minneapolis. Having been put on the cover of *Time* magazine, knowing that he was in large part responsible for Truman's victory and being national chairman of the Americans for Democratic Action, Humphrey may have expected special treatment and results in pushing his programs through the Senate . This was not to be, however, due to the rigid rules of the Senate "Club." As a newcomer, Humphrey was expected to be quiet, and this, of course, was against his very nature. He wanted reform on Taft-Hartley and he wanted Civil Rights action. He also expected the Democratic majority in the Senate to sanction Southerners who did not carry out the Democratic platform. His insistence on this and his lack of understanding for the "Club" rules brought him a chastisement which he found hard to understand and which deeply hurt his feelings. Senators, regardless of political persuasion, were expected to stand by senior members such as Strom Thurmond of South Carolina and Richard Russell of Georgia, irregardless of their beliefs. Humphrey's calls for action found him the outcast, with Vice President Barkley at one point saying, "they [Minnesota] first send us their [Sen.] Ball, then they send us their [Sen.] Thye, and now they've sent us their goddamn ass." Senator

Russell asked, "How in the hell could Minnesota elect a damn fool like that to the Senate of the United States?" And Senator Jenner of Indiana openly attacked Humphrey for his ADA chairmanship and for his leanings toward the English Labour Party. Matters were not helped when a shoving match between Humphrey and Sen. Homer Capehart of Indiana developed after a radio program. But when Humphrey attacked Sen. Harry Byrd of Virginia for maintaining a costly and unused committee, his chastisement was worse than ever, with the whole "Club" attacking Humphrey and defending Byrd. During a four hour Senate session wrath was heaped on Humphrey by Senator after Senator. Humphrey rose time and time again to protest, but each time the presiding officer would look the other way and recognize another Senator who would continue the attack.

Humphrey later found some measure of relief by entering the Senate Dining Room with a black assistant and insisting that the aide be served, an action that resulted in integrating that facility. But Humphrey's acceptance as a Senator began only when the Majority Leader, Lyndon Johnson, decided to take him under his wing and show him the Senate ropes. Humphrey was distrustful of his mentor, but gradually an affection and respect was to develop. Moreover, Humphrey began to understand that to "get along he had to go along." Thus he was able to disagree with Johnson on Civil Rights but agree on other social legislation. He was also able to gain favored committee appointments, such as the Foreign Relations Committee. And he learned that the Senate would hear him if he spoke in favor of issues rather than against his fellow Senators.

Humphrey offered several major pieces of legislation that were adopted before he left the Senate to become Vice President. One bill allowed underdeveloped nations to buy farm surpluses with foreign currencies. He offered the legislation that was to eventually become Medicaid. And of course his leadership led eventually to Civil Rights Bills in 1958 and 1964 that instituted profound changes for minorities in the United States. Though unsuccessful in having the Taft-Hartley Act repealed, he worked relentlessly to do so. Indeed, labor's legislative champion was not John Kennedy or Lyndon Johnson, but Hubert Humphrey.

He was a strong advocate of a national defense, voting for NATO, the Marshall Plan and foreign aid, and supporting the Truman Doctrine. He resisted the moves of Joseph McCarthy and led the movement that censured the Wisconsin Republican. He served as a UN delegate in 1956 and was a strong supporter of Israel (he was also probably the largest recipient of Jewish donations in the country). He struck hard at the Eisenhower Administration when it reduced price supports for dairy farmers. He was unsuccessful in having a Missouri Valley Authority (similar to the Tennessee Valley Authority) enacted, in large part due to the brashness he displayed to fellow "Club" members in his early Senate years. It was Humphrey's idealism that led to the eventual establishment of the Peace Corps, although John Kennedy was to receive the plaudits.

He was also an early exponent of nuclear disarmament. But when the Russians launched Sputnik, he, as a Foreign Relations Committee member, was one of the Democrat's chief spokesmen against the Republican Administration. By 1960, he would be echoing the Democratic refrains about a "missile gap."

Politically ambitious, Humphrey tried to force himself to the top of Democratic politics. In 1952, he established himself as the kingpin of Minnesota politics when he persuaded President Truman, within twenty-four hours of the death of the incumbent District of Columbia Federal Judge, to appoint to the new vacancy the Republican Governor of Minnesota, who challenged him in popularity. Next he had himself named a "Favorite Son" candidate for President, but Adlai Stevenson swept the Minnesota delegates away from him. In 1956, Humphrey thought he had made a deal with Stevenson to obtain the Vice Presidential nomination. Apparently thinking his chances were good, he opened, of all things, a "Humphrey for Vice President" headquarters in Washington, D.C. The deal that Stevenson had with Humphrey was based on the premise that Humphrey would deliver Minnesota's primary votes for Stevenson. When Minnesota Republicans got wind of this, they promptly "switched over" to Estes Kefauver, and Humphrey's deal was forgotten when he could not deliver delegates to Stevenson. He still had hopes for the nod, but then Stevenson "opened" the convention, and Humphrey was crushed in a mad rush of ambitious fellow Democrats. John Kennedy, who had nominated Stevenson, became a national figure at this convention and almost won the nomination, but in the end, Humphrey swung his support to Tennessee's Kefauver. The team of Stevenson and Kefauver then went down to a crushing defeat at the hands of Eisenhower and Nixon.

THE PRESIDENTIAL ELECTION OF 1960

It was ironic that international affairs — not domestic issues such as labor policy or civil rights or federal aid to the poor — put Humphrey in the limelight for the Democratic nomination for President in 1960. Humphrey, sensing Republican weakness after the launching of Sputnik and the recession of 1958, decided to actively seek the Presidency. Eleanor Roosevelt thought of Humphrey as having "the spark of greatness" over all his potential opponents, including John Kennedy and Lyndon Johnson. Perhaps what had brought Humphrey to the spotlight was a trip to Moscow in 1958. There Humphrey had had a day long conference with Nikita Khrushechev, with frank exchanges being made by each. Upon return Humphrey was featured on numerous television and radio programs, and he was also pictured on the front covers of a host of periodicals. Far and away, Hubert Horatio Humphrey was the front runner for the Democratic nomination in 1960.

But Humphrey's major obstacle was John F. Kennedy, who had youthful vision, charisma and lots of money. Minor obstacles included Lyndon Johnson and Adlai Stevenson, although the latter was neither campaigning actively nor seeking to be another William Jennings Bryan. Humphrey never made Kennedy's Catholicism an issue, but he surely took delight in stating, "It's not the Pope but the Pop..." that he was against. Campaigning hard in the primaries of New Hampshire, Wisconsin and West Virginia, Humphrey found himself out-organized and out-spent. Surprisingly, he also found himself without support from labor, which, under the leadership of his ADA friend Walter Reuther, was for Kennedy. He also found to his chagrin that the Kennedys were pointing to his lack of service in World War II. Humphrey boldly proposed his liberal ideas: Food Stamps, Health Care for Senior Citizens, a Youth Conservation Corps, and a higher minimum wage. But the voters would not heed him, and he went down to devastating defeats both in his neighboring Wisconsin and then in West Virginia. Humphrey withdrew from the campaign, deeply in debt and deeply distressed. He hoped for a Vice Presidential nomination, but that faded when he would not release his delegates to Kennedy, who was favoring Gov. Orville Freeman. Freeman seemed assured of getting the nomination but Lyndon Johnson, who was believed not to be interested in being Vice President, surprised everyone when he accepted the nomination that was supposed to be being offered merely as a courtesy for party unity.

Humphrey ran again for Senator and was re-elected in a landslide. When he returned to the Senate in 1961, he became Majority Whip, and he began to exert more power and influence than ever before. President Kennedy invited him at the White House regularly for consultations, and it was Humphrey who pushed through key pieces of New Frontier legislation. Many of Humphrey's ideas, such as the Peace Corps and Food for Peace, were, of course, enacted during this period with Kennedy gaining the credit. Humphrey used his influence to have two key appointments made—Walter Heller as the Administration's Chief Economist and George McGovern as director of the Food for Peace program. Undoubtedly, though, Humphrey's major contribution to President Kennedy was getting the Senate to ratify the "Limited" Test Ban Treaty.

Although Humphrey was an extremely hard driving Senator, he had become Majority Whip because he had mellowed. His liberalism had not waned, however, and he was still active in the ADA. In 1963, an invitation was extended for Humphrey to attend an assemblage of socialist European leaders, including the Socialist Prime Ministers of England, Sweden, Denmark and Norway, as well as Berlin Mayor Willy Brandt and Walter Reuther. This left a lasting impression with many that Humphrey, who was at ease with this cast, was for all purposes a Socialist himself.

The tragic death of John Kennedy caused Humphrey to sincerely grieve. But even before Kennedy was buried, he was plotting his own political future. He held a strategy session with key advisers, telling them that because of his lack of money he needed to become Vice President under Johnson in 1965 and then spring to the Presidency from that platform. To gain Johnson's favor, Humphrey became a close adviser and the new President's chief liaison in Congress. The Civil Rights Bill of 1964, proposed by Johnson as a memorial to the slain Kennedy, had been a goal of Humphrey since 1948, and he diligently put together the coalition necessary for passage, and then patiently out-maneuvered the Southerners, led by Richard Russell (who had branded Humphrey a "damned fool" in 1949). No doubt Hubert Horatio Humphrey considered this legislation the crowning achievement of his life.

THE ELECTION 0F 1964

The legislative support and personal counseling of Humphrey endeared him to Johnson. But Humphrey was convenient for another reason. Bobby Kennedy, the dead President's brother who was despised by the new President, was maneuvering to get the Vice Presidential nomination by riding a wave of sympathy from the American people. Johnson conveniently announced that his Cabinet members would be too busy with their duties to seek the Vice Presidency, and from then on virtually everyone knew that Humphrey was Johnson's choice. Johnson withheld his official recommendation until the last moment for publicity reasons, and the moments of waiting were anxious ones for the man who had been rejected by Stevenson in 1956 and Kennedy in 1960. Johnson required a pledge of loyalty from Humphrey that was simple but plain. By saying, "You can trust me, Mr. President," Humphrey obtained the nomination and agreed to place loyalty above cause, trusting that this move would eventually lead him to the Presidency of the United States.

The campaign that followed was probably the most enjoyable one of Humphrey's career. His role was to attack Sen. Goldwater, and this he carried out masterfully, beginning with his acceptance speech in Atlantic City, which, along with his Philadelphia speech sixteen years earlier, is remembered as one of his most effective and well-known speeches: "...Most Democrats and Republicans voted ... for the Civil Rights Act. But not Senator Goldwater." [etc.] His kicker was, "It's back to the store [for Goldwater] in '64". Knowledgeable, confident, witty and with the assurance that the voters were Democratic, Humphrey traveled the country in his plane dubbed "The Happy Warrior" and presented the Democratic cause with vitality. For once, he had enough money to keep his mind on issues rather than finances. Johnson kept a tight rein, but this was to Humphrey a small price to pay for a future chance at the Presidency. Johnson and Humphrey won one of the most overwhelming victories in history in 1964. They had a popular margin of 15 million votes and won in the electoral college by 486 votes to only 52 for the Goldwater-Miller ticket.

VICE PRESIDENT (1965-69)

Once he had assumed office, Humphrey found the Vice Presidency less to his liking than he anticipated. Johnson, he found, demanded a loyalty akin to subservience. When, for example, Winston Churchill died, Johnson chose Supreme Court Chief Justice Earl Warren — not the Vice President — to lead the American delegation to the funeral and felt no obligation to explain the omission of the Vice President. When Muriel Humphrey questioned why, Johnson ignored Humphrey for a month, excluding him from important meetings. On another occasion Humphrey advised against the bombing of North Viet Nam while Soviet President Kosygin was in Hanoi, and Johnson proceeded to keep Humphrey away from various high level conferences for an extended period of time. It was a hard price for the proud Humphrey to pay, but he paid it without revealing his dissatisfaction publicly and only privately to the most intimate of friends. He was intent on remaining loyal to the President, and this he did, especially on Viet Nam. He spoke consistently in favor of the President's policies on the war, and a loud cry from various liberal groups came out against him personally. Yet, he maintained his loyalty until the campaign of 1968, when political necessity made him announce that he would end the bombing of North Viet Nam.

The Johnson Administration was much more successful on domestic matters than in foreign affairs, with a host of social legislation being enacted. Johnson's Great Society, consisting of the Job Corps, Model Cities, Head Start, the Office of Economic Opportunity, and various Civil Rights bills, was the most dramatic change in government since the New Deal.

Many of the programs were the ideas Humphrey brought with him to the Senate in 1948. Of course, it was to be another person who would get the credit for his programs.

THE ELECTION OF 1968

President Johnson startled the nation when he announced in March of 1968 that he would not run again for President. Already, Sen. Eugene McCarthy, Humphrey's Minnesota protege, was mounting a formidable drive against Johnson. Soon Robert Kennedy, drawing upon the sympathy of his dead brother, decided to also enter the race for the nomination.

Although the nation was in turmoil due to demonstrations on matters ranging from the Viet Nam War to civil rights (there were some especially bad rights in Los Angeles, New York, Detroit and Newark), Humphrey did not view the turmoil as a reason not to seek to fulfill his lifelong dream. Because of Johnson's late withdrawal, his strategy was to avoid primaries and gain party machinery delegates. During the campaign a host of traumatic events took place. Martin Luther King was assassinated first and then Bobby Kennedy was also murdered. Demonstrations against "Johnson's War" reached an emotional peak at the Democratic Convention in Chicago, where thousands of "hippies" clashed with police on national television. Just four years earlier, Barry Goldwater was finished in San Francisco. In 1968, Hubert Humphrey was finished in Chicago.

The Republicans chose Richard Nixon and Spiro Agnew to vie against Humphrey and Sen. Edmond Muskie, chosen by Humphrey because he was Catholic and from New England. Trailing in the polls by a vast margin, Humphrey finally decided to break with Johnson on the war, pledging to end the bombing of North Viet Nam if he were President. Although his following picked up immediately due to support from the peace faction, he was still haunted by his lack of military service in World War II as well as the lack of service by any of his sons in the Viet Nam era, although each was a military academy graduate. The race was exceptionally close, but Nixon won with 43 percent of the popular vote, a margin of only one-half million popular votes, and an electoral margin of 301 to 191. Gov. George Wallace of Alabama and his newly formed American Independent Party received 14 percent of the popular vote and 46 electoral votes, which would probably have gone to the more conservative Nixon in a two man race.

LAST YEARS

Deeply disappointed at losing in 1968, Humphrey still resisted inclinations to be bitter. He met with President-Elect Nixon and genuinely wished him well, though he turned down an offer to be UN Ambassador. He returned to his Minnesota home and was closer to his family than in years. He had, for example, not attended his father-in-law's funeral because of Minnesota party business; he had also stayed in the Senate during the most crucial time of voting on the Civil Rights Act of 1964 rather than return to Minnesota during an operation on his son Bob for cancer. One granddaughter was mentally impaired. The compassionate Humphrey, whose life work was meant to resolve these woes, now concentrated on re-establishing the ties of love. Out of work and not well off financially, he needed employment, which was provided by several Minnesota teaching appointments and a position with *Encyclopedia Britannica;* he then was better off financially than in many years. He was still restive and anxious for action that could lead him to the Presidency. Ted Kennedy, the Democratic "heir apparent," was expected to receive the nomination in 1972. While on a trip to Russia, however, two events occurred which made Humphrey a contender for '72. First, he received the news of Ted Kennedy's Chappaquidick episode. Then, within a week, Sen. Eugene McCarthy announced that he would not seek re-election to his Minnesota seat in 1970. Of course, Humphrey ran and won the Senate seat with no opponent being close.

Returning to the Senate in 1971, Humphrey was without the previous power he had held as a Senator and Vice President. Moreover, he found himself treated harshly, being unable to secure his old appointments to the Foreign Relations or Appropriations Committees. Humphrey soon found that there was a wing of the Democratic party even more liberal than he, and it was intent on a change in the national leadership.

Yet Humphrey still held strong national appeal with the masses, and he decided to make a challenge again in 1972. This time his major opponents for the Democratic nomination were his former running mate, Edmond Muskie, Alabama Governor George Wallace and George McGovern, who had started his Washington career under the tutelage of Humphrey. McGovern, who had served as Chairman of a Party committee to redistribute delegates and who knew best what was required to win the nomination, turned out to be the best organized of all the candidates. In 1972 the primaries, as in 1960, were to be Humphrey's undoing. Wallace took critical votes from Humphrey in Wisconsin, where McGovern gained a momentum that was never stopped. Wallace won Michigan and Maryland, but an assassin's bullets ended his campaign. Humphrey won several primaries, but the crucial state of California went to McGovern.

The convention and subsequent election of 1972 turned out to be one of the most devastating periods in the history of the Democratic Party. Having rejected Humphrey, who had won more primary votes than McGovern, the Party then nominated Sen. Thomas Eagleton, who turned out to have had a nervous disorder requiring treatment. The Republicans had a field day as McGovern, who first announced that he was "one-thousand percent behind [Eagleton]," forced Eagleton to withdraw and then selected Sargent Shriver, whose chief asset was that he was a brother-in-law of the Kennedys, as his running mate.

Watergate became the burning issue that consumed the nation after the election of '72. Humphrey was not an early open advocate of Nixon's departure. To be sure, there had been some improprieties in his earlier campaigns, with one aide going to prison and Humphrey being embarrassed as the Senate looked into illegal contributions from corporations and especially from Howard Hughes. As the 1976 election approached, he decided to make one last run for the highest office in the land. Unfortunately Humphrey by this time was out of touch with both the party machinery and the party rank and file. He was also seriously ill, the effects of an old bladder problem starting to flare up again. The nation strongly wanted an outsider, and thus all of the old professionals, Humphrey, Muskie, McCarthy and McGovern, were rejected in favor of a political newcomer from Georgia, Jimmy Carter. Carter, showing a facile ability for organization, captured early caucuses and primaries and won the nomination with ease. Inexperienced, he turned to Humphrey for advice on the coming campaign and on Humphrey's protege, Walter Mondale, as his running mate. Humphrey was elated to see the pair unseat Gerald Ford from the Presidency.

For some years Humphrey had been receiving treatments for his bladder problems. In 1977 cancer was detected, and surgery was performed, but unfortunately the dreaded disease had already spread to other parts of his body. Chemotherapy was tried, which left him deathly sick, pale and balding. Yet he kept his up his good cheer and encouragement for others. Sensing his demise, the Senate established a new position just for Humphrey — Senate Deputy President Pro Tem. As he worsened, most of his time was spent in confinement at his Waverly, Minnesota home. He made constant calls to friends and adversaries alike on a WATS line given him as a Christmas present. He was able especially to have a meaningful — even loving — correspondence with his old nemesis, Richard Nixon.

A CELEBRATION OF LIFE

The time came for Humphrey to say his final good-byes to Washington. President Carter arranged for the man who had wanted so much to be President to fly to Washington aboard "Air Force One." A trip to Camp

David was also arranged. Humphrey spoke to the House of Representatives and to the Senate, and he was deeply moved when Senators who had initially rejected his strong overtures now extended a rare display of affection, with moving tributes being rendered from both sides of the Senate aisle. The new Health, Education and Welfare Building was named, appropriately, in his honor.

He returned home, accompanied by Vice President Mondale, but succumbed within a month. As he intended, his funeral was a celebration. His coffin was displayed in the Capitol, and his family, certainly carrying out his feelings of love for a former foe, welcomed Richard Nixon to the memorial services. Appropriately enough, after over thirty years of the most active and sometimes distasteful political proceedings, the death of the man who had grown from obscurity in search of a teaching position only to end up seeking the Presidency could show above all else that he had been a man of compassion.

George McGovern
The Election of 1972

George McGovern was an arrogant and abrasive political personality who tried in vain for the Presidency only to suffer one of the most humiliating defeats in American history. Against Richard Nixon, whom he loathed, McGovern could carry only Massachusetts and Washington, D.C. He had been able for many years to maintain his Senate office in conservative South Dakota while keeping liberal views contrary to his constituents, but when it was necessary to reveal his innermost thoughts to seek national office, he lost even his home state. George McGovern is a study of a political opportunist losing badly.

SOUTH DAKOTA CHILDHOOD

The son of a professional baseball player turned minister, George McGovern was born July 19, 1922 in Avon, South Dakota, where his father, a Methodist circuit preacher, was presently "called." George was the second of four children in the McGovern family. His father's ancestors had reached South Dakota from Pennsylvania coal mines and Iowa farms, while his mother, who was only one-half her husband's age, was of Canadian lineage.

The McGovern household was often short on income, with food or chickens sometimes being supplied rather than a salary for the minister-father, but some degree of comfort was achieved by the frugal management of Rev. McGovern, who rented part of the house to supplement earnings. Though poor, the McGovern house was not lacking in discipline. The children were expected to attend all church services and could question their father's judgement only at the risk of corporal punishment. George often would sneak into the movies, but he did so at great peril, relying upon the alibis of his brother and sisters for protection.

When the Great Depression hit the McGoverns in the early 1930's, young George felt the effects, and he never forgot them. His family was poverty stricken, and he saw countless South Dakota farmers lose their property as dust storms and drought kept crops from being harvested. One of his most vivid remembrances was that of a farmer weeping openly because the earnings of an entire farm season had barely been enough to pay for the bill to truck his hogs to market. Such experiences inevitably shaped the thinking of the sensitive lad.

At first George was not a good student, almost failing the first grade due to shyness, but his teachers seemed to bring out the best in him. By the time he was in high school, he was participating in his school's debate society. In the midwest, debating was considered *the* premier extra-curricular activity, and George McGovern was one of the best of his time at the forensic activity. He had a special ability to stand on his feet and present a reasoned and orderly verbal dissertation. He traveled hundreds of miles to participate in contests and on several occasions was judged by a school teacher named Karl Mundt. Mundt later became renowned both as a forensic expert and as a Republican United States Senator whom McGovern, ironically, would unsuccessfully face in a Senate race.

The ability to debate shaped the course of George McGovern's life. His high school record earned him a scholarship to Dakota Wesleyan College in 1940, where he refined his forensic abilities and began to also develop leadership abilities, being elected class president at the college his last three years. While at Wesleyan McGovern began dating Eleanor Stegeberg, a nursing student and daughter of a Democratic Party County Chairman. They soon became quite serious and made plans to be wed, but World War II, another event which was to shape the course of McGovern's life, was to intervene.

McGovern was listening to the radio when newscaster John Daly interrupted with news of Japan's sneak attack on Pearl Harbor. Declining to volunteer at the outbreak of hostilities, he continued his college education, not knowing when he, like countless other young Americans, would receive his call to armed duty. In college his ability to speak sharpened, and he won South Dakota's Peace Oratory Contest, selecting the title "My Brother's Keeper." His remarks were also adjudged by the National Council of Churches as one of the twelve best orations on peace in 1942. In 1943 he traveled to Minnesota and placed first in a five state debate tournament. Upon return to his home campus, an induction notice into the Army was awaiting the first semester junior.

WAR HERO

At the outset of World War II, McGovern had joined the Civil Air Patrol and received flying instructions. Upon entering the Army, he was enrolled in Flight Cadet School at Muskogee, Oklahoma. He was quite lonely, and soon he and Eleanor were seriously contemplating marriage. They were wed on his first leave, and she began following him to a number of training camps across the Midwest. Their existence was meager at times, but they were content. They were expecting their first child when George received orders that he was being shipped overseas as the pilot and crew commander of a B-24 Liberator, the largest of America's World War II bomber aircraft.

McGovern quickly earned a reputation as a competent pilot and as one who was cool under fire. Though not getting into action until the latter stages of the war in 1944, he flew thirty-five combat missions, many of them under hostile enemy fire. On several occasions his craft was imperiled. Once a tire blew out upon take-off, yet the dependable McGovern carried out his mission, returned, and landed safely. On a mission over Czechoslovakia, the nose of his craft was blown away and his controls disabled. He decided to try to head his B-24 to his Italian base some 600 miles away, although he was rapidly losing altitude. It appeared that his crew might have to parachute out, but McGovern was finally able to land his craft on a tiny Mediterranean island controlled by the British. Had his flying not been exact, the crew would have crashed into a mountain at the far end of the runway; instead, McGovern received the Distinguished Flying Cross.

Never missing a mission, McGovern even flew the same day he received news that his father had died of a heart attack. His last mission was memorable: the nose of his plane was blasted away by flak and some members of his crew were injured, but McGovern headed his Liberator toward home. The landing gear was cranked down by hand, and he landed the craft by making his approach at the beginning of the runway, quickly reversing engines, and letting the craft roll and roll until it finally came to rest on a fail-safe embankment at the far end. His calmness and expertness under this difficulty earned him the Air Medal.

HOME TO SCHOOL AND THE MINISTRY

McGovern had taken many of his textbooks with him to Europe, and he studied them assiduously while off duty. His experience with the many horrors of war, including one incident where his bombardier had apparently intentionally unloaded some bombs on a farmhouse (this bombardier never flew for McGovern again), had seriously affected his sensitive outlook. He now vowed not only not to fly or fight again but to join with other former servicemen in putting together a world order dedicated to peace. To this end he decided to complete his Bachelor's degree and then go to Seminary and become a Methodist preacher.

McGovern re-enrolled in Dakota Wesleyan. Soon he was engaging in debate and public speaking again, and he once more won the South Dakota Peace Oratory Contest with an address entitled "From Cave to Cave." In that address, McGovern first expressed the social-political philosophy that would mark his future political platforms. McGovern graduated from Dakota Wesleyan in August of 1946 and then entered Garrett Theological Seminary at Northwestern University in Chicago. He also accepted an appointment as a student minister at Diamond Lake Methodist Church.

The new student preacher seemed to be secure and content with his new station. He not only had income from stipends and his ministerial position, but he was receiving aid through the GI Bill. More importantly, he felt that he could preach the "social gospel," which he had been studying since his return from World War II. That study had included serious reviews of Hegel and Marx and, more importantly to McGovern, of an American philosopher named Walter Rauchenbusch. Preaching the social gospel, McGovern felt, would allow him to spread the idealism of world peace, one world government, and the rights of working men to organize labor unions to provide for domestic welfare.

What the ministry did not provide McGovern, according to some (including his mother), was a "call" to preach in accordance with traditional church doctrine. McGovern, who had already abandoned the conservative Methodism of his father for more modern doctrine, was not as interested in tending a flock as he was in expressing his social and political views. Some friendly professors at Northwestern, where McGovern was also taking some history courses, pointed out to McGovern that he should pursue the study and teaching of history instead of preaching. During this period, according to McGovern, he was attending a lecture on the "Intellectual History of the United States" and was so enthralled by it that he decided to drop the ministry — after only nine months of service — to pursue a Doctorate in History. It was a decision that he never regretted.

INTO POLITICS

McGovern entered Northwestern's graduate school in late 1947 and delved into his advance studies with unusual determination and vigor. His professors for the most part were "left wing," and the combination of his social gospel background and the study of history from the liberal viewpoint soon had him thinking of actively engaging in politics.

His personal life style, never luxurious, was still limited and had him feeling that he was a "working man." His wife pulled in what money she could through odd jobs. The rest of the income of the family, now numbering four, came from George's stipends and his GI Bill subsistence. These financial conditions probably influenced McGovern to choose the "Ludlow Massacre," the 1913-14 riot-filled labor uprising against a Rockefeller owned Colorado mine, as the subject for his doctoral thesis.

In 1948, while still a doctoral student, McGovern began his long climb up the political ladder by supporting Henry Wallace, the radical former Vice President of FDR who favored strong ties to the Soviet Union, instead of Harry Truman, the incumbent Democratic President. McGovern was to later refuse to speak of his role in the '48 campaign, but there is no doubt that he was at first active for Wallace, writing "letters to the editor" of South Dakota papers and making public speeches there also. He attended the Progressive Convention in Philadelphia as a delegate. It was there that he finally realized that Wallace was being misled by the Russians; McGovern, who throughout his career had a nifty ability to know when to change political positions, decided not to vote for Wallace or support him further.

In 1949 McGovern finished his basic doctoral studies and returned to his hometown of Mitchell to accept a teaching position at Dakota Wesleyan while completing his thesis. Teaching debate and history, he continued his political activities, now as a Democrat, and made public his views on a cease fire in Korea and recognition of Communist China. In 1952 he became a devotee of Adlai Stevenson, naming his son Steven after the Democratic nominee and campaigning throughout his home state for the Party. Toward the end of the campaign, McGovern had a conversation with the state chairman of the Party concerning its future. The chairman, realizing that the Democrats would be trounced once again in 1952, wanted McGovern to quit teaching and accept a position as state Executive Secretary to rebuild the Party. McGovern knew that the job would be difficult — he would even have to raise his own salary through contributions — but he knew that this would allow him to be in politics full-time. After some consideration, he announced that he would take the job.

McGovern's took on his difficult new job with zeal. He contacted all of the state's county chairman to let them know that he was on the job. He also traveled the state continuously, making speeches to various civic clubs extolling his party's virtues and calling for an effective two-party system. In a short time an effective organization was built which was winning more and more legislative seats. Once more Democrats were in the legislature, he coordinated their efforts there. He also spearheaded the opposition of Republican farm policies, being careful not to condemn President Eisenhower but making Ike's Secretary of Agriculture, Ezra Taft Benson, an object of ridicule in South Dakota. By 1954, the party was strong enough to run close, though unsuccessful, statewide races for Governor. Personally ambitious, it was McGovern's goal to run for the U.S. Senate in 1956 and go to Washington to pursue his social agenda. Party interests, however, dictated that he run for the House instead.

Campaigning down the backroads of the state and using a person-to-person approach, McGovern soon made headway against a popular incumbent. Finding that they were in trouble, the Republicans resorted to smear tactics, charging that McGovern was too sympathetic to communism and the policies of former Vice President Henry Wallace. But his war record, especially his Distinguished Flying Cross, served him well, and in the end McGovern won his District by an impressive 12,000 votes.

CONGRESSMAN

McGovern and his family moved into a house next door to Hubert Humphrey when they settled in Washington. While his congressional record was not outstanding, he was able to maintain contact with his constituents in a novel way. Newsletters and other communications not only informed voters of what was going on in Washington but who might be the parents of twins or who the local high school valedictorians were. This was effective politics, and when McGovern ran for re-election in 1958 against an incumbent Republican Governor, a World War II ace pilot who could not succeed himself, he was able to run a better race than in 1956. This campaign was bitter, but McGovern's ability to debate served him well. He clearly bested his opponent, whose media experience was extremely limited, and handily won a second term to Congress.

IN THE KENNEDY ADMINISTRATION

Congressman McGovern began making some influential friends in Washington, including John and Robert Kennedy, with whom he worked on labor reform legislation. These contacts helped him when he decided to challenge Senator Karl Mundt, his political antitheses, for the Senate in 1960. However, McGovern met his match in Senator Mundt, not faring well at all in debates with the founder of the National Forensic Society. Mundt was particularly effective in pointing out McGovern's past ties with liberal causes and Henry Wallace, his connections with Kennedy and Catholicism, and a devious McGovern attempt to smear him with a "black book" publication. Bitter at losing, McGovern was to later say, "...I knew I hated his guts."

McGovern had run on a ticket with John F. Kennedy. Though he lost South Dakota, John Kennedy became the President-Elect in 1960, and the new President was sensitive to McGovern's loss, feeling that his Catholicism and liberal views had destroyed any chances for McGovern's success in the normally conservative South Dakota. Soon an offer was extended for McGovern to stay in Washington as head of the New Frontier's "Food for

Peace" program. McGovern quickly accepted the offer, knowing that it would not only provide him with the opportunity to expand his social agenda but also offer him a political position that would keep him in close contact with the large block of farm voters in his home state.

FOOD FOR PEACE

Working as "Special Assistant to the President," McGovern quickly assembled a team to ship America's abundant harvests to underdeveloped nations around the world. The importance of his mission was not diminished by the fact that the new Chief Executive had created the Food for Peace program by his second executive order. But the new Director must have been taken aback a bit when he chose some offices in the old Executive Office Building only to have them claimed by the new Vice President, Lyndon Johnson. Nonetheless, he approached his job with fervor. He wanted to ship wheat to Communist China, then in the midst of a famine, but the Chinese firmly declined an offer from the capitalistic U.S. A mission was undertaken to South America, and the results were encouraging. McGovern had supplies sent to countries, such as Brazil, where starvation was rampant. Later, he arranged a school lunch program for Peru.

The Food for Peace Director was soon sending shipments to other parts of the world. India especially received enormous amounts of aid. Other assistance was given to countries in Africa, Asia and the Soviet Union, and dramatic drops in hunger and disease were recorded. Pope John XXIII personally commended McGovern for his leadership. In 1964 McGovern wrote a short book entitled *War Against Want*, in which he explained both the policy and plans that he had for the Food for Peace project as well as the future directions the United States should take in such endeavors.

McGovern's style of leadership was not especially suited to some New Frontier leaders. Often the South Dakotan would bluntly lambast a superior official who did not see things as he did. He did not get along well with Orville Freeman, the Secretary of Agriculture (McGovern had originally wanted this position himself), and he forcefully resisted any efforts to have the Food for Peace measure absorbed into larger programs. Partly because of the Cabinet opposition he faced but more so because he wanted to further his career, McGovern resigned his position in 1962 to run for the United States Senate.

When the incumbent Republican Senator died unexpectedly in June of 1962, McGovern's campaign was helped inestimably. Seven Republicans offered themselves as candidates for the vacancy, and as they divided, Mc-

Govern conquered. The resulting GOP nominee was charged with being a drunkard, not an enviable image in conservative South Dakota, while McGovern was able to portray the reputation of having been a high White House official who had traveled around the world not only feeding people but selling American agricultural products. Not taking any chances in the normally Republican state, McGovern canvassed the public unceasingly, extolling his war record, his ministerial background, his South Dakota roots, and his White House work. On election day, the hard campaigning paid off as McGovern won by 121,581 votes to 121,481, a margin of exactly one-hundred votes. A recount demanded by his opponent increased the new Senator's margin to 504 votes.

UNITED STATES SENATOR (1963-1975)

The new Democratic Senator asked for and received appointments to the Agriculture and Interior Committees, posts which were vital to his constituents back home. But he soon moved in other areas to establish himself as one of the most liberal Senators in the nation's history. Almost immediately he called for cuts in military spending, asking that the funds be used for foreign aid to depressed countries — even Cuba, which, he indicated, was less responsible than certain capitalist countries for the current state of bad relations. Believing that the United States had an overkill nuclear capability, McGovern proposed in a 1973 Senate speech that defense contractors stop manufacturing war materials within twelve months and also come up with plans to convert their plants to the production of products for peace. Time and time again he voted against various military spending proposals: bombers; anti-ballistic missiles; new ships; the C5-A transport; NASA; and any increase in general military appropriations. By 1968, when the United States was deeply involved in the War in Vietnam, he would be calling for an "excess profits" tax on defense industries. He was careful to oppose, however, any cuts for installations in his native South Dakota.

McGovern engineered a notable victory in the Agriculture Committee. In 1964, though a "free trader," he had legislation passed which limited imports on beef, a product essential to the South Dakota economy. He also had restrictions lifted on compulsory subsidies on wheat, a practice offensive to his home state farmers. Most of the New Frontier and Great Society programs received McGovern's support, including the War on Poverty, the Manpower Training Act, the Job Corps, Office of Economic Opportunity, and a host of welfare and educational aid bills. Ironically, the liberal Senator who believed in the rights of working men violated his conscience for political expediency and opposed a move to repeal the Taft-Hartley Labor Act, since his constituents did not favor labor unions as much as he did. This vote would cost him dearly when he received the Democratic nomination in 1972.

McGovern's national reputation surged when he began to openly oppose Lyndon Johnson on the Viet Nam War. McGovern made a number of speeches — including in 1963 the first Senate speech condemning American involvement in Southeast Asia — indicating that America was wrong to be in Viet Nam, and he then voted against the "draft" as being forced labor. By 1965 he was calling for unilateral cessation of the bombing of North Viet Nam, claiming, based on his military background, that such a move would lead to negotiations. When President Johnson finally relented to pressures for such a move and made such an offer to Hanoi, McGovern and other "doves" without hesitation pressed unrelentingly for other concessions to the communist Vietnamese. The President deeply resented such bold affronts to his leadership, but McGovern continued to oppose what he considered a mad war. An inspection trip only confirmed to him that his position was right. In 1969, after Nixon was President, he called for a unilateral cease fire and complete withdrawal of U.S. forces from the Asian battlefield. But the South Dakota Senator's opposition to the War did not stop there. He began to speak to huge anti-war rallies. He also consulted with "think tank" professor Daniel Ellsburg on the so-called "Pentagon Papers" and, after refusing to release the classified documents himself for fear of losing his credibility and his security clearance, he suggested that Ellsburg take them either to the Washington *Post* or the New York *Times*. Finally, in an interview with *Playboy* magazine, the former minister compared the North Vietnamese role to that of the United States during the Revolutionary War, indicating further that North Vietnamese communist leader Ho Chi Minh was the George Washington of his country.

The South Dakota Senator joined with other liberals in calling for an end to poverty in the United States. Often traveling to destitute communities, without giving local or state governments any notice of the visit, McGovern and his colleagues would survey homes for signs of malnutrition. Soon he was on the floor of the Senate lobbying for legislation to increase the size of food stamp allotments. When opposition to his thinking arose, he self-righteously condemned his opponents. Increases were passed, but not to the extent that the former minister desired.

RUNNING FOR PRESIDENT IN 1972

Always an ally of the Kennedys, McGovern, after doing some necessary homework to keep his South Dakota support intact, supported Robert Kennedy in 1968 after Lyndon Johnson, who had received considerable opposition from Minnesota Senator Eugene McCarthy, removed himself from the race for the Democratic nomination. When RFK was assassinated in Los Angeles, McGovern was deeply hurt, and he rode on the funeral train of Robert Kennedy from New York City to Washington. On the trip, McGovern was approached by RFK supporters who maintained that McGovern should carry on Bobby's mission and seek the Democratic nomination in Bobby's place. After consideration, McGovern decided to seek the 1968 Democratic nomination for President.

Hubert Humphrey, an old friend but as Vice President under Lyndon Johnson a political enemy, and Sen. McCarthy were McGovern's chief adversaries in the race. The incumbent Vice President had gotten into the race late and decided to bypass most of the preferential primaries, concentrating instead on traditional party support to gain the nod for President. McGovern, lacking the charisma of the Kennedys as well as their organizational skills, soon found that he had an uphill fight. He went to the Chicago convention well behind in delegates but refused to give up the fight. A debate among Humphrey, McGovern and McCarthy was arranged by friends in the California delegation, and McGovern, seizing the initiative, boldly (and probably rightly) stated that had he not been shot, Robert Kennedy would have easily been the Democratic nominee in 1968. His performance in this debate endeared him to many liberals for the future.

The story of the 1968 Chicago convention was not the debate, though, but rather the demonstrations in the streets of Chicago protesting the War in Viet Nam. Communist radicals had clearly organized riots that were provoking the police of Chicago. For several nights, chaos, visible to the entire nation via television, reigned outside the convention center. Inside, political chaos was erupting. McGovern and other liberals were chastising President Johnson, Vice President Humphrey, Chicago Mayor Daley and other "establishment" leaders both for their parts in the war and for any abuse the demonstrators were receiving. Sen. McGovern himself referred to Chicago policemen who were arresting the demonstrators as "son-of- bitches" and "bastards." His stance helped leave the Democratic party in disarray; it also cost him dearly in the future.

No sooner had Richard Nixon defeated Hubert Humphrey in 1968 than did George McGovern, who won Senate re-election the same year, decide to seek the Presidency again in 1972. McGovern became more and more active in party organization and accepted one post, Chairman of the Democratic Reform Commission, which became pivotal to his 1972 chances. As Chairman, candidate McGovern pushed for changes in the selection of delegates — proportional changes in the number of women and minorities — to the next nominating convention. The rules he proposed were adopted, and McGovern quickly set about organizing a strategy to gain the nomination, even if the composition of the convention did not match national sentiment.

At first his major opposition appeared to be Teddy Kennedy, but McGovern, who did not feel the same loyalty to the younger Kennedy as he had to JFK and RFK, decided that he should not back off from running. When a female campaign worker of Kennedy died in the famous car accident at Chappaquidick bridge, leaving the impression that the Massachusetts Senator was both drinking and womanizing, Kennedy withdrew from the race. Hubert Humphrey decided to make another bid for the nomination, but he no longer had the support needed to win. However, Humphrey's '68 running mate, Sen. Edmond Muskie of Maine, had considerable support and was the apparent front runner until charges emerged during the primary season, probably planted by Nixon operatives, that Muskie had been unfaithful to his wife.

Many Democrats knew that the chances of unseating Richard Nixon, who had been an able and successful first term President, were slim. McGovern, though, felt that the sitting President was sinfully wrong on both the War in Viet Nam and domestic economic programs to aid the poor. All through the primary campaign, he hammered over and over on the themes of unilaterally ending the war and eliminating poverty. On the latter issue, McGovern even proposed a guaranteed annual income for every citizen.

Rolling over all opposition, he still had a confused campaign organization. At the national convention, his forces could not control the agenda. The convention became embroiled in various debates, and the new nominee was not able to deliver his acceptance speech until 3:00 in the morning, with no prime time television audience available to hear his "Come Home, America" message. When the convention was over, the candidate found himself woefully behind in public opinion polls. Indignant, he continued to charge his opposition with heinous sins, assuming a role that forbade him to speak of love for his country, its soldiers in Viet Nam, or the flag. On election day in November, he suffered a humiliating defeat: Nixon, whom he detested, had won "Four More Years" and the hearts of American voters, receiving 61 percent of the popular votes (a margin of over 16,000,000 out of over 70,000,000 cast) and winning all but one state for an Electoral College margin of 521 to 17. Even South Dakota went for Richard Nixon.

OPPONENT OF THE PRESIDENT

McGovern appeared bitter after the election and continued his quest to end the War in Viet Nam. A new issue had emerged during the '72 election which he was quick to press: Watergate. Even during the campaign McGovern had raised the possibility of political crimes, but Richard Nixon had been able to manage the issues to his advantage. After the campaign was over, however, the Democratic Congress, perhaps a bit wary of the popularity of the Republican President, began probing more deeply into the break in of the Democratic Party headquarters. As soon as it became apparent that Nixon was culpable, McGovern issued a statement calling for the President to resign. He supported later moves for impeachment and indicated he was willing to vote for conviction if Nixon did not resign. Not realizing that issues, not personalities, had defeated him in 1972, he seemed to indicate that Nixon's resignation had justified his past positions and that the voters in retrospect had wanted him all along.

In 1974 McGovern was able to capitalize on "Watergate" and won a third six-year Senate term, but soon afterwards his conservative home state voters finally began to realize that he was out of touch with their views. For too long he had espoused causes not in tune with South Dakota. With a disdain for the beliefs of his constituents, McGovern made a trip to Cuba, where he smoked cigars with Fidel Castro and was happily photographed with the communist boss, leaving the impression that the United States had much to be ashamed of while leftist nations were on the right path to world order. A fourth campaign in 1980 found the venerable Senator unable to sell his enlightened liberalism to the conservatives of his state, and he decisively lost his seat to a conservative Republican. McGovern then became a Washington consultant and lobbyist, and he began to appear on various public television programs to debate the issues of the day. In the 1980's, perhaps to supplement his income, he made some television commercials for a razor blade company. Later, newspapers noted that McGovern, never wealthy, had opened a tourist "bed-and-breakfast" hotel to supplement his retirement income. He attended and spoke to national Democratic conventions every four years and hinted from time to time that he might seek the presidency again, but he was not taken seriously by party leaders or the people. The former minister-turned-politician who had fomented much discontent in his thwarted rise to power had lost the audience for his views on peace and aid to the poor.

Walter Mondale

The Election of 1984

Since 1960, six former Vice Presidents have vied for the post of Chief Magistrate. Only two — George Bush as the first "incumbent" since Martin Van Buren and Richard Nixon, who scored perhaps the greatest political comeback in American history — have been successful in their bids for Chief Executive. Walter Mondale, the protege of Hubert Humphrey, decided to try his luck in 1984 but went down to one of the most devastating defeats in the history of the United States. Overwhelmed from the beginning by the ever-popular Ronald Reagan, Mondale tried campaign gimmicks, such as attack debating and the selection of the first woman for Vice President, but the views of the aspirant and his beloved Democratic Party were woefully out of tune with the people.

His rise to the pinnacle of political power is still fascinating, and at an earlier time, when perhaps the New Deal was more popular, he might have become President. His obstacles to power when he ran, though, were too great to overcome.

FROM A MINNESOTA FARM

"Fritz" Mondale was born to a Minnesota country family of Viking Norwegian descent. His father was reared a Lutheran but joined the Methodist Church because he did not agree with the predestination views of the Lutheran Church. He later had a mystical experience while plowing and became a circuit Methodist preacher. Because of his lack of education and his rudimentary manners, he never pastored a very large congregation, and his family moved constantly from small town to small town.

Rev. Mondale was a poor farmer before his call to the ministry, and politically he was a populist. He had lost two farms to foreclosure when farm prices dropped after World War I. When his first wife, to whom he was devoted, died slowly of encephalitis, he was left with three sons and one adopted daughter to raise. Almost at the same time he developed lockjaw, and was able to survive only by his own persistence, using a home-made tool to prize his jaw open. To compound his misery, the church he was pastoring burned, and Rev. Mondale had to lead its rebuilding.

His fortunes changed when he married again. His second bride was Claribel Cowan, a college educated music teacher, who bore him another son, Walter Frederick, on January 5, 1928, at the small Minnesota town of Ceylon, just a few miles north of the Iowa state line. Another son was later born to the family.

Rearing a large family on a meager parson's salary was a difficult task, and the boys were required to work to help support the family during the Great Depression and World War II. "Fritz" Mondale knew what it was to scrounge corncobs to burn in lieu of coal. To earn money to help support his poor family, he became a newspaper boy, worked at the corner grocery store, assisted a veterinarian castrating calves and vaccinating hogs, became a "pea lice" inspector checking plant stems for infestations, and picked corn side by side with Mexican immigrants. He joined in a strike with the Mexicans at one point but found that management held the upper hand when it sent the Mexicans back to Mexico; such experiences molded his future political actions.

He was a popular student, being elected President of his Junior Class in High School, although losing the Senior Class Presidency. He was co-captain of the football team with the nickname of "Crazylegs," and was captain and an All-Conference guard on the basketball team. He also ran track. He sang to the accompaniment of his mother at church gatherings such as weddings, even winning singing contests. Mischievous at times, he smoked cigarettes, only to be caught by his father and made to smoke cigars until sick, and he pilfered pennies from the collection plate, for which he received a switching that brought forth blood. Such an upbringing mixed with the family's constant conversations about FDR, Norman Thomas and social issues blended with humanitarian concern, in large part formulated the philosophy of Walter Mondale. A family trip to Washington, D.C. which allowed the Mondales to visit the institutions of government sparked the youth's interest in politics.

TO COLLEGE AND INTO POLITICS

Mondale enrolled in both Macallaster College and the Democratic-Farm-Labor Party in 1946. Macallaster was chosen because it was a Presbyterian school that was compatible, in the eyes of his parents, with his Methodist background. Once on campus, Mondale began attending DFL meetings. At one meeting in a union hall, Mondale became acquainted with Hubert Humphrey, the newly elected Mayor of Minneapolis who had formed the DFL coalition and was becoming a national force. A future Governor and Secretary of Agriculture, Orville Freeman, used Mondale as a door-to-door worker, and Mondale as well dutifully passed out campaign fliers and solicited votes.

In 1947, Mondale organized the Students for Democratic Action at Macallester as the student wing of the Americans for Democratic Action, which Humphrey had helped organize. He also became an organizer in the Student DFL and swung critical young support to Humphrey in his 1948 Senate bid. In an uphill battle, the Humphrey forces first had to rid the DFL of communists and socialists before electing Humphrey to the Senate. Mondale was gleefully participating in all of these activities and making important connections for the future. For a while he sported a William O. Douglas for President pin instead of supporting Harry Truman, but this changed when the Democratic nomination went to Truman.

A major opportunity for Mondale developed when, since he had no funds to pay his next term's tuition to Macallester, he requested permission of Humphrey to canvass the traditionally Republican Second District near his home town in Humphrey's 1948 election. The assignment was granted provided he raise his own funds. He eagerly accepted, raised funds, borrowed a car from a friendly Democrat who was a car dealer, and solicited the District, which went for Humphrey by 8,500 votes. At the time, Walter Mondale was only twenty years of age and not even able to vote.

Shortly after the election of 1948, Mondale's father passed away after a lengthy illness. Faced with a lack of funds and also restless, he decided to take a salaried position ($250.00 per month) with the newly formed National Students for Democratic Action in Washington, D.C. This experienced allowed the young Mondale to travel widely, exposing himself to a wide range of acquaintances and events. At first he had hoped to get close to his hero, Humphrey, and he was hurt deeply when the new Senator, so busy with his own adventures, inadvertently snubbed him. But this did not deter him in his many other endeavors. He visited England and met the Labour Party Prime Minister, Clement Atlee, but was not very impressed with the British system of socialist economics. He joined with Allard Lowenstein, later to leave a radical image nationally for liberal Democrats who opposed the War in Viet Nam, in building the National Students Association as an anti-communist organization. In a move reminiscent of Humphrey, he went to a National Young Democrats Convention held in Chattanooga, Tennessee and worked day and night to get a minority report on Civil Rights brought to the convention floor where, after he made an impassioned speech, it was adopted by a 2 to 1 margin. At the time only twenty-two, Mondale was recruited by Orville Freeman to be his campaign manager in his 1950 campaign for Attorney General. Freeman lost, but when he later became

Governor he would not forget that the young Mondale had worked his heart out for him.

Mondale decided to enter the University of Minnesota in 1950 and complete his Bachelor's degree. He graduated with honors in 1951 and then enlisted in the Army for two years of undistinguished service. The day after he was discharged he enrolled in the University of Minnesota Law School, determined to get the tools necessary to get himself into active politics. He worked hard, and he graduated at the top of his law school class, doing particularly well in classes concerning personal issues as opposed to property issues.

He met his future wife on a blind date. She was from St. Paul's most exclusive society, but her family was Democratic. After eight or nine dates, he proposed and they were married by her father, a Presbyterian Chaplain at Macallaster College, in December of 1955.

After completing law school, Mondale again indulged in politics, joining Orville Freeman's campaign team. The DFL was somewhat in disarray, having supported Adlai Stevenson rather than Estes Kefauver of Tennessee in the Minnesota Primary in hopes of having Humphrey nominated for Vice President in 1956. When Minnesota Republicans got wind of this deal, they "switched," and Freeman's chances for re-election waned. It was Mondale who came to the fore, pulling the DFL machinery together to allow Freeman a narrow victory.

Freeman had arranged for Mondale to become an associate in his old Minneapolis law firm after the 1956 election. The firm encouraged young attorneys to be politically active, but the environment was not totally to Mondale's liking. He and another associate, Harry McLaughlin, set up their own firm with the understanding that each was free to pursue outside goals. In 1958, Freeman appointed Mondale, considered now the top political strategist in the state, to be his Campaign Manager for re-election, and the bid for re-election was a smoothly run campaign against a foe that was doing his best to get the normally combative Freeman to fight back. Mondale advised restraint, a policy that worked for Freeman, who won this time with 56 percent of the vote. Mondale, only thirty years of age, was a state power. He became state DFL finance director and continued to make contacts for the future.

INTO OFFICE

When Walter Mondale ran for President, one issue that haunted him was that he had never ran for a political office to which he had not received appointment, which was a fact. The first appointment was that of State Attorney General, made by Governor Freeman, partly out of repayment for having been Freeman's Campaign Manager but also because Freeman felt Mondale was qualified and was destined to a higher role in politics. Upon entering office, Mondale discovered a file showing that an investigation into the Sister Elizabeth Kenny Foundation had revealed mammoth corruption. Marvin Kline, the former Mayor of Minneapolis whom Hubert Humphrey had defeated, and other prominent citizens had been taking illicit gratuities. Mondale seized upon the opportunity to prosecute and build for himself an honest name. Republicans had hoped to expose Mondale as an inexperienced administrator and political hatchetman when he ran for Attorney General in his own right some six months after entering the office, but Mondale won by a quarter-million votes. He had run on the same ticket with John Kennedy and Hubert Humphrey, who also won, and with Orville Freeman, who, without Mondale as his Campaign Manager this time, lost narrowly. (Freeman, who had made JFK's nominating speech at the 1960 Los Angeles convention, was then made Secretary of Agriculture.)

Mondale wanted to run for the Governorship in 1962 but found that organized labor favored the current DFL Lieutenant Governor over himself. He continued to conduct the affairs of the Attorney General's office for the benefit of consumers and against big business. Indeed a pattern was emerging that would eventually lead to Mondale being labeled the most liberal Senator in the United States. He had opposed a move by the Florida's Attorney General to deny a hearing for a Florida prisoner who claimed he had been denied due process of law because he had no attorney; the Supreme Court sided with the more liberal Mondale in a landmark decision. He was re-elected Attorney General in 1962.

John Kennedy's death had a profound impact on Minnesota politics. Hubert Humphrey was the front runner to be the next Vice President under Lyndon Johnson, and he sat out at once to be Johnson's legislative lieutenant in the Senate as well as a close political counselor. Johnson had some delicate political work for Humphrey to do, including keeping the 1964 Atlantic City convention peaceful. When the Mississippi Freedom Democratic Party delegation appeared before the Credentials Committee to challenge the regular Mississippi delegation, Johnson called on Humphrey to settle the matter — or possibly lose the Vice Presidential nomination. Sitting on the Credentials Committee was none other than ... Walter Mondale. Humphrey immediately enlisted Mondale, whose sympathy lay with the Mississippi blacks but who knew that Humphrey's chances depended on compromise, to work out a complicated conciliation, which allowed the blacks two at-large delegates and a proper seating at the next convention while keeping the regular Mississippi delegation in place. His plan was adopted, and Humphrey became Vice President.

SENATOR (1965-1977)

Humphrey's election created a Senate vacancy for Minnesota, and Walter Mondale was appointed to that vacancy. The Vice President himself let it be known that the thirty-six year old Mondale should be selected over older aspirants. A lifelong bond between the two was now in effect that would first see Mondale serving in the Senate with Humphrey as Vice President and then Humphrey again serving in the Senate with Mondale as Vice President. Mondale would be haunted time and again about being appointed to office, but he won convincing re-election victories in 1966 and 1972.

When Hubert Humphrey entered the Senate in 1949, he was brash and brusque with senior Senators. Some sixteen years later in 1965, he had some sound advice for the young Mondale, which was heeded. Fritz Mondale, though poles apart on the social issues of the day, made friends readily with the elderly, Southern Senators that controlled the "Club." When he did not receive the key committee appointments he desired, he did not raise a fuss. Soon, he was intimately involved with Senators such as Eastland and Russell, careful always to attack issues but not personalities. Later he would get key committee assignments by following this strategy.

A social activist, Mondale's positions often attacked big business and entrenched segregationist policies. He allied himself with Ralph Nader in attacking the automobile manufacturers, which led to enactment of "Fair Warnings" for motorists about motor vehicles. He was supportive of the Great Society programs calling for food stamps, expanded aid for education, and increased Social Security benefits and Medicaid. But it was on "Open Housing" that Mondale scored his greatest legislative victory. A small group of liberal Senators asked Mondale to take on the task of promoting this sensitive legislation. Mondale worked hard on the bill, using all his parliamentary skills to guide the legislation through the right committee and present it to the Senate floor. There cloture was invoked by Southern senators, but Mondale, like Humphrey before him in 1964, patiently prodded key Senators to change their positions. Finally, he persuaded Republican Minority Leader Everett Dirksen to join the cause after some compromises were made, and the hallmark of his legislative career was passed into law. People were beginning to think of Fritz Mondale as a future contender for higher office.

The war in Viet Nam placed Mondale in a sensitive and delicate position. In the beginning he supported the conflict out of loyalty to Humphrey. At one point he considered going public against American involvement, but Humphrey intervened to change this. When President Johnson, whose conduct of the war had led students to riot and burn draft cards, announced that he would not run for President, Humphrey enlisted Mondale to be his national Co-Chairman for President. Starting out late, the strategy for Humphrey was to gather machine support and sit out the primaries. The assassinations of Robert Kennedy and Martin Luther King created havoc for the campaign, but Mondale patiently canvassed state party caucuses, and the nomination was secured for Humphrey, although the ensuing chaos at Chicago ruined Humphrey's life-long dream to be President. Seeing the futility of Humphrey trying to defend Johnson's position, Mondale and others advised a change in tactics, and Humphrey made his famous Salt Lake City speech, claiming he would stop bombing North Viet Nam if he became President. The tactic almost worked, but 1968 belonged to Richard Nixon, who rose from a political grave to narrowly defeat Hubert Humphrey in a three way race that also included George Wallace, whose votes, if he had not run, probably would have gone to Nixon and made him a landslide winner.

Mondale resumed his Senate tenure by taking up the cause of the hungry and migrant workers. He felt that Mexicans were being ill-treated in California and called for hearings on Coca-Cola, whose subsidiaries controlled the wages of migrants. A breakthrough occurred, and wages and conditions improved. Mondale also championed the cause of hungry children, becoming a member of George McGovern's Hunger Committee and sponsoring other initiatives for children through the "Justice for Children" program. He then introduced legislation which would establish day care centers on a graduated income basis, but President Nixon vetoed this as too costly and "communal." The veto was upheld. Attempts by Mondale and other liberals to attack the "oil-depletion" allowance met with no success whatsoever.

A "white backlash" began sweeping the nation during Nixon's administration, and the President called upon the "great silent majority" of Americans to speak out. The most burning issue of the day was school busing, and a strange alliance, led by John Eastland of Mississippi and Abraham Ribacoff of Connecticut, joined hands to have desegregation measures applied evenly throughout the land. Northerners were in a quandary when it came to calling for the same treatment for their states as for Southern states. Mondale saw things clearly, stating, "...The amendment offered by the Senator from Mississippi would do nothing about de facto desegregation.

Its sole purpose is to paralyze and hamper efforts to eliminate the dual school systems wherever they exist." Mondale was right about the South, but he also probably made a fatal mistake for his political future when he would not call on Northern states to accept equal treatment.

A continuing and burning issue of the day was the Viet Nam War, but McGovern was not too vocal about it. True enough, he joined other liberals in opposition, but his forum was for domestic social issues, and he was dismayed to see that George McGovern could sweep Humphrey and others aside during the 1972 nominating season, especially since he had no chance at all of defeating Nixon. The devastating defeat in 1972 convinced many long term "New Deal" Democrats to return to candidates who would mandate the past. Walter Mondale was considered a prime candidate for such a role, and in 1974 he probed the political climate of the nation for a 1976 bid. What he found was that while he stood an excellent chance of getting the Democratic nomination, the nation at large was opposed to the whole Washington scene. "Watergate" extended to insiders of both parties, with even Hubert Humphrey having to explain some campaign misdeeds and seeing an aide go to prison. Therefore, Mondale, after conducting what appeared to be a successful beginning canvass, startled everyone, including his wife, when he announced that he would not run for the nomination in 1976.

Dropping out probably helped Jimmy Carter, though not by design, capture badly needed early delegates in the Iowa caucus. After the former Georgia Governor swept New Hampshire, did away with George Wallace in Florida, captured key delegates in Pennsylvania and mowed down every Washington insider to seal the Democratic nomination, Hubert Humphrey went to bat for Mondale. With his strong ties to labor, Humphrey let it be known that he would be highly pleased if Mondale were the Vice Presidential nominee. "I've got lots of friends who might not be Governor Carter's friends — now. But they could be..." Choosing Mondale was a plus and a balance for Carter, who was from the deep South, a Baptist, not strongly tied to labor, and a Washington outsider who knew very little of the workings of the federal government and who ultimately showed his ineptness at managing the affairs of state.

The Vice Presidential nomination for Mondale was another "appointment" to haunt his future. But for the present, he showed himself to be a formidable campaigner. Carter left the New York Democratic convention with a commanding lead in the polls, but then President Gerald Ford, out of desperation, challenged the "challenger" to a series of debates. Except for a enormous guffaw over Poland and other eastern European nations not being under communist control, Ford handled Carter with ease and regained considerable support in the polls. The 1976 debates offered a first in American politics, a debate between the Vice Presidential nominees. Senators Robert Dole and Walter Mondale met in Houston before a national television audience. Dole revealed himself as a combative, somewhat "cut-throat" attacker, while Mondale displayed a calm demeanor, counter-attacking Dole when it was suggested that Watergate should be no more of an issue for Republicans than all of the wars of the twentieth century being started under Democratic administrations. The race was extremely tight, but Carter and Mondale were elected to office.

VICE PRESIDENT (1977-81)

Mondale had certain conditions for accepting the Vice Presidential nomination, but the main one was that he not languish like his close friend Hubert Humphrey. For the outsider from Plains, this was fortunate, for Jimmy Carter knew very little about Washington and neither did most of his staff. A close working relationship was formed from the beginning, and President Carter, while keeping Mondale out of the political spotlight, allowed his Vice President to have a continuing voice in the selection of key appointments and to sit in on all high level strategy and security meetings. Carter also let it be known that he would not hesitate to dispatch the new Vice President on a moment's notice to a key spot such as Moscow and resolve disputes with the same authority as the President.

Perhaps the saddest duty for Mondale was to see his old mentor, Hubert Humphrey, be slowed from his former vigor by a deadly bout with cancer. They became closer than ever, and Mondale was instrumental in arranging a "good-bye" tour of Washington for Humphrey, who was flown to the Capital aboard Air Force One to make farewell speeches to the Senate and the House and to see the Health, Education and Welfare Building named in his honor. Mondale delivered an emotional eulogy while Humphrey's body lay in the Capitol Rotunda, and he accompanied his body back to Minnesota for final rites and burial. He resolved to carry on the traditions that were inspired in him by Humphrey when they first met in 1946.

Early in his administration President Carter began to disappoint his constituency. In the campaign "Grits and Fritz" had spoken of a "misery index," which was formulated by adding the inflation and interest rates. Soon the economy under Carter was out of control. The "misery index" doubled that under President Ford. For a while Carter experienced some success in foreign affairs, having Anwar Sadat of Egypt and Menachim Begin of Israel sign the Camp David Accord, but public opinion for Carter dipped badly when he mishandled the Iranian crisis, sitting by more-or-less idly while the Shah was deposed for the anti-American Ayatolla Kholmeni, and then appearing helpless to do anything about the capture of American Embassy employees in Tehran after allowing the Shah to enter the United States to receive medical treatment for cancer. After a mission to rescue the hostages resulted in American helicopters crushed and abandoned in the Iranian desert with military men dead, the 1980 race was over.

THE ELECTION OF 1980

Teddy Kennedy, with Chappaquidick some time behind him but with an unsure marriage ahead of him, decided to take on Carter for the nomination. Carter, though, was in firm control of the party machinery and won renomination. His only choice for Vice President was Mondale. However, they found the general election to be much tougher than gaining renomination. This time Ronald Reagan, the "Great Communicator," was the Republican nominee, and his charisma, backed by a splendid record as Governor of California, made him an early leader in the polls. A debate, arranged by Carter out of desperation, was held toward the end of the campaign, but this proved to be even more fatal for Carter and Mondale. Ronald Reagan and George Bush swept the nation, delivering the most humiliating defeat to an incumbent since the defeat of Herbert Hoover in 1932.

THE ELECTION OF 1984

Prospects of the Democrats unseating Ronald Reagan in 1984 were dim, but Walter Mondale decided that if ever there were to be a time for him, it would have to be against the immensely popular, patriotic, and fatherly sitting President. Gathering the nomination was not too much of a problem, for Teddy Kennedy, embarrassed by a divorce in a Catholic family and still bearing the scars of Chappaquidick, was not running. The main opposition came from Sen. Gary Hart of Colorado, former campaign manager of George McGovern's ill-fated attempt against Richard Nixon in 1972. The Democratic Party machinery was still clinging to New Deal idealism, while the rank and file Democrats were looking to John Kennedy's Camelot image. Neither was a match for the actor-turned-politician who, like Franklin Roosevelt some forty years before him, had captured the imagination of the people, while making lasting reforms.

The pragmatic Mondale planned a simple but pragmatic campaign, believing principles presented forthrightly would sway the American people back to the Democratic fold. He boldly told the American people that a tax increase would be necessary to combat the massive deficits under Reagan, but the American people could not believe that a Democratic candidate would be interested in balancing the budget. Moreover, Reagan had become immensely popular by reducing the "misery index" alluded to by Jimmy Carter in 1976: both inflation and interest rates were down. Deregulation of various industries was having a positive economic impact, and the unemployment rate had come down, although the nation had suffered a severe recession, which Reagan had succinctly pinned on the Democrats.

In a dramatic gesture, Mondale selected as his running mate the first woman nominee for Vice President, Congresswoman Geraldine Ferraro of New York. Tough and attractive, Ms. Ferraro did not, however, possess the political savvy so desperately needed in national politics. Soon the media discovered that her husband had been involved in some questionable business deals that might lead to indictment, and Mondale was faced with a decision akin to George McGovern's in 1972. Mondale, to the delight of Republicans, decided to retain Ferraro, and the Grand Old Party had a field day rhyming tidbits about the duo and exposing Ferraro as an unqualified ploy by a Democratic Party in desperate need of votes.

The customary debates were arranged, and Mondale went on the attack against Reagan in their first meeting. The press built up suspense by indicating that Mondale was making a charge on Reagan, but the astute President used his ability with mass communication to offset any gains. A debate between Vice President Bush and Congresswoman Ferraro showed her as brash and unqualified, and it seemed to seal Mondale's fate. A final debate between Reagan and Mondale showed a confident President in control of the entire situation.

Election night in 1980 brought the most disastrous defeat in the history of the Democratic Party. "Reagonomics" was ratified in every state except Mondale's home state of Minnesota, and there only barely after much campaigning by the Minnesota candidate. (The District of Columbia also cast its votes for Mondale.) The Senate stayed Republican, although the House remained under the Democrat's control. Walter Mondale, the son of the Methodist minister who had worked so hard and long to reach the Presidency, would not attain his goal.

After leaving the Vice Presidency in 1981, Mondale accepted a partnership in a prestigious Texas law firm. All his life he had been poor, and he left office with few assets, the chief one being the equity in his Washington home. Like Hubert Humphrey before him, Walter Mondale had risen from

Minnesota obscurity to enter the political stage, rise almost to the apex of power only to fade and then find the means to seek a fortune and become wealthy.   Now, in political retirement, he could give his wife and three children many of the comforts he had wanted to give the American people but was unable to do so.

Michael Dukakis

The Election of 1988

Michael Dukakis, the son of immigrants, often spoke of his Greek heritage, and in many ways the multi-faceted "Duke" was an "all-around" man, just as the successful ancient Greek was. Disciplined and determined, he ran his political life like the ancient marathon runner, which he also was, achieving lasting acclaim with many in his native Massachusetts, although his quest for the Presidency of the United States was denied.

A BOSTON YOUTH

Boston, Massachusetts, is an old American city, steeped in Irish and English traditions. It is also a city of many ethnic backgrounds, because Boston is a city of immigrants. Two immigrants from Greece were to come to the "land of opportunity" in the early part of the twentieth century and eventually settle in Boston. This couple was Panagis Dukakis, who would graduate from the American International College at Springfield and Harvard Medical School, becoming a medical doctor, and Euterp Boukis, who would graduate Phi Beta Kappa from Bates College in Maine and become a junior high school teacher. As fate would have it, the two would be introduced and then become romantically involved. In early 1929, Dr. Dukakis proposed marriage to Euterpe, and the two were married later in the year. The couple settled in Brookline, a middle class suburb of Boston, and had two sons, Stelian, born in 1931, and Michael, born on November 3, 1933. Michael Dukakis would devote his life to government and politics, and become the Democratic nominee for President of the United States in 1988.

Even as a youth, Mike Dukakis would show the hallmarks of seriousness that would be evident throughout his adult life. He was elected president of his third grade class in elementary school, where he also participated in various sports, especially enjoying baseball (his position was catcher). At Brookline High School, Mike was elected vice president of his freshman, sophomore and junior classes. In his senior year, he decided to run for president but was defeated. Undeterred, he then ran for Student Council president and was elected. Mike was also involved in the school's athletic program, playing baseball, basketball, running cross country, and serving as captain of the tennis team. In 1951, the seventeen year old track man lied about his age to enter the Boston Marathon and finished fifty-seventh in a field of 151. The all-around student also played the trumpet in the school band. In addition to his extra-curricular achievements, Mike was elected president of Alpha Pi, a distinction granted to the member of the school's honor society who had earned the most A's. He also became an Eagle Scout.

TO COLLEGE AND INTO POLITICS

Although the brightest students in the Boston area were expected to go to Harvard, Michael Dukakis decided to attend Swarthmore College, a Quaker liberal arts college just outside of Philadelphia. Expecting to be a doctor like his father before him, Mike initially took a pre-medicine curriculum, but a "D" in freshman physics made him wonder if he were in the field of study he really desired. During this same year (1951), Mike enlisted in the campaign of Joe Clark, a reform Democrat who was running for Mayor of Philadelphia. He organized some Swarthmore College students into a group of election day poll watchers and was thrilled when Clark became the first non-Republican Mayor in decades. The following year found the young new Democratic enthusiast supporting Adlai Stevenson against Dwight Eisenhower. Dukakis organized some Swarthmore students for the Democratic candidate and was disappointed when Ike won by a landslide.

Dukakis found time to participate in many campus activities, being elected to the school's Student Council and lettering in cross country, basketball and tennis. Already a liberal philosophically, he joined the Students for Democratic Action, leading a protest against fraternities because of their discrimination practices against minorities and setting up a barbershop in his dormitory room to serve blacks who could not get haircuts in the town of Swarthmore. His new-found political interest was helping Dukakis to establish his life's goals. He confided to friends that he wanted to go into politics and become Governor of Massachusetts. He changed his major to Political Science, attended special political science seminars and became completely immersed in his political studies. An outstanding student, Michael Dukakis graduated with highest honors and, in the tradition of his mother, was elected to Phi Beta Kappa.

The bright Swarthmore graduate emerged from college with his goal in life firmly set, and he methodically set about attaining it. He first decided to dispose of his military obligation and joined the army, serving as an enlisted man in post-war Korea. Not at all suited for military service, he was happy when his two-year tour of duty was completed in 1957 so that he could attend law school at the most prestigious school in the nation — Harvard — in his home town of Boston.

The pressures of Harvard were surmounted rather easily by the cool Dukakis, who commuted from Brookline to his classes on a motor scooter and again excelled in his studies, graduating *cum laude* in 1960. Although an excellent law student, he perhaps excelled even more in politics, both on and off campus. He became an active member of the Harvard Law Graduate Democrat Club, which in 1958 had as a guest one of the school's most illustrious alumni, Senator John F. Kennedy, who had already started his run for the Presidency in 1960. Michael Dukakis was enthralled by the Boston Senator and immediately adopted him as a political hero. In 1960, just after graduating from law school, he and Paul Brontas, a fellow student at Harvard and a future Senator from Maryland, drove to the Democratic National Convention in Los Angeles to share in the joy of John Kennedy's nomination.

Dukakis did not wait for graduation or a career to become actively involved in politics himself. In 1958, the twenty-five year old law student decided to be a candidate for the four member Brookline Redevelopment Authority. Receiving help from his fellow students in the Harvard Democratic Club, Dukakis waged a vigorous campaign, but finished fifth in his first political race. The loss did not keep him from plodding ahead, for in the spring of 1959 he was running for office again, this time for membership on the Brookline Town Council. Dukakis emerged a victor, gaining his first public office. Not too long after this victory, Dukakis helped organize a group of reform minded Democrats to run as a slate to wrest control of the Democratic Town Committee from old line ward politicians. The young group of feisty reformers were not expected to win, but they were a part of the Kennedy machine in Massachusetts which was becoming unstoppable as the fever to elect a local man to the White House became contagious. The entire slate of Dukakis candidates won, and the word was soon spreading through the Boston area and the entire state that a young Democrat from Brookline appeared to be carving out an outstanding future for himself.

With an eye to reforming a state Democratic party that had been guilty of widespread corruption for some time, Mike Dukakis in 1960 helped organize the Commonwealth of Democrats (COD), a group of highly educated young liberal Democrats who wanted to improve the democratic process. The young activist began traveling the entire state, outlining a series of reforms needed to change many outdated election procedures. The COD coalition grew in strength, and in 1962 it decided to target for support certain candidates for the state legislature. Michael Dukakis was one of those selected to run for three open seats from the Brookline area. With dedication and earnest support from his allies, the twenty-nine year old Dukakis was elected to membership in the Massachusetts State Assembly. He had taken another step toward his life's ambition.

PERSONAL LIFE

All through his high school, college and law school years, Dukakis remained too busy with his academic and political pursuits to become very serious romantically with any one girl. In 1961 Mike began dating Kitty Chaffetz, a twenty-five year old divorcee and mother of one son who was of the Jewish religious faith. The two soon became deeply attached to each other and were wed in June, 1963, after he completed his first session in the state House. The son from Kitty's first marriage became so attached to Michael that he was eventually adopted by his step-father and took the Dukakis name as his own. Mike and Kitty also had two children from their own marriage.

A problem for Michael through most of the 1960's was his brother, Stelian. The two boys had been close during their boyhood years, but periods of depression haunted the older brother, who attempted suicide in 1955 while a student at Bates College, and the two became estranged over the years. In 1964 Stelian, who had himself unsuccessfully sought public office and who had threatened to challenge future House Speaker "Tip" O'Neill for his Congressional seat, distributed leaflets urging Brookline voters not to vote for his brother's re-election. Psychological counseling over the years did not provide relief for the emotional problems. Unfortunately, Stelian Dukakis was killed in a hit-and-run accident in 1973. The driver was never apprehended. During the 1988 Presidential campaign, Dukakis admitted that this relationship with his brother had been one of the most agonizing experiences of his life.

Upon his graduation from Harvard's law school, Michael became affiliated with an elite Boston legal firm. Over the years he would conduct a law practice when not occupying a full time office, but his heart would always be devoted to the reform of government rather than the legal profession. Eventually he would become a partner in a firm, but while he was not serving in office, and being sought more for his connections than for his legal abilities.

LEGISLATIVE REFORMER

Dukakis was interested in ridding Massachusetts state government of both corruption and antiquated laws. His first effort in this direction was to join forces with other reformers to oppose the re-election of the incumbent Speaker, who owed his position to the sinister forces of Massachusetts machine politics. Despite reform opposition, the Speaker was re-elected only to be indicted the following year and survive another vote of confidence by the state House. He finally vacated the office in disgrace several years later. Dukakis also called for an investigation into the highly corrupt Department of Public Works, where contracts for payoffs were routine. He applied the pressure to have a special crime commission created to investigate this agency. Later, scores of indictments which led to convictions were laid down, involving officials of the Boston Underground Garage and the Boston Turnpike Authority, architects and other professional who received contracts for paybacks, and other public works officers who took part in money laundering scams. The whole episode was so widespread that the *Saturday Evening Post* produced a comprehensive article on the matter. Michael Dukakis' influence was significant enough that his picture was featured in the article, and he was cited as a young lawmaker who was striving to change the Massachusetts Legislature's corrupt reputation. He was also denoted as the type of future politician that was required in Massachusetts if reform were to be achieved. Mike Dukakis was making his mark in life.

The young reformer, who would be easily re-elected to three more two-year terms, delved into many areas of inner-city reforms, successfully supporting rent controls, sponsoring the nation's first "condominium" legislation, and having the Governor and Lieutenant Governor elected as a ticket to four year rather than two year terms. The young liberal was also the sponsor of laws adopting "no-fault" automobile insurance in Massachusetts, the first state to adopt such legislation. He also called for changes not only in the operations of the Department of Public Works but in its policies, proposing at first a halt to the freeway system, which was creating a mass displacement of lower income citizens and substituting a new system of trolleys and subways, and later a halt to an entire new mass transit system. He also unsuccessfully opposed the Turnpike Authority's drive to obtain "air rights" over freeways, feeling this would further disrupt low income families.

Dukakis had been plotting his own path to the Governor's chair for some time. In 1966, he decided to run for state Attorney General to replace Ed Brooke, the Republican Negro Attorney General who was successfully seeking a U.S. Senate seat. But he was overwhelmed for his party's nomination by Francis Bellotti, a former Lt. Governor and former nominee for Governor. Dukakis unrelentingly continued his quest. In 1970, he surprised many seasoned professionals when he sought and received, by using superb campaign organization and personally contacting many convention delegates, the nomination for Lt. Governor. Unfortunately, the young state Representative was on a ticket headed by Boston Mayor Kevin White, who refused to coordinate campaign strategy and who had to take time out from his campaigning because of a bleeding ulcer. In addition, the incumbent Republican Governor had policies about as liberal as the Democrats, with a record of performance to go with it. White and Dukakis lost in a landslide, collecting only 43 percent of the popular vote.

As a part of the Kennedy legacy, Dukakis joined the anti-Viet Nam war efforts that began in the late 1960's. Part of the legacy was a natural opposition to Robert Kennedy's old nemesis, Lyndon Johnson. Dukakis was an early supporter of Minnesota's anti-war Senator, Eugene McCarthy, in his quest for the Democratic Presidential nomination in 1968. He endorsed a huge anti-war rally in Boston and supported the successful candidacy of a fellow state House member, Mike Harrington, over William Saltonstall, the son of a former long time Republican Senator. He also supported a bill (later overturned by the Supreme Court) which stated that Massachusetts citizens were not obligated to served in Viet Nam. Not at all pleased with the election of Richard Nixon, Dukakis was nonetheless presented some interesting options after Nixon picked Gov. Peter Volpe to be in his Cabinet and the Bay State Attorney General, Elliot Richardson, to be a deputy Secretary of State.

Shortly after the 1970 election, Dukakis announced the formation of the "Dukakis Raiders," a group to monitor the performance of the re-elected Governor. Now out of the legislature, since he had been unable to run for Lt. Governor and the House simultaneously, Dukakis for the first time began the full-time practice of law. He and his wife bought an apartment house, which they divided into units and sold as condominiums under the legislation he had originally sponsored. Dukakis also secured a highly visible position as a moderator of the popular public television program, "The Advocates," which featured many of the nation's political leaders in a debate forum. Though a partisan liberal Democrat, Dukakis received high marks for his knowledge of subject matter and his objectivity in presiding over the programs. He also achieved a high degree of political visibility and popularity in Massachusetts.

The former candidate for Lt. Governor was planning another run for state Attorney General in 1974. In the political maneuverings of the time, Dukakis' old ally, Mike Harrington, planned to himself announce early for Governor so that the incumbent Democratic Attorney General, Bill Quinn, would not also announce for Governor. The Dukakis camp, realizing that the incumbent Attorney General might mess up the Democratic nomination process by entering a one-man race, began to put out statements that their man was interested in the Governor's chair. Soon, word was circulating that Dukakis was a serious candidate, and the "Duke" decided to make a serious run for the position he had long coveted.

Hiring a full-time campaign manager in late 1972, the Governor-to-be began to pull together an efficient campaign organization. He ran as a reform candidate against the politics of the past and developed the campaign slogan that "Mike Dukakis Should Be Governor." His opposition ended up being Attorney General Bill Quinn, the man that he had feared would oppose him for Attorney General. With hard work, Dukakis soon pulled into a dead heat with Quinn in the polls. He challenged Quinn to a debate, but the challenge was denied. Then Dukakis began attacking Quinn's record on crime. Soon, the polls shifted in his favor, and Quinn responded by making a number of charges against Dukakis' legislative positions on abortion, Racial Imbalance laws, and the Viet Nam war. This strategy failed miserably, for on election day Dukakis won the nomination by a landslide, with 58 percent of the popular vote. The nominee, who had as his running mate for Lt. Governor the eldest son of House Speaker "Tip" O'Neill, then took on the incumbent Governor, Frank Sargent. With an organization of both reformers and regulars (through the influence of Tip O'Neill), and with a recession, high unemployment and runaway inflation creating serious problems for Massachusetts Republicans, Mike Dukakis' chances for winning the election were high, with a 25 point lead in the polls. Sargent, a seasoned politician, quickly closed the huge gap when he called out state guardsmen to quell anti-busing riots. The campaign turned into a brawl, especially over budget concerns. Dukakis, in a move he would later greatly regret, pledged that he would solve the state budget deficits by cutting spending and promised *not* to raise taxes. When the final ballots were counted on election day, Michael Dukakis had achieved his life's dream, winning the Governorship of Massachusetts in a landslide, with over 55 percent of the vote.

AN UNPOPULAR GOVERNOR

After taking the oath of office on January 2, 1975 at the famous Bullfinch House, Dukakis announced that the portrait of Samuel Adams, the Revolutionary War hero who was simple, frugal and of unbending character, would be placed on the wall behind the Governor's desk. Dukakis himself meant to be revolutionary in his reforms. The next day he surprised everyone, including his own Cabinet members, when he held his first Cabinet session in public—and announced that all future Cabinet meetings would be held under the same condition. As time went by, he produced other surprises, such as riding the subway to his office each day rather than using a state limousine, abolishing patronage (even close campaign workers had to apply for state positions through written applications and formal interviews), and, in order to keep politics out of the Judiciary, creating a Judicial Nominating Commission that was non-political in makeup.

Dukakis assumed his duties amidst a sea of controversy on budget matters. During his campaign he had assumed that deficit projections of $150 million were fairly accurate, but he soon learned that the deficits were far greater, more in the neighborhood of $500 million. The spending policies of Massachusetts lawmakers, which provided liberal payments to the unemployed, the sick, and those on welfare, had the state on the verge of bankruptcy. Now, Dukakis' spartan plans for increasing government productivity and holding the line on spending increases to balance the budget were in jeopardy. In a television address to the people of Massachusetts a year and one day after taking office, the beleaguered Governor, who had already cut spending and raised taxes on tobacco and gasoline, admitted that he had been wrong to pledge no new taxes. Now he proposed a program to increase new sales and income taxes. To the chagrin of his fellow liberals, he also announced that there would have to be cuts in benefits to "employables," and this so angered certain elements of his party that he almost did not get the much needed revenue bill passed.

Relations with his supporters, already wary, now were strained to the limit. Rather than solicit the support of legislators, Governor Dukakis maintained a self-righteous and arrogant atmosphere, so alienating his fellow Democrats in the legislature that they yearned for his term of office to come to an end so that they could help replace him. When he sought the party's nod in 1978, his diminished respect was evident. In a televised debate, Ed King, the Executive Director of the Massachusetts Port Authority, rebuked him, calling for massive reductions in taxes, a tougher crime policy and the end to funded abortions. Dukakis, who was refusing to use paid media advertising and was already suffering an image problem, clearly lost the debate and any chance for re-election. When the ballots for the nomination were counted, the incumbent Governor, who had gathered 58 percent of his party's votes four years before, was a clear loser, this time winning only 41 percent of the Democratic electorate.

PLANNING A RETURN

The stoic Dukakis did not blame those around him for his defeat, but he also did not endorse Ed King for the general election. Perhaps with an eye toward the 1982 race, he kept the remnants of a political organization intact. Out of a job, he accepted a teaching position at Harvard's John F. Kennedy School of Government, renewing old acquaintances and, more importantly, learning through the teaching process to listen to others rather than expect them to blindly accept his tenets. He also resumed his post as moderator of the highly acclaimed public television show, "The Advocates," and talk soon emerged that he might run again for Governor.

As time went by, Dukakis had meetings with many of the state's liberal leaders, and a new understanding evolved between the former Governor and these influential officials. In the meantime, Ed King's administration was being exposed with many cases of corruption and incompetence. Soon, there was a widespread call for Dukakis, with a reputation for honesty and ability, to oppose King in the '82 Primary. Even a name for the contest had been created by the media. It would be called "The Rematch."

Dukakis took one further step to insure his ties with liberals. He hired John Sasso, an organizer for Sen. Teddy Kennedy, (controversial) Congressman Gerry Studds and other liberal candidates and programs, as his campaign manager. The two would remain associates for many years. While talented, Sasso was also ruthless in dealing with opposition and would create many embarrassments for Dukakis over the years. Nonetheless, he provided the drive and organization, as well as the connections, needed for re-election. He also saw to it that Dukakis had the necessary funds raised to finance the most expensive Governor's campaign in Massachusetts history.

"Tip" O'Neill's son, who had served as Lt. Governor under both Dukakis and King, also hoped to gain the nod, but Dukakis stymied his efforts by gaining the early endorsement of groups such as the Americans for Democratic Action. O'Neill was knocked out of the race and King severely hurt when a television debate among the three was held in April, 1981. In this round of the campaign, the Duke was at his best, asking O'Neill if he preferred to be remembered as the Lt. Governor of Dukakis or King, and pouncing on King both for the acts of corruption which took place during his tenure and for being friendly to Ronald Reagan, who was anathema to Massachusetts liberals. Dukakis went on to gather the endorsement of the state convention by a 2 to 1 margin, and he held a 57 percentage point lead in the polls at the end of the Democratic conclave. However, this huge lead soon shrank (a characteristic of Dukakis campaigns) as King began to focus on issues, such as Dukakis' tax increases. As the lead in the polls narrowed, Dukakis brought forward a new theme — competence — and it appeared that he was coasting to victory until it was revealed that John Sasso had allowed two very nasty acts to occur. The first was the release of a television ad referring to King as a son-of-a-[bleep!]; the second made fun of King's sexual relationship with his wife, who had been a victim of polio and who had recovered, as Massachusetts voters well knew, through the encouragement and support of her husband. Soon, the 57 point lead was gone, and it appeared that King would retain his position. But fate intervened when a state official and friend of King committed suicide amid new charges of corruption in state government. When the ballots of "The Rematch" were tabulated, the "Duke" had knocked out his rival, receiving 53 percent of the votes. Unlike Dukakis four years before, King endorsed his rival, and with only token opposition in the highly Democratic state, Dukakis was easily elected to his second term as Governor.

GOVERNOR FROM 1983-1991

Saying that he was "very grateful" for his "second chance," Dukakis was from the beginning of his second term more relaxed and less arrogant than during his first term of office. He would no longer hold public Cabinet meetings, and he would make courtesy calls to legislative leaders and others of influence before executing controversial policies. He and John Sasso would be the chief officers of government, but he would recruit from Harvard many new officials for his new administration. His whole set of guidelines were different -- he even started using a government limousine rather than riding the subway.

But his zealous desire for reform and liberal causes had not faded. In his inaugural address he announced a program to aid the homeless, and a task force was immediately implemented for this purpose. To alleviate traffic congestion and increase economic development, Dukakis proposed, at a cost of $2 billion to be funded primarily from Washington, a new tunnel under Boston harbor. The creation of a program to train welfare recipients for useful work was implemented, while welfare payments went up almost one-third. As the nation began to come out of a national recession and ease into the long economic recovery of the Reagan era, the Governor also pushed for the development of Massachusetts into a "high-tech" corridor, and the state prospered. Again faced with a budget crisis, Dukakis in 1983 refused to raise tax rates, proposing instead a bill to collect taxes from those who had not been paying their fair share. The new law was a success, with government revenues increasing by $500 million annually.

Dukakis was now more popular than ever in Massachusetts. As the Presidential Election of 1984 approached, his support was solicited by a number of potential candidates. The Governor decided to support former Vice President Walter Mondale. When Mondale lost the New Hampshire primary to Gary Hart, Dukakis rallied to his cause, actively campaigning throughout the Bay State for Jimmy Carter's legatee. Massachusetts ignored its popular Chief Executive, however, choosing instead to vote for the Kennedy look-alike, Gary Hart. At the Democratic National Convention, Dukakis was chosen to present the party's platform to the delegates, while the national media was on hand to report on his demeanor during prime time national television. When Mondale ultimately won the nomination, Dukakis was one of the final candidates for the Vice Presidential selection. Of course Mondale made the fatal mistake of choosing Geraldine Ferraro, but John Sasso was recruited to run her campaign. While Sasso diligently pursued his duties, he was also performing another task. His boss, the forty-one year Governor of Massachusetts, was now a national political figure. Sasso was using the Ferraro campaign to make the necessary contacts to see that Michael Dukakis was elected President of the United State in 1988.

Dukakis would discuss Presidential ambitions with no one, not even his wife, preferring to concentrate on the '86 Governor's race and ratification from the voters that his policies had been right. His program for aid to the homeless gained momentum, and a drug prevention program was given high priority. He pressed forward with his plans for revitalizing his state's economy and also instituted a tax cut. His economic program was dubbed "The Miracle of Massachusetts," and President Ronald Reagan compared the efforts of Dukakis to his own when he was Governor of California. Dukakis, to the satisfaction of Democrats, disavowed such a connection, and national Democrats took note of his willingness to challenge the popular President. He was appointed Chairman of his party's Committee on Industrial and Entrepreneurial Economy, fostering many important national contacts. When the gubernatorial election of 1986 came around, the "Duke" was unopposed in the Democratic convention and primary, and in the general election he overwhelmed a Greek Republican with credibility problems who was already a replacement for another candidate who had withdrawn after admitting that he had lied about his military record. Collecting an impressive 69 percent of the popular vote, Mike Dukakis was now being viewed nationally as a contender for the 1988 Presidential nomination.

RUNNING FOR PRESIDENT

Shortly before he delivered his third inaugural in 1986, Governor Dukakis inserted some language into his address that hinted of his intentions to seek the Presidency in 1988. An avalanche of media attention soon followed his every action, awaiting his formal entry. The early favorite for the nomination was former Colorado Sen. Gary Hart, but a possible sex scandal with a model did in his candidacy immediately, although he re-entered the campaign at a later date. Other contenders were Senators Albert Gore of Tennessee, Joseph Biden of New Jersey, Paul Simon of Illinois, John Glenn of Ohio (the first American astronaut to circle the globe), Rep. Richard Gephardt of Missouri and the black activist Preacher, Jesse Jackson.

Shortly after the contest for Iowa caucus delegates had begun, an article was published showing Sen. Biden to be guilty of plagiarism in a speech. This was a death blow to Biden's candidacy, and he soon withdrew from the race. However, it was soon revealed that the person behind the revelation was none other than John Sasso — the campaign manager of Michael Dukakis. Dukakis did not want to fire Sasso, but the astute manager him- self realized that he had to resign if Dukakis were to win. He did so, and Dukakis then appointed Susan Estrich, a Harvard professor, to be his campaign manager, the first woman to hold such a position for a major party.

Dukakis did not fare well in the Iowa caucuses, but he gained momentum when he won the New Hampshire primary, the first in the nation. In one grueling primary after another, he picked up strength, gaining in the liberal Northeast and then, surprisingly, also in parts of the South by winning both Florida and Texas on "Super Tuesday," the date when many Southern primaries were held. Soon there were only three candidates, Gore, Jackson, and Dukakis. Gore tested the political waters a while longer and then withdrew. Although the nomination was in effect then decided, Jackson, to the great chagrin of Dukakis, who needed no animosity from black or liberal voters, proclaimed that he was in the race all the way to the convention. When it appeared that Dukakis would have enough delegates to win the nomination on the first ballot, Jackson then announced that he felt he should get the Vice Presidential nomination. The "Duke," realizing that his campaign would be doomed if he agreed to this, stated promptly and flatly that Jackson would not receive the nod. The Dukakis forces at the convention, firmly in control but not wanting to lose Jackson's support, agreed to certain planks demanded by the Black activist and then let the black leader deliver an emotional address during prime television time.

The Democratic National Convention, meeting in Atlanta, heard a host of speakers attack Ronald Reagan and George Bush, the nominee-to-be of the Republicans, in sharp, unsavory rhetoric. Leading the attack was Sen. Teddy Kennedy, who derisively asked, to the delight of Democrats, "Where was George?" as a reminder of a blundered attempt by the Reagan administration to retrieve some hostages from Iran by suppling weapons to the middle-east terrorist regime. The convention issued a simply written campaign platform which included none of the divisive language that many past conventions, such as those in 1968 and 1972, had contained. Then Michael Dukakis delivered a simple and eloquent acceptance speech, also being sure not to alienate any factions of his party, and proclaimed that competence would be the issue in the campaign. Pulling some pages from the successful campaigns of Ronald Reagan, he had U.S. Flags and red, white and blue balloons in prominent view throughout the convention. He also had Texas Sen. Lloyd Bentsen, a conservative with many differing viewpoints than his own but with some foreign policy expertise, named as his Vice Presidential running mate.

Dukakis left the Democratic convention with a seventeen point lead in public opinion polls and expected to coast to an easy victory over George Bush, Ronald Reagan's two term Vice President, who was gathering the Republican nomination with relative ease. In a feisty mood, he was comparing the 1988 campaign to 1960, saying that a President from Massachusetts and a Vice President from Texas were going to keep an incumbent Vice President who had served under an aged President from gaining the White House, just as John Kennedy and Lyndon Johnson had done in 1960 when Dwight Eisenhower was President and Richard Nixon was Vice President.

But George Bush quickly and easily turned the tables on the Massachusetts Governor. In his acceptance speech and in later addresses, he focused on issues on which Dukakis was extremely vulnerable. He chastised the Massachusetts Governor for having refused to sign a law requiring teachers to lead the Pledge to the Flag. The Vice President further claimed that Dukakis had opposed the American invasion of Grenada and the bombing of terrorist Libya, and then charged that Dukakis himself had no foreign policy experience. He claimed that Dukakis was soft on crime, pointing out that the Massachusetts "weekend release" program had let out on leave hardened criminals who had committed violent crimes, including rape, while released. And then George Bush, not considered an environmentalist, charged that Boston's harbor was the dirtiest waterway in the nation and that Dukakis had pursued waste disposal policies for Massachusetts that had been polluting nearby states.

Almost immediately, the campaign polls were even, and George Bush was gaining momentum. Dukakis, who had before seen his leads in Massachusetts fade and rise, seemed to feel that a temporary aberration had occurred. For the next part of the campaign he stayed mostly in Massachusetts and refused to attack Bush, although he did make an issue of Bush's running mate, Sen. Dan Quayle of Indiana, who appeared to have used the influence of his wealthy family to gain an appointment to the Army National Guard during the late 1960's to avoid duty in Viet Nam. Dukakis, perhaps remembering the 1960 election, felt that when the Presidential debates took place, he would, like Jack Kennedy, seize the initiative and go on to victory in November. But by the time of the first debate, George Bush's campaign had already put together one of the most effective media campaigns in memory, effectively establishing Dukakis as a member of the American

Civil Liberties Union and thus a liberal with a capital "L," a big spender who might raise taxes, and an opponent of Ronald Reagan's defense measures against communism. Most observers felt that Dukakis won the first debate, but it was not a "knockout," and Bush maintained his commanding lead in the polls. A debate between Lloyd Bentsen and Dan Quayle seemed to be even more decisive for the Democrats, but the Republican ticket, leaning on the popularity of Ronald Reagan, who was leading the country in the longest period of economic prosperity in its history while at the same time negotiating a nuclear arms reduction treaty with the Soviet Union, crept even further ahead in the polls. A second debate between the two Presidential candidates about a month before the election would be crucial to Dukakis. This time, however, George Bush showed his mastery of foreign and domestic issues, and, furthermore, he came off as the warmer human being of the two. Last minute non-stop campaigning by the Democratic team was to no avail. George Bush did not fall to Michael Dukakis as had Richard Nixon to John Kennedy in 1960. Instead, Bush won by a landslide, gathering 54 percent of the popular vote, with a margin of 7,000,000 out of 95,000,000 votes cast. The Vice President carried 40 states with 426 electoral votes to only 10 states and the District of Columbia for Dukakis, who received only 112 electoral ballots.[1]

RETURN TO MASSACHUSETTS

On election night Dukakis was gracious in conceding defeat to Bush, but his supporters were chanting, "'92! '92! '92!" He returned to his Governor's office the next morning and resumed his duties, continuing his agenda for reform in Massachusetts and indicating that he was leaving his options on a future race for the White House open. While most observers felt that his defeat was so devastating that his future chances for nomination were minute, they nonetheless felt certain he would run again for the office of Governor, a position he had always coveted. A good deal of curiosity was therefore aroused when he announced in January of 1989 that he would not be a candidate for re-election to the Governor's chair.

As time went by, the "Massachusetts Miracle" that Dukakis had supposedly created showed signs of financial collapse, and Michael Dukakis was chastised by fellow liberals in his home state. Adding to these woes were drug and alcohol related problems of his wife, who was admitted to treatment programs on several occasion. Dukakis through all of his troubles maintained his stoic Greek poise. While he would not reveal his future plans, most observers felt that the Greek son of immigrants, born in John Kennedy's home town of Brookline, devoted to liberal principles and participant in numerous elections as both victor and vanquished, might somehow be involved in the future political affairs of Massachusetts, if not the United States of America.

---

[1] *When the Electoral College met, the ballot of one Democratic Elector was cast for Lloyd Bentsen.*

BIBLIOGRAPHY
(By Chapters)

Chapter 1 - CHARLES COTESWORTH PINCKNEY
Zahniser, Marvin R. *CHARLES COTESWORTH PINCKNEY,*
"FOUNDING FATHER" . Chapel Hill:
University of North Carolina Press, 1967.

Chapter 2 - DeWITT CLINTON
Bobbe, Dorothy. *DEWITT CLINTON.* New York:
Minton, Balch and Company, 1933.

Chapter 3 - RUFUS KING
Ernst, Robert. *RUFUS KING, American Federalist.*
Institute of Early American History and Culture. Chapel Hill:
University of North Carolina Press, 1969.

Wilson, Vincent, Jr. *The Book of the Founding Fathers.*
Crawfordsville, Indiana: R.R. Donnelly and Sons Company, 1962.

Chapter 4 - HENRY CLAY
Schurz, Carl. *HENRY CLAY (Volumes I & II).*
New York: Chelsea House Publishers, 1980.

Chapter 5 - LEWIS CASS
McLaughlin, Andrew *C. LEWIS CASS (The American*
Statesman Series). Boston: HOUGHMAN MIFFLIN COMPANY
(The Riverside Press Cambridge),1891 and 1899.

Chapter 6 - WINFIELD SCOTT
Elliot, Charles Winslow. *WINFIELD SCOTT, The Soldier*
and the Man. New York: The Macmillan Company, 1937.

Chapter 7 - JOHN CHARLES FREMONT
Egan, Ferol. *FREMONT, Explorer for a Restless Nation.*
Garden City, New York: Doubleday & Company, Inc., 1977.

Chapter 8 - STEPHEN A. DOUGLAS
Johannsen, Robert W. *STEPHEN A. DOUGLAS.* New York:
Oxford University Press, 1973.

BIBLIOGRAPHY
(By Chapters)

Chapter 9 - GEORGE B. McCLELLAN
Sears, Stephen *W. GEORGE B. MCCLELLAN, The Young Napoleon.*
New York: Ticknor & Fields, 1988.

Chapter 10 - HORATIO SEYMOUR
Mitchell, Stewart. *HORATIO SEYMOUR OF NEW YORK.*
New York: Da Capo Press, 1970.

Chapter 11 - HORACE GREELEY
Hale, William Harlan. *HORACE GREELEY.* New York:
Harper & Bros., 1950.

Chapter 12 - SAMUEL TILDEN
Flick, Alexander Clarence. *SAMUEL JONES TILDEN,*
A Study in Political Sagacity. Port Washington, NY:
Kennikat Press, Inc., 1963.

Chapter 13 - WINFIELD SCOTT HANCOCK
Fourney, John W. *LIFE AND MILITARY CAREER*
OF WINFIELD SCOTT HANCOCK. Philadelphia:
J.C. McCurdy and Co., 1880.

Chapter 14 - JAMES G. BLAINE
Stanwood, Edward. *JAMES GILLESPIE BLAINE*
(American Statesman Series). Boston: HOUGHTON MIFFLIN COMPANY
(The Riverside Press), 1905.

Chapter 15 - WILLIAM JENNINGS BRYAN
Hibben, Paxton. *THE PEERLESS LEADER, WILLIAM*
JENNINGS BRYAN. New York: Russell and Russell, 1967.

Kosner, Alice. *THE VOICE OF THE PEOPLE,*
WILLIAM JENNINGS BRYAN. New York: Julian Messner, 1970.

Chapter 16 - ALTON BROOKS PARKER
Creelman, James. "Alton B. Parker: A Character Sketch."
Atlantic Monthly Review of Reviews, Vol XXX
(August, 1904) pp 163-71.

Chapter 17 - CHARLES EVANS HUGHES
Glad, Betty. *CHARLES EVANS HUGHES and The Illusions of*
Innocence. Urbana and London: University of Illinois Press, 1966.

BIBLIOGRAPHY
(By Chapters)

Perkins, Dexter. *CHARLES EVANS HUGHES and American Democratic Statesmanship*. Boston: Little, Brown and Company, 1956.

Chapter 18 - JAMES M. COX
Cebula, James E. *JAMES M. COX, Journalist and Politician*. New York: Garland Publishing, Inc., 1985.

Chapter 19 - JOHN W. DAVIS
Harbaugh, William H. *LAWYER'S LAWYER, THE LIFE OF JOHN W. DAVIS*. New York: Oxford University Press, 1973.

Chapter 20 - ALFRED E. SMITH
O'Connor, Richard. *THE FIRST HURRAH, A BIOGRAPHY OF ALFRED E. SMITH*. New York: G.P. Putnam's Sons, New York, 1970.

Chapter 21 - ALFRED M. LANDON
McCoy, Donald R. *LANDON OF KANSAS*. Lincoln: University of Nebraska Press, 1966.

Palmer, Frederich. *THIS MAN LANDON*. New York: Dodd, Mead, 1936.

Chapter 22 - WENDELL WILLKIE
Barnes, Joseph. *WILLKIE*. New York: Simon and Schuster, 1952.

Chapter 23 - THOMAS E. DEWEY
Smith, Richard Norton. *THOMAS E. DEWEY AND HIS TIMES*. New York: Simon & Schuster, 1982.

Chapter 24 - ADLAI STEVENSON
Cochran, Bert. *Adlai Stevenson, Patrician Among the Politicians*. New York: Funk & Wagnalls, 1969.

Martin, John B. *Adlai Stevenson and the World*. Garden City, NY: Doubleday & Company, Inc., 1977.

BIBLIOGRAPHY
(By Chapters)

Chapter 25 - BARRY GOLDWATER
Goldwater, Barry M. *WITH NO APOLOGIES*. New York: William
Morrow and Company, Inc., 1979

Chapter 26 - HUBERT HORATIO HUMPHREY
Solberg, Carl. *HUBERT HORATIO HUMPHREY* New York:
W.W. Norton & Company, 1984.

Chapter 27 - GEORGE McGOVERN
Anson, Robert Sam. *McGovern, A Biography*. New York,
San Francisco: Holt, Rinehart and Winston, 1972.

Chapter 28 - WALTER MONDALE
Lewis, Finley. *Mondale - Portrait of an American Politician*. New York:
Harper & Row Publishers, 1980.

Chapter 29 - MICHAEL DUKAKIS
Gaines, Richard and Segal, Michael. *DUKAKIS, The Man
Who Would Be President*. New York: Avon Books - New York, 1987.

BIBLIOGRAPHY
(General)

Boller, Paul F., Jr. *PRESIDENTIAL ANECDOTES*. New York:
Oxford University Press, 1981.

THE NEW COLUMBIA ENCYCLOPEDIA. Eds. William H.
Harris and Judith S. Lively. New York: Columbia University Press, 1975.

Whitney, David C. *THE AMERICAN PRESIDENTS*. Garden City,
New York: Doubleday& Company, Inc., 1967.